McLaren

A Racing History

McLAREN

A Racing History

GEOFFREY WILLIAMS

The Crowood Press

First published in 1991 by
The Crowood Press Ltd
Ramsbury, Marlborough,
Wiltshire SN8 2HR

British Library Cataloguing in Publication Data
Williams, Geoffrey
  McLaren: a racing history.
  1. Cars. Racing
  I. Title
  796.72

ISBN 1 85223 603 5

Typeset by Inforum Typesetting, Portsmouth
Printed and bound in Great Britain by BPCC Hazell Books, Aylesbury

Contents

Dedication

This book is dedicated to Timothy (Tim) James Bennett, 1964–1990. A great friend, considerate person, enthusiast of life, and wonderful human being.

Acknowledgements

It is only when one comes to thanking all those who have helped with this book that one realizes just how important their contributions are. This book divides neatly into three sections: the text, the appendices, and the photographs, and it was with the latter that I needed the most help. Bruce Grant-Braham, whose book on the Williams Team served as a 'model', was very helpful in providing photographs that otherwise would have been short on both quality and quantity.

As for the text, without the assistance of the staff at The National Motor Museum library, Beaulieu – and without the library's collection – there would have been no book, as simple as that. Their help with research was invaluable.

On the occasions when the National Motor Museum library was unable to assist, my local library in Portswood, Southampton, managed to fill the breech. The Librarian seemed to treat my many requests as a personal challenge, and not once, whether stocked by the county or not, did a book fail to arrive. Despite all his efforts on my behalf, he still does not hide under the counter when I walk in.

Naturally enough, many people connected with McLaren, past and present, were able to assist in a variety of ways. Two of these, John Watson and Ron Dennis, will be very familiar to you. The former took a day off from his Performance Driving Centre to fill in all kinds of gaps; while the latter went to great lengths to ensure that I got what I needed.

Indispensible to the book though, was Peter Stayner, the head of Tag/McLaren Marketing Services. Peter could not have been more helpful – he would have said 'professional'! – and made a great individual contribution to the book, taking each request in his stride, and then adding a few suggestions of his own. As for Mclaren being a 'humourless' organization, at least Peter's section must be a lively place to work in.

Shell's Video and Film Unit provided transcripts of interviews with McLaren personnel, which helped a great deal.

The Appendices are based on the research of Christine Sieniawska. She has absolutely no interest in motor racing whatsoever but, as you know, scientists are good, diligent, thorough people, and she assures me that she really did enjoy wading through thousands of magazines, books and programmes to gather and check all the information. Rather her than me.

Finally, credit is due to Dolly, Beattie, and Celia – a Daimler, Riley, and my bicycle – for conveying me all around the country for the book.

Introduction

'Everyone's got a book inside them', or so the saying goes, but not too many publishers would show any sympathy with this. No, you have either got to be interesting, or successful, and who could be more successful than the Mc-Laren Grand Prix team? Now they are worth writing about.

Why choose McLaren though? I could say that I have been a lifelong motor racing enthusiast, and have followed McLaren's fortunes every inch of the way, but that would be a lie. Oh yes, I have been a racing driver of sorts, and have followed motor racing, in general, for years, but if I am serious about one thing in life – and it is a big 'if' – that is history. Most of the sport or transport books I have read treat history as nothing more than 'recall'. Personally I prefer to look at *why* something happened, *what* caused it to happen, what were the *effects* of the happening, and so on. I felt that this would be a good approach to bear on Grand Prix racing, and as McLaren have long been a favourite team, who better to be my 'victims'?

So, here you are; a book which tells the story of the McLaren Grand Prix team, incorporating some of the leading issues of any given period, and which tries to give a flavour of the Grand Prix world, all from my own perspective. If you do not agree with all that is written, good, but write and tell me, and not Ron Dennis, all about it.

There was also a secondary aim for the book, that germinated during the research stages. This was to counter what I increasingly saw as inaccurate, biased, occasionally mocking and demeaning press reports about McLaren. Everyone loves the 'Boys Own' stuff of sports stars who spend all night partying, then get up and run through the opposition. There are not too many of that ilk around though, and to win in Grand Prix racing, as indeed all sports, you need to be prepared. For one thing, the roar of a Grand Prix engine would play havoc with your hangover!

Nobody prepares more thoroughly in the Grand Prix world than McLaren, and that is why they are doing all the winning. They do not need my help against a hostile press, but I think it needs saying once again, 'Do not believe all that you read'.

CHAPTER 1

From Tiny Acorns . . .

'Anyone for racing?' There was a time, during the 1950s and 1960s, when it seemed that almost anybody could take up motor racing. I mean, all you had to do was purchase your chassis, 'off the shelf' from say Lotus or Cooper, stick in an engine, and off you went. Teams seemed to set up almost overnight, some even tasting success for a period. These days, before you can begin Grand Prix racing, a few million pounds would not go amiss.

Of the Grand Prix teams that started during those decades only two have survived: Mclaren, and Brabham. Neither of these retain any serious links with their origins, though a distinct lineage can be followed and, significantly, both were founded by contemporary Grand Prix drivers. The 1980s saw a number of teams enter Grand Prix racing; how many will remain in twenty years' time remains to be seen.

A new era dawned for Grand Prix racing in 1966. The 1.5-litre formula of 1961–1965 was replaced by one allowing engines of up to 3 litres. The initially unpopular 1.5-litre formula had become well established, thanks to some excitingly close races and the Drivers' Championship. Race speeds had risen well beyond those attained by the previous 2.5-litre cars, but this was mainly due to chassis and suspension improvements. Netherthless, the decision to change to a 3-litre engine formula was rather hasty, suggesting some political jiggery-pokery in certain quarters.

As ever when change is in the air, there are those who oppose new ideas. The British contingent of the Grand Prix fraternity, who made up the bulk of the grids, were understandably less than pleased when Coventry Climax, the com-

pany which provided most teams with engines, announced they would not be building a 3-litre engine. This opened the door for a number of firms with engines to offer, but the late announcement ensured that few teams would have an engine fully developed and ready to race. It was into this new world that the McLaren Grand Prix team was to make its debut.

NOT QUITE AS PLANNED

Bruce McLaren was one of the most popular and friendly drivers of the 1960s. He had raced in Grand Prix with the Cooper team since 1959, having arrived from New Zealand the year before, and became the team leader after Jack Brabham left to found that team, in 1962. Unfortunately, Cooper had declined from their pre-eminent position of 1959/1960 and the Lotus, Ferrari, and BRM teams had dominated the 1.5-litre formula. Bruce's career had begun to founder.

In 1963 Bruce floated the idea of forming his own team with a young American lawyer named Teddy Mayer, whose brother, Tim, was a promising driver. Another American, Tyler Alexander, became a party to these discussions and, despite the death of Tim Mayer, the McLaren team was set up in the spring of 1964. Premises were obtained at Colnbrook, near Heathrow Airport, and work began. Meanwhile Bruce was to race for two more seasons with Cooper, in Grand Prix, while racing McLaren sports cars.

Robin Herd, a young aerospace engineer, joined the team and designed the Grand Prix

Teddy Mayer's expression does not suggest unbridled optimism. This is the all new M2B with the Ford Indy V8 engine, reduced from 4.2 to 3 litres. It is standing here at Monaco prior to its race debut. The excellence of McLaren preparation is evident right from the start.

car for the 1966 season. This became the M2B and broke new ground in racing car design, having a full monocoque chassis made out of balsa-wood enclosed in aluminium, known as Mallite. This was used in aircraft manufacture, and the M2B proved to be one of the most rigid open racing cars built at that time, though conventional in most other respects.

So far so good, but there remained the problem, shared by most teams in 1966, of a suitable engine. Through their sports car connections, McLaren pinned their hopes on a Ford V8 4.2-litre Indy car engine, linered down to a 3-litre capacity. The option of a Ford engine looked

excellent on paper, but was to be their undoing, ruining their first season in Grand Prix.

Initial testing proved the unit to be unreliable, not particularly powerful with around 300bhp, and 'peaky'. This last problem was exacerbated by the use of a four-speed gearbox, thus allowing power to fall off when changing gears, and it was a heavy engine. Three M2B cars were built, to be driven by Bruce McLaren and his young compatriot Chris Amon.

McLaren were not alone in experiencing serious problems with the heart of the car. Works teams from Ferrari, BRM, Lotus,

Cooper, Brabham and Eagle made up the field, but nearly all were in a state of limbo as far as the engine was concerned. BRM used their Formula 2 V8 2-litre engine, while their over-complicated H16 was being developed, and later breaking down with alarming regularity. Lotus were making do with a 2-litre Climax engine, and later tried the BRM H16, to record its only victory. Cooper used the Maserati V12, and Dan Gurney's Eagle team used the Weslake-developed V12, neither of which were outstanding. Even Ferrari with their new V12, who were favourites in 1966, were experiencing engine problems. So the door was left ajar for Jack Brabham's team to sweep the board with their reliable, if not particularly powerful, Repco V8 engine.

As far as McLaren were concerned, 1966 was a virtual disaster. Only one car was entered in the first race, at Monaco, for Bruce. After a disappointing practice and race, in which the engine was distinctly off the pace, Bruce retired well down the field without any oil pressure. Clearly, the engine needed much more development. In fact, it underwent a total redesign by Ford (US) themselves. As can be imagined, this would leave a Grand Prix team in a pretty precarious position today, with the wide variety of engines in use. Back in 1966, with a dearth of suitable engines, things did not look at all promising.

A crisis loomed, but rather than temporarily pulling out, it was decided to try Count Volpi's Serenissima V8 M166 sports car engine, developed by Stirling Moss's ex-mechanic Alf Francis. Displacing 2,996cc and allegedly pro-

After the failure of the Ford V8 engine, McLaren tried the Serenissima sports car engine in the M2B chassis. This was an even bigger disaster, though at this stage, in June, only one race had been missed.

11

ducing 350bhp at 8,600rpm, it seemed a reasonable replacement. Indeed, if it was as good as was supposed, why had it not been taken up by other teams? Perhaps because its actual output was only 260bhp; and on its debut, at the Belgian Grand Prix, it ran its bearings in practice, and so Bruce did not make the race. This was jumping out of the frying pan into the fire.

While trying to sort out the Serenissima's lubrication problems, McLaren missed the last French Grand Prix to be held on the Reims road circuit, in order to appear at the British Grand Prix. By this time Brabham, with their reliable Repco engine, were turning more than a few heads, as the established front runners of

Lotus, BRM, and Ferrari all struggled. If only McLaren could make their engine reliable, there was a good chance of achieving some success. As it happened, the Serenissima engine survived the British Grand Prix, but Bruce came home a distant sixth, to record McLaren's first World Championship point. The manner of its achievement, though, did not exactly raise expectations for the future.

At the following Dutch Grand Prix Bruce failed to start, due to the Serenissima engine letting him down. This could not go on, throwing good money after bad, so they decided to withdraw until the Ford engine was ready again. Poor Chris Amon had not even started a

The British Grand Prix saw the Serenissima-engined M2B start its only race in four attempts. Bruce McLaren finished sixth, miles adrift, and that ill-fated car is seen in the paddock at Brands Hatch, during the meeting.

The final race for the Ford Indy V8 engine was in Mexico. Plagued by overheating problems, the rear bodywork has been cut away, leaving the engine fully exposed.

race yet! The season had collapsed around their ears, but there was still the redesigned Ford engine to look forward to.

By the time McLaren were ready to resume racing, at the United States Grand Prix, Jack Brabham had all but won his third World Championship. Lotus, in desperation, had tried using BRM's H16 engine, and neither of these teams had won since BRM's victory at Monaco. Even Ferrari were in disarray, with their V12 failing to meet expectations, and team leader John Surtees had left abruptly and joined Cooper. A 'tyre war' had developed as well, with Dunlop dominating the early races, only for Goodyear and new entrants Firestone to catch them up. Even the racing was becoming more closely fought as the season progressed and the new Formula established itself.

The most surprising thing about the United States Grand Prix was that the BRM H16 engine held together to allow Jim Clark to record his only victory of the year. As for McLaren, a well-off-the-pace fifth place did little for morale. The 312bhp at 9,500rpm of the redesigned Ford engine was clearly not a match for the leading opposition. The final race, in Mexico, saw Bruce retire once again with engine problems, to bring down the curtain on a pretty dismal first season. True, they had gained three Championship points, and several teams these days go through a whole season without getting any, but they had not 'won' them.

Aside from the Grand Prix racing, 1966 had not been without its successes for McLaren. Bruce had finally teamed up with Chris Amon and won the Le Mans 24-hour race, in a 7-litre Ford GT40 MkII. Ford's sports car successes, and their disappointment with their Indy car engine in Grand Prix, had encouraged them to back a new V8 3-litre engine project, especially designed for Grand Prix by Cosworth Engineering. Lotus would have sole use of this for 1967, and it was to be made more widely available the following year. McLaren had their eyes on this.

Another success of 1966 had been the M2B car. While not an outstanding chassis, it was sturdy, competitive and, in between engine failures, reliable. Moreover, the McLaren standard of preparation and finish was of the highest order, beginning a tradition which has been carried forward to this day. Clearly, there was a solid base on which to build, but the problem of a decent engine still remained. Added to this was the old story of economics. At this time, the McLaren Grand Prix operation was financially dependent on their sports car efforts in America.

Funds were thus restricted, so it did not make sense to design a brand-new car, not knowing which engines would be available.

LET'S TRY AGAIN

Negotiations were opened with BRM, who had laid their unreliable H16 to one side and were designing a new V12 engine. This would not be ready for the start of 1967, so BRM offered their V8 2.1-litre Formula 2 engine to

Grand Prix Results 1966

GRAND PRIX	DRIVER	CAR	NO	1ST PRACTICE Time/Posn	2ND PRACTICE Time/Posn	3RD PRACTICE Time/Posn	FINAL GRID POSN	FINAL PLACING	RETIRED CAUSE OF	HIGHEST POSN IN RACE
MONACO Monte Carlo 22.5.66	B. McLaren	Ford M2B/2 3-litre	2	1min 35.1sec 5/12	1min 34.3sec 9/17	1min 32.8sec 9/19	9–16		Lp 10 Oil leak	7th
	C. Amon	Ford M2B	1	Did not appear						
BELGIAN Spa Fran-corchamps 12.6.66	B. McLaren	McLaren-Serenissima V8 M2B/2	24	3min 56.7sec 14/17	4min 36.1sec 15/15		Did not start			
	C. Amon	Ford M2B	25	Did not appear						
FRENCH Reims 3.7.66	B. McLaren	McLaren-Serenissima V8 M2B/2	28	Did not appear						
BRITISH Brands Hatch 16.7.66	B. McLaren	McLaren-Serenissima M2B	14			1min 38.5sec 11/20	13–20	6/12		6th
	C. Amon	Ford M2B	15	Did not appear						
DUTCH Zandvoort 24.7.66	B. McLaren	McLaren-Serenissima M2B	20	1min 40.1sec 12/16	1min 32.2sec 14/17	1min 31.7sec 13/18	Did not start			
	C. Amon	Ford M2B	22	Did not attend						
GERMAN Nürburgring 7.8.66	B. McLaren	Ford M2B/2	16	Entry withdrawn						
ITALIAN Monza 4.9.66	B. McLaren	Ford M2B/21 BRM		Entry withdrawn						
USA Watkins Glen 21.10.66	B. McLaren	Ford M2B/1	17	1min 13.0sec 18/21	1min 10.57sec 13/21		11–19	5/6		4th
MEXICAN Mexico City 23.10.66	B. McLaren	Ford M2B/1	17	2min 0.68sec 18/19	1min 66.84sec 16/20		14–18		Lp 40 Engine	9th

Key to abbreviations

FL   Fastest Lap
Lp   Lap

Teddy Mayer

Of all the Grand Prix team bosses down the years, Teddy Mayer is probably the most overtly competitive. Of course, to many owners, the team is their life, but Mayer *shows* that his team and Grand Prix racing mean everything to him. Thus when one of his cars wins, none of the old hackneyed phrases such as 'pleased to win' pour forth; you can see his delight written all over his face: the look of the true enthusiast.

Teddy Mayer is an American law graduate who got involved in motor racing by looking after the interests of his brother Tim. It was not exactly planned, but the deeper Tim got involved, so too did Teddy. By 1961 Teddy was managing the Formula Junior Rev-Em Racing Team, with Tim, and later McLaren pilot Peter Revson, as drivers, and from that point on Teddy's fate was sealed. Two years later the Mayers met up with Bruce McLaren, and with Tyler Alexander as their mechanic. The four of them hatched plans to form the McLaren team.

During the winter of 1963/64 Bruce McLaren and Tim Mayer competed in the Tasman Championship, when Tim was killed. This shook Teddy terribly and he returned home. But the time away from the racing fraternity hardened his resolve and ambition, and he returned to Britain to join Bruce McLaren Racing. With Tyler Alexander, and later Phil Kerr, he then began the long haul to the top of Grand Prix.

The death of Bruce McLaren, in 1970, meant that Teddy Mayer increasingly took responsibility for running the team, even extending his influence to engineering matters. The mid-1970s saw Team McLaren at their peak, but thanks to Colin Chapman, Grand Prix racing was entering a new era. As Gordon Coppuck and the other McLaren engineers floundered around with this new technology, so Mayer – by this time one of the most experienced race engineers at the time – took over. After a disastrous 1979 season, Mayer managed to persuade Marlboro that McLaren could be turned round, and that their tentative proposal to merge with Project 4 need not go ahead. It did not work out though, but Mayer was astute enough to know when to say 'Yes' to Marlboro, and he became joint Managing Director of McLaren International with Ron Dennis a year later.

Mayer was responsible for de Cesaris's car in 1981, and the following year was race engineer for John Watson, a fact not fully appreciated by the Ulsterman, after the latter's poor treatment in 1980. However, Mayer's sheer competitive instincts came to the fore and, determined to prove that he could do more for Watson than John Barnard could for Lauda, Mayer rose to the occasion and, in Watson's words:

'. . . did a very good job indeed in 1982. At that time he was probably a better race engineer than Barnard, despite his lack of formal technical training. He had an imense experience of what was needed in a race, and set up my car accordingly for those conditions.'

Watson finished as joint runner-up in the Drivers' Championship that year and, with a bit of luck, might well have won.

At the end of that season Mayer sold his share in McLaren to Ron Dennis and, along with Alexander, he left. Teddy could not be kept down though, and in 1985 was back with the Carl Haas-Lola team, with Ford turbo power. Progress was made but success, in the highly competitive turbo era, eluded them, and they withdrew at the end of 1986. However, like the fabled boxer who never knows when to lie down, Mayer bounced back once again, in 1989, as Managing Director of the resurgent Brabham team, only for that team to be sold a year later.

Teddy Mayer is a man of extremes. The worried, almost pained expression he often wears at race meetings clearly shows the importance he attaches to racing and the effort he puts into it. On the other hand, his delight in success is not the cool, almost nonchalant 'just doing our job' reaction of certain team bosses. Mayer is ultra-competitive and likes to make things happen, and such is his determination to get things right that it would be no surprise to find him behind the wheel, when he thinks his drivers are failing to deliver. If his heart occasionally rules his head, he is certainly no fool, and the fact is that McLaren owe their very existence and much of their earlier success directly to Teddy Mayer. He is possibly the single most important person in their history.

hold the fort. McLaren were not over-enthusiastic about this, but had little alternative, the Ford engine having been completely abandoned.

Robin Herd developed the M4A Formula 2 car into the M4B, to accept the small BRM engine, while the team anxiously awaited the BRM V12. A new car was designed for this, the M5A, and though not over-optimistic for the start of the season, an improvement on the previous year's performance was hoped for.

The effective opposition for 1967 was also

expected to amount to more than just Brabham-Repco and the occasional good performance from one of the other teams. Lotus were to have the new Ford-Cosworth engine when it was ready, with all the attendant benefits – and problems – that would bring, while Colin Chapman was busy penning one of his brilliant designs around it, the Lotus 49. Perhaps it was unreasonable to expect McLaren to keep up with Lotus, especially with a Formula 2 engine, but could a Lotus finish every race? Then, there was the reliable Brabham team, who certainly intended to be front runners again. The other teams from 1966 were all present and would, no doubt, have improved. Obviously BRM were effectively in the same boat as McLaren, and Ferrari, though never to be completely dismissed, were somewhat less than an harmonious unit. Perhaps of most interest was the Honda team, with their new V12 engine,

which was definitely not up for sale. After appearing in 1964–1965, and re-emerging late in 1966, they were to enter fully into the fray. Much was expected of them, especially with former World Champion John Surtees as their driver.

At this time, Grand Prix racing had not quite lost all of its sporting dimension, and an element of fun was still apparent. Characters, such as Jim Clark and Graham Hill, who enjoyed any form of racing and were seemingly full of life, abounded. The hard-nosed 'professionals', who were about to have their day, had not quite arrived.

Many of the teams did not restrict their activities to Grand Prix racing either, as is the case today; nearly all ran Formula 2 teams and some, such as McLaren, sports car teams. Variety, no doubt, apart from adding spice to life, also offered other options if a team failed in one category. McLaren, in 1967, were a prime example

An undressed lady! The M4B/BRM stands in the paddock at an early season British non-championship Formula 1 race.

Eyes down, and prepare yourselves for another disappointment. The interim M4B/1 car, comprising a modified Formula 2 chassis and a 2.1-litre V8 BRM Formula 2 engine.

of this, their success in the Can-Am series standing in marked contrast to their Grands Prix results.

Commercial sponsorship was still relatively restricted and limited to automobile-associated products, such as tyres, fuel, brakes, etc. There were more smiling faces around the pits area than there are today. The motivation to succeed usually came from within the team, a desire to prove themselves, not to promote some commercial product. Life in a Grand Prix racing team must have been more pleasurable, if not so financially rewarding, twenty-five years ago.

The 1967 season opened with the usual non-championship races, before the first Grand Prix, at Monaco. Bruce was entered as the only works driver – a sensible decision considering

the finances – and only one M4B was built. He acquitted himself well enough in these early races, and then produced a good performance to finish fourth at Monaco.

At the Dutch Grand Prix – where Jim Clark gave the Lotus 49 with Ford-Cosworth engine its maiden, debut victory – disaster struck. Bruce crashed and, although not seriously hurt, the only raceworthy car was burnt out. The team was in a quandary. The M5A car was designed to take the BRM V12 engine which was not yet available, but any time and effort invested in building a second M4B would have given a poor return. Fortunately, Dan Gurney offered Bruce an Eagle-Weslake car, which was gratefully accepted. The pressure on the team was eased, and having a proper 3-litre engine car

Lap 2 of the 1967 German Grand Prix, and Bruce McLaren, in the Eagle-Weslake V12 102, has passed reigning World Champion Jack Brabham. It did not last and he retired two laps later, his last drive in one of Dan Gurney's cars.

enhanced Bruce's chances. Regrettably, three retirements in three Grands Prix rather spoiled the record books.

Finally, for the Canadian Grand Prix the M5A, with BRM V12 engine, was ready to race. This engine initially developed 370bhp at 9,750rpm, and compared favourably with the Repco engine in the Brabham cars, if not with the Ford-Cosworth unit. The latter was mated to a Hewland DG 5-speed gearbox, unlike BRM who, as usual, used their own. McLaren's fortunes were transformed for, although Bruce finished seventh, he might have won, had not the alternator been omitted in order to save weight. As a result, the battery boiled dry, but a McLaren had challenged strongly in a Grand Prix for the first time.

For much of the Italian Grand Prix McLaren hopes were raised still further. Bruce, who had qualified a McLaren on the front row of the grid for the first time, was challenging John Surtees, in the Honda, for the lead. The fine handling M5A was ideally suited to the fast Monza bends, and a real battle was in progress when, with only twenty laps to go, a cylinder liner cracked and Bruce was out.

POTENTIAL GALORE

Clearly the new car/engine combination had the potential to do well, but doubts about the engine were beginning to surface. After two more engine-related retirements in the final

Bruce McLaren

Just as Jackie Stewart came to personify the increasing professionalism, commercialism, and safety consciousness of Grand Prix racing in the 1970s and similarly so with Ayrton Senna as the dedicated professional of the 1990s, so Bruce McLaren typified the happy, often comradely spirit prevalent during earlier times. The most universally liked driver of his era, Bruce's background suggested he might have something out of the ordinary to offer the sport.

Born in New Zealand in 1937, McLaren won that country's first Driver to Europe scholarship in 1958, and had his first race in a Formula 2 Cooper at the Aintree 200. He scored his first international win later that year, in the Formula F2 section of the German Grand Prix, before returning to New Zealand and winning the national championships that winter.

The following year saw Bruce McLaren alongside Jack Brabham in the Cooper Grand Prix team. He won the United States Grand Prix to become the youngest driver to win a Grand Prix, aged twenty-two, a distinction he still holds. The following season, McLaren was runner-up to Brabham in the second of his Championship triumphs.

Then came the 1.5-litre formula, and the end of Cooper's brief flourish; Ferrari, BRM, and especially Lotus, were the new top dogs. McLaren led Cooper after Brabham had left to form his own outfit, but they were very much 'also-rans' most of the time, McLaren claiming his last Grand Prix victory in 1962.

In those days, Grand Prix drivers were not paid anywhere near as much as today, and to keep the wolf from the door, both teams and drivers entered non-championship, Formula 2, and sports car races. It was to this latter category that Bruce McLaren turned when thinking about starting his own team. He was fortunate to meet Teddy Mayer and Tyler Alexander, these three really setting the McLaren team on its way. Once it was decided to aim for Grand Prix racing, with the onset of the 3-litre formula in 1966, Bruce's days with Cooper were numbered.

As a driver, Bruce was one notch short of the highest class. Like Denny Hulme, he was consistent, fast, dependable, looked after his cars, and was among the leading drivers of his day. Bruce was also versatile, being Can-Am Champion, driving his own cars, in 1967 and 1969, while he won the Le Mans 24-hour race in 1966. He was also an outstanding test driver for the time.

Perhaps his greatest achievement was in opening the long McLaren account of victories, by winning the Belgian Grand Prix in 1968 – only the second driver to win in his own car. The following year Bruce was third in the Drivers' Championship, though he did not win a single race, such was his consistency of performance.

Bruce was an essential member of the McLaren management team, and with Denny Hulme formed perhaps the most harmonious driving partnership of all time; that the Can-Am series became known as the 'Bruce and Denny show' was not solely due to their hegemony, but also reflected their working relationship. In a sport which is dominated by individuals' egos, this was indeed a rare combination.

It was in fact while testing the 1970 M8D Can-Am car, at Goodwood, on the 2nd of June that year, that Bruce was killed. Round he went, on a routine test session, but this time the rear body section was, unknowingly, not secured properly, and it came adrift at high speed. The air got underneath, ripped the body and rear wing away, and the car left the road and hit a concrete marshall's post, killing Bruce instantly. The shock waves which swept through the world of motor racing were equally forceful.

During an era when there were a great many deaths among racing drivers, the loss of Bruce shocked everyone. It would have been no surprise if Team McLaren had folded there and then. That they developed to the level of dominance reached today is a fitting memorial to a man who, ironically, might have felt out of place in the modern era of the totally dedicated professional.

two races of the year, in the USA and Mexico, options were being re-cast elsewhere. The BRM engine had too many niggling problems, experienced by BRM themselves, and which they failed to cure. Furthermore, it was not noticeably any quicker than the Ford-Cosworth engine which, despite a few reliability problems, had still powered Jim Clark to four victories during the year. This engine was to be made available to other teams for 1968, and Bruce McLaren and Teddy Mayer saw this as a better alternative than the BRM. Subsequent events

Stripped to its bare essentials, the M5A-BRM promised much but, like so many things from Bourne, reality proved rather different. At least McLaren were able to escape to a Ford-Cosworth engine.

showed this to have been the correct road to take.

In other respects McLaren, though experiencing much ill luck, had made a number of mistakes, but most importantly, they seemed to learn from them. Their idea of running a two-car team in 1966, when problems were experienced with the Ford V8 engine, proved too ambitious. Similarly, the building of only one M4B chassis, even when only a stopgap, was shown to be a marginal decision, after it had burned out.

Inevitably, there were other errors of a lesser magnitude which, considering the leap into the dark which was taken when entering Grand Prix racing, were understandable. Indeed, despite the poor showing of only six Championship points from two seasons' racing, there was much to be optimistic about. Bruce had won the Can-Am Championship in a McLaren and

his partner, new World Champion Denny Hulme, had won three of the six races in the series to finish runner-up. Mainly as a result of this experience with McLaren, Denny signed up to drive alongside Bruce in Grand Prix racing for 1968. Gulf Oil, who were mainly interested in the Can-Am series, increased their level of support, while Goodyear and Reynolds Aluminium also contributed to their coffers. Not a bad list of backers for a moderately successful team.

Of course, apart from the driver line-up of Bruce and Denny, the team pinned their hopes for 1968 on the Ford-Cosworth engine and on the M7A car being designed by Robin Herd to take this. If this proved to be an advance on the M5A, and there was no reason to suggest it would not, then with a top class driver line-up and competitive and reliable engines, here was the evidence on which their optimism was

Grand Prix Results 1967

GRAND PRIX	DRIVER	CAR	NO	1ST PRACTICE Time/Posn	2ND PRACTICE Time/Posn	3RD PRACTICE Time/Posn	FINAL GRID POSN	FINAL PLACING	RETIRED CAUSE OF	HIGHEST POSN IN RACE
SOUTH AFRICAN Kyalami 2.1.67	Not entered									
MONACO Monte Carlo 7.5.67	B. McLaren	BRM V8 M4B/1	16	1min 33.4sec 12/20	1min 30.5sec 9/21	1min 30.0sec 6/21	10-16	4/6		3rd
DUTCH Zandvoort 4.6.67	B. McLaren	BRM V8 M4B/1	17	1min 28.2sec 7/16	1min 27.9sec 10/15	1min 27.7sec 12/17	15-17		Lp 2 Accident	16th
BELGIAN Spa Fran-corchamps 18.6.67	Not entered									
FRENCH Le Mans-Bugatti 2.7.67	B. McLaren (Anglo-American Racers)	Eagle-Weslake V12 102	8	1min 40.2sec 6/13	1min 37.6sec 5/15		4-15		Lp 26 Ignition	6th
BRITISH Silverstone 15.7.67	B. McLaren (Anglo-American Racers)	Eagle-Weslake V12 102	10	1min 29.3sec 9/20	2min 01.5sec 19/19	1min 28.1sec 10/20	9-21		Lp 15 Engine	7th
GERMAN Nürburgring 6.8.67	B. McLaren (Anglo-American Racers)	Eagle-Weslake V12 102	10		8min 36.7sec 13/25	8min 17.7sec 4/25	7-17		Lp 4 Oil leak	4th
CANADIAN Mosport 27.8.67	B. McLaren	BRM V12 M5A/1	19	1min 24.8sec 5/15	1min 23.5sec 6/18		8-17	7/12		4th
ITALIAN Monza 10.9.67	B. McLaren	BRM V12 M5A/1	4	1min 32.0sec 11/16	1min 29.3sec 2/18		3-18		Lp 48 Engine	4th
USA Watkins Glen 1.10.67	B. McLaren	BRM V12 M5A/1	14	1min 08.05sec 3/19	1min 09.60sec 16/22		10-18		Lp 17 Water hose	7th
MEXICAN Mexico City 22.10.67	B. McLaren	BRM V12 M5A/1	14	1min 51.30sec 7/18	1min 50.06sec 8/19		7-19	13/13	Oil pressure	6th

based. The triumvirate of Bruce McLaren, Teddy Mayer and Tyler Alexander, though perhaps lacking the design genius of Colin Chapman, formed as astute a management team as any in Grand Prix at that time. They were shortly to be joined by Phil Kerr, as joint Managing Director, from Brabham, and were not likely to squander the opportunities the team had gained for itself.

As 1968 dawned McLaren, with their premises at Colnbrook and the McLaren Engines concern in the USA, were ready to take a big stride up the Grand Prix grid. There was just one unexpected problem to overcome . . .

CHAPTER 2

A New Dawn

If McLaren's formative years in Grand Prix had been their first faltering steps, then the next three seasons were very much the age of adolescence. By the end of 1970 McLaren had come of age and were learning to cope with tragedy. Far from being also-rans, it was expected that a McLaren car would be challenging for the lead of at least a few races each season. Their reputation for building reliable, dependable and immaculately prepared, if conventional, cars became firmly established. One felt that were it not for the genius of Colin Chapman, a McLaren driver would be a regular visitor to the winners' podium. McLaren had firmly established themselves towards the forefront of the Grand Prix fraternity.

Prior to this, however, there was a bit of a shock in store for the team. In a team/group situation no one person is usually indispensible, though the equilibrium can easily be upset by the loss of one member. Thus it was a surprised, upset, and disappointed Bruce McLaren who learned that his talented young designer, Robin Herd, was to join Cosworth Engineering to help them design their own Grand Prix car.

Bruce undoubtedly felt let down as much as cheated at a time when the team, with the new personnel, were looking forward to the 1968 season so optimistically; furthermore, the design details of the new M7A car were far from settled. Robin Herd's departure could have proved a serious loss, coming when it did, but the Swiss born, ex-Lotus engineer Jo Marquart was recruited in his place and Herd's assistant, Gordon Coppuck, stepped in to fill the breach.

TEETHING TROUBLES

For many enthusiasts the three seasons ending in 1970 proved to be a time of mixed blessings. On the one hand, grids were filled with competitive cars as never before, and one was being continually excited by the seemingly endless stream of technical innovations. New ideas seemed to be emerging with each passing race, and what was competitive at the beginning of a season could be decidedly old hat by the end.

On the other hand, the 'romance' seemed to go out of racing. Mainly due to the increasing race speeds and level of competition, Grand Prix racing became far more professional and began to distance itself from some of its traditions. Perhaps the most obvious sign of this change came with the circuits themselves. Reims was last used for the French Grand Prix in 1966, and two years later the Rouen-les-Essarts circuit took its final bow. 1970 saw the long Spa circuit dropped from the calendar, and others, such as the Nürburgring, were altered. Though this was sad to see, much of this was due to the need for improved safety features. Still, the sight of Grand Prix cars dicing through the streets, or on roads on which you could drive your own car, was part of the heritage of the sport and of the romantic attraction.

Safety, for both drivers and spectators, has been an important factor for motor racing ever since the 1903 Paris to Madrid race was stopped by the French authorities after several fatalities. Motor racing has always been and always will be a dangerous sport, yet if spectators deserve to be protected, as far as is reasonably possible, so do the driving heroes.

During the 1950s spectators enjoyed an un-impeded view of the drivers sitting up in their cars, working away to control them. Then came the 1955 Le Mans disaster, when Levagh's Mercedes somersaulted into the crowd, causing mayhem. Gradually people in either central government, or the governing bodies of motor sport, began to realize the dangers involved, and road races were either curtailed or restricted.

Drivers remained scantily protected though helmets were compulsory, as were roll bars, from 1961. These went some way towards protecting the driver in the event of an accident, but as speeds rose with the 3-litre formula, so did the dangers, especially on road circuits. The drawback with the technological advances of the last years of the sixties, particularly as regards brakes, tyres, and aerodynamics, was that cars were cornering much faster than had previously been the case. With the steadily increasing power of the 3-litre engines, the cars were arriving at corners much faster as well, and the margin for error was reduced. Those pretty trees, signposts, blind corners and brows of hills became potential hazards as never before. The period of 1968–1970 saw drivers and others really getting to grips with the safety problem. Many times these people were referred to in often unsympathetic terms by the press, circuit owners, and even team owners. However, safety became something of a crusade and an increasingly dominant factor in motor sport, thanks to the effort of drivers such as Jackie Stewart, Graham Hill and Jo Siffert.

If the changing face of the circuits failed to register with racing enthusiasts, sponsorship did not. Cars traditionally wore the national colours of the country in which the team was based, for example, Ferrari: Italian red, BRM: British green, etc. In 1968 the McLaren cars were painted in a yellow/orange colour, known as 'papaya', representing the Gulf Oil Company, their major sponsors. This was as nothing compared to the Lotus team, whose cars suddenly appeared in the red, white and gold of the Gold Leaf cigarette brand. A new era was dawning,

when the traditional supporters of motor racing – automotive-based companies – would gradually be replaced by a diverse selection of firms requiring an 'image' for a product. Cigarette companies stole the early limelight, but airlines, photographic equipment and even contraceptives, have been represented since. At least this has made the cars easy to distinguish, and makes a colourful grid.

The dawn of more prominently displayed advertising on Grand Prix cars went hand in glove with the rapidly increasing costs of racing. Cosworth's DFV engine gave the opportunity for more teams to enter Grand Prix racing, at a price, increasing the competitive pressure on established teams. Extra testing was necessary to try out new ideas, or improve an existing car and find a small advantage over opponents. Teams became more technically biased, gaining in professionalism what had been lost of the fun side of the sport. All this cost money, and if the revenue from the paying spectator was finite, other sources needed to be found.

To attract sponsors though, Grand Prix racing needed to appeal to a wider public. Television came to be seen as the ideal vehicle for reaching that audience, and if cigarette adverts were banned from the screen, the brightly painted racing cars identified the product easily enough. Unfortunately, all this came at a price, and the 'tail' began to have more influence on the 'dog' than ought to be the case.

FIRST TASTE OF VICTORY

As the 1968 season got under way, much of this was only a dot on the horizon, as the serious business of racing came to the fore. The opening round of the Championship, the South African Grand Prix, was held on New Year's Day, and McLaren's new car was not ready. Denny Hulme made his debut for the team with the M5A and the BRM V12 engine. He drove a typically stubborn race, finishing fifth, to give the car its first Championship points.

23

Bruce McLaren, sitting on the wheel of his M7A, with Denny Hulme behind in no. 1, in this 1968 pit scene, typical of that era. In the distance, Teddy Mayer seems to be interested in the Cooper offering.

The race itself was won by Jim Clark, his twenty-fifth and final Grand Prix win before his death.

Back at Colnbrook, bolstered by this surprise result, work continued on the new Cosworth-powered M7A. McLaren had used the Gulf money to purchase five DFV engines at £7,500 each for the season; a far cry from today's top teams. The M7A was a fairly conventional design, but worked well right from the start. Unlike most cars, it used Lockheed and not Girling brakes, but it continued the McLaren standard of a good, sound design, excellently prepared.

And what a debut. At the non-championship Race of Champions at Brands Hatch, Bruce had the perfect meeting, claiming pole position and setting fastest lap on his way to a memorable victory. Denny Hulme came home third, to round off an excellent day. Five weeks later at Silverstone's International Trophy, the result was even better. Denny, after claiming the pole, led home Bruce in a 1–2 victory.

These results confirmed the car's potential and greatly added to the team's confidence, but the real test for the M7A came with the Spanish

Grand Prix. There, Denny Hulme put the car on the front row of the grid and finished in a fine second place, although Bruce retired with no oil pressure. At the following Monaco Grand Prix, Denny's fifth place was not particularly outstanding, especially since Bruce crashed.

A third chassis was built, to be used by Bruce McLaren at the Belgian Grand Prix. This was a momentous race for the team as Bruce, quite appropriately, but unbeknown to him as he crossed the finishing line, gave his team its maiden victory. This great achievement was only slightly tempered by Denny Hulme's failure to finish, and everyone in racing was genuinely pleased for Bruce. This was also his

first Grand Prix victory since 1962. Who knew what might be possible for McLaren?

As it happened, results were placed on hold as McLaren seemed to fall off the pace a bit. Both cars retired, for the only time that season, at the Dutch Grand Prix, bringing them quickly down to earth. During the next few races Graham Hill and Jackie Stewart began to draw ahead in the Drivers' Championship. The M7A had already been modified to carry its fuel in side panniers, giving it a better balance as well as distinctive looks. For the French Grand Prix, following the lead of Ferrari and Brabham, the McLarens sported rear wings and nose fins. These were intended to increase the download on the tyres to raise cornering speeds and

The rear end of Bruce McLaren's M7A, with which he won the Belgian Grand Prix to open the McLaren account for Grands Prix wins.

This is the front of Bruce McLaren's Belgian Grand Prix winning M7A/1. The three gauges record engine speed, oil and water temperature, and oil pressure, and what more does a driver need to know? Oh for the simple life.

shorten braking distances. At this stage of the season aerodynamic aids were very much a black art, with some teams doing better than others in their guesswork/calculations. Wings grew ever higher as the season progressed, and suddenly, McLaren seemed to get it right.

Denny Hulme was not a driver with the genius of Clark, or the precision of Stewart. He was nicknamed 'The Bear' and certainly had the persistence of that animal. He had become World Champion in 1967 not by being the fastest driver around, but by nearly always col-

lecting a few points at each race. In 1968 he displayed these abilities again, picking up points in mid-season when the car was 'off'. With the M7A working better again and Bruce McLaren taking a front row position for the Italian Grand Prix, it was Denny Hulme who won the race. When Denny led Bruce home in the following Canadian Grand Prix, to record the first McLaren 1–2, he moved into the lead of the World Championship alongside Graham Hill. Could Hulme become Champion again? What a turnaround for the team that would be.

No, this is not Cleethorpes beach. Bruce McLaren comes back to earth with a bump in Holland, after his Belgian victory. He has spun during practice and needs the willing assistance of these Dutchmen to get going again.

Within McLaren, optimism ran high during the weeks before the United States Grand Prix to be held at Watkins Glen. Swiss driver Jo Bonnier had used the BRM-engined M5A to secure sixth place in Italy, and was to race in America. Dan Gurney, who ran his own Eagle team, had used the M7A/3 car in Canada – as he had run out of Weslake V12 engines – and was to race this car in America and Mexico, thus aiding Denny Hulme's championship chances.

Despite the grids' lack of depth during 1968, the season was coming nicely to the boil for the climax. Terrific interest and excitement were generated at Watkins Glen, as all the possible permutations were worked out. Lotus's earlier superiority had diminished, but who could discount such a determined driver as Graham Hill? Jackie Stewart, in the Matra, looked an even-money bet as well; the title could go to either of

Denny Hulme

New Zealander Denny Hulme joined the Mc-Laren team in 1968 as reigning World Champion, from the front-running Brabham-Repco team. It seemed quite a strange move at the time, and a distinctly downward one since McLaren had hardly shone in the premier league of motor sport. However, the New Zealander had driven for McLaren in the 1967 Can-Am series, finishing as runner-up, and was well aware of the potential of the team.

Known as 'The Bear', Hulme was a well controlled, smooth, yet determined driver. Though not quite in the 'ace' class, Hulme was a good team man, ideally suited as a partner to Bruce McLaren, and perhaps less so to the meritocratic 1970s. Occasionally Denny seemed to go off the boil, when the cars were poor, and he made no secret of his hatred of racing in the rain. In this respect he was not a complete racer, like Stirling Moss, for example, but once things began to pick up, Hulme was soon up among the front runners again.

Hulme's first season with McLaren was his most successful, and he failed to retain his World Champion title only in the last race. However, he always ran well alongside Bruce, whether it be in Grand Prix or sports cars. Following the death of Bruce, an understandable decline set in at McLaren, and Hulme, unfortunately, succumbed to this. But with the arrival of Peter Revson, Hulme rose to the new challenge in typical fashion. The two forged a good working partnership, and restored McLaren's position towards the top of the Grand Prix tree.

However, during 1974, the New Zealander seldom came to grips with the car and Fittipaldi's speed, and as the season wore on it became clear that he had lost the urge of previous years. Perhaps it was age; perhaps it was the setting up of the car, or simply that Fittipaldi was the faster driver. In any case the team had to give Fittipaldi his title chance, and Hulme probably could not have coped with number two treatment.

McLaren thus lost a valued team member; one who had stuck by them through thick and thin, and had contributed a great deal to the sport. For many, a McLaren without Denny was unthinkable, but he was one of a long line of distinguished drivers to bring a McLaren first past the chequered flag. His retirement was a great loss to the sport but, after so many seasons at the top, well deserved.

'Oh, for the wings, for the . . .' Lap 5 of the British Grand Prix at Brands Hatch, and Bruce McLaren, in seventh place, leads Jochen Rindt and Denny Hulme. Two laps later, Hulme passed the pair of them.

these deserving drivers, or to Denny Hulme. In the event, Stewart's win seemed to confuse the issue; the possible permutations increased. Though Bruce McLaren and Dan Gurney secured points finishes, Denny Hulme unluckily had a half-shaft break, causing him to crash. The wrecked chassis had to be returned to Colnbrook to be rebuilt before being sent to Mexico City for the final round. This was another example of how thorough McLaren were with their race preparation.

Depending on the result of the Mexican Grand Prix, either Hulme, Hill or Stewart could win the World Championship. Then, just at the wrong moment, the car let Denny Hulme down. A damper broke while he was well set, and he crashed again, rounding off his season on a disappointing note. Graham Hill,

to widespread acclaim, went on to win the race and with it the World Championship for the second time, while Bruce McLaren secured some consolation by coming second in the race.

Even more important was McLaren's position of runners-up to Lotus in the Constructors' Championship. This was an outstanding performance, based on good teamwork, thoughtful leadership, getting the best out of a car, and not least, two highly determined drivers. Though mostly optimistic, few team members could have expected such a momentous season when the first race got under way. This achievement was doubly impressive as Hulme won the Can-Am series, with Bruce coming second – as emphatic a victory as one could get.

Back at Colnbrook, there was much work to

Denny Hulme, as reigning World Champion, proudly wears the no. 1 on his M7A at Brands Hatch. Compare this to the modern pictures to see just how much, and yet how little, has changed.

'Ring out the old, ring in the new.' Denny Hulme, in his M7A, has just lapped Piers Courage in a BRM in the British Grand Prix. Two more years were to pass before the Bourne outfit would win another Grand Prix.

Grand Prix Results 1968

GRAND PRIX	DRIVER	CAR	NO	1ST PRACTICE Time/Posn	2ND PRACTICE Time/Posn	3RD PRACTICE Time/Posn	FINAL GRID POSN	FINAL PLACING	RETIRED CAUSE OF	HIGHEST POSN IN RACE
SOUTH AFRICAN Kyalami 1.1.68	D. Hulme	McLaren-BRM V12 M5A/1	1	1min 27.5sec 6/14	1min 26.0sec 10/24	1min 24.0sec 9/24	9-23	5/10		5th
SPANISH Jarama 12.5.68	D. Hulme	Ford V8 M7A-DFV M7A/2	1	1min 29.1sec 4/12	1min 28.3sec 1/13	1min 28.3sec 7/14	3–13	2/5		2nd
	B. McLaren	Ford V8 M7A-DFV M7A/2	2	1min 28.9sec 3/12	1min 28.6sec 3/13	1min 29.1sec 2/14	4-13		Lp 78 Loss of oil	3rd
MONACO Monte Carlo 25.5.68	D. Hulme	Ford V8 M7A-DFV M7A/2	12	1min 32.2sec 9/18	1min 30.4sec 8/18	1min 54.8sec 19/19	10-16	5/5		3rd
	B. McLaren	Ford V8 M7A-DFV M7A/1	14	1min 31.0sec 5/18	1min 32.9sec 14/18	1min 29.6sec 1/19	7-16		Lp 1 Spun exiting tunnel, hit barrier	
BELGIAN Francorchamps 9.6.68	D. Hulme	Ford V8 M7A-DFV M7A/2	6	3min 35.4sec 5/19			5-18		Lp 19 Inboard driveshaft pin	1st
	B. McLaren	Ford V8 M7A-DFV M7A/1	5	3min 37.1sec 6/19			6-18	1/8 WINNER		1st
	J. Bonnier (own entry)	McLaren-BRM V12 M5A/1	17	9min 02.2sec 18/19	4min 34.3sec 4/11		16-18		Lp 2 Broken wheel stud	18th
DUTCH Zandvoort 23.6.68	D. Hulme	Ford V8 M7A-DFV M7A/2	1	1min 24.59sec 1/16	1min 24.45sec 7/18	1min 25.54sec 8/19	7-19		Lp 1 Damping	13th
	B. McLaren	Ford V8 M7A-DFV M7A/3	2	1min 25.07sec 4/16	1min 24.58sec 8/18	1min 24.97sec 6/19	6-19		Lp 20 Crashed at Tarzan hairpin	6th
	J. Bonnier (own entry)	McLaren-BRM V12 M5A/1	19	1min 33.75sec 15/16	1min 29.22sec 18/18	1min 28.43sec 16/19	19-19	8/9		8th
FRENCH Rouen 7.7.68	D. Hulme	Ford V8 M7A-DFV M7A/2	8	1min 58.2sec 4/18	1min 57.7sec 2/18		5-17	5/12		5th
	B. McLaren	Ford V8 M7A-DFV M7A/3	10	1min 38.4sec 6/18	1min 58.0sec 3/18		8-17	8/12		6th
BRITISH Brands Hatch 20.7.68	D. Hulme	Ford V8 M7A-DFV M7A/2	1	1min 31.2sec 7/19	1min 30.4sec 4/16	1min 30.7sec 10/24	13-20	4/9		4th
	B. McLaren	Ford V8 M7A-DFV M7A/3	2	1min 31.2sec 8/19	1min 30.4sec 5/16	1min 31.9sec 15/24	9-20	7/9		7th
		Ford V8 M7A-DFV M7A/1	34			1min 30.4sec 9/24	Practice only			
	J. Bonnier (own entry)	McLaren-BRM V12 M5A/1	23			1min 36.8sec 24/24	19-20		Lp 7 Suspected dropped valve	17th

Race	Driver	Car	No.					Notes	Pos.
GERMAN Nürburgring 4.8.68	D. Hulme	Ford V8 M7A-DFV M7A/2	1		10min 52.9sec 14/20	10min 16.0sec 2/12	13–20	7/14	7th
	B. McLaren	Ford V8 M7A-DFV M7A/1	2		11min 01.4sec 17/20	10min 33.0sec 6/12	18–20	13/14	13th
ITALIAN Monza 8.9.68	D. Hulme	Ford V8 M7A-DFV M7A/2	1	1min 26.67sec 3/25	1min 27.0sec 7/23		7–20	1/6 WINNER	1st
	B. McLaren	Ford V8 M7A-DFV M7A/1	2	1min 24.4sec 10/25	1min 26.11sec 2/23		2–20	6/6	Lp 35 Loss of oil	1st
	J. Bonnier (own entry)	McLaren-BRM V12 M5A/1	3	1min 31.2sec 22/25	1min 30.55sec 18/23		19–20		6th
CANADIAN Mont Tremblant St Jovite 22.9.68	D. Hulme	Ford V8 M7A-DFV M7A/2	1	1min 35.8sec 6/22	1min 34.9sec 5/21		8–21	1/7 WINNER 2/7	1st
	B. McLaren	Ford V8 M7A-DFV M7A/1	2	1min 37.4sec 12/22	1min 35.0sec 7/21		6–21		2nd
	D. Gurney	Ford V8 M7A-DFV M7A/3	11	1min 37.2sec 11/22	1min 34.5sec 4/21		5–21	Lp 29 Overheating	4th
	J. Bonnier (own entry)	McLaren-BRM V12 M5A/1	22	1min 41.7sec 19/22	1min 39.6sec 16/21		17–21	Lp 1 Metering unit seized	
USA Watkins Glen 6.10.68	D. Hulme	Ford V8 M7A-DFV M7A/2	1	1min 05.44sec 6/24	1min 04.57sec 5/23		6–20	Lp 93 Damaged after spinning off course	3rd
	B. McLaren	Ford V8 M7A-DFV M7A/1	2	1min 08.15sec 17/24	1min 05.69sec 10/23		9–20	6/8	5th
	D. Gurney (Anglo-Amer, Racers)	Ford V8 M7A-DFV M7A/3	14	1min 05.84sec 9/24	1min 05.22sec 7/23		8–20	4/8	3rd
	J. Bonnier (own entry)	McLaren-BRM V12 M5A/1	17	1min 08.93sec 19/24	1min 09.20sec 20/20		17–20	Still running at finish officially classified as 14th	11th
MEXICAN Mexico City 3.11.68	D. Hulme	Ford V8 M7A-DFV M7A/2	1	1min 48.96sec 10/20	1min 46.04sec 3/21		3–21	Lp 11 Accident after suspension failed	3rd
	B. McLaren	Ford V8 M7A-DFV M7A/1	2	1min 48.28sec 7/20	1min 47.00sec 9/21		10–21	2/21	2nd
	D. Gurney (Anglo-Amer, Racers)	Ford V8 M7A-DFV M7A/3	14	1min 50.75sec 15/20	1min 46.15sec 6/21		6–21	Lp 29 Lower rear wishbone failure	3rd
	J. Bonnier (own entry)	McLaren-BRM V12 M5A/1	17	1min 52.30sec 19/20	1min 46.96sec 12/21		17–21	5/21	5th

be done. The Cosworth engine had dominated, winning eleven out of twelve races in 1968. Ferrari and BRM were overwhelmed, as was the Matra engine. Lotus, Matra, and Rob Walker's Dulacher Racing Lotus also used the Cosworth DFV, and designers were now looking at further ways of using all the available power. The route most favoured was four-wheel drive, the very path engine builders Cosworth themselves were following. If McLaren were not to be left behind, and many seasoned observers of Grand Prix racing were of the opinion that four-wheel drive would take over, they too had to design a car. Of course, the problem was keeping the M7A competitive in the meantime, while still running the lucrative and successful Can-Am team.

The whole question of four-wheel drive was emmeshed in the fluctuating fortunes of the Grand Prix teams. During 1968, Lotus had not dominated so completely so as to demoralize everyone else, as it had seemed might be the case. The established teams of BRM and Ferrari had lurched from one disappointment to another and, though they could never be discounted, looked less threatening than they ought to have been. Even Brabham who had largely dominated the previous two years, had not made much of a showing, their Repco V8 not really being a match for the Cosworth engine. In place of these, McLaren came to the fore, as did Ken Tyrrell's Matra-Ford driven by Jackie Stewart. Both teams produced front-running cars, utilizing the Cosworth engine, and for 1969 it did seem as though you might as well not bother entering if you did not use one of these.

RETRENCHMENT

So it was that Lotus, McLaren, Matra-Ford, and Cosworth themselves, followed the four-wheel drive path. As has been suggested, this appeared the way to go, provided of course that you had a DFV with power to spare. If four-wheel drive was a success, and a team ignored the option, then that team would be out of the picture in terms of really competing at Grand Prix level.

In all cases though, and to varying degrees, four-wheel drive was a failure. The systems used tended to be heavy, complicated, expensive, and required a quite different driving technique to that of the ordinary car. None of these problems would have proved to be either individually, or collectively, insurmountable, but aero-

dynamic aids were rapidly losing their witches' brew reputation and were becoming a science in themselves. After several setbacks, teams hit the right note and wings were used to much greater effect, and totally outperformed four-wheel drive in nearly every aspect of performance and practicality.

So for those teams involved, four-wheel drive proved to be an expensive failure – though Lotus persisted for a year or two – and the experiment has never been repeated since. However, a question remains. Could four-wheel drive work with today's more powerful engines, better manufacturing materials, and techniques? It has been proven in rallying, so why not Grand Prix racing? Perhaps we could return to a wingless era.

As the 1969 season approached, McLaren were busy working on their four-wheel drive car, the M9A, while seeking to keep the M7A competitive in the meantime. This was a similar problem to that faced by Lotus and Matra,

Teddy Mayer leans over Denny Hulme and a half-stripped M7. In the background somebody seems to be setting about the engine with a tuning fork, while this view shows the attachments for the slab-sided fuel panniers.

This shot shows the ill-fated four-wheel drive M9A car raced by Derek Bell at the 1969 British Grand Prix. Behind is Denny Hulme's M7A car from 1968.

while others, such as Ferrari and BRM, were more concerned with mundane matters, such as engine horsepower. McLaren also had their Can-Am cars to develop, but at least here they had a winning formula on which to work.

McLaren entered three cars for the opening race of 1969, the South African Grand Prix, all from the previous season. Local driver Basil van Rooyen was the third driver alongside Bruce McLaren and Denny Hulme, and things got off to a reasonable start, with two points finishes.

Wings were now on tall, spindly struts at both the front and rear, and looked very precarious and odd indeed. The Spanish Grand Prix saw both Bruce and Denny in the points, but a horrific accident caused by wings breaking

up marred the race, and thrust safety to the fore again. There were many arguments for and against wings, some being a foretaste of those used a decade later concerning 'ground effects'. Wings were fine when they worked, but the problems occurred when a driver arrived at a corner, expecting to brake and take it normally, and suddenly found that a wing strut had broken. Robbed of the downforce, the car would be going too fast for the corner, and an accident was inevitable.

While the arguments raged and occasionally boiled over, a compromise on wing heights was reached, resulting in them having a much lower profile and appearing as part of the bodywork. As well as being safer, these new wings were

The two pictures on this page make an interesting comparison in the attitude of the McLaren cars. Here Denny Hulme brakes hard at Monaco, in his M7A, the nose nearly scraping the circuit . . .

. . . while Bruce McLaren's M7C nose points upwards as he accelerates hard out of the tunnel at Monaco, on his way to fifth place. The small fixed wing on the rear is also visible.

lighter annd worked better, and hastened the demise of four-wheel drive.

In Spain, Bruce had been driving a F5000 M10A chassis re-built to Grand Prix specification and designated an M7C. He raced this thereafter, while Denny Hulme continued with his M7A/2. As the season progressed, the McLarens were always among the leading bunch, but were being outclassed by Stewart's Matra-Ford and the Lotus team. Hulme in particular suffered with a string of retirements in mid-season, despite several good grid positions, but team morale remained high.

During 1969, M7A/3 was sold to Colin Crabbe's Antique Automobiles team, for Vic Elford to drive. Though not in the works team, the car was competitive and featured slab-sided fuel tanks, and was designated an M7B. Elford

put up some good performances, picking up Championship points at the French and British Grands Prix. Rather unfortunately, and ironically, his season ended at the German Grand Prix, when Mario Andretti's four-wheel drive Lotus 63 crashed. A wheel came off and hit Elford, who then crashed and wrote off his car, injuring himself.

Appropriately, the four-wheel drive M9A was finally ready to race at the British Grand Prix, to be driven by young Derek Bell. It was not a success; the car proved to be quite uncompetitive and retired with suspension failure. The car was never raced again, and marked one of the few failures in McLaren's history. The same could also be said in the career of Derek Bell who went on to become one of sports car racing's greats.

Denny Hulme scored his only win of 1969 in the final race, in Mexico. Here, with a full-face helmet, he leads with no pursuers in sight.

Bruce McLaren in his M7C, on the way to fifth at Monaco.

By the second half of the season, the World Championship was virtually sewn up by Stewart. The M7s were usually fast but inconsistent. Bruce was doing well however, and despite not recording a victory picked up points regularly. Perhaps the Italian Grand Prix typified his season, when he finished a blink of an eye behind the winner, Stewart, yet came fourth. It was left to Denny Hulme to achieve a tangible reward for their efforts by winning the final race of the year, in Mexico. Bruce McLaren finished third in the Driver's Championship, with Denny Hulme sixth, and McLaren were fourth in the

Constructors' Championship. Perhaps not as good as hoped for when the season began, but as Bruce won the Can-Am Championship it was hardly a failure. With the four-wheel drive project out of the way, McLaren could now concentrate on a conventional replacement for the M7A and its variants.

Grand Prix racing had, in Jackie Stewart, a new World Champion. 1969 was a successful season for Grand Prix, with many technical advances and some thrilling racing, none more so than the dramatic finish at Monza. Once again though, there had been several very serious ac-

Denny Hulme's front-winged M7A, also at Monaco.

cidents, the consequences of which gave the publicity-conscious sport a bad press. More than any previous World Champion, Stewart was to use this position to highlight the safety issue. It was no longer realistic to accept death or serious injury as a consequence of a misjudgement on the race track.

GROWING PAINS

The 1970 season was to confirm Grand Prix's arrival into the modern era. After years of small

grids and few truly competitive cars, things were changing, and an automatic qualification by just turning up was not guaranteed. Sponsorship was an obvious reason for this, and cars were increasingly wearing the colours of their sponsors. Another reason was the founding of March Racing. This company was started by a number of racing people, of whom Robin Herd, the ex-McLaren designer, provided the 'H'. Apart from their own team, they sold off-the-shelf cars to teams who could then install a Cosworth/Hewland package and be ready to race. Their major customer, at least temporarily,

Grand Prix Results 1969

GRAND PRIX	DRIVER	CAR	NO	1ST PRACTICE Time/Posn	2ND PRACTICE Time/Posn	3RD PRACTICE Time/Posn	FINAL GRID POSN	FINAL PLACING	RETIRED CAUSE OF	HIGHEST POSN IN RACE
SOUTH AFRICAN Kyalami 1.3.69	D. Hulme	Ford-V8 M7A-DFV M7A/2	5	1min 21.8sec 1/15	1min 20.5sec 3/17	1min 21.5sec 2/19	3-18	3/8		3rd
	B. McLaren	Ford-V8 M7A-DFV M7A/3	6	1min 21.3sec 6/15	1min 21.1sec 8/17	1min 22.2sec 3/19	8-18	5/8		5th
	B. van Rooyen	Ford-V8 M7A-DFV M7A/1	18	1min 21.8sec 8/15		1min 24.4sec 7/19	3-18		Lp 12 Brakes	3rd
SPANISH Barcelona 4.5.69	D. Hulme	Ford-V8 M7A-DFV M7A/2	5	1 min 30.6sec 6/12	1min 29.3sec 5/14	1min 28.6sec 9/15	8-14	4/5		4th
	B. McLaren	Ford-V8 M7C-DFV M7A/4	6	1min 32.6sec 10/12	1min 30.0sec 6/14	1min 29.7sec 14/15	13-14	2/5		2nd
MONACO Monte carlo 18.5.69	D. Hulme	Ford-V8 M7A-DFV M7A/2	3	1min 29.0sec 8/15	1min 27.8sec 7/17	1min 26.7sec 11/17	12-16	6/7		6th
	B. McLaren	Ford-V8 M7C-DFV M7A/4	6	1min 27.6sec 6/15	1min 29.2sec 11/17	1min 26.5sec 8/17	11-16	5/7		4th
DUTCH Zandvoort 21.6.69	B. McLaren	Ford-V8 M7C-DFV M7A/4	6	1min 23.71sec 5/15	1min 24.07sec 8/15	1min 22.87sec 2/13	6-18		Lp 25 Front hub	6th
	D. Hulme	Ford-V8 M7A-DFV M7A/2	7	1min 23.28sec 3/15	1min 23.07sec 4/15	1min 26.08sec 12/13	7-18	4/10		3rd
	V. Elford (Antique Automobiles)	Ford-V8 M7A-DFV M7A/3	18	1min 35.17sec 15/15	1min 28.8sec 15/15	1min 28.47sec 13/13	18-18	10/10		10th
FRENCH Clermont Ferrand 6.7.69	D. Hulme	Ford-V8 M7A-DFV M7A/2	5	3min 04.7sec 2/12	3min 06.7sec 7/13	3min 02.4sec 2/13	2-13	8/10		2nd
	B. McLaren	Ford-V8 M7C-DFV M7A/4	6	3min 13.0sec 8/13	3min 09.5sec 10/13	3min 05.5sec 7/13	8-13	4/10		4th
	V. Elford (Antique Automobiles)	Ford-V8 M7A-DFV M7A/3	10	3min 17.7sec 11/12	3min 11.1sec 11/13	3min 08.0sec 10/13	9-13	5/10		5th
BRITISH Silverstone 19.7.69	D. Hulme	Ford-V8 M7A-DFV M7A/2	5	1min 24.0sec 7/16	1min 22.394sec 2/16	1min 21.5sec 4/21	3-17		Lp 27 Ignition	3rd
	B. McLaren	Ford-V8 M7C-DFV M7A/4	6	1min 23.9sec 6/16	1min 23.5sec 8/16	1min 22.6sec 9/21	7-17	3/10 6/10		3rd
	V. Elford (Antique Automobiles)	Ford-V8 M7A-DFV M7A/3	19	1min 19.3sec 15/16	1min 26.7sec 13/16	1min 23.3sec 13/21	11-17			6th
	D. Bell	Ford-V8 M9A-DFV 4WD M9A/1	20	1min 26.9sec 14/16	1min 26.1sec 12/16	3min 01.3sec 21/21	21-21		Lp 5 Rear suspension	21st

Race	Driver	Car	No.							Result
GERMAN Nürburgring 3.8.69	D. Hulme	Ford-V8 M7A-DFV M7A/2	9		8min 01.4sec 8/13	7min 52.8sec 4/13	5-14		Lp 11 Broken transmission	5th
	B. McLaren	Ford-V8 M7C-DFV M7A/4	10	8min 09.3sec 6/10	7min 59.5sec 5/13	7min 56.5sec 8/13	8-14	3/4		
	V. Elford	Ford-V8 M7A-DFV M7A/3	12	8min 09.8sec 6/10	8min 06.6sec 11/13	7min 54.8sec 5/13	6-14		Lp 1 Crash	
ITALIAN Monza 7.9.69	D. Hulme	Ford-V8 M7A-DFV M7A/2	16	1min 26.57sec 3/16	1min 25.69sec 2/17		2-15	7/11		2nd
	B. McLaren	Ford-V8 M7C-DFV M7A/4	18	1min 27.54 sec 9/16	1min 26.48sec 4/17		5-15	4/11		3rd
CANADIAN Mosport Park 20.9.69	B. McLaren	Ford-V8 M7C-DFV M7A/4	4	1min 18.6sec 8/18	1min 18.5sec 4/19		9-20	5/8		5th
	D. Hulme	Ford-V8 M7A-DFV M7A/2	5	1min 18.0sec 4/18	1min 18.5sec 4/19		5-20		Lp 10 Ignition Distributor	5th
USA Watkins Glen 5.10.69	D. Hulme	Ford-V8 M7A-DFV M7A/2	5	–	1min 03.65sec 2/18		2-18		Lp 52 Gear leakage	2nd
	B. McLaren	Ford-V8 M7C-DFV M7A/4	6	1min 15.65sec 6/17	1min 04.22sec 6/18		6-18	Did not start		
MEXICO Mexico City 19.10.69	D. Hulme	Ford-V8 M7A-DFV M7A/2	5	1min 43.7sec 4/15	1min 44.7sec 5/17		4-17	1 WINNER		1st
	B. McLaren	Ford-V8 M7C-DFV M7A/4	6	1min 45.5sec 6/15	1min 44.75sec 4/17		7-17	Did not start. Fuel system		

was Ken Tyrrell, who had left the Matra team to found Tyrrell Racing. World Champions Matra wanted to use their own V12 engine, while Stewart and Tyrrell were contracted to Ford and the Cosworth engine, but this new all-French team was to provide good publicity for the sport in that country which pioneered motor sport.

Several drivers made their Grand Prix debuts in 1970, and the list makes impressive reading: Emerson Fittipaldi, François Cevert, Ronnie Peterson, Clay Regazzoni and Rolf Stommolen. Seldom has such a talented array of drivers come to the fore in the same season. (Four of them went on to win Grand Prix races.) Perhaps the most significant event, though, was the introduction of Ferrari's flat-12 engine to replace the inconsistent V12. This engine was to survive until the turbo era and to power three future World Champions. It was also to provide the main opposition to Cosworth throughout the ensuing decade. And, in case we forget, the BRM V12 also became a winner for the first time.

On the car/chassis front, wings continued to be fitted, front and rear, to 1960s-type chassis. Though clearly improving performance, something new was always on the cards. As ever, it was the genius of Colin Chapman who provided the breakthrough, and Lotus with a significant advantage. Throughout 1969 Jochen Rindt and Graham Hill, until his accident, had battled manfully against the Matra-Ford with their Lotus 49s. This car was no longer at the top of the field, and Chapman came up with the Lotus 72, the first car to be designed with wings as an integral part of the chassis/body. Even now, that car looks so far in advance of its rivals as to be from a more recent year. This car, as much as anything, heralded the dawn of the modern era. Rindt used it, to such effect that he was to have the Drivers' Championship virtually sewn up by the Italian Grand Prix, but then fate took a hand.

Simultaneously with car and engine development went that of tyres. Rain tyres had been introduced in 1968, and the major companies, Dunlop, Firestone, and Goodyear, were spending increasing sums competing against each other. Tyre widths had increased and their performance had improved dramatically, perhaps becoming the single most important factor in car cornering and braking speeds. Unfortunately, these ever-rising costs forced the long established Dunlop to reconsider its racing/advertising policies, and they pulled out at the end of the season.

McLaren's main hopes for 1970 lay in a new car, the M14A. It was evolved from the M7A, incorporating certain Can-Am developments, and did not, unlike the Lotus 72, mark any radical change. As such, it ought to have been an improvement over its predecessor. This was the case in pre-season testing, but you never know how good a car is until it is raced against the opposition. Two chassis were built to this design for the start of the season.

McLaren also had two other irons in the fire. The most important of these was the use of the Alfa Romeo-backed, Autodelta-prepared V8 engine developed from the Tipo 33 sports car. It produced around 430bhp at 10,500rpm, but they proved to be fairly unreliable horses. This was mated to a modified M7A chassis, designated M7D, and made its debut at the Spanish Grand Prix, where it failed to qualify, driven by the inexperienced Andrea de Adamich. In fact, this same misfortune befell it at Monaco, and it was only when an M14A chassis was built, as an M14D, that the car finally made the starting grid.

The other 'iron' was the setting up by John

Tyler Alexander

Alexander first met Tim and Teddy Mayer before Bruce McLaren did, back in the early sixties in America. He was an aircraft engineer who got into racing by preparing 500cc engines for friends, and eventually became the Mayers' mechanic. Coming to England in 1963, Alexander rejoined the brothers and entered the initial discussions about the possibility of forming McLaren Racing. He stayed on after the death of Tim Mayer to become successively: Chief Mechanic, Chief Engineer, and a director.

Increasingly, Tyler Alexander became involved in the American racing arm of McLaren, and his Grand Prix appearances dried up, especially when based at McLaren Engines Incorporated at Livonia, to run the USAC and IMSA teams. As such, he was not a well known face on the Grand Prix circuit.

Then in 1980, with the Grand Prix effort floundering, Alexander was recalled to assist Mayer in his efforts to turn the team's performances round. However, a new era had dawned: that of the ground effects, and Alexander, like Mayer, was very much of the 'old school' of practical mechanical engineers. He remained with McLaren International until the end of 1982, when Ron Dennis bought out his small shareholding and, like Mayer, Alexander left the company. He continued through 1983 at McLaren Engines, working on the Buick Indy project, before parting company for good. Two years later he was back in Grand Prix racing with the Carl Haas-Lola team, alongside Teddy Mayer again, but this project folded at the end of 1986.

Tyler Alexander played a central role in the birth and growth of McLaren for, without their successful American operations, the Grand Prix team might never have reached its later heights. While Teddy Mayer ran the show and Gordon Coppuck designed the cars (both obvious targets for the press), Alexander kept out of the limelight. Most successful operations need a solid rock to keep things in check and perspective, and Alexander performed this dutiful role for McLaren, especially in the USA.

Surtees of his own Grand Prix team. He bought Bruce McLaren's old M7A/4, and used it himself in the first three Grands Prix of the year. This car was later raced by Jo Bonnier, and

Denny Hulme leads Jackie Stewart and Jean-Pierre Beltoise in fourth place at the British Grand Prix. The M14 was not a great car and never matched the Lotus 72, but Hulme finished third at Brands Hatch.

continued to be used by him on occasions until the end of 1971. This car had the unusual record of starting sixteen Grands Prix for two teams, featuring three drivers, in three years; and did not record a single victory.

TRAGEDY

As the cars lined up on the grid for the South African Grand Prix, the signs were there that 1970 may become a watershed in Grand Prix racing: new teams, new drivers, a revolutionary new car on its way, more competitors, and more sponsorship. Despite retirements for Bruce McLaren and John Surtees, Denny

Hulme brought the new car home second in South Africa. In Spain, Hulme again qualified and raced well, but retired, along with Surtees, while Bruce came second – two good results without really setting the pace. At Monaco, despite Bruce McLaren crashing and John Surtees retiring again, Denny Hulme came fourth. But then, disaster struck.

McLaren had never restricted themselves to Grand Prix racing, entering works cars in Can-Am, F5000 and F2, and contracting out the building of cars for customers. There was thus a great deal of testing to undertake, for the time, and on 2 June 1970, Bruce was trying out a Can-Am car at Goodwood, when he crashed fatally. The announcement of his death stunned

Denny Hulme leads Clay Regazzoni during the early stages of the British Grand Prix. He beat the forceful Swiss driver in the end, despite 'Regga' trying to outbrake him and shooting across his bows, fortunately missing him.

motor racing, much as Jim Clark's did, two years earlier. Whereas Clark was in the 'genius' category of drivers, McLaren was perhaps the most well liked and popular of drivers, and the loss of such a character was a great blow to the sport.

Needless to say, the effect on the team was well nigh catastrophic. Entries to the forthcoming Belgian Grand Prix were withdrawn and the whole question of the team continuing was raised. Despite the management of McLaren being very much a team effort, Bruce's role and

influence were central to their existence. Continuing without the founder seemed to be out of the question, and yet would not Bruce have expected them to carry on? Had the decision to do so not been taken, Grand Prix racing would surely have taken a different path to the one it has trodden down the years. It may, or may not, have been 'better', but Grand Prix racing would have certainly been less colourful and entertaining.

The team decided to resume racing for the Dutch Grand Prix, though Denny Hulme was also absent, having suffered burns to the hands while racing at Indianapolis. F5000 driver Peter Gethin temporarily replaced Denny, while old friend Dan Gurney came in for Bruce. The whole meeting was something of a disappointment with Gethin crashing, Gurney retiring, and de Adamich in the new M14/D failing to qualify for the third race in succession.

Hulme returned at the French Grand Prix, and both he and Gurney recorded points finishes without even seriously challenging the leaders. Even de Adamich, in the M7/D, started a race only to finish fifteenth. Denny used the

M14/D chassis with the DFV engine for this race and the following British Grand Prix, while his own car was rebuilt after Gethin's crash. His results suggest that it was a good job he did not use the Alfa engine as well.

As a sign of changing times, with increasing commercial influence in the sport, there was a problem over Dan Gurney as Bruce McLaren's replacement. McLaren were sponsored by Gulf Oil and wore their colours, while Gurney was sponsored by Castrol. There were contractual problems which could not be resolved, and so Gurney had to stand down, to be replaced by

Dan Gurney, in his last drive for McLaren, leads Chris Amon, raising his hand, and Jean-François Cevert at Brands Hatch. It was not to be a happy ending, and Gurney retired from seventh place with low oil pressure.

Grand Prix Results 1970

GRAND PRIX	DRIVER	CAR	NO	1ST PRACTICE Time/Posn	2ND PRACTICE Time/Posn	3RD PRACTICE Time/Posn	FINAL GRID POSN	FINAL PLACING	RETIRED CAUSE OF	HIGHEST POSN IN RACE
SOUTH AFRICAN KYALAMI 7.3.70	B. McLaren	Ford V8 M24A-DFV M14A/1	5	1min 20.5 sec 4/21	1min 20.3sec 7/19	1min 20.7sec 9/23	10–23		Lp 39 Engine	4th
	D. Hulme	Ford V8 M14A-DFV M14A/2	6	1min 20.1sec 1/21	1min 20.1sec 5/19	1min 20.2sec 4/23	6–23	2/13		2th
	J. Surtees (own entry)	Ford V8 M7C-DFV M7A/4	7	1min 20.5sec 5/21	1min 20.2sec 6/19		7–23		Lp 59 Engine	4th
SPANISH Jarama 19.4.70	D. Hulme	Ford V8 M14A-DFV M14A/2	5	1min 24.1sec 1/22	1min 24.1sec 1/22	1min 24.3sec 3/22	2–16		Lp 1 Rotor arm shaft	2nd
	J. Surtees (own entry)	Ford V8 M7C-DFV M7A/4	8	1min 25.2sec 8/22	1min 25.2sec 8/11	1min 26.0sec 2/22	12–16		Lp 77 Gearbox	3rd
	B. McLaren	Ford V8 M14A/1	11	1min 25.7sec 12/22	1min 25.7sec 12/22	1min 24.5sec 6/22	11–16	2/5		2nd
	A. Adamich	Alfa-Romeo V8 20 M70/1	20	1min 25.8sec 14/22	1min 25.8sec 14/22	1min 25.15sec 16/22	Did not qualify			
MONACO Monte Carlo 10.5.70	A.Adamich	Alfa-Romeo V8 M7D/1	10	1min 27.6sec 14/20	1min 54.7sec 18/20	1min 29.3sec 18/22	Did not qualify 3–16			
	D. Hulme	Ford V8 M14A-DFV M14A/2	11	1min 25.1sec 3/20		1min 29.4sec 21/22	10–16	4/8		3rd
	B. McLaren	Ford V8 M14A-DFV M14A/1	12	1min 26.6sec 8/20		1min 26.1sec 6/22	13–16		Lp 20 Damaged suspension after accident	10th
	J. Surtees (own entry)	Ford V8 M7C-DFV M7A/4	14	1min 27.4sec 11/20	1min 40.9sec 6/22	1min 28.7sec 15/22			Lp 15 Engine-oil pressure	11th
BELGIAN Spa-Francor-champs 7.6.70	B. McLaren	Ford V8 M14A-DFV	4	Entry withdrawn						
	D. Hulme	Ford V8 M14A-DFV	5	Entry withdrawn						
	A. Adamich	Alfa-Romeo V8 M7D	6	Entry withdrawn						
	J.Surtees (own entry)	Ford V8 M7C-DFV	17	Entry withdrawn						
DUTCH Zandvort 21.6.70	P. Gethin	Ford V8 M14A-DFV M14A/2	20	1min 24.93sec 23/26	1min 20.41sec 4/23		13–20		Lp 19 Accident	9th
	A.Adamich	Alpha-Romeo V8 M7D/1	21	1min 22.23sec 15/26	1min 21.55sec 3/23	1min 21.36sec 17/23	Did not qualify 20–20			
	D. Gurney	Ford V8 M14A-DFV M14A/1	22	1min 21.61sec 11/26	1min 21.59sec 14/23	1min 21.36sec 16/23	15–20		Lp 3 Engine-timing gear	19th
	J. Surtees (own entry)	Ford V8 M7C-DFV M7A/4	16	1min 22.16sec 14/26	1min 21.50sec 12/23	1m 21.18sec 12/23		6/11		5th
FRENCH Clermont Ferrand 5.7.70	A. Adamich	Alfa-Romeo V8 M7D/1	16	3min 07.09 sec 17/22	3min 05.10sec 14/23	3min 04.04sec 13/23	15–20	Not classified as finisher		15th
	D.Gurney	Ford V8 M14A-DFV M14A/1	17	3min 04.87sec 10/22		3min 04.04sec 15/23	17–20	6/14		6th
	D. Hulme	Ford V8 M14A-DFV M14A/2	19	3min 01.06sec 3/22	3min 01.06sec 3/22	3min 04.73sec 10/23	7–20	4/14		4th

Race	Driver	Car	No.	Practice 1	Practice 2	Practice 3	Grid/Pos		Retirement	Result
BRITISH Brands Hatch 19.7.70	D. Hulme	Ford V8 M14A-DFV M14D/1	9	1min 25.6sec 3/27	1min 27.5sec 18/24	–	4-22	3/9		**3rd**
	D. Gurney	Ford V8 M7A-DFV M7A/1	10	1min 26.6sec 7/27	1min 26.8sec 12/24	–	13-22		Lp 61 Engine	**7th**
	A. Adamich	Alfa Romeo V8 M7D/1	11	Did not start	Fuel leak					
GERMAN Hockenheim-ring 2.8.70	D. Hulme	Ford V8 M4A-DFV M14A/2	4	2min 03.1sec 10/26	2min 02.8sec 17/27	2min 02.1sec 13/23	16-21	3/9		**3rd**
	A. Adamich	Alfa Romeo V8 M14D/1	20	2min 04.1sec 17/26	2min 05.5sec 24/27	2min 03.0sec 21/23	Did not qualify			
	P. Gethin	Ford V8 M14A-DFV M14A/1	24	2min 04.2sec 18/26	2min 06.8sec 26/27	2min 02.2sec 14/23	17-21		Lp 4 Engine	**20th**
AUSTRIAN Österreich-ring 16.8.70	D. Hulme	Ford V8 M4A-DFV M14A/2	21	1min 42.50sec 7/18	1min 41.49sec 10/25	1min 43.00sec 15/24	11-24		Lp 31 Engine	**6th**
	A. Adamich	Alfa Romeo V8 M14D/1	22	1min 47.40sec 16/18	1min 41.82sec 12/25	1min 42.17sec 12/24	15-24	12/15		**12th**
	P. Gethin	Ford V8 M14A-DFV M14A/1	23	1min 43.60sec 13/18	1min 42.79sec 17/25	1min 42.90sec 14/24	21-24	10/15		**8th**
ITALIAN Monza 6.9.70	D. Hulme	Ford V8 M4A-DFV M14A/2	30	1min 29.30sec 22/26	1min 27.59sec 21/27	1min 25.47sec 9/25	9-20	4/9		**1st**
	P. Gethin	Ford V8 M14A-DFV M14A/1	32	1min 30.31sec 24/26	1min 29.13sec 25/27	1min 26.19sec 13/25	16-20	9/9		**9th**
	A. Adamich	Alfa Romeo V8 M14D/1	34	1min 27.91sec 17/26	1min 25.91sec 7/27	1min 26.86sec 17/25	12-20	8/9		**8th**
	G. Galli	Ford V8 M70-DFV M7D/1	36	1min 31.78sec 25/26			Did not qualify			
CANADIAN St Jovite 20.9.70	D. Hulme	Ford V8 M4A-DFV M4A/2	5	1min 34.1sec 5/18	1min 33.9sec 13/20	1min 33.9sec 16/22	16-20		Lp 59 Flywheel	**6th**
	P. Gethin	Ford V8 M14A-DFV M14A/1	6	1min 36.4sec 12/18	1min 33.4sec 10/20	1min 33.2sec 11/22	12-20	6/10		**6th**
	A. Adamich	Alfa Romeo V8 M14D/1	8	1min 36.3sec 11/18	1min 33.9sec 14/20	1min 33.2sec 12/22	11-20		Lp 69 Oil pressure	**8th**
USA Watkins Glen 4.10.70	D. Hulme	Ford V8 M14A-DFV M14A/2	8	1min 05.91sec 16/29	1min 04.84sec 10/30		12-24	7		**6th**
	P. Gethin	Ford V8 M14A-DFV M14A/1	9	1min 06.12sec 18/29	1min 06.13sec 17/30		22-24	14		**13th**
	A. Adamich	Alfa Romeo V8 M14D/1	10	1min 20.40sec 29/29	1min 16.77sec 29/30		Did not qualify			
	J. Bonnier (own entry)	Ford V8 M7A-DFV M7A/4	27	1min 07.16sec 23/29	1min 06.46sec 21/30		23-24		Lp 51 Water pipe	**20th**
MEXICO Mexico City 18.10.70	D. Hulme	Ford V8 M4A-DFV M14A/2	8	1min 45.81sec 12/18	1min 44.95sec 11/18		13-18	3/9		**3rd**
	P. Gethin	Ford V8 M14A-DFV M14A/1	9	1min 45.11sec 9/18	1min 44.46sec 8/18		9-18		Lp 28 Engine	**8th**

Peter Gethin. Though one can understand the two oil companies not wanting to waste their money promoting each other, this event brought home the 'he who pays the piper calls the tune' mentality rather brusquely.

As from the German Grand Prix Gethin partnered Hulme, with de Adamich restored to the M14/D. It would have been too much to expect a major improvement in team performance, though Denny, as ever, continued to doggedly pick up points. Then in practice for the Italian Grand Prix, World Championship leader Jochen Rindt was killed in his Lotus. This affair turned quite nasty, with allegations being made against Lotus, but suddenly Rindt's Championship was subject to doubt, with four races remaining. Jacky Ickx in the resurgent Ferrari was looking competitive and could, with the right results, still become Champion. All this seemed to add a certain messiness to the sport at a time when stability was needed.

Perhaps it was fate, but new Lotus protégé Fittipaldi went on to record his first victory in the United States Grand Prix, to secure the Drivers' Championship, posthumously, for Rindt. With this, Grand Prix racing regained much of its lost dignity.

The safety argument raged back and forth again, one significant victim being the Spa-Francorchamps circuit, which oozed history; unless a circuit could be made 'safe' for the modern commercialized sport, it was likely to be axed. Of course, the larger the circuit, the more expensive to make 'safe', and thus the likelihood of it being replaced. The loss of Spa was a pointer to the future.

McLaren's season ended respectably with Denny Hulme picking up a third place in Mexico, but there were no victories this time around, though Denny Hulme again won the Can-Am Championship as compensation. The M14 had not been a front-running car, and clearly a replacement would be needed for 1971. Mechanical reliability was not all it should have been, Peter Gethin, in particular, suffering in this respect. However, the team had survived the loss of its founder. Wisely, the Alfa engine project was quietly dropped – its poor showing being a combination of McLaren not being able to do their best, indifferent quality from Alfa themselves, and the use of an inexperienced driver. Perhaps if Bruce McLaren had not been killed, and if Denny and Bruce had driven the car . . .

By the end of 1970 Grand Prix racing had made the transition into the new commercial era. It would be wrong to suggest this was anywhere near complete and that all aspects of the 'old' had been eradicated, but an era had passed, and many of the changes were for the better. Four-wheel drive had come and virtually gone, and the Ford-Cosworth engine made for more competitive teams and racing, without completely overwhelming developments elsewhere. Perhaps most importantly, the 3-litre formula had put the 'oomph' back into Grand Prix racing, enabling it to justify the title 'Grand Prix' once again.

Despite their dominance of Can-Am, Grand Prix racing was never more important to McLaren. They would return, along with the ever-expanding number of teams, giving their best in the new season, and now that Lotus had shown the way, everyone was sure to follow. Besides, Tyrrell had their new car ready, Ferrari their new engine, and even BRM were winning again. The racing promised to be more open than it had been for years.

CHAPTER 3

Life After Bruce

On reflection, the two seasons following the death of Bruce McLaren were very much a period of regrouping and coming to terms with life in a rapidly changing environment. In a word, Grand Prix racing was becoming commercialized. It was not a case of money not being important before – witness Jim Clark being forced to live abroad because of high taxation in Britain – but that costs were in a rapidly increasing, upward spiral. Drivers were also beginning to reap an adequate reward for their talents, not to say putting their lives at risk, and this also put an additional strain on team finances. Not that this was driving teams away from Grand Prix, far from it. In fact, the grids were becoming ever longer and brighter coloured, as any number of cars wearing sponsors' logos appeared. Grand prix racing was looking healthier than ever.

SLOW RECOVERY

This was not, like all impressions and images, entirely true. The quantity of cars on the starting grid may have been high, but the quality was little better than in previous years. There were only a few really competitive cars, as usual, and in 1971, this was abysmally small. Ferrari once again appeared to be back-pedalling; their lovely flat-12 engine not really being made use of by an indifferent chassis. March were still on the learning curve, along with the many other novice teams, and it was BRM who offered any, albeit unreliable, opposition to the dominant Tyrrell team. Even this success for the Bourne outfit was laced with poison, as their

top driver, Pedro Rodriguez, was to lose his life.

Lotus, the standard setters of the previous season, were a wayward outfit. Colin Chapman was tinkering with the gas-turbine driven, four-wheel drive Lotus 56, in an ultimately unsuccessful attempt to push the technical boundaries of Grand Prix cars even further. Who knows what might have happened if . . . It is all history now, but it was typical of Chapman not to just evolve his epoch-making 72, but to try and leave the opposition really floundering in his wake. As it was with the four-wheel drive experiments of 1969, it was his standard race car, the 72, which suffered. For the first time in over a decade, a Lotus did not win a Grand Prix and, in reality, did not look likely to. The door was thus left ajar for Tyrrell to sweep the board. They won seven out of eleven Grands Prix, in a dominating run more usually associated with Lotus themselves, six of which went to Stewart.

The standard of driving was not of the highest order either. Many of the new tyro's were still feeling their way about, showing promise for the future, but not ready to stake their claim yet. Retirements and deaths had robbed the sport of some former greats and, sadly, some of the senior drivers such as Graham Hill and even Denny Hulme, appeared to be on the wane.

Through all this Stewart, in his Tyrrell, cut a great swathe, his smooth driving and masterful car control masking the ability to outrun the fastest 'charger'. Here was a champion who, given a competitive car, could run the fastest opposition ragged, and did so almost to the point of boredom. 'If only there were some real opposition', it was thought. Well, if there were,

Gordon Coppuck

Behind every successful organization there is always one, if not more, leading figure who eschews the limelight; in McLaren's case, this was Gordon Coppuck. He stood almost permanently in the shadows of the other extrovert members of the team, and yet he more than played his part.

Having known Robin Herd from his days at the National Gas Turbine Establishment, Coppuck joined McLaren as Herd's assistant at the end of 1965, when the team moved to their new Colnbrook premises. When Herd left at the beginning of 1968, Coppuck worked alongside, rather than under, his new boss Jo Marquart. Coppuck designed the M10A F5000 car and its successors. These proved an immediate success: the outstanding Can-Am cars, the M15 Indy/USAC car and its M16 series descendant. Marquart, meanwhile, concentrated on Grand Prix and Formula 2 cars. Ralph Bellamy took over from Jo Marquart in 1971, but when he left Coppuck was in charge, with John Barnard as an assistant.

The design tradition at McLaren was unlike that at Lotus, where one leading personality prevailed. Coppuck was in charge of design, but with forceful characters such as Teddy Mayer around, others had their say; good in terms of keeping the situation fluid, but risking the 'Too many cooks . . .' syndrome. Coppuck made this system work – with his M16B winning the Indianapolis 500 for the Penske team – and then he penned his first Grand Prix car, the M23. Here, Coppuck's approach reached its zenith, with an M16 and M19 laid out side by side; and the M23 grew in his mind's eye. And what a car it was.

Over a remarkable career spanning four-and-a-half years as a front-line Grand Prix car, the M23 won seventeen Grands Prix, and four non-championship races. Though the 1973 cars were not identical to those running four years later, they were modified either to keep them competitive or to suit the regulations. In this respect, the M23 ranks alongside the Lotus 72 and McLaren's own Barnard-designed MP4 cars for competitive longevity.

Yet Gordon Coppuck had more to offer. His M16D won the 1974 Indianapolis 500, while the M26 won three Grands Prix. But there the success stopped. The hideous, supposedly 'ground effect' M28 was a disaster and the two follow-up cars were little better. When McLaren International was formed Gordon Coppuck was left out, no doubt weary after years of multitudinous pressures spent working in the hottest of hothouses.

Thereafter, Coppuck worked for Robin Herd on the new March Grand Prix car, and later still his Spirit team was the vehicle selected by Honda for their re-introduction into Grand Prix racing, in 1983. When Honda moved to Williams the following year, Spirit gamely tried to continue before finally being forced out of the top echelon of motor racing. In 1986, Coppuck was in charge of the March GP–P cars project, and still later was back in Grand Prix racing – the move away from the single-designer car allowing him to find a niche again.

Gordon Coppuck falls somewhere between the original 'nice guy' and the archetypal 'boffin', but do not be fooled by the quiet manner; here is one of the most successful of Grand Prix car designers. Furthermore, his string of successful designs in other categories of racing (Can-Am, F5000 and USAC) is virtually unrivalled, giving Coppuck a unique place in motor racing history.

Stewart would have destroyed them as well, such was his mastery in 1971.

More than just a driver though, Stewart was becoming the sport's ambassador. Perhaps the most professional racing driver of all time, Stewart was the perfect front man for his sponsors, the sport in general, his team, and for carrying the torch in the safety crusade, to which he devoted much energy. Grand Prix racing looked as though it was becoming a one-man show.

By 1971, sponsorship in Grand Prix was the norm. Drivers, teams, circuits and races dis-

played sponsorship as costs soared. As a result, a more professional attitude was demanded and teams and drivers had to devote time to their sponsors. All this added to their workload and, of course, sponsors wanted more races for their money. There are more Grand Prix races these days than there were in 1971, but in that year there were eight non-championship races, not all of which attracted good entries. More countries were wanting to be represented on the Grand Prix calendar, and sponsors were usually only too glad of the added exposure. All this led to an increased competitiveness within the sport, and further pressure to do well. Hence the loss of some of the 'sportingness' within Grand Prix.

McLaren were in quite a different position to most teams as the 1971 season approached. While coming to terms with the loss of their founder, Bruce was such an important figure within the team that he could not be totally replaced. More than this, though, the M14 car had proved to be off the pace and a new car was needed urgently. Secrecy within Grand Prix racing is not particularly easy, and a straightforward Lotus copy might have seemed the safe

road for McLaren to take, all things considered. Instead, with the new car designated M19, Ralph Bellamy tried to steal a march on the rivals by using rising rate suspension.

The car itself was longer and wider than the M14 and had a full, coke-bottle shaped monocoque, with a distinctly modern look. Unfortunately, the decision to proceed with the rising rate suspension proved to be McLaren's undoing and, along with the wings, made the M19 very difficult to set up correctly. The car oversteered badly out of corners, after usually having understeered into them, and was difficult to

The 1971 M19 makes its press debut. Naturally full of optimism, especially with the rising rate suspension expected to work wonders, McLaren's fortunes were soon to change – for the worse.

drive consistently and quickly. Furthermore, only one chassis was completed before the Dutch Grand Prix in June.

Another innovation was the founding of the Nicholson-McLaren Cosworth engine rebuilding operation, with John Nicholson at Colnbrook. Previously, Cosworth had undertaken this themselves but, due to the increasing number of engines in use, they had begun to farm this work out, offering the opportunity for teams to secure some small horsepower advantage over their rivals.

On the driving front, Denny Hulme was to lead the team with Peter Gethin, who had stepped into the breach after the problems with Dan Gurney. It was not to be a happy season though, as Gethin soldiered on with an M14 until the Dutch Grand Prix and then crashed at the German Grand Prix. He felt he was made the scapegoat for the M19 failure, in particular the problems with the rising rate suspension, which he could just not get on with. Gethin was told that he would not be needed after Italy, but luck was on his side and BRM offered him a drive for Austria, and he took great pleasure in telling Teddy Mayer to 'stuff the job'. Gethin's re-

---

Peter Gethin

Peter who? You might well ask. Peter Gethin's motor racing career seems to be one long series of contradictions: a Grand Prix winner, yet barely remembered; highly talented, yet relatively unsuccessful at the upper level of motor sport; landing two top Grand Prix drives, but at the wrong time . . . The list could go on.

Born in Surrey and son of the jockey Ken Gethin, Peter graduated into Grand Prix from F5000. Using a semi-works McLaren, Gethin won the European 5000 crown in 1969 and 1970, earning himself the title 'King of F5000', before Bruce McLaren invited him to replace Denny Hulme for the Belgian Grand Prix. Bruce McLaren was killed shortly afterwards, and the McLaren entries were withdrawn, but Gethin made his Grand Prix debut in Holland. Hulme then returned, and Dan Gurney had taken McLaren's place, so Gethin was out. But not for long. Following the dispute between Gulf and Castrol over Gurney's presence in the team, Gethin took over as number two to Hulme from the German Grand Prix onwards, but the M14 let him down badly, and he only managed one sixth-place finish.

For 1971 Gethin lost his Can-Am seat to Peter Revson, and was faced with racing the M19 and its awkward 'rising rate' suspension, though he used an M14 in the early rounds. Gethin, who was not too happy at McLaren, just could not get on with the 'rising rate' suspension, and as the team became less competitive by the race, Teddy Mayer informed him that he would not be needed after the Italian Grand Prix. Word of this must have leaked, because Louis Stanley telephoned to ask if he would be free for Austria. Gethin took great pleasure in being able to tell McLaren to 'stuff the drive', and moved to BRM.

His second race for BRM was in Italy at the final Monza slip-streamer, and towards the end he hauled himself up into the leading bunch. Then, on the final dash out of the *Parabolica*, Gethin got his BRM in front, to cross the line barely 2 feet ahead of Peterson and win at a record 150.75mph (242.55kph) average speed – a record that still stands. With great presence of mind, Gethin threw his arm aloft as he crossed the line, to make extra sure of his victory. One can never be too prudent . . .

Gethin looked to have landed on his feet, but it was not to be. The 'great white hoax' of British racing was about to go into terminal decline, and in 1972 Gethin was a victim of BRM ineptitude. He returned to F5000 in 1973, winning the Race of Champions against a good field of Grand Prix cars, and was runner-up in the European F5000 Championship in 1974 and 1975. He won the 1974 Tasman Series and was runner-up in the 1977 Can-Am Championship. Yet, despite all this, and his obvious talent, Gethin only managed one Grand Prix drive in 1974, and that was his lot; he retired.

After a brief foray into management, Gethin left the sport, to return in 1983 as Team Manager of Toleman, only to depart the sport for good when Benetton took over. Gethin's Grand Prix record of one win from twenty-eight races, and his dismal McLaren record of only 1 point from fourteen starts, do not reflect his talent; his success in the lesser formulae are rather more indicative in this respect. Had he landed either the McLaren or BRM drives at another time, we might have been talking about Peter Gethin, ex-World Champion, instead of Peter who?

Denny Hulme driving the unsuccessful rising rate suspensioned M19 at a mid-season race. The car's handling was not consistent, changing from understeer to oversteer in corners, with the result that the drivers were not able to commit themselves totally. It never really worked well, and as the season wore on, so the team seemed lost and confused.

This view of Denny Hulme in his M19 shows the front rising rate suspension under braking. The Coke bottle shape of the car, its low waistline and new slick tyres can be seen clearly.

Peter Gethin in his last race for McLaren (the German Grand Prix) lead the BRMs of Vic Elford and Howden Ganley. It did not last long and he went off the road on lap 5. Two weeks later, Gethin was racing for BRM in Austria.

venge was complete when he won the Italian Grand Prix for BRM in one of the closest ever finishes, at an average speed of 150.754mph (242.55kph), still the fastest Grand Prix ever run. Gethin was initially replaced by Jackie Oliver, while Mark Donohue and David Hobbs also took turns behind the wheel. This make-do-and-mend situation only added to their woes, and did not make for a happy team atmosphere.

Yet it all began well enough. Denny actually led the South African Grand Prix until four laps from the end, when a suspension bolt fell out and he finished in sixth position. This was followed by a fifth place in Spain, and a surprising fourth at Monaco, before the season began to fall apart with a series of retirements and lowly placings.

The rising rate suspension, particularly on the rear, was causing all sorts of problems and rather than solving these, McLaren were falling further and further behind. It was also proving difficult to set the wing angles to suit the car for all parts of a given circuit. The result was a car which was inconsistent, difficult to drive and did not inspire confidence.

On top of this, Denny Hulme also seemed to go off the boil a bit. He was no less a driver than in previous years, but given an unreliable car which was off the pace, Denny's motivation seemed to, naturally, dip. This is not to suggest that he was a fair-weather driver, far from it in fact, but battling away in the mid-field was not really his scene, after so long a time at the top.

Elsewhere, Stewart was dominating proceedings almost at will. Goodyear had introduced slick tyres during the season, and Stewart's Tyrrell responded well to this latest innovation. Firestone were being left behind and their teams were floundering even more than other Goodyear runners.

Unfortunately, the safety question raised its head again during the season. Pedro Rodriguez, Piers Courage and Jo Siffert were killed, and Spa was dropped from the calendar. Watkins

All was not doom and gloom in 1971. Hulme leads at the United States Grand Prix away from Cevert, Stewart, Regazzoni and the rest. He eventually crashed out to round off a very disappointing season.

53

Grand Prix Results 1971

GRAND PRIX	DRIVER	CAR	NO	1ST PRACTICE★ Time/Posn	2ND PRACTICE★ Time/Posn	3RD PRACTICE★ Time/Posn	FINAL GRID POSN	FINAL PLACING	RETIRED CAUSE OF	HIGHEST POSN IN RACE
SOUTH AFRICAN Kyalami 6.3.71	D. Hulme	Ford V8 M19A-DFV M19A/1	11	1min 20.8sec 7/17	1min 20.4sec 11/22	1min 19.1sec 4/25	7-25	6/13		1st
	P. Gethin	Ford V8 M14A-DFV M14A/1	12	1min 21.2sec 13/17	1min 20.1sec 9/22	1min 19.6sec 10/25	11-25		Lp7 Loose fuel line	18th
	J. Bonnier (own entry)	Ford V8 M7C-DFV M7A/4	23	1min 24.6sec 17/17	1min 22.3sec 22/25	1min 22.3sec 22/25	23-25		Lp5 Suspension	22nd
SPANISH Barcelona 18.4.71	D. Hulme	Ford V8 M19A-DFV M19A/1	9	1min 32.7sec 20/21	1min 27.1sec 9/22	1min 37.4sec 2/19		5/10		5th
	P. Gethin	Ford V8 M14A-DFV M14A/2	10		1min 26.8sec 7/22	1min42.9sec 9/19		8/10		8th
MONACO Monte Carlo 23.5.71	D. Hulme	Ford V8 M19A-DFV M19A/1	9		1min 25.3sec 5/18	1min 36.9sec 13/18	5-18	4/10		4th
	P. Gethin	Ford V8 M14A-DFV M14A/2	10	102min 08.1sec 10/12	1min 26.9sec 16/18	1min 46.4sec 18/18	13-18		Lp 23 Suspension	11th
DUTCH Zandvoort 10.6.71	D. Hulme	Ford V8 M19A-DFV M19A/2	26	1min 19.74sec 13/22		1min 21.14sec 17/25	15-24	12/12		11th
	P. Gethin	Ford V8 M19A-DFV M19A/1	28	1min 22.07sec 21/22		1min 23.12sec 22/25	21-24	21/24	Running not classified	15th
FRENCH Ricard-Castellet 4.7.71	D. Hulme	Ford V8 M19A-DFV M19A/2	9		1min 53.24sec 9/23	1min 53.70sec 12/20	13-23		Lp 16 Ignition	12th
	P. Gethin	Ford V8 M19A-DFV M19A/1	10		1min 55.71sec 18/23	1min 54.90sec 15/20	20-23	9/13		9th
BRITISH Silverstone 17.7.71	D. Hulme	Ford V8 M19A-DFV M19A/2	9	1min 20.9sec 11/21	1min 19.6sec 15/22	1min 19.9sec 6/22	9-22		Lp 23 Engine	
	P. Gethin	Ford V8 M19A-DFV M19A/1	10	1min 20.9sec 5/21	1min 20.6sec 8/22	1min 20.1sec 16/22	17-22		Lp 53 Engine	
	J. Oliver	Ford V8 M14A-DFV M14A/2	11	1min 22.0sec 18/21	1min 21.0sec 17/22	1min 21.2sec 16/22	18-22		Start-line accident	
GERMAN Nürburgring 1.8.71	D. Hulme	Ford V8 M19A-DFV M19A/2	18	7min 40.0sec 6/21	7min 31.2sec 5/19	7min 26.0sec	5-22		Lp 3 Fuel leak	6th
	P. Gethin	Ford V8 M19A-DFV M19A/2	20	7min 45.6sec 13/21	7min 45.6sec 18/19	7min 41.4sec 18/22	20-22		Lp 5 Accident	11th
AUSTRIAN Österreichring 15.8.71	D. Hulme	Ford V8 M19A-DFV M19A/2	9	1min 38.88sec 5/18	1min 38.95sec 4/17	1min 39.98sec 16/21	9-21		Lp 5 Engine	11th
	J. Oliver	Ford V8 M19A-DFV M19A/1	10			1min 44.22sec 22/22	21-21	9/12		9th
	J. Bonnier (own entry)	Ford V8 M7C-DFV M7A/4	28	1min 42.88sec 19/22	1min 43.03sec 21/21	1min 41.66sec 22/24	Practice only			

Race	Driver	Car	No.						Result
ITALIAN Monza 5.9.71	J. Oliver	Ford V8 M14A-DFV M14A/2	14	1min 26.99sec 12/20	1min 26.76sec 9/12	1min 24.09sec 12/23	13-23	7/10	**7th**
	J. Bonnier (Scuderia Filipinetti)	Ford V8 M7C-DFV M17A/4	28	1min 30.44sec 20/20	1min27.86sec 11/12	1min 26.14sec 21/23	21-23	10/10	**10th**
CANADIAN Mosport Park 19.9.71	D. Hulme	Ford V8 M19A-DFV M19A/2	9		1min 16.5sec 2/25	1min 16.4sec 5/23	1min 16.9sec 9-20 7-20	4/15	**FL 4th**
	M. Donohue (Penske-White Racing)	Ford V8 M19A-DFV M19A/1	10		1min 17.0sec 6/25	1min 16.3sec 3/23	1min 16.7sec 6-25	3/15	**3rd**
USA Watkins Glen 3.10.71	D. Hulme	Ford V8 M19A-DFV M19A/2	7	1min 44.54sec 5/27	1min 42.93sec 3/29		3-28		Lp 47 Spun on oil **2nd**
	J. Bonnier	Ford V8 M7A-DFV M7A/3	20	1min 51.21sec 26/27	1min 49.29sec 28/29		28-28	16/17	**16th**
	D. Hobbs (Penske-White Racing)	Ford V8 M19A-DFV M19A/1	31	1min 49.00sec 22/27	1min 46.26sec 21/29		22-28	10/17	**10th**
	M. Donohue (Penske-White Racing)	Ford V8 M19A-DFV M19A/1	10		1min 45.38sec 18/34		Practice only		

* Some races ran four practices. A driver's best three times are counted.

Glen and the Nürburgring were also altered, trees being chopped down and armco barriers fitted at the most dangerous places. It may be impossible to make motor racing absolutely safe, but at least measures were being taken in this direction.

The racing, despite Stewart's domination, did have its moments. The jockeying for position behind Stewart was as fierce as ever, and in Italy the front five cars crossed the line in a blur of speed and sound, led by Peter Gethin. Then for the final two races of the season, McLaren came back into the running. In Canada the Penske run car of Mark Donohue was an impressive third, ahead of Denny Hulme, who set the fastest lap. The final round of the season, at Watkins Glen, saw Denny qualify on the front row of the grid for the first time that season and, although he crashed in the race, new boy David Hobbs finished in tenth place. Not a great ending, but one showing potential for the future. In addition, Donohue had shown them a way out of the woods with the rear suspension problem.

BACK IN THE WINNERS' CIRCLE

The season over, thankfully for the most part, decisions had to be taken quickly. There was no time to lose, for the 1972 season opened in January with the new Argentinian Grand Prix. In between, there were to be many changes for McLaren. After sponsoring BRM, the Yardley cosmetics company took their coffers to Colnbrook for two seasons with an option for 1974. Further sponsorship came from Gulf and Goodyear, so at least the finances appeared to be strong.

Ralph Bellamy had returned to Brabham, and so Gordon Coppuck was entrusted with modifying the M19, while beginning a new design for the future. The M19 was adapted to take a conventional rear suspension, though the rising rate system was retained at the front. The wings were raised, with a big one fitted at the back, and though a heavy car, it handled noticeably better, aided by Goodyear tyres. Although firm knowledge of the opposition was limited, the improvements were enough to raise

The 1972 Yardley-liveried M19 makes its press debut.

the team's hopes. Furthermore, a new 'C' specification M19 was on the drawing board to be introduced at the Monaco Grand Prix.

After the calamities of 1971 concerning the drivers, Teddy Mayer recruited American oval racer Peter Revson, and once again McLaren had a promising driver line-up. Revson was committed to certain races in the US, and his replacement was to be young Briton, Brian Redman. Of course much would depend on Denny Hulme, and if he was motivated, anything was possible.

As the teams gathered in Argentina, the signs suggested that, though in a healthy enough

shape, Grand Prix racing was evolving, for a second season, rather than launching any serious new technical breakthrough. The dominant Tyrrell team had updated their cars, and of course Stewart was unlikely to relinquish his title without a fight. The most likely challenge to Tyrrell was from Lotus, with Fittipaldi behind the wheel of the revised Lotus 72D. Once Chapman came around to abandoning the Lotus 56 turbine four-wheel drive project, and his energies were focused on a conventional update of the Lotus 72, a serious challenge to the Tyrrell car would surely be made. Elsewhere, the same story of technical evolution was the norm, although the March 721X set new standards of low polar movement, but was mostly a makeweight.

Thus to the racing. After the disappointment of the previous year, McLaren came up trumps from the start. Perhaps goaded by the arrival of Revson, Hulme finished a credit-worthy second in Argentina and followed this up with his first victory for two years, in South Africa; Peter coming third. This fine start could not be maintained, and once the Stewart/Fittipaldi battle got into full swing, Hulme and Revson were slightly off the pace.

The racing was more open than for many years, and while the Lotus was, marginally, the best car, several other teams were always in contention. The two McLarens were picking up points regularly, and when Redman replaced Revson at Monaco, he came a fine fifth, Hulme being way back. He repeated this again in Germany. The only truly disappointing race was in France where both Hulme and Redman failed to finish in the points. For the rest of the season the Mclarens were a model of consistency and reliability. Hulme and Revson seemed to be scoring off each other and for the last half of the

Peter Revson

When Peter Revson was chosen to partner Denny Hulme for 1972, it caused more than a few eyebrows to be raised. Here was an American 'oval' racer, fast, but not the best, whose driving style would surely be too rugged for Grand Prix racing. McLaren would need to do better than this if they were to halt the steady decline in performance of the previous two seasons. In the event, Revson caused even more eyebrows to be raised, in admiration!

Revson was no newcomer to either Grand Prix racing, or McLaren. In the early sixties he raced alongside Tim Mayer, Teddy's brother, in Formula Junior, the forerunner of Formula 3, with the Rev-Em team. Revson then went into Grand Prix in 1963/64, though not helped by decidedly uncompetitive cars. He returned to the American scene, racing Can-Am, Trans-Am, USAC 'ovals', and Ford GT40 sports cars.

In 1970 Revson landed a McLaren drive at Indianapolis, through Denny Hulme's accident and Chris Amon's withdrawal from the race, to forge new links with the team. He raced for McLaren in Can-Am the following year, and beat Hulme for the Championship, and drove for Tyrrell in the United States Grand Prix. With McLaren having a vacancy alongside Denny Hulme for 1972, Peter Revson was thus a more than eligible candidate.

Revson quickly found his feet in the more precise world of Grand Prix, and by the end of the season was nearly the equal of Hulme, who had raised his own performance somewhat to meet the new challenge. The next season saw the two drivers neck and neck, Revson winning two Grands Prix, and beating Hulme in the Drivers' Championship. The two were very much 'team' men though, and whereas Revson's arrival had spurred Hulme to drive at his best, the team atmosphere at McLaren mellowed Revson's slightly arrogant demeanor. The combination seemed to work perfectly, and was an example of Teddy Mayer's often inspired management.

All looked settled for 1974, when Fittipaldi arrived in the new Texaco-Marlboro sponsored team, meaning that Revson would drive the sole Yardley car. Peter was not happy with this arrangement, erroneously thinking that he would get inferior equipment, and left for the Shadow team. He was killed in only his third Grand Prix for his new team, in South Africa.

As events turned out, the Yardley drivers, Hailwood, Hobbs and Mass, did better than Hulme when it came to equipment, often having two cars at their disposal. Revson would have no doubt performed well in such an environment, and may well have embarrassed the Texaco-Marlboro team.

Far from being an unwise choice, Peter Revson might well have been the spark that McLaren needed to set them back on the winning trail, which ultimately led them to the top. Peter was never the most popular of drivers within the USAC ranks, heralding from a wealthy background, but he more than earned the respect of his Grand Prix peers in his all too brief second spell. He single-handedly rounded off his rough edges, and silenced all the critics of his initial appointment where it mattered: out on the circuits. Of the American 'oval' racers who have tried their hand in Grand Prix, only Mario Andretti has equalled the performances of Peter Revson; high praise indeed.

A rear end view of the new M19. Without its rising rate suspension, success was not too long in coming.

year, one, the other, or both, featured on the winners' podium, for one of the placings at most races.

Besides the Lotus and Tyrrell battle for the Championship, with McLaren just behind, other teams were featuring, if only irregularly. BRM, who finished third from bottom in the Constructors' Championship, secured one Grand Prix and one non-championship race victory, and even Brabham, who finished bottom, secured a non-championship race win. This openness made for occasionally thrilling racing, and enhanced interest in Grand Prix, both from spectators' and sponsors' points of view. This is just what the sport needed, after all the off-field battles which bedevilled the season.

As ever, the safety problem was never far from the surface, but the real battle was between the teams and the sport's governing body, the Commission Sportive Internationale (CSI). This was motor sport's version of similar battles being enacted in many sports around this time: football, tennis, etc. An antiquated, authoritarian governing body, seemingly out of step with reality and the needs of the sport for the future still trying to impose its will on all concerned. The old exclusive gentlemen's club/ amateur ethic versus modern commercial reality battles made Grand Prix the loser in the short term, but the safety improvements demanded by drivers and team owners seemed to be working. Better prize money was sought from race organizers and circuit owners, to offset the rising costs of racing teams, grudgingly fought all the way. Grand Prix racing was anything but dull in 1972.

If there was no dominating or technically outstanding car at this time, and ace drivers were thin on the ground, at least 1972 saw several novices make their bow in Grand Prix. The South American pair Carlos Pace and Carlos Reuteman showed much promise, while McLaren gave Peter Revson and the fiery young Jody Scheckter their chances. These four all went on to win Grand Prix races in the future, and Mike Hailwood, the great motorcycle racer, came to the fore on several occasions. These all showed great promise for the future, both for themselves and the sport.

Whatever the reality of slightly below-par cars and drivers, Grand Prix racing seemed to be booming. The safety problems were being dealt with, and teams were both more professional and financially sound than before. Mandatory monocoque chassis, though expensive to build, were safer and, along with circuit improvements, gave the driver who made a mistake a better chance of survival.

The drivers themselves, or at least the top few, were, like their counterparts in other sports, becoming superstars. They were featured endorsing the use of all sorts of products, and of

The opening lap of the Argentinian Grand Prix, with Peter Revson leading Tim Schenken,
Henri Pescarolo, Jacky Ickx and the rest. A new season, new optimism, and new hopes all.

Revson, on his way to a very pleasing third place in the South African Grand Prix. With
Hulme's victory, it was a real red letter day for McLaren.

Denny Hulme disliked racing in the rain, and Monaco only made matters worse. He trails around
on his way to fifteenth place, about to be lapped by Hailwood in a Surtees.

Brian Redman had his first race for McLaren at Monaco and, after dropping to eighteenth place,
fought back to finish a good fifth, showing Denny Hulme what could be achieved if he tried.
Here, he passes Mike Beuttler, in a March. Jean-Pierre Beltoise won in a BRM to give the team
its final Grand Prix win.

The Austrian Grand Prix saw another worthy performance from Revson, to finish third. Here he leads Amon, Schenken, Hailwood, Hill and Peterson, on the opening lap.

A fine study of Denny Hulme on his way to third at the Italian Grand Prix.

Lap 5 of the Canadian Grand Prix, and the battle for sixth place between Reutemann, Cevert, and Hulme, which ultimately became that for third place. After Reutemann ran out of petrol near the end, Hulme came through to clinch the four points.

course they became public property. The benefit was money at the cost of their private lives, and few would shun this opportunity; sponsorship had become an essential element within the sport's financial budgets.

For McLaren, the year was highly successful. They had re-established themselves as one of the top teams, and proved that there was, indeed, life after Bruce McLaren. Their reliability record throughout the season had been the best of all the teams, restoring their reputation in this direction. After the difficulties of the two previous seasons, this transformation was a relief, and much appreciated by many within the sport.

Quite how this change in fortune came about is difficult to assess; it was almost as great a

surprise as their 1968 performance had been. The effort put in behind the scenes by team members could hardly have been improved upon for 1972, yet retirements were limited to just four during the season. The M19, though the same two chassis were used throughout 1971/1972, benefited by having the rising rate suspension removed from the rear. Apart from being more reliable in a race, it was also far easier to set up and the team were not thrashing around in the dark, as they had been doing to a certain extent. With the fitting of a large rear wing, the M19 was thus transformed in its cornering abilities, making it a fine-handling, consistent car out of the corners, if a little slow on the straights.

Perhaps this was the single most important

Emerson Fittipaldi

Emerson Fittipaldi burst on to the Grand Prix scene with Lotus in 1970, winning the United States Grand Prix before the year was out. His rise to fame was meteoric and during the early 1970s he was one of the sporting world's most popular figures.

If 1971 proved to be a difficult learning year, with the Lotus being off the pace, he came back with a vengeance. After a season-long battle with Jackie Stewart, Fittipaldi became the youngest ever World Champion, at the age of twenty-five. Another of Chapman's special relationships with 'his' driver looked to be capable of dominating Grand Prix racing for the foreseeable future, but in 1973 Ronnie Peterson arrived at Lotus. Peterson's natural speed, flair, and highly popular image, began to ebb away at the Chapman/Fittipaldi relationship, and Emerson decided to leave for the new Texaco-Marlboro sponsored McLaren team.

Fittipaldi undertook an intensive winter testing programme with the M23, getting it sorted to his liking. He began to eclipse Denny Hulme and emerged as a front runner for the title. Though the Brabham was the faster car, and the inconsistent Ferraris of Lauda and Regazzoni started to win races, Emerson became World Champion for the second time, aided, as much as anything, by the immaculate preparation of the team. It was not an inspiring win though, achieved more through collecting points than going out to win races.

The following season saw Fittipaldi give best to the dominant Lauda/Ferrari combination, but he still proved he could be a force when the urge took him. His neat and tidy driving style was not wearing on a car, and as a result he was able to pick up points regularly, while not seriously challenging for the lead.

As World Champion, Fittipaldi took the question of safety very seriously, some said too seriously. His integrity in this matter was upheld when he alone refused to race at the ill-fated Spanish Grand Prix of 1975. Unfortunately, there were other occasions when the Brazilian seemed to be more interested in safety than actually racing.

The shock of that winter came when Emerson left McLaren to join his family Fittipaldi team, a decision he has subsequently described as, 'The biggest mistake of my life'. Fittipaldi's demise in Grand Prix racing was almost as dramatic as his entrance. The heavy, uncompetitive Fittipaldi cars left Emerson with little chance to race at the front again, and sadly he drifted almost unnoticed into retirement in 1980.

Four years later, Emerson re-emerged in the American Indycar series, and he won both the Indianapolis 500 and CART Championship in 1989. This shows that the initial talent, which became dimmed through the politics of Grand Prix racing, is still very much to the fore, and at the age of forty-four he is barely in middle age by American racing driver standards.

Peter Revson leads the future World Champion, Emerson Fittipaldi, in third place in Canada.
The Brazilian dropped back later, while Revson went on to finish second.

Grand Prix Results 1972

GRAND PRIX	DRIVER	CAR	NO	1ST PRACTICE★ Time/Posn	2ND PRACTICE★ Time/Posn	3RD PRACTICE★ Time/Posn	FINAL GRID POSN	FINAL PLACING	RETIRED CAUSE OF	HIGHEST POSN IN RACE
ARGENTINIAN Buenos Aires 23.1.72	D. Hulme	Ford V8 M19A-DFV M19A/2	17	1min 13.56sec 2/22	1min 12.99sec 4/22		3-22	2/11		2nd
	P. Revson	Ford V8 M19A-DFV M19A/1	18	1min 14.51sec 8/22	1min 12.74sec 3/22		4-22		Lp 49 Engine seized after spin	8th
SOUTH AFRICAN Kyalami 4.3.72	D. Hulme	Ford V8 M19A-DFV M19A/2	12	1min 18.1sec 4/23	1min 18.1sec 8/25	1min 17.4sec 4/26	5-26	1/17 WINNER		1st
	P. Revson	Ford V8 M19A-DFV M19A/1	14	1min 28.2sec 23/23	1min 18.5sec 13/25	1min 18.0sec 11/26	12-26	3/17		3rd
SPANISH Jarama 1.5.72	D. Hulme	Ford V8 M19A-DFV M19A/1	11		1min 19.18sec 1/25		2-25		Lp 48 Gearbox piston bearing	1st
		Ford V8 M19C-DFV M19C/5	11	1min 20.37sec 4/29 1min 21.30sec 7/24	1min 19.99sec 9/32					
	P. Revson	Ford V8 M19A-DFV M19A/2	20		1min 20.1sec 10/25		11-25	5/11		5th
MONACO Monte Carlo 14.5.72	D. Hulme	Ford V8 M19C-DFV M19C/1	14		1min 22.7sec 7/25		7-25	15/17		8th
		Ford V8 M19C-DFV M19C/1	14	1min 23.5sec 2/25	1min 22.7sec 7/30					
	B. Redman	Ford V8 M19A-DFV M19A/2	15	1min 25.1sec 7/22	1min 23.1sec 10/25	1min 49.4sec 6/21	10-25	5/17		5th
BELGIAN Nivelles 4.6.72	D. Hulme	Ford V8 M19C-DFV M19C/1	9	1min 12.1sec 3/23	1min 12.9sec 11/25	1min 11.8sec 6/23	3-24	3/14		3rd
	P. Revson	Ford V8 M19A-DFV M19A/1	10	1min 12.5sec 6/23	1min 12.2sec 5/25	1min 12.19sec 8/23	7-25	7/14		7th
FRENCH Clermont Ferrand 2.7.72	D. Hulme	Ford V8 M19C-DFV M19C/1	2	2min 54.7sec 3/22	2min 59.7sec 8/23	2min 54.2sec 2/20	2-24	7/18		2nd
		Ford V8 DFV M19A/1	2	2min 55.6sec 2/34		2min 59.4sec 10/20				
	B. Redman	Ford V8 19A-DFV M19A/1	11		3min 0.8sec 15/23		15-24	9/18		9th
		Ford V8 M19A-DFV M19A/1	11	3min 4.3sec 23/34						
BRITISH Brands Hatch 5.7.72	D. Hulme	Ford V8 M19C-DFV M19C/1	18	1min 24.4sec 13/25	1min 23.9sec 7/25	1min 24.0sec 7/25	12-26	5/13		5th
	P. Revson	Ford V8 M19A-DFV M19A/1	19	1min 23.6sec 2/22	1min 22.7sec 1/25	1min 23.1sec 2/25	4-26	3/13		2nd

GERMAN Nürburgring 30.7.72	D. Hulme	Ford V8 M19C-DFV M19C/1	3	7min 31.0sec 13/26	7min 19.4sec 9/24	7min 14.5sec 8/25	9-27		Lp 8 Engine	**10th**
	B. Redman	Ford V8 M19A-DFV M19A/1	5	7min 33.1sec 17/26		7min 23.2sec 15/25	20-27	5/15		**5th**
AUSTRIAN Österreichring 30.7.72	D. Hulme	Ford V8 M19C-DFV M19C/1	12	1min 37.20sec 4/25	1min 37.65sec 10/25		7-25	2/14		**FL 2nd**
		Ford V8 M19A-DFV M19A/1	12T		1min 37.94sec 13/29					
	P. Revson	Ford V8 M19C-DFV M19C/2	14	1min 36.98sec 3/25	1min 36.63sec 2/25		4-25	3/14		**3rd**
		Ford V8 M19A-DFV M19A/1	14T		1min 38.37sec 15/29					
ITALIAN Monza 10.9.72	D. Hulme	Ford V8 M19C-DFV M19C/1	14	1min 35.97sec 2/25	1min 34.84sec 10/25		5-25	3/13		**3rd**
		Ford V8 M19A-DFV M19A/1	14T		1min 36.96sec 11/31					
	P. Revson	Ford V8 M19C-DFV M19C/2	15	1min 36.42sec 7/25	1min 36.82sec 9/25		8-25	4/13		**4th**
		Ford V8 M19A-DFV M19A/1	15T		1min 38.61sec 6/31					
CANADIAN Mosport Park 24.9.72	D. Hulme	Ford V8 M19C-DFV M19C/1	18	1min 14.7sec 2/24	1min 13.9sec 2/23	1min 14.9sec 11/24	2-24	3/13		**3rd**
		Ford V8 M19A-DFV M19A/1	18T		1min 13.6sec 1/23	1min 15.6sec 13/29				
	P. Revson	Ford V8 M19C-DFV M19C/2	19	1min 15.0sec 4/24		1min 14.5sec 7/24	3-24	2/13		**2nd**
		Ford V8 M19A-DFV M19A/1	19T			1min 15.1sec 8/29				
USA Watkins Glen 8.10.72	D. Hulme	Ford V8 M19C-DFV M19C/1	19	1min 41.084sec 3/30		2min 15.829sec 13/31	3-31	3/19		**2nd**
	P. Revson	Ford V8 M19C-DFV M19C/2	20	1min 40.527sec 2/30		1min 56.477sec 4/31	2-31	Not running. Classified 18th	Lp 54 Ign failure	**6th**
	J. Scheckter	Ford V8 M19A-DFV M19A/1	21	1min 42.058sec 7/30		2min 7.828sec 24/31	6-31	9/19		**3rd**

* Some races ran four practices. A driver's best three times are counted

factor in the re-emergence of McLaren. A good car to work with, constantly being improved in minor ways, enhanced team morale – the team knew where they were heading, and Peter Revson's perceived challenge to Denny Hulme, which he rose to meet in typical fashion, was also a boost. All these factors contributed to the overall improvement in performance and established a strong base for future seasons. Indeed, the 1972 season was just the launching pad required, from which to aim and reach new heights within Grand Prix.

CHAPTER 4

The Road to the Top

Following the revival of McLaren's fortunes in 1972, positive steps needed to be taken to ensure this was built on, and that there was no drift back to the dark days of 1971. On the surface, little appeared to have changed. The management team and the drivers remained, as did Yardley, the main sponsors. Even the cars were the same, at least for the first few races of the season, but it was here that McLaren held an ace up their sleeve.

As from the Spanish Grand Prix, to be held at the end of April, all Grand Prix cars had to have a single monocoque structure and deformable fuel tank, these being positive steps in driver safety at long last. A new car, designated the M23, was designed by Gordon Coppuck to meet with the letter and spirit of these requirements. It was inspired by a combination of Coppuck's M16 Indy car and the M19. As the story goes, two chassis of these cars were laid beside each other at Colnbrook, and the new car took shape in Coppuck's mind's eye. As he said, 'It just had to work. . .'. Whether this is true or not is unimportant, but it gives an insight into racing car design in those days; an 'If it looks right, it is right' approach, as opposed to today's highly technical, thoroughly researched teamwork design.

BIRTH OF A LEGEND

The new M23 was not ready for the start of the 1973 season, but when it did make its debut, in South Africa, it was immediately competitive and was to remain so for a further four-and-a-half seasons, not taking its final bow until the end of 1978. Seldom in the history of Grand Prix racing has a single design, though continuously developed, remained competitive for so long. Without wishing to take the story too far ahead, during its life as a front-line team car, the M23 won seventeen Grands Prix, though one was later officially expunged, and four non-championship races. Two drivers won the World Championship with the car, and the team also won the Constructors' Championship. An outstanding record.

Yet the M23 was seldom, if ever, the car to beat. Throughout its Grand Prix life there was always another car/driver combination the equal of, if not superior to, that at McLaren; yet the car still kept winning. The M23 was, by Grand Prix standards, a fairly simple, conventional design, thoroughly tested. With each passing season Coppuck revised and cunningly modified the design to keep it towards, if not at, the forefront of the pack. Its longevity was undoubtedly helped by this period being one of almost technical stagnation, with a few noteworthy and not too successful exceptions. The drivers who won in the M23 (namely, Denny Hulme, Peter Revson, Emerson Fittipaldi, James Hunt, and Jochen Mass) were no mugs either, though only Hunt, at his best, was clearly the fastest driver of his day.

Perhaps the deciding factor with the continuing good fortunes of the M23 was the immaculate preparation and attention to detail of the McLaren team, carrying on the principles established by Bruce McLaren. Without doubt, it was the combination of these factors which made McLaren such a force in Grand Prix over the next five seasons. One wonders if, in

Young Jody Scheckter leads his home South African Grand Prix, in only his second race in the M19. The year 1973 was nearly as eventful for Scheckter as was his Championship year of 1979.

another team, the M23 would have achieved quite the level of success that made it one of the all-time great Grand Prix cars.

Denny Hulme and Peter Revson were to continue in harness again in 1973. This made good sense, as Peter had defied all expectations of an American oval racer and quickly adapted to the neat and precise driving style needed in Grand Prix racing. These were to be joined for a few races by the young South African Jody Scheckter, who had shown immense potential. Jackie Ickx also had a one-off drive at the German Grand Prix, when Ferrari decided not to race there. Denny Hulme also became President of the Grand Prix Drivers' Association, a position of some importance at that time, and fully justified by his standing within the sport.

Elsewhere, the position did not look too rosy. Tyrrell, with Stewart and the fast improving Cevert as drivers, were always likely to be front runners. Reigning World Champion Fittipaldi, still with Lotus, would undoubtedly be a man to beat, but alongside him Chapman had brought in the new starlet and potential champion in the making, Ronnie Peterson. There was no more flamboyant driver in Grand Prix racing at that, or possibly any other, time and given a competitive car, as the Lotus most certainly was, a real challenge was expected from him. The question remained whether Lotus could cater for two top drivers, or would their efforts be dissipated between them?

Regrettably, truly strong challenges from other teams were not expected. The Old Boys of Ferrari and BRM were, once again, in various stages of disarray, the former to eventually recover and the latter, sadly, on their way out. BRM had among their team of drivers Clay Regazzoni and young blood Niki Lauda and began the season well enough, only to quickly fall away. It says much for their state of affairs that even though Lauda was still a relative novice, this pair of drivers, who the next season went on to achieve so much, could not pull any rabbits out of the hat. A new all-American team based in England, Shadow, appeared showing promise for the future, and Techno, with their flat-12 engine, also joined in. But Matra with their V12 engine were losing ground, leaving the rest of the field to Cosworth/Hewland runners.

The racing was to be almost a side issue for much of the season, as Grand Prix lurched from one crisis to the next. At the forefront was the political wrangling, which at times made the House of Commons look like a quiet orderly debating society. The Western world economy was going through one of its inflationary periods, and team costs were rising remarkably. Most teams, but not all, had joined the Formula One Constructors Association (FOCA), to represent them as a body, and had threatened to strike for more starting and prize money. Circuit owners and race organizers then retaliated by threatening to throw open the World Championship to Formula 2, F5000, and USAC cars. At one time we all sat and wondered if there was going to be any racing at all, or if the World Champion was going to be the person who could shout loudest.

As an aside to this argument and kerfuffle, but intertwined within it, was the question of safety. Once again circuit owners, FOCA, and the CSI, the sport's governing body, battled over the need for improvements and, more particularly, the cost of making these. Most people had an opinion on the need to improve safety conditions where reasonably possible – for Grand Prix racing cannot ever be truly safe or else it would not be Grand Prix racing – but when it comes down to putting hands into pockets and paying for the improvements, well, that is another matter. The Grand Prix Drivers' Association (GPDA), naturally enough as they were the ones most at risk, threw in their twopence's worth and threatened to strike over cir-

Denny Hulme climbs into his nice, shiny new M23, while Teddy Mayer wears that all too familiar worried face of his.

cuit safety, the position of photographers and facilities, or lack of them. If everyone had decided to strike, the circuit owners, FOCA, and the GPDA, perhaps we would have seen representatives of the teams' sponsors racing each other on a running track. Now that would have been interesting!

The important part of Grand Prix, the racing, got off to a good start in Argentina at the end of January. The M19s were improved by having M23 rear suspension fitted. Neither made much impression on the results, as Fittipaldi chalked up his first win of the season and Stewart suffered the first important puncture endured by leading runners during the year. In Brazil, Hulme restored the status quo by finishing third in his final race with the M19, behind Fittipaldi – winning his home Grand Prix – and Stewart.

THE M23 BREAKS OUT

The debut for the M23 came at the South African Grand Prix, though only one car was available. Sensationally, and surprisingly for such a distinguished driver, Denny Hulme claimed the pole position for the only time in his Grand Prix career. Local boy Jody Scheckter joined the team for his second Grand Prix, in Denny's old car, qualifying an impressive third on the grid. Hulme, using his new-found advantage of pole position, roared off to lead the race in fine style, until a puncture slowed him and he finished a

disappointed fifth. Not so for Scheckter, though. Driving with all the natural skill he so clearly possessed and all the unconcern of youth for established reputations, young Scheckter briefly led the race at one stage.

Order was quickly restored, and the big guns edged him back to fourth place when, with only four laps to go, his engine failed. Peter Revson upheld the M19's honours in its last Grand Prix by splitting Stewart and Fittipaldi to come second. Stewart, incidentally, was a somewhat fortuitous winner as, following Regazzoni's accident, he overtook under the

Down in deepest Colnbrook, work goes on with the new M23. In the background sits a partially dismantled M19.

yellow flag. Teddy Mayer filed a protest and Stewart was severely reprimanded, but the result was allowed to stand. One wonders if, had it been any other driver, he would have got off so lightly? The accident involving Regazzoni was one of several during the year which served to illustrate the dangers of motor racing. He was rescued by Mike Hailwood, who later received the George Medal for his bravery.

Neither McLaren featured strongly in the Spanish Grand Prix, though both Hulme and Revson now had M23s. Fittipaldi won again to increase his lead in the Championship. It was the same for the Belgian Grand Prix, the first to be run at the Zolder circuit. This was one of those events where the actual racing nearly took a back seat. The track surface broke up dangerously and as the politicians leapt to the fore, prospects for the race looked glum. Naturally Stewart had much to say on this, but then he proved that he spoke from a position of strength as he won in masterly fashion. Controversy raged afterwards; Peter Revson had crashed due to the track surface, and been hit by Jarier's March later. As it all came out in the wash, nobody was seriously hurt and the damage was not too bad. Amidst all this, nobody seemed to notice the Techno team's debut.

There was no mistaking the arrival of the Hesketh team at the Monaco Grand Prix, though. Lord Hesketh and his band of merry men had a customer March 731, with the usual Cosworth/Hewland package, for young Briton James Hunt to drive. Hunt, in his first Grand Prix, got himself into sixth position before his engine expired towards the end of the race. However, it was the team, with their yacht, helicopter, and Rolls Royce, which seemed to make the greatest impact.

This was also the year the new Monaco circuit came into being, another of the so-called 'Mickey Mouse' brigade. Stewart drove a typically calculating race to beat Fittipaldi and ensure that the Championship remained a two-horse event. Once again, neither of the McLarens featured strongly, though Monaco had never been a particularly favourite circuit of the team. This was now the fourth race in which the M23 had promised so much, and yet failed to deliver. The car was clearly good, but not as good as the Lotus or the Tyrrell.

Then, at the inaugural Swedish Grand Prix, McLaren's luck changed. Peterson had been comfortably and stylishly leading his home race until he picked up a puncture near the end. This time it was Hulme who benefited. He sailed into the lead on the penultimate lap, after having held a good second place, to give the M23 its first victory. Denny Hulme deserved his lucky break, though one felt terribly sorry for Peterson to be so close, and yet end up as bridesmaid once again. Denny's win was just what the doctor ordered. The Stewart/Fittipaldi stranglehold of Grand Prix had been broken; both the Lotus and Tyrrell teams were beatable, and it was the McLaren team who were most likely to do the beating.

Peter Revson was to miss the French Grand Prix through his American commitments, to be replaced by Jody Scheckter. If ever McLaren needed to be convinced as to how good their M23 was, the young South African was about to provide the evidence. In his first race with his car, Scheckter qualified firmly in the middle of the front row, right in between the two heavyweight Championship contenders, Stewart and Fittipaldi. This had all been seen before, in South Africa, and the big guns would soon blow the young upstart away, or so it was thought.

No doubt this same thought was going through most people's mind as the upstart led cleanly from the flag: 'Let him have his moment of glory, it won't last long'. Stewart and Fittipaldi thrashed around behind Scheckter for lap after lap, all to no avail as Scheckter was not going to fall off the track, nor did he feel obliged to let them pass. Eventually, only Fittipaldi was able to give chase, even though giving chase was all he could do. Then with twelve laps remaining, Fittipaldi, no doubt getting increasingly desperate, tried to squeeze through on the inside of a slow corner; Scheckter refused to budge and that was that, both cars were out, handing the race to, of all people, Peterson for his long-overdue maiden victory.

Fittipaldi, as was typical of the fashionable showbiz image of the time, indulged in post-race histrionics, accusing Scheckter of this, that and the other, but most independent observers thought the incident fifty: fifty. Surely though, as reigning World Champion, Fittipaldi ought to have known better than to try such a man-oeuvre, or did he think that his mere presence was enough for Scheckter to let him by? What was worse for him was that Stewart had finished fourth and taken over the lead in the Drivers' Championship.

THRILLS AND SPILLS

If this was all fun and games and part of the learning process for Scheckter, the British Grand Prix provided the opportunity for him to make his mark in an even more notable way. Teddy Mayer, with Peter Revson back from America, could hardly ignore Scheckter now, and so all three drivers were entered for the race. Practice only seemed to justify this deci-sion, as Hulme and Revson were both on the front row of the grid, with Scheckter on the third. Scheckter got off well and was waved through by Denny Hulme in pursuit of the leaders.

Coming into the long, fast, right-hander that was the old Woodcote Corner, Scheckter ran wide, putting his two left-hand wheels on to the grass as he came on to the straight. Since rubber does not grip so well on grass, Scheckter had to turn the wheels at a greater angle than normal to try and get back on to the tarmac, when sud-denly, the wheels gripped. Scheckter was head-ing across the circuit towards the pit wall (how long ago was it when drivers were derided for wanting barriers to protect the pits at all cir-cuits?), at 100-plus-God-knows miles per hour,

This is how the McLaren team greeted Peter Revson, as he won the British Grand Prix – his first victory at this level.

and for a split second it looked as though there would be a huge collision. The rear wing of Peter Revson's car was knocked off and Denny Hulme just squeezed through. His was the last car, as the catastrophe that looked imminent occurred when Scheckter's car careered back across the track just as the pack was arriving; mayhem! Suddenly, there were cars, bits of cars, catch fence posts and wire everywhere. You can understand why James Hunt gave Scheckter the nickname 'Fletcher', Jonathan Swift's accident-prone bird, though coming from 'Hunt the shunt' no less, that was a bit much.

That was not the end of the proceedings by a long way. Despite the fact that young Jody had managed to eliminate nine cars, including his own, the race was restarted as though the warm-up proceedings had not happened. Mind you, in future years Silverstone used to hire professional stunt drivers to entertain the crowds, rather than rely on impromptu performances by an obliging racing driver. This time Peterson shot off into the lead and a furious battle ensued with Stewart. After thrilling the crowds with this no-holds-barred contest, which showed that for all his safety consciousness, Stewart was every much a racer, Stewart spun off, leaving Peterson in the lead.

Still there was more to come. Slowly but surely, the McLarens of Revson and Hulme hauled Peterson in, with Revson finally managing to squeeze through into the lead. But there behind Denny Hulme was England's young charger James Hunt, grimly hanging on to Denny's rear wing for all he was worth. Revson began to pull away from this trio, who continued to grab everyone's attention with their exciting battle. Coming into the old Woodcote Corner for the last time in a Grand Prix, Peterson, Hulme and Hunt were a blur of speed and sound. Could Hulme make it a McLaren 1–2, or could Hunt do the impossible? Not quite. Peterson crossed the finish line a blink ahead of Hulme, who was himself two blinks ahead of Hunt. After all this, one could be forgiven for forgetting that Revson had won

his first Grand Prix, and that the M23 had now led the last three races.

The teams had two weeks in which to put right all the damage caused by Scheckter's shunt, in time for the Dutch Grand Prix. McLaren had Denny Hulme and Peter Revson as their sole entries, but neither made much of an impression. The race was notable for Stewart notching up his record twenty-sixth victory, and the lack of a Ferrari entry. Fittipaldi had a huge crash in practice, and once again failed to score points. More importantly, during the race Roger Williamson had a bad crash – the armco barriers collapsed and caused his car to turn over and catch fire. He was trapped inside, as the fire-fighting facilities proved to be hopelessly inadequate, and for lap after lap the cars had to drive past the burning wreck, with the knowledge that a fellow driver had needlessly burned

Denny Hulme had several skirmishes with James Hunt, in his Hesketh-entered March 731. Here at Zandvoort they do battle, with the future McLaren driver all too aware of 'The Bear' in his mirrors.

Peter Revson leads Jean-Pierre Beltoise, in a BRM, and Carlos Pace, in a Surtees, at the Dutch Grand Prix. Revson eventually finished fourth, and Marlboro were to switch their allegiance to McLaren at the end of the season. BRM were the losers once again.

to death. Little wonder the safety question would not go away.

TRIVIAL PURSUIT?

A week later the teams assembled at the Nürburgring for the German Grand Prix and McLaren had a new M23 to replace the car wrecked by Scheckter. Wisely, they did not offer this to Scheckter, on such a long and demanding circuit, but gave the drive to Ickx, as Ferrari were once again absent. Ickx was as familiar with the great Nürburgring as anybody, yet even he could not prevent Stewart notching

up yet another brilliant victory and virtually ensuring himself of his third World Championship. Neither Denny Hulme nor Peter Revson really came to terms with the race, and both finished in lowly positions.

The Austrian Grand Prix provided more disappointment for McLaren, the M23s being strangely off the pace. Peterson was really coming into his own at this stage of the season and he led with some ease. He waved Fittipaldi through to lead, in his hunt for points in the Championship race, but he then retired, leaving Peterson to another win.

Gordon Coppuck had revised the suspension geometry of the M23 after the British Grand

Prix but, despite recent indifferent showings, this remained unaltered for the Italian Grand Prix at the 'emasculated' Monza. From 1971 the introduction of chicanes on this high-speed circuit had slowed things down quite a bit, but it was still a real challenge. The race was important in the World Championship, for if Stewart picked up enough points, the title was his. This did not seem too likely when Stewart sufered a puncture early on, dropping him to twentieth place. Thereafter though he showed what a truly great driver he was, again by weaving his unspectacular way through the field to finish fourth. As Peterson had pipped Fittipaldi by less than a second for another win, Stewart became World Champion for the third time, with two races still to run. McLaren were on the up as well for, despite Denny Hulme's lowly showing, Peter Revson finished third behind the Lotus twins, edging in front of Denny in the Championship table.

For the two North American races, McLaren brought Scheckter back into the team with an eye to the following season. That he had talent was beyond doubt and was demonstrated again at the Canadian Grand Prix. He qualified third on the grid, just behind Revson and well ahead of Hulme. The race started in the rain, and Lauda dominated the first part in the hitherto uncompetitive BRM, to lead a Grand Prix for the first time. Hulme, who disliked racing in the rain and was plagued with punctures from the word go, was nowhere, but as the track dried there was a chance for Scheckter and Revson. Once this happened, that was the end of Lauda's glory, but then Scheckter and Cevert collided, just as everyone was heading to the pits for slick tyres. Scheckter had done it again.

Amidst all the confusion the pace car came out in front of the wrong car, instead of the leader. Nobody seemed to know what was going on and the cars all closed up together. Significantly, Revson virtually made up a whole lap at this stage. This was Grand Prix racing? The race went on until someone decided to hang out the chequered flag, and then the

serious business began. Many hours later, when all sense of meaning had gone out of the window, Revson was declared the winner. Once again he had profited from Scheckter's antics.

For the final race of this fifteen-round contest, appropriately in America – a contest which seemed to have more in common with the Muhammed Ali/Joe Frazier boxing match of that year than with motor racing – McLaren once again fielded three cars. Things got off to a disastrous start when Cevert was killed in a horrifying practice accident. Jackie Stewart, for whom this was to be his 100th and final race, did not start. He had planned carefully from early in the season the moment when 'Uncle' Ken Tyrrell would inform Stewart's wife that Jackie had retired, and when Stewart would then tell Cevert he was to be number one. Now, in one dreadful instant, all this was taken away, and racing had lost yet another driver.

But the race went ahead. Scheckter had his customary spin, though this time it was caused by a wishbone breaking, and he ended up, harmlessly, out of the race. Hulme and Revson finished in the points together for the first time since Silverstone, only in fourth and fifth position. The main interest once again featured Peterson, who swept to his fourth victory of the season, but it was not solely centred on him. He was chased to the flag by Hunt, in his Hesketh-March, who really had no right to be up there. The year before, Peterson himself had been the young charger, and now here he was as the established front man being pressed to within a second at the end of a thrilling race by another young blood. What could Hunt have done with an M23?

The teams and Grand Prix racing in general seemed to be reeling from the effects of the season. The racing had occasionally been thrilling, but too often this had been overshadowed by what ought to have been peripheral events. Despite the retirement of Stewart and the loss of Cevert, prospects on the driving front looked to be better than for many years. Peterson had finally established himself in the winners' circle, and the emergence of Hunt, Scheckter and

During the winter of 1973/74 Emerson Fittipaldi undertook a great deal of testing for the McLaren team. Here he is at Paul Ricard in France, waiting to go out for another spin in his M23, once adjustments have been made.

Lauda promised much for the future. From the standpoint of the cars, things seemed to be at a standstill; a period of consolidation. However, over the previous few seasons speeds had increased so much that this was no bad thing. Technical marking time was of the order, as if waiting for Colin Chapman to pull his next trick out of the hat. It was an open secret that work was already in progress on the new Lotus. Perhaps surprisingly, this very lack of technical advance was to lead to a period of unprecedented competition at the front of Grand Prix racing.

As ever though, there was not long for the teams to recover from the traumas of 1973, gather themselves together and prepare for the start of the following season. Grand Prix racing had suffered a little from the domination of Lotus, Tyrrell and McLaren – each of the fifteen races having been won by cars from these teams – but McLaren's fortunes had been rather mixed. True, they had won more races than in the previous year, but neither their other placings nor reliability had been as good. The M23 had proved to be a good car and an improvement on the M19, but did not appear to be able to match the Lotus 72 which, despite being four seasons old, was still the car to beat.

Grand Prix Results 1973

GRAND PRIX	DRIVER	CAR	NO	1ST PRACTICE★ Time/Posn	2ND PRACTICE★ Time/Posn	3RD PRACTICE★ Time/Posn	FINAL GRID POSN	FINAL PLACING	RETIRED CAUSE OF	HIGHEST POSN IN RACE
ARGENTINE Buenos Aires 28.1.73	D. Hulme	Ford V8 M19C-DFV M19C/1	14	1min 11.88sec 6/16	1min 15.67sec 16/18	1min 11.7sec 7/17	8-19	5/10		5th
	P. Revson	Ford V8 M19C-DFV M19C/2	16	1min 14.21sec 14/19	1min 12.22sec 8/16	1min 12.79sec 7/18	11-19	8/10		8th
BRAZILIAN Interlagos 11.2.73	D. Hulme	Ford V8 M19C-DFV M19C/1	7	2min 34.5sec 4/17	2min 32.7sec 5/19	2min 35.8sec 9/17	5-20	3/12		3rd
	P. Revson	Ford V8 M19C-DFV M19C/2	8		2min 35.4sec 5/17	2min 34.3sec 6/18	12-20		Lp 3 Gearbox	7th
SOUTH AFRICAN Kyalami 3.3.73	D. Hulme	Ford V8 M23-DFV M23/1	5	1min 16.42sec 1/26	1min 16.79sec 4/24	1min 16.28sec 1/23	Pole	5/11		1st
	P. Revson	Ford V8 M19C-DFV M19C/2	6	1min 16.72sec 2/26	1min 16.87sec 5/24		6-25	6/25		6th
	J. Scheckter	Ford V8 M19C-DFV M19C/1	7	1min 16.87sec 3/26	1min 16.77sec 3/24	1min 16.43sec 4/23	3-25		Lp 76 Engine	1st
SPANISH Barcelona 29.4.73	D. Hulme	Ford V8 M23-DFV M23/1	5	1min 23.5sec 3/23	1min 22.5sec 2/24	1min 23.5sec 5/25	2-22	6/12		2nd
		Ford V8 M23-DFV M23/3	5T			1min 26.5sec 20/25				
	P. Revson	Ford V8 M23-DFV M23/2	6	1min 24.8sec 6/23	2min 0.6sec 24/24	1min 23.4sec 4/25	5-22	4/12		4th
		Ford V8 M23-DFV M23/3	6T		1min 42.5sec 23/24					
BELGIAN Zolder 20.5.73	D. Hulme	Ford V8 M23-DFV M23/1	7	1min 42.64sec 22/22	1min 27.1sec 18/23	1min 23.0sec 2/21	2-23	7/12		7th
	P. Revson	Ford V8 M23-DFV M23/2	8	1min 27.79sec 6/22	1min 24.43sec 6/23	1min 23.57sec 9/21	10-23		Lp 36 Accident. Spin	3rd
MONACO Monte Carlo 3.6.73	D. Hulme	Ford V8 M23-DFV M23/1	7	1min 32.3sec 18/29	1min 27.8sec 3/27	1min 30.0sec 14/29	3-25	6/10		6th
		Ford V8 M23-DFV M23/2	7T	1min 33.8sec 21/29						
	P. Revson	Ford V8 M23-DFV M23/2	8			1min 29.4sec 9/29	15-25	5/10		5th
SWEDISH Anderstorp 17.6.73	D. Hulme	Ford V8 M23-DFV M23/1	7	1min 25.46sec 5/19	1min 24.63sec 6/20		6-21	1/14 WINNER		FL 1st
		Ford V8 M23-DFV M23/2	7T			1min 24.71sec 4/12				

Race	Driver	Car	No.							Result
	P. Revson	Ford V8 M23-DFV M23/2	8	1min 25.73sec 7/19	1min 24.94sec 8/20		7-21	7/14		**7th**
FRENCH Ricard–Castellet 1.7.73	D. Hulme	Ford V8 M23-DFV M23/1	7	1min 50.27sec 5/30	1min 49.68sec 1/27	1min 50.08sec 4/28	6-25	8/16		**2nd**
		Ford V8 M23-DFV M23/2	7T	1min 49.65sec 4/30						
	J. Scheckter	Ford V8 M23-DFV M23/3	8	1min 50.29sec 6/30	1min 49.97sec 2/27	1min 49.18sec 1/28	2-25		Lp 43 Accident	**1st**
		Ford V8 M23-DFV M23/2	8T			1min 51.23sec 11/28				
BRITISH Silverstone 14.7.73	D. Hulme	Ford V8 M23-DFV M23/1	7	1min 16.5sec 1/30	1min 17.2sec 6/32		2-29	3/13		**3rd**
	P. Revson	Ford V8 M23-DFV M23/2	8	1min 17.5sec 5/30	1min 16.5sec 2/32		3-29	1/13 WINNER		**1st**
	J. Scheckter	Ford V8 M23-DFV M23/3	30	1min 17.5sec 5/30	1min 16.9sec 5/32		6-29		Lp 1 Crash	
DUTCH Zandvoort 29.7.73	D. Hulme	Ford V8 M23-DFV M23/1	7		1min 20.31sec 2/23	1min 21.2sec 10/26	4-24		Lp 32 engine	**4th**
		Ford V8 M23-DFV M23/4	7T			1min 21.47sec 13/26				
	P. Revson	Ford V8 M23-DFV M23/2	8	1min 36.05sec 16/17	1min 21.26sec 4/23	1min 20.6sec 5/26	6-24	4/12		**4th**
		Ford V8 M23-DFV M23/4	8T			1min 21.82sec 15/26				
GERMAN Nürburgring 5.8.73	D. Hulme	Ford V8 M23-DFV M23/1	7	7min 20.8sec 14/23	7min 16.5sec 3/24		8-23	12/16		**6th**
	P. Revson	Ford V8 M23-DFV M23/2	8	7min 15.9sec 7/23	8min 04.9sec 23/24		7-23	9/16		**6th**
	J. Ickx	Ford V8 M23-DFV M23/4	30	7min 09.7sec 4/23	7min 10.3sec 1/24		4-23	3/16		**3rd**
AUSTRIAN Österreichring 19.8.73	D. Hulme	Ford V8 M23-DFV M23/1	7	1min 35.69sec 2/29	1min 35.75sec 2/28		3-23	8/11		**2nd**
		Ford V8 M23-DFV M23/4	35	1min 35.91sec 4/29						
	P. Revson	Ford V8 M23-DFV M23/2	8	1min 35.86sec 3/29	1min 36.41sec 5/28		4-23		Lp 1 Clutch	
		Ford V8 M23-DFV M23/4	35	1min 36.52sec 7/29	1min 36.84sec 10/28					

ITALIAN Monza 9.9.73	D. Hulme	Ford V8 M23-DFV M23/1	7	1min 37.97sec 4/23	1min 36.02sec 1/27	1min 35.45sec 3/24	3-24	15/16		**3rd**
		Ford V8 M23-DFV M23/4	7T			1min 36.33sec 6/27				
	P. Revson	Ford V8 M23-DFV M23/4	8	1min 36.75sec 1/23	1min 36.74sec 1/23	1min 35.29sec 2/24	2-24	3/16		**3rd**
		Ford V8 M23-DFV M23/4	8T			1min 37.45sec 12/27				
CANADIAN Mosport Park 23.9.73	J. Scheckter	Ford V8 M23-DFV M23/2	0	1min 15.18sec 2/26	1min 14.76sec 3/26	1min 15.39sec 5/26	3-26		Lp 33 Accident Puncture	**2nd**
	D. Hulme	Ford V8 M23-DFV M23/1	7	1min 35.89sec 25/26	1min 16.59sec 14/26	1min 15.32sec 4/26	7-26	13/18		**13th**
	P. Revson	Ford V8 M23-DFV M23/4	8	1min 15.79sec 5/26	1min 14.74sec 2/26	1min 15.51sec 6/26	2-26	1/18 WINNER		**1st**
USA Watkins Glen 7.10.73	J Scheckter	Ford V8 M23-DFV M23/2	0	1min 41.8sec 5/28	1min 41.32sec 10/28 1min 41.21sec	1min 41.71sec 5/28	10-27		Lp 40 Suspension	**5th**
	D. Hulme	Ford V8 M23-DFV M23/1	7	1min 41.92sec 7/28	9/28	1min 43.08sec 11/28	8-27	4/17		**4th**
	P. Revson	Ford V8 M23-DFV M23/4	8	1min 41.87sec 6/28	1min 40.90sec 5/28	1min 42.42sec 9/28	7-27	5/17		**5th**

★ Some races ran four practices. A driver's best three times are counted.

In America McLaren had not competed in Can-Am, as they could not seriously challenge the powerful Porsche cars. Roger McCluskey had finished third in the Indianapolis 500, with an ex-works M16, and though the works team did not do so well, other teams won USAC races with McLaren cars. Unfortunately, McLaren lost the Gulf Oil sponsorship at the end of the year. Elsewhere, however, dramatic changes were afoot with sponsors.

TWO TEAMS, TWO WORLD CHAMPIONSHIPS

At the end of 1971, in slightly acrimonious circumstances, the Yardley Cosmetics firm took their money from BRM to McLaren. BRM were then sponsored by Marlboro Cigarettes, but steadily went downhill. As 1973 drew to a close, a tie-up was proposed between Texaco, Marlboro and McLaren to run a two-car team which would include Emerson Fittipaldi, who was not too happy with his position at Lotus. BRM were, as one might expect, less than thrilled at the idea, but there was nothing they could do about it. However, Yardley had an option for a third year with McLaren and they were most keen to exercise this.

Yardley's budget, after inflation had cut into it, could no longer support a two-car team, and it was thanks to this that a compromise was worked out. McLaren in effect became two teams, with the Texaco-Marlboro team being run by Teddy Mayer, with Hulme and Emerson driving, and the one-car Yardley team run by Phil Kerr, with Revson as the driver. Revson was doubtful as to how this would work out; he did not want to have to put up with second-class treatment or machinery and so took himself off to join Shadow.

This left McLaren in a bit of a pickle as,

naturally, Yardley wanted their car to have a top-class driver. Fortune again smiled kindly. Mike 'the bike' Hailwood, who had had enough of his Surtees breaking down on him (he used to joke that he always carried a book with him in the car, so that when it broke down he had something to do; or perhaps he was not joking!) leapt at the chance to drive a reliable, front-running car; a solution acceptable to Yardley.

Through the close season Gordon Coppuck worked on modifying the M23 to keep it competitive. It was designed with an intended three-year lifespan in mind and 1974 ought to see it at its best. The wheelbase was lengthened by 3in (76mm) to give it more stability and make it easier to drive, and the rear track was widened by 2in (50mm). But, by using different-length spacers between the engine and gearbox, the wheelbase could be varied to suit the circuit. Finally, the rear suspension was revised.

All the winter testing, of which there was a considerable amount for those days, was undertaken by Fittipaldi, Hulme spending the time at home in New Zealand. Though this was ideal for Denny, as he used to do much of the testing workload, it led to problems on his return. Fittipaldi preferred the car to be set more towards oversteer, whereas Hulme liked the car to understeer slightly. This minor handling characteristic might make little difference to you or me, but then again we are not trying to corner a car at speeds of 160mph. This appears to have blighted Denny's season, especially as, with Emerson's title challenge, the spare car was set up for Emerson. This meant that if Denny's race car was not right, he had no other car to drive.

The two McLaren teams enjoyed an almost schizophrenic existence; working alongside each other and sharing technical modifications at Colnbrook, yet competing when at a circuit. Perhaps this was an almost ideal situation for drivers to compete with identical machinery, though Denny Hulme might not have agreed. One advantage for the Yardley team was that Mike Hailwood had a spare car all to himself, once the season was underway.

The real opposition was more than enough to keep Teddy Mayer and his men on their toes. Everyone knew that what was presumed to be Colin Chapman's new masterpiece, the Lotus 76, would be introduced soon. This was expected to break new ground and Lotus looked very strong indeed, especially as the old 72 was still competitive. Tyrrell had a new car on the drawing boards to introduce when appropriate, though of course they had lost both drivers from the previous season. Brabham, March, Shadow, Surtees and Hesketh were all preparing new cars. Even the 'old couple', Ferrari and BRM, were getting new designs ready. Finally, on the team front, new entries were expected from Trojan, the ex-McLaren Can-Am customer car builders, Amon and Lyncar, and Lola had designed cars for the Embassy-Hill team.

On the driving front the new Texaco-Marlboro McLaren team had the strongest line-up on paper, now that Stewart had left the arena. With Mike Hailwood joining the Yardley team, McLaren had a real opportunity to challenge for the Constructors' Championship. Of the competitors Lotus (with Peterson and Ickx) looked particularly powerful. Elsewhere, there were a lot of drivers on the way up, but few truly established winners, such was the hiatus left with Stewart's retirement.

Brabham had an interesting pairing with Reutemann and Pace, and the Hexagon team were running an ex-works Brabham for John Watson. Shadow had ex-McLaren driver Peter Revson and Formula 2 Champion, the undoubtedly fast Jean-Pierre Jarier. Tyrrell, perhaps the unluckiest team as regards drivers, had taken a brave step. 'Uncle' Ken had taken a long deep breath, counted to ten and, to the surprise of the Grand Prix fraternity, given Jody Scheckter his chance, after Teddy Mayer had decided against him. Here was a driver with the talent of Peterson, who needed to apply this over the full distance of a race, not just the beginning, to become a winner. Ken Tyrrell no doubt felt that his calming influence would encourage just that. Their other driver was Patrick

Depailler, who many thought was selected to keep Elf, Tyrrell's main sponsors, happy. This was not the case though, and Depailler proved to be another of the young drivers of talent discovered by Ken Tyrrell over the years.

Over at Ferrari, the 'Old Man' had been astute enough to snatch Regazzoni and the young Austrian Niki Lauda from his old-time rivals, BRM. Regazzoni was a known quantity, a race winner with Ferrari and 'hard' driver, but his team-mate was something of a gamble. He had hardly made his mark in Grand Prix racing, but then by driving March and BRM cars that was hard to do. There was the soaking wet start of the Canadian Grand Prix, though, when Lauda in his BRM had led with impunity, almost as though it was a Lotus he was driving. Had Ferrari seen more in Lauda than the other team owners had noticed?

Before the new season got under way there was one more major problem to overcome. Following the Yom Kippur war in 1973, the world was plunged into an oil crisis, with supplies seriously disrupted while the cost doubled. There was also the threat of another war, with the Western world's need to safeguard its vital energy needs. Furthermore, most of the racing teams were, and indeed are still, based in Britain, and during that winter of 1973/1974 there was the three-day working week to conserve energy, during the successful miners' strike which brought down the Conservative government. This was of no benefit to the teams trying to prepare for the Argentinian Grand Prix in January (if, indeed, racing was to go ahead at all). Who says that sport and politics are unrelated?

Go ahead the racing did, though, and the Argentinian Grand Prix proved to be an excellent pipe opener. Fittipaldi was in great form, but as the race got under way a plug lead came off and he had to go into the pits to have it replaced. He roared back into the race determined to make up for this, but then succeeded in knocking the steering-wheel mounted ignition switch off, cutting out the engine. Not knowing this, and

having assumed some sort of ignition failure, he pulled off the circuit, unstrapped his safety harness and then noticed his error. He started up the car, drove round to the pits to have his harness buckled up and, no doubt red-faced, got back into the race to finish tenth.

Mike Hailwood also had an incident-strewn race, having a contretemps with Regazzoni at the start which posed more than a few problems for those behind, but managed to continue. Later, a stone punctured a radiator and he had to slow down a bit. However, he still finished a creditable fourth, and if Hailwood carried a book with him, it was not needed in the M23!

But what of Denny Hulme? He settled into mid-field, as Reutemann roared off in the new Brabham BT44, and soon closed on the other front runners. This was Hulme at his best, as he seemed happy enough with the car. Gradually, he passed those cars in front of him until he was in second place, but half a minute down on Reutemann. Then the gremlins struck at the Brabham; first the engine airbox worked loose, and then a plug lead came off. Reutemann was in trouble and Hulme saw his chance. He quickly caught and then, on the penultimate lap, passed the sick (in both respects) Brabham, and if any of those following thought that they could take the lead from Denny, they could forget it. 'The Bear' was certainly not going to be an obliging Yogi.

This was a debut victory for the Texaco-Marlboro team, but there was more to come as Emerson claimed the pole for his home Brazilian Grand Prix. Peterson, before he got a puncture, and Reutemann were the early front runners, but Emerson eased ahead on lap 16, and was still there when a heavy downpour caused the race to be stopped after thirty-two laps. Two races, and two wins! Denny Hulme was way back with tyre problems, right from the start, and Mike Hailwood recorded another points finish. Interestingly, in second place was that unknown Austrian, Lauda.

A few teams remained in Brazil for the non-championship President Medici Grand Prix in

Mike Hailwood in his Yardley-sponsored M23, on his way to fourth place in the Argentinian Grand Prix, his first, impressive race for his new team.

Brasilia, where Reutemann claimed the pole. Once again the Brabham led a race, only for its engine to give up, leaving Emerson to record a hat-trick of wins for McLaren. This feat was achieved despite the Brabham being the faster car, and the M23 not being noticeably better than either the Ferrari, or the Lotus. McLaren's teamwork was standing them in good stead.

After the success of previous seasons, the McLaren team looked forward to the South African Grand Prix. Tyrrell introduced their new 007 car, nothing to do with James Bond, and Hesketh gave their first design, the 308, its debut with Hunt at the wheel. It was also nice to note that BRM had at last got a new design out, the P201, even if they were still handicapped by their own V12 engine.

The meeting was marred by the death of Peter Revson. This happened while testing his Shadow before the official business began, when his car hit the armco barriers. It was following this accident that calls went out for more catch fencing and sand traps to be installed. Both McLaren teams were experimenting with the cars and neither of the Marlboro-sponsored cars featured strongly at the meeting. Mike Hailwood came a satisfactory third behind Reutemann's victorious Brabham and Beltoise, who performed heroics in the new BRM. Another point of significance was that Lauda had claimed the pole position.

Following another lack-lustre McLaren performance at Silverstone's International Trophy, which Hunt won in his Hesketh, the teams

*Lap 47 of the South African Grand Prix, Emerson Fittipaldi is hounded for fourth place by
Mike Hailwood in the Yardley car. It was Hailwood who came out on top, as he finished third,
while Fittipaldi fell back to finish seventh.*

*Everybody seemed to spin on the greasy, wet surface at Jarama, in Spain. Mike Hailwood could
not have picked a worse moment for his, just in front of Fittipaldi.*

assembled in Spain for the European series of races. Ferrari had their new 312B3 for both drivers, serving notice of their intentions. The Trojan and Amon teams made their respective debuts as well, filling out the grids still further. It was a wet race due to run to the two-hour rule. Peterson romped off into the lead, but then the rain stopped and the circuit began to dry out. As this happened most drivers headed for the pits to change tyres, and bedlam broke out with the time-keeping, just like in Canada in 1973. The Ferraris of Lauda and Regazzoni took the lead, but all the other positions were in doubt. To confuse matters more, it might have been possible to run the full distance, but the 2-hour rule was invoked.

For forty laps all the cars were equal, and nobody allowed themselves to be passed or pushed aside. Everyone had a chance here; this was open, unfettered racing and all the drivers seemed to be enjoying themselves. The Ferraris were clearly dominant though, and as the time-keepers sorted themselves out, it was Emerson Fittipaldi who was awarded third position, enhancing his title challenge, while Denny Hulme also came home in the points.

Aside from on-circuit events, the pitstops offered great entertainment. Nearly every team came a cropper at some stage, but none so bad as Lotus. Ickx was still having his tyres changed when told to go. He made to set off, but the car was still on the jack, having a rear wheel tightened. Tools and mechanics flew in all directions as the Lotus set off up the pit lane, but the offending wheel worked loose and the car ground to a halt outside the Trojan pit, just as their car was due in. The Lotus boys ran after their car in the pouring rain and, to a barrage of abuse from Trojan and jeers elsewhere, completed the job. Then, for an encore, Ickx hit the fire extinguisher button instead of the starter and covered everything and everyone in foam. Just to cap it all, this got into the fuel intakes and the engine would not fire cleanly.

For the Belgian Grand Prix McLaren had all their cars in long-wheelbase form, though adjusted to each driver's liking. The race was hardly a classic, as some had been at Spa, but Fittipaldi and Lauda fought a long, hard battle, with the McLaren driver just holding off the Ferrari at the finish. Fittipaldi was now a clear leader in the Championship.

François Migault, driving hard in his BRM, is about to be lapped by Denny Hulme, on the Nevelles circuit in Belgium. One team well on the way up, the other firmly on the slippery slope down.

Victorious Emerson Fittipaldi steps from his car after winning the Belgian Grand Prix by 0.35 seconds from Lauda.

Monaco was never a favourite McLaren circuit in those days, and their cars were all set up differently. This was aimed to maximize opportunity on this tight and twisty circuit, but also suggested a bit of indecisiveness within the team(s). Fittipaldi was a bit under the weather for the whole meeting, and amidst the usual high rate of attrition in Monaco, came a distant fifth. Hulme and Hailwood both crashed out. Peterson, back in the Lotus 72, chalked up his first win of the season, with Jarier an impressive third in the Shadow.

The six races run in 1974 had, in sharp contrast to previous seasons, produced five different winners driving for four teams. The Swedish Grand Prix was to add to this tally, as Scheckter won in the Tyrrell, closely followed by teammate Depailler. Hunt came third in his Hesketh, three seconds behind, and then came Emerson in fourth, a minute adrift; Hulme and Hailwood both retired. Not a great result for McLaren, but Fittipaldi was still leading the Championship.

Recent seasons had witnessed the increasing use of relatively short, twisty, 'Mickey Mouse' circuits, following the safety crusade. The Dutch Grand Prix, held almost continuously since 1949 at the Zandvoort Circuit among the sand dunes was, somewhat regrettably, being tarred with the same brush. When races were run on circuits such as Monza, Monaco, Spa, and Reims, Zandvoort was unique. Now, as similar circuits such as Jarama, Paul Ricard, and Nivelles came into use, Zandvoort was losing its individuality.

Thus far, the season had been remarkably free of controversy. This came to an abrupt end in Holland with, of all things, arguments raging over the number of entries accepted for the meeting. Considering the oil crisis and the general state of the Western economies, perhaps Grand Prix racing did not appreciate when it was well off. However, the root of the problem was safety, and you could not have too many cars trying to qualify all at the same time when the speed differential was enormous.

After all the fuss had died down and the racing was under way, Lauda and Regazzoni in

84

Patrick Depailler leads Emerson Fittipaldi, followed by Mike Hailwood and Jody Scheckter, in their battle for third place in Holland. The two McLarens came out on top in the end, with Fittipaldi taking the third place.

Depailler and Fittipaldi resumed their battle in the following French Grand Prix, though this time for eighth position. Here they are on the opening lap, but Fittipaldi's engine failed, and put him out.

their Ferraris proceeded to dominate the event, leaving Fittipaldi and Hailwood to pick up third and fourth places, with steady drives. Hulme had a miserable time, going out with ignition failure but, unusually, the first five finishers took the flag in their grid positions.

Once again, at the French Grand Prix, FOCA were concerned about the number of entries accepted for the race. Though their arguments were justified on the grounds of safety, if not finance, they were viewed as an attempt at restrictive practices and did not win much sympathy among the uncommitted, and brought many a knowing smile from some of those who were. In one sense, practice times served to pull the rug from under the FOCA arguments, as barely two seconds separated the first and last cars on the grid, indicating a high level of competence throughout.

McLaren had meanwhile introduced a Ferrari-like, taller, slimmer engine airbox cover on the M23. During tests, this had increased the downforce on to the rear wheels, as the air was less disturbed when it reached the rear wing. Their hopes were reasonably high as the race began, only for Pryce, sitting in third place on the grid, to be too busy watching his instruments when the green light flashed, and to be rammed from behind by Hunt. Peterson drove off into the distance, while Fittipaldi went out with an engine failure. Hulme and Hailwood were both off the pace, finishing in sixth and seventh places respectively, and to round off a fairly miserable day for McLaren, Lauda and Regazzoni came second and third, to overhaul Fittipaldi in the Drivers' Championship.

After the débâcle of the previous year, the RAC hoped for a less dramatic British Grand Prix, held at Brands Hatch. The potion looked good; a large-sized entry, without the squabbles of the last couple of races, a four-way drivers' title fight, not forgetting Peterson, and a new revised McLaren M23. This, the eighth car built, featured a totally new rear suspension layout, lowered front suspension and revised steering, and was to be used by Fittipaldi in an attempt to regain his lead in the Championship.

New leader, Lauda, notched up yet another pole position with Peterson alongside in the Lotus 72, and stormed off to lead comfortably. As another Ferrari victory seemed likely, Lauda picked up a puncture and elected not to change the tyre. He fell to third place and then, with one lap remaining, the tyre virtually lost all its air and Lauda headed for the pits. After a quick wheel change, Lauda was prevented from rejoining the race, in fifth place, as the RAC blocked the end of the pit road. All sorts of people who should not have been in the pits had thus prevented a justifiably enraged Lauda claiming vital Championship points. In any event, he lost his lead after this unseemly incident. Ironically after the events of the previous year, Scheckter won the race, while Fittipaldi was a steady second with Hulme in seventh place. Mike was running fourth when he spun off, and was unable to restart the engine.

As the teams gathered at the Nürburgring for the German Grand Prix, the Drivers' Championship had not been so closely contested for many years. There were four main title contenders, and a royal battle looked in prospect at this most demanding of circuits. Fittipaldi's spare car was fitted with the new suspension, while Hulme's and Hailwood's were unchanged. Mike Hailwood had an accident during practice, possibly the result of something breaking, and this proved to be a precursor to a disastrous meeting for the team(s). On the short warm-up lap Fittipaldi's engine began to play up, and it required some desperate work on his part to take his place on the grid. Then at the start, he could not select first gear, and the world and his neighbour went past. Inevitably though, with Fittipaldi marooned in the middle of the track, someone had to hit him. It was a bit unfortunate for that someone to be Denny Hulme, who promptly jumped out of his car and took the spare car from the pits, only to be disqualified shortly afterwards. That was one in the eye for those who had been suggesting that Denny had lost the will to race anymore!

Denny Hulme seemed to go off the boil a bit in 1974. Here he follows Jochen Mass and Jean-Pierre Jarier, in sixteenth place, ahead of Henri Pescarolo's BRM. Hulme managed to finish seventh by the end, but it was not a great final season for 'The Bear'.

Emerson Fittipaldi, with the benefit of Denny Hulme's 'bump start', got away, but had a puncture and was forced to go straight to the pits. He retired a few laps later with gearbox failure, probably the result of Hulme's attention. However, Mike Hailwood was doing much better and had got himself into fifth position. Then, following one of the many humps on that circuit, he went straight into the armco barriers. Hailwood was trapped in the wrecked car and suffered severe leg injuries. He was not expected to race for the rest of the season, but in fact this accident finished his motor racing career, so bad were the injuries. The fact that

Regazzoni had become the seventh driver to win a Grand prix that season seemed lost on McLaren at the time; it was certainly not a race to be recalled in a hurry.

The Yardley team now had two problems; first both cars were damaged, and second they needed a driver. The first problem was solved simply enough by borrowing one of the Texaco-Marlboro cars, while British driver David Hobbs took over from Mike Hailwood in time for the Austrian Grand Prix, where local hero Lauda claimed the pole once again. Watson used a Brabham BT44 for the first time, with the Hexagon team, and the works cars were showing a welcome return to form with Reutemann alongside Lauda on the grid.

Fittipaldi badly needed the points at this stage of the season, but like the year before when set for a good finish, out he went with an engine failure. Fortunately for him, only Regazzoni of his main rivals picked up any points, and he only came fifth, as Reutemann chalked up an easy win, followed by Hulme with his best result since the opening round. Hobbs meanwhile claimed seventh place.

Regazzoni led the Drivers' Championship by five points from Scheckter, and nine from Fittipaldi, on the eve of his home Italian Grand Prix. Lauda achieved his ninth pole position of the season and romped off into the lead. It looked like it was Ferrari's day, until his engine failed after thirty laps, but Regazzoni took over the torch. If Regazzoni won, Fittipaldi could forget about his title chances. But, as had happened many times that season, the Ferrari car let its driver down yet again, and Regazzoni went the same way as Lauda.

This left Peterson leading Fittipaldi, who began to attack his former team-mate. It made little difference though, as despite a couple of passing attempts, showing that Fittipaldi still had the racer instinct in him, Peterson calmly took the victory laurels by a comfortable few car lengths. With Scheckter claiming third place, the Drivers' Championship had opened up once again. Hulme picked up sixth place, though was lapped in the process, while Hobbs finished ninth.

Before the journey across the Atlantic for the final races of the season, ex-Surtees driver Jochen Mass was recruited to drive the Yardley car. However, everything had to be put behind Fittipaldi's and McLaren's own title challenge, and the Brazilian driver responded magnificently by ending Lauda's monopoly of the pole, in Canada.

It was Lauda who led the race easily enough from Fittipaldi, then the gremlins struck again. This time Lauda was the first to arrive on the scene after Watson had gone off the track. The

Austrian hit the debris and went off himself. Fittipaldi, given Lauda's warning, got through safely to record his third win of the season and join 'Regga' at the top of the Championship. Denny Hulme came in sixth again, and poor Jochen had the sort of car and race he must have associated with his Surtees days. Of particular importance, though, was McLaren's six-point lead in the Constructors' Championship.

For the first time since 1968 it was a three-horse race going into the final hurdle. True, Scheckter lay seven points adrift of Fittipaldi and Regazzoni, but if he won, and if . . . well, you never know your luck. Grid positions offered little by way of what to expect in the race. Reutemann was on the pole with Hunt alongside, and Andretti, in the new Parnelli, an astonishing third. Of the Championship contenders, Scheckter qualified highest, a row in front of Fittipaldi, who was himself a row in front of the 'out-psyched' Regazzoni, who was fighting with his car as much as with his rivals.

The race became a Brabham *tour de force*, with Reutemann leading team-mate Pace home, followed by Hunt. Scheckter led Fittipaldi, but his main rival, Regazzoni, was effectively out of the running with a car which must have felt as though the McLaren mechanics had prepared it. All Emerson had to do was finish behind the Tyrrell driver, but Scheckter, with fuel problems, was forced to retire, and that was that. Fittipaldi cruised home fourth to take his second title and confirm McLaren as the Constructors' Champions for the first time. It was sad that Hulme had to retire with an engine failure after only four laps, and not share in the double triumph, for he left the scene almost immediately to retire. He had contributed so much over the years to this great moment for the team, yet was not there to take his just reward.

Jochen finished seventh to round off a disappointing year for Yardley, if not their team, but he had impressed as a stand in. The one black mark over the whole event was the death of Surtees driver Koinigg, when his car was trapped between the armco barriers after he left the circuit – another reminder of the dangers of racing.

Winning Grand Prix titles was one thing, but McLaren's success was not limited to Grand Prix racing. Customer Can-Am cars only managed one win, but the works USAC team won four races, including the most famous of the lot, the Indianapolis 500, with Johnny Rutherford at the wheel. The Penske team won this event two years earlier with a McLaren car, but this was different again. There was much to cheer at Colnbrook but, amazingly, all this success was necessary to turn in a profit. The money from Texaco, Marlboro, Yardley, and Goodyear did not cover expenses, and prize and starting money was as important as ever, such were the soaring costs of a top-flight racing team at that time. Yet, teams such as Hesketh and March had managed to run near the front on a shoestring budget; it seemed a strange world.

Fittipaldi became Champion for the second time, no doubt greatly helped, as has already

been suggested, by the McLaren team preparation. He was the first World Champion since Graham Hill in 1968 who had not won more races than any other driver, setting a pattern which became more familiar over the next decade. He was also the first of the 'accountant Champions' who concentrated on collecting points, rather than simply winning races. This is not as damning as is first apparent because, for one thing, it was quite innovative for Fittipaldi to look at racing in this way. Also, unlike many previous World Champions, his car was seldom, if ever, the fastest in a race and reliability was ever more important. Furthermore, competition had never been greater. Over sixty drivers and seventy cars were entered for races during the year. Not all, by a long way, started, but seven different drivers won a race, and several others looked like they would shortly be joining the ranks of Grand Prix winners. Those young bloods of earlier years were maturing quite nicely, thank you very much.

Grand Prix Results 1974

GRAND PRIX	DRIVER	CAR	NO	1ST PRACTICE* Time/Posn	2ND PRACTICE* Time/Posn	3RD PRACTICE* Time/Posn	FINAL GRID POSN	FINAL PLACING	RETIRED CAUSE OF	HIGHEST POSN IN RACE
ARGENTINIAN Buenos Aires 13.1.74	E. Fittipaldi	Ford V8 M23-DFV M23/5	5	1min 53.92sec 1/24	1min 53.25sec 5/25	1min 51.06sec 2/24	4-15	10/13		**3rd**
	D. Hulme	Ford V8 M23-DFV M23/6	6	1min 55.30sec 8/24	1min 53.43sec 4/25	1min 52.06sec 4/24	9-25	1/13 WINNER		**1st**
	M. Hailwood	Ford V8 M23-DFV M23/1	33	1min 54.68sec 4/24	1min 51.86sec 5/24	1min 52.09sec 4/24	10-25	4/13		**3rd**
BRAZILIAN Interlagos 27.1.74	E. Fittipaldi	Ford V8 M23-DFV M23/5	5	2min 32.97sec 2/25	2min 33.0sec 1/25	2min 33.65sec 1/25	1-24	1/17 WINNER		**1st**
	D. Hulme	Ford V8 M23-DFV M23/6	6	2min 35.54sec 7/25	2min 36.12sec 9/25	2min 35.56sec 9/25	10-24	12/17		**8th**
	M. Hailwood	Ford V8 M23-DFV M23/1	33	2min 34.95sec 4/25	2min 35.05sec 6/25	2min 35.35sec 4/25	7-24	5/17		**5th**
SOUTH AFRICAN Kyalami 30.374	E. Fittipaldi	Ford V8 M23-DFV M23/4	5	1min 16.82sec 4/27	1min 17.39sec 9/27		5-27	7/19		**4th**
	D. Hulme	Ford V8 M23-DFV M23/6	6	1min 17.43sec 10/27	1min 17.11sec 5/27		9-27	9/19		**9th**

Race	Driver	Car	No.							
	D. Charlton (Lucky Strike)	Ford V8 M23-DFV M23/2	23	1min 18.375sec 17/27	1min 19.20sec 22/27		20-27	19/19		**15th**
	M. Hailwood	Ford V8 M23-DFV M23/1	33	1min 17.38sec 9/27	1min 17.34sec 8/27		12-27	3/19		**3rd**
SPANISH Jarama 28.4.74	E. Fittipaldi	Ford V8 M23-DFV M23/5	5	1min 20.34sec 7/22	1min 19.25sec 5/24	1min 20.01sec 7/23	3-25	3/14		**3rd**
	D. Hulme	Ford V8 M23-DFV M23/4	6	1min 20.83sec 9/22	1min 19.66sec 6/24	1min 20.48sec 11/23	7-25	6/14		**6th**
	M. Hailwood	Ford V8 M23-DFV M23/7	33	1min 21.63sec 15/22	1min 20.65sec 15/24	1min 20.94sec 14/23	20-25	9/14		**9th**
BELGIAN Nivelles 12.5.74	E. Fittipaldi	Ford V8 M23-DFV M23/5	5	1min 20.19sec 1/27	1min 17.07sec 4/27	1min 11.07sec 2/28	3-31	1/18 WINNER		**1st**
	D. Hulme	Ford V8 M23-DFV M23/6	6	1min 26.53sec 17/27	1min 22.29sec 11/29	1min 11.61sec 10/28	11-31	6/18		**FL 6th**
	M. Hailwood	Ford V8 M23-DFV M23/7	33	1min 22.60sec 17/27	1min 12.13sec 7/29	1min 11.98sec 11/28	14-31	7/18		**6th**
MONACO Monte Carlo 26.5.74	E. Fittipaldi	Ford V8 M23-DFV M23/5	5	1min 31.7sec 13/23	1min 29.5sec 16/24	1min 28.2sec 10/24	12-25	5/15		**5th**
		Ford V8 M23-DFV M23/4	5T	1min 33.7sec 31/33						
	D. Hulme	Ford V8 M23-DFV M23/6	6	1min 31.0sec 7/23	1min 28.2sec 6/24	1min 29.0sec 14/24	11-25		Lp 1 Multiple accident	
	M. Hailwood	Ford V8 M23-DFV M23/1	33	1min 28.6sec 1/23	1min 28.4sec 8/24	1min 28.1sec 8/24	9-25		Lp 11 Accident	**5th**
		Ford V8 M23-DFV M23/7	33	1min 29.5sec 6/33	1min 29.4sec 18/30	1min 28.1sec 11/32				
SWEDISH Anderstorp 9.6.74	E. Fittipaldi	Ford V8 M23-DFV M23/4	5			1min 25.96sec 6/23	10-24	4/11		**4th**
		Ford V8 M23-DFV M23/5	5T	1min 27.72sec 5/27	1min 30.80sec 8/27	1min 25.94sec 7/23				
	D. Hulme	Ford V8 M23-DFV M23/6	6	1min 28.01sec 5/22	1min 26.48sec 8/23	1min 26.18sec 8/23	11-24		Lp 56 Suspension	**6th**
	M. Hailwood	Ford V8 M23-DFV M23/7	33	1min 28.11sec 6/22	1min 26.04sec 7/23	1min 26.19sec 9/23	12-24		Lp 5 Fuel line	**12th**
		Ford V8 M23-DFV M23/1	33T		1min 44.14sec 26/27	1min 25.96sec 10/23				
DUTCH Zandvoort 23.6.74	E. Fittipaldi	Ford V8 M23-DFV M23/5	5	1min 20.64sec 4/22	1min 20.94sec 8/21	1min 19.56sec 2/24	4-25	3/12		**3rd**
	D. Hulme	Ford V8 M23-DFV M23/6	6	1min 20.77sec 5/22	1min 20.40sec 6/21	1min 20.15sec 7/24	10-25		Lp 65 Ignition	**7th**

	Driver	Car	No.							
	M. Hailwood	Ford V8 M23-DFV M23/7	33	1min 21.52sec 8/22	1min 79.68sec 4/24	1min 20.75sec 9/23	3-25	4/12		**2nd**
		Ford V8 M23-DFV M23/1	33T			1min 24.20sec 28/28				
FRENCH Dijon-Prenois 7.7.74	E. Fittipaldi	Ford V8 M23-DFV M23/5	5	59.20sec 1/18	59.41sec 3/20	59.70sec 7/21	6-22		Lp 27 Engine	**4th**
		Ford V8 M23-DFV M23/4	5T		1min 1.72sec 27/32	1min 0.17sec 12/34				
	D. Hulme	Ford V8 M23-DFV M23/6	6	1min 1.58sec 15/18	1min 0.08sec 9/20	1min 0.22sec 8/21	12-22	6/16		**6th**
		Ford V8 M23-DFV M23/4	6T	1min 2.30sec 26/30						
	M. Hailwood	Ford V8 M23-DFV M23/1	33	1min 5.10sec 18/18	59.22sec 3/21	59.74sec 6/21	5-22	7/16		**4th**
	M. Hailwood	Ford V8 M23-DFV M23/1	33T	1min 1.30sec 16/30	1min 0.02sec 8/32	59.59sec 5/31				
BRITISH Brands Hatch 20.7.74	E. Fittipaldi	Ford V8 M23-DFV M23/8	5	1min 22.0sec 5/22	1min 21.5sec 6/23	1min 20.5sec 7/22	7-25	2/14		**2nd**
		Ford V8 M23-DFV M23/5	5T	1min 23.7sec 19/37	1min 23.0sec 24/37					
	D. Hulme	Ford V8 M23-DFV M23/6	6	1min 24.9sec 16/22	1min 21.7sec 9/23	1min 22.6sec 21/22	20-25	7/14		**7th**
		Ford V8 M23-DFV M23/5	6T	1min 23.2sec 16/37	1min 23.4sec 26/37		Practice only			
	M. Hailwood	Ford V8 M23-DFV M23/1	33	1min 22.2sec 8/22	1min 21.2sec 5/23	1min 21.7sec 11/22	12-25		Lp 57 Spun, unable to restart	**5th**
	E. Fittipaldi	Ford V8 M23-DFV M23/5	5T	1min 23.7sec 19/37	1min 23.0sec 24/37		Practice only			
GERMAN Nürburgring 4.8.74	E. Fittipaldi	Ford V8 M23-DFV M23/8	5	7min 7.5sec 6/23	7min 2.3sec 2/25		3-26		Lp 2 Accident damage	**24th**
	D. Hulme	Ford V8 M23-DFV M23/6	6	7min 16.2sec 15/23	7min 8.8sec 5/25		7-26		Lp 1 Accident	
	M. Hailwood	Ford V8 M23-DFV M23/7	33		7min 13.7sec 14/25		12-26	15/15		**5th**
	D. Hulme	Ford V8 M23-DFV M23/5	5T	7min 16.4sec 14/34		Practice only				
	E. Fittipaldi	Ford V8 M23-DFV M23/5	5T	7min 8.4sec 8/34		Practice only				
	M. Hailwood	Ford V8 M23-DFV M23/1	33T	7min 10.1sec 12/34		Practice only				

AUSTRIAN Österreichring 18.8.74	E. Fittipaldi	Ford V8 M23-DFV M23/8	5	1min 36.17sec 4/21	1min 36.27sec 3/24	1min 35.76sec 3/22	4-23		Lp 37 Engine	**3rd**
	D. Hulme	Ford V8 M23-DFV M23/6	6	1min 37.18sec 3/23	1min 37.29sec 7/21	1min 36.39sec 4/24	9-23	2/12		**2nd**
		Ford V8 M23-DFV M23/5	6T	1min 42.90sec 29/29						
	D. Hobbs	Ford V8 M23-DFV M23/4	33	1min 39.89sec 18/21	1min 38.63sec 21/24	1min 37.44sec 15/22	18-23	7/12		**7th**
ITALIAN Monza 8.9.74	E. Fittipaldi	Ford V8 M23-DFV M23/8	5	1min 34.15sec 3/22	1min 33.95sec 4/22	1min 34.27sec 5/24	6-25	2/11		**2nd**
	D. Hulme	Ford V8 M23-DFV M23/6	6	1min 35.63sec 8/22	1min 35.73sec 13/22	1min 39.00sec 23/24	19-25	6/11		**5th**
		Ford V8 M23-DFV M23/5	6T		1min 36.12sec 18/29					
	D. Hobbs	Ford V8 M23-DFV M23/4	33	1min 36.31sec 12/22	1min 38.04sec 21/23	1min 36.30sec 19/22	23-25	9/11		**7th**
CANADIAN Mosport Park 22.9.74	E. Fittipaldi	Ford V8 M23-DFV M23/8	5	1min 14.5sec 5/26	1min 13.62sec 4/26	1min 13.19sec 1/24	2-26	1/16 WINNER		**1st**
	D. Hulme	Ford V8 M23-DFV M23/6	6	1min 15.07sec 11/25	1min 14.75sec 11/26	1min 15.31sec 17/24	13-26	6/16		**6th**
	J. Mass	Ford V8 M23-DFV M23/4	33	1min 14.84sec 10/25	1min 14.486sec 9/26	1min 14.50sec 11/24	11-26	16/16		**12th**
USA Watkins Glen 6.10.74	E. Fittipaldi	Ford V8 M23-DFV M23/8	5	1min 39.86sec 6/25	1min 39.57sec 2/27	1min 39.57sec 4/25	7-27	4/12		**4th**
	D. Hulme	Ford V8 M23-DFV M23/6	6	1min 42.97sec 20/25	1min 41.82sec 18/27	1min 41.03sec 11/25	18-27		Lp 4 Engine	**20th**
	J. Mass	Ford V8 M23-DFV M23/4	33	1min 41.87sec 17/25	1min 41.90sec 19/27	1min 41.3sec 16/25	19-27	7/12		**7th**

★ Some races ran four practices. A driver's best three results are counted.

GIVING SECOND BEST TO FERRARI

But the Grand Prix world quickly moves on and neither McLaren nor Emerson Fittipaldi could sit and rest on their laurels. If they did, you could bet that everyone else would soon surpass them. The Mayer-Coppuck partnership had worked marvellously well, and with continued Texaco and Marlboro support, there was little reason to start changing things. Of course,

Denny Hulme's retirement meant that a new driver had to be found, but this problem was solved easily enough when Yardley ended their sponsorship and Jochen Mass simply transferred to the other team. With Emerson Fittipaldi still number one, this looked to be an ideal pairing.

The M23 was modified into C specification, the most notable change being the Brabham-like front suspension. Other minor aerodynamic alterations were made to keep the cars competitive, while a new design was to be prepared

The opening lap of the 1975 Brazilian Grand Prix, and Regazzoni, in fourth place, leads Lauda, Scheckter and Fittipaldi in his home race.

during the season. Other teams had followed a similar path, and at the Argentinian Grand Prix only Brabham and Shadow had new cars. Most teams remained the same with single car entries from March, Hesketh, Surtees, BRM (what a come-down), Penske, Parnelli, and new boys Fittipaldi, the team run by Emerson's brother, Wilson. Trojan, Hexagon, Amon, and Ensign had all departed the scene, but Token and Lyncar expected to resume at a later stage of the season.

Perhaps surprisingly, the only driver change among the leading five teams was the retirement of Denny Hulme. Nearly all of these, with the possible exceptions of Mass (too inexperienced) and Ickx (losing interest) were of the front rank, though none were quite yet 'aces'. If you included the likes of Hunt, Andretti and Jarier, you had a set of drivers, the quality of which had never been seen before, and they were all still improving.

Two things that did change as the teams settled in the Argentinian Grand Prix were sponsors. While Firestone Tyres had withdrawn from the fray, many teams had changed their sponsors in the annual merry-go-round, though significantly, none of the leading five teams had switched, except for the withdrawal of Yardley. Firestone had been thoroughly trounced by Goodyear and, while reflecting on the cost to them of Grand Prix racing, and possibly contemplating the effect of the publicity they were gaining as losers, decided to quit, leaving Goodyear a clear road ahead.

Jarier, in the new Shadow, claimed the first pole position of the year, but thanks to this car, was unable to start the race from this hard-earned place. Off they went in the debilitating heat and as things settled down, it was Hunt leading in his Hesketh. Fittipaldi closed steadily though, and Hunt finally spun on lap 34 under the pressure, leaving Emerson to win comfortably. Hunt recovered to finish second, having been taught a salutory lesson by the established 'master'.

Jarier took the pole again in Brazil, with Fit-

The ecstatic Brazilian fans celebrate a local triumph as Emerson Fittipaldi finishes second, to fellow-countryman Carlos Pace.

tipaldi alongside him. Next came the Brabhams, Ferraris and Tyrrells, with Hunt as the cat among the pigeons once more. Lotus were way back in midfield. Emerson Fittipaldi was desperately keen to win his home race again but, after another gruelling battle, had to give best to fellow Brazilian Pace, who notched up his first and, as it happened only, win. But who should pop up in third place? Jochen Mass drove a steady race, displacing his more illustrious rivals

to score his first points for McLaren. The team left South America extremely pleased with their rewards, and with a good lead in the two Championships.

The South African Grand Prix was noteworthy for several reasons. In terms of history, Lella Lombardi, driving a March, became the first lady to qualify for a modern Grand Prix. This did not open the floodgates or even begin the merest trickle of the fair sex into Grand Prix racing, as had been hoped. Of more significance were Ferrari's two brand new 312T cars. These were most definitely going to have an effect on Grand Prix racing, as three of the next six seasons were to see cars of this series win the World Championship.

The meeting was hardly memorable from the McLaren point of view. Fittipaldi qualified in mid-grid, following an engine failure, and finished miles back, having spent a good deal of the race in the pits while the mechanics tried to find the cause of a misfire. Jochen Mass came sixth as the Tyrrell and Brabham teams dominated the race.

Three races and three different winners; the prospects looked good for the season. Hiding under this veneer though, and not too deeply either, were the problems created by safety and the muscle-flexing of the various representative bodies: FOCA, GPDA, and CSI (who?), the sport's governing body. The Spanish Grand Prix was due to return to Montjuich Park in Barcelona, and it would be nice to recall simply the racing, as if all the other miserable events did not happen. As the McLaren drivers were prominently involved in both the racing and the extra-curricular activities, we might cast a glance over them.

The demands in the circuit safety battle had grown ever higher from the days of tree removal and armco barrier erection. The latter, through a combination of faulty installation or positioning, had been the cause of the death of some drivers, and weaknesses had been shown. The GPDA had called for wire catch fencing to be erected at certain points on circuits, to pre-

Jochen Mass on the way to his only Grand Prix victory, in Spain, passes a Ferrari. This makes for an interesting comparison in the rear end of the two leading cars of 1975.

vent wayward drivers hitting the barriers hard. These did not always meet with unmitigated success, so further demands were put forward for sand traps and larger run-off areas. On top of this, drivers wanted wire nets installed at critical points, to protect spectators from flying debris. Once again, there were cries of 'cissy' from certain quarters of the press, but members of the press do not risk their lives, unduly, when at work.

Montjuich Park failed even the barest minimum of safety requirements, and the steel barriers lining the circuit were found to be dreadfully installed. The drivers quite reasonably, in view of the dangers presented to them, went on strike. The organizers agreed to secure the barriers overnight, but in the morning this was found to be nothing more than hot air.

The drivers again refused to go out, but the CSI, despite the hood-winking of the organizers, declared that the circuit was up to standard . . . The organizers insisted that the team owners honour their contracts to race, but that was a little difficult without drivers. The organizers retaliated, not by securing the barriers to make them safe, but by petulantly threatening

to impound all the FOCA equipment in the paddock and sue for compensation. The FOCA members then made up work parties of their own personnel to secure the barriers, and virtually forced the drivers to race.

The whole affair was a shambles of the highest order, and had far-reaching effects. The drivers did not come out of the event covered in glory either, but they had made their point. The GPDA became a bit of a spent force and FOCA took it under its mantle. FOCA themselves, led by Brabham boss Bernie Ecclestone, was engaged in a long-running war with the CSI (later FISA) to gain greater control over Grand Prix racing for the participants.

As with the prelude to the race, the Spanish Grand Prix remains memorable for all the wrong reasons. Practice finally went ahead to establish grid positions, but Emerson Fittipaldi stood by his principles by refusing to race, as he still considered the safety precautions to be inadequate. As reigning World Champion and current Championship leader, Emerson took this stand from a position of strength, but it could also be argued that he had the most to lose by refusing to race.

During the middle section of the Belgian Grand Prix, Fittipaldi held fourth place, ahead of Depailler, but it was the latter who eventually finished in that position.

The race did get under way though, and eventually Stommelen was leading Pace, in his Hill GH–1, when the rear aerofoil came adrift. Bereft of downforce at the rear, Stommelen's car hit the armco barriers, which bent, but did not break, shot back across the track, ran along the top of the barriers opposite, and destroyed itself, badly injuring Stommelen; Pace also crashed. Unfortunately, a marshall and four spectators were killed, and the ill-fated race was brought to an end after only twenty-nine laps, with Mass declared the winner. The whole sorry event was capped by the awarding of only half points, and racing was a clear loser. It might have been a fiasco, but there was more to come.

Normality, whatever that might be, returned for the Monaco Grand Prix, as did Fittipaldi. A new gadget was fitted so that he could adjust the front anti-roll bar during the race. This seemed to make little difference, as he lined up in ninth place on the staggered grid, but by dint of perseverance and a bit of luck, he finished second to Lauda (the fifth different winner in five races) while Mass came sixth.

Lauda repeated this performance at both the Belgian and Swedish Grands Prix, with neither

McLaren driver featuring in the points. Lauda took over the lead in the Championship, and with the M23s not handling well, nothing seemed to stand in his way. But then came the Dutch Grand Prix. The Ferraris of Lauda and Regazzoni occupied the front row of the grid, as usual, with Fittipaldi back in sixth place. Another Lauda victory looked imminent.

The race began in the wet, a sure-fire joker in the pack, and on lap 7 Hunt went and changed on to slick tyres. This put him way down in the running but, as the track was drying fast, everyone would have to change their tyres. After all the pitstops, Hunt emerged with a big lead over Lauda, but it did not take long for the new 'master' to close up on the Hesketh. It seemed only a matter of time before Lauda would pass the gallant, but vulnerable when leading, Englishman, as Fittipaldi had pressured him into an error when he led the Argentinian Grand Prix. This time Hunt held on for lap after lap, Lauda having a good look past on many occasions; while at other times it seemed as if he had a tow rope attached to the Hesketh. Then, finally, Hunt won his first Grand Prix, but this did not help Fittipaldi as neither McLaren finished, once again.

The suspension modifications and body alterations to the M23 had been of little use in stopping the recent onslaught of Lauda and Ferrari. Fittipaldi needed a change of fortune if he was to stay in the title hunt. For the French Grand Prix there was little sign of this, as Lauda sat on the pole again, with Fittipaldi nowhere, and Lotus not even that far. How the mighty had fallen. The race was almost a continuation of the previous one, except that Lauda was leading Hunt, and this time Mass was hard on their tails, gatecrashing their private party. These three finished in this order, while Fittipaldi came fourth, some 30 seconds adrift; his title challenge looked to be over.

Change was afoot for the British Grand Prix, held at Silverstone. Woodcote Corner had been replaced by a chicane, following Scheckter's accident in 1973, while Ickx had upped and left

Lotus and gone into retirement, though he had been accused of effectively 'retiring' rather earlier. Jim Crawford took his place, and Lotus also fielded Brian Henton for a one-off drive. Another nice change was to see Welshman Tom Pryce on the pole in his Shadow; but rest assured, Lauda was still in third place.

Normal service was quickly restored with the Ferraris in command, but after fifteen laps it began to rain. Out spun Regazzoni, leading a race once again, and into the pits for wet tyres went some of the drivers. These did not include Emerson and Hunt, however, and Hunt took over the lead. A real battle was now under way and Emerson demoted the Englishman on lap 43. Ten laps later catastrophe paid the RAC another visit, as a downpour engulfed the back of the circuit. Cars slowed right down and nearly half the field slithered off at Stowe and Club Corners. Amidst all the confusion, with few cars running and Fittipaldi in the pits for rain tyres, the race was called off after fifty-five laps. Fittipaldi was declared the winner, but the results were protested and it took another two days before the final results were announced. Grand Prix racing could have done without this bother, quite apart from the RAC; this was their hat trick of controversial races.

Remembering their unhappy time at the Nürburgring in 1974, McLaren could be forgiven for just going through the motions. Instead, with a few aerodynamic aids, including another attempt at evaluating skirts at this undulating circuit, spirits were high; it is amazing what a win can do. Jochen Mass, as keen as mustard, overdid it a bit in practice, comprehensively wrecking his newly rebuilt car. Fortunately he was relatively unhurt and qualified sixth, ahead of Fittipaldi, though Lauda claimed his customary pole position once again.

Despite its undoubted dangers, everyone wanted to do well at the Nürburgring – the ultimate test for a driver – and none more so than Jochen. However, he had another major crash on the first lap, after a tyre failed. His car

Early in the German Grand Prix, at the Nürburgring, Mass holds fourth position ahead of Scheckter, before he crashed later on the opening lap.

was destroyed, but at least he escaped serious injury again. Fittipaldi's race was little better; he collected a puncture and retired shortly afterwards with damaged suspension caused by this incident. Disappointment for McLaren then, but the demanding nature of the course threw up some surprising and well earned results. Reutemann became the seventh winner of a Grand Prix that season, with Laffite finishing second in his Williams. A number of punctures allowed some unaccustomed drivers into the points; Pryce came fourth in his Shadow, followed by Jones in the Hill, and one van Lennup claimed sixth place in the Ensign. All of these were drivers who rightly earned their moment of glory.

With only two weeks before the Austrian Grand Prix it was all that the McLaren mechanics could do to get two cars ready, so there was no spare – one way of encouraging the drivers to stay out of trouble. Stommelen was to make

his return after recovering from his injuries, but Mark Donohue was seriously injured in the warm-up, and died a short while later.

There was not much luck in the race either, as it got off to a wet start. Racing of sorts took place until another heavy downpour hit the circuit, and the race was stopped on lap 29. The tough Italian, Brambilla, was leading in his March, but as he crossed the finishing line, arms raised in triumph, he lost control and collided with a wall. It must have brought a bit of a welcome smile to the soaked, hardy spectators, as the winner toured round with the front of his car deranged, accepting all their plaudits, when they last saw him in one piece. This could only have happened to 'Brambles' Brambilla.

The excitement was only just beginning, though. A little later it stopped raining, and some teams wanted to continue, but the original race had covered more than half the distance and a winner was declared! Another controversy followed, with arguments raging back and forth, and all the while the poor spectators were ignored. In the event nothing happened, and for the second time that season only half points were awarded. If ever a sport seemed to have its finger poised over the self-destruct button, it was Grand Prix racing.

Before the Italian Grand Prix a non-championship race was held at Dijon, and Fittipaldi had a new M23 for this. It was here that a bit of confusion arose concerning chassis numbers as, instead of becoming M23–10, the new car became M23–8/2. This car became quite famous, but that is jumping the gun somewhat.

The Italian Grand Prix was, not unexpectedly, dominated by Ferrari. Lauda claimed his, by now, customary pole position with Regazzoni alongside, but Fittipaldi was third, ably supported by Mass in fifth place. A Ferrari showpiece was expected but Fittipaldi, while not exactly extinguishing Ferrari celebrations, certainly put a damper on them. As expected the two Ferraris took off like there was no to-morrow, but Fittipaldi showed his skill by keeping pace with, and finally passing Champion elect, Lauda. For the third year in succession Fittipaldi finished second in this race, but this did not prevent Lauda becoming the new World Champion, nor Ferrari the Constructors' Champions.

There was now a month to wait before the United States Grand Prix, the last of the year, as uncertain finances had caused the Canadian race to be cancelled. Needless to say, this did not happen quietly, and yet another row between FOCA and the organizers kept things on the boil. Apart from the loss of the race and the cost of travelling across the Atlantic for just one race, the fans lost out yet again, although nobody seemed to care much for them.

There were no new tweaks for the M23 cars, but Fittipaldi still ran Lauda very close indeed for the pole. The race began in the same way, with Lauda leading a revitalized Emerson, who was looking for a way past into the lead. Then they came behind a delayed Regazzoni who let

Lauda pass but, like a good team-mate, held Fittipaldi up for five laps so that he dropped out of serious contention. Good old Regazzoni was eventually black-flagged and was brought in to be told off. There is nothing wrong with helping out a team-mate but, apart from killing off the race, he overdid it a bit. Fittipaldi finished second again, with Mass coming third, ahead of Hunt and Peterson who was in the points once again after a dismal season.

There were times during the season, especially from Monaco onwards, when it seemed that Grand Prix was a Ferrari and especially Lauda benefit. Yet out of fourteen races, nine drivers had won, from six teams. The racing was usually competitive and closely fought, but the season really belonged to Lauda. He was undoubtedly aided by the new 312T Ferrari, which he was prominent in developing, and he won four more races than his team-mate Regazzoni, who was an established front runner. Other opponents had matured nicely, most obviously Hunt, but Pace and Scheckter as well, while drivers of the calibre of Andretti, Watson, Depailler, Laffite, Mass, Pryce, and Jarier, among others, all showed considerable progress. Curiously enough, one highly respected journalist said of Lauda '. . . he is hardly likely to go down in history as a great Champion'. How many times must Denis Jenkinson have eaten those words over the years!

Fittipaldi had a bit of an indifferent year, going off the boil at times, especially when Lauda was into his winning streak. He finished the season on a high note, though, and there were other occasions when he shone, but he did seem to lose interest occasionally. Jochen Mass really improved. He drove with enthusiasm, and though rarely upstaging his senior partner, seemed keen to learn.

The M23 looked a bit dated by the end of the year, and its successor, the M26, was needed if the team were going to mount a serious challenge to Ferrari and others in 1976; or so it appeared. The Lotus 72 was a case in point, a car that had outlived its useful life and was now languishing at the wrong end of the grid, despite the efforts of Peterson. If McLaren did not act soon, the downward path was clearly marked out by Lotus.

McLaren had finished third in the Constructors' Championship behind Ferrari and Brabham, but their chief weapon had been, once again, reliability. Out of twenty-seven

starts, in fourteen races, they achieved 11 points finishes, with neither car finishing in only two events. When one considered the sheer depth of similar opposition, this was impressive. In America the factory team achieved two USAC race wins, and Johnny Rutherford finished second in the Indianapolis 500 with the M16E, that team having a similar reputation as the

Grand Prix Results 1975											
GRAND PRIX	DRIVER	CAR	NO	1ST PRACTICE★ Time/Posn	2ND PRACTICE★ Time/Posn	3RD PRACTICE★ Time/Posn	FINAL GRID POSN	FINAL PLACING	RETIRED CAUSE OF	HIGHEST POSN IN RACE
ARGENTINIAN Buenos Aires 12.1.75	E. Fittipaldi	Ford V8 M23-DFV M23/9	1	1min 50.74sec 4/23	1min 50.02sec 1/23	1min 51.75sec 11/23	5-22	1/14 WINNER		1st
	J. Mass	Ford V8 M23-DFV M23/8	2	1min 52.49sec 12/23	1min 53.01sec 16/23	1min 51.82sec 12/23	13-22	14/14		14th
BRAZILIAN Interlagos 26.1.75	E. Fittipaldi	Ford V8 M23-DFV M23/9	1	2min 31.0sec 3/21	1min 32.28sec 6/23	2min 30.68sec 1/22	2-23	2/15		2nd
	J. Mass	Ford V8 M23-DFV M23/8	2	2min 34.09sec 10/21	2min 33.68sec 11/23	2min 33.06sec 8/22	10-23	3/15		3rd
SOUTH AFRICAN Kyalami 1.3.75	E. Fittipaldi	Ford V8 M23-DFV M23/9	1	1min 17.29sec 6/25	1min 17.22sec 2/25	1min 17.68sec 3/25	9-24		Lp 65 Running not classified	4th
		Ford V8 M23-DFV M23/6	1T	1min 18.17sec 15/24						
	J. Mass	Ford V8 M23-DFV M23/8	2	1min 18.01sec 12/25	1min 17.79sec 5/25	1min 18.17sec 13/20	14-24	6/17		6th
	D. Charlton (Lucky Strike)	Ford V8 M23-DFV M23/2	31	1min 21.10sec 21/25	1min 18.51sec 17/25	1min 21.57sec 24/25	18-24	14/17		14th
SPANISH Barcelona 27.4.75	E. Fittipaldi	Ford V8 M23-DFV M23/9	1			2min 10.2sec 27/27	Did not race. Protest concerning safety arguments			
	J. Mass	Ford V8 M23-DFV M23/8	2			1min 25.4sec 11/27	11-25	1/8 WINNER		1st
MONACO Monte Carlo 11.5.75	E. Fittipaldi	Ford V8 M23-DFV M23/9	1	1min 30.3sec 13/16	1min 29.72sec 13/16	1min 27.77sec 9/17	9-18	2/9		2nd
	J. Mass	Ford V8 M23-DFV M23/8	2	1min 29.5sec 8/16	1min 28.61sec 7/16	1min 28.49sec 15/17	15-18	6/9		5th
BELGIAN Zolder 25.5.75	E. Fittipaldi	Ford V8 M23-DFV M23/9	1	1min 26.82sec 2/23	1min 26.26sec 2/22	1min 26.58sec 9/23	8-24	7/12		4th
	J. Mass	Ford V8 M23-DFV M23/8	2	1min 28.48sec 14/23	1min 27.93sec 14/22	1min 27.38sec 15/23	15-24		Lp 1 Collided broke steering	

Race	Driver	Car		Practice 1	Practice 2	Practice 3	Grid		Notes	Result
SWEDISH Anderstorp 8.6.75	E. Fittipaldi	Ford V8 M23-DFV M23/9	1	1min 26.35sec 8/25	1min 26.09sec 8/24	1min 26.82sec 7/21	12-26	8/17		**5th**
		Ford V8 M23-DFV M23/6	1T	1min 41.85sec 28/28						
	J. Mass	Ford V8 M23-DFV M23/8	2	1min 27.38sec 13/25	1min 27.33sec 13/24	1min 26.77sec 6/21	13-26		Lp 34 Water leak	**11th**
DUTCH Zandvoort 22.6.75	E. Fittipaldi	Ford V8 M23-DFV M23/9	1	1min 21.04sec 6/24	1min 20.91sec 2/24	1min 20.95sec 2/23	5-24		Lp 40 Engine	**4th**
	J. Mass	Ford V8 M23-DFV M23/8	2	1min 21.28sec 4/23	1min 21.48sec 4/24	1min 21.01sec 5/24	7-24		Lp 61 Accident Engine cut out	**5th FL**
		Ford V8 M23-DFV M23/4	2T	1min 22.36sec 17/27						
FRENCH Ricard- Castellet 6.7.75	E. Fittipaldi	Ford V8 M23-DFV M23/9	1	1min 48.75sec 3/22	1min 49.64sec 11/23	1min 49.48sec 12/24	10-25	4/18		**4th**
	J. Mass	Ford V8 M23-DFV M23/6	2	1min 49.51sec 11/22	1min 48.68sec 5/23	1min 48.54sec 5/24	7-25	3/18		**3rd**
BRITISH Silverstone 19.7.75	E. Fittipaldi	Ford V8 M23-DFV M23/9	1	1min 20.0sec 1/24	1min 19.9sec 5/24	1min 19.9sec 5/24	8-26	1/19 WINNER		**1st**
	J. Mass	Ford V8 M23-DFV M23/6	2	1min 20.7sec 12/24	1min 20.3sec 9/24	1min 20.2sec 9/24	9-26	7/19		**2nd**
GERMAN Nürburgring 3.8.75	E. Fittipaldi	Ford V8 M23-DFV M23/9	1	7min 2.7sec 2/22	7min 2.8sec 5/22	7min 3.6sec 9/23	8-22		Lp 3 Damaged susp following puncture	**7th**
	J. Mass	Ford V8 M23-DFV M23/4	2			7min 3.0sec 8/23	8-22		Lp 1 Accident tyre failure	
		Ford V8 M23-DFV M23/4	2T	7min 1.8sec 2/26	7min 6.3sec 1/25	7min 4.2sec 8/27	6-22			
AUSTRIAN Österreichring 17.8.75	E. Fittipaldi	Ford V8 M23-DFV M23/9	1	1min 35.21sec 2/23	1min 35.41sec 3/19	1min 36.36sec 4/22	4-26	9/17		**5th**
	J. Mass	Ford V8 M23-DFV M23/6	2	1min 36.88sec 10/23	1min 36.70sec 10/19	1min 36.12sec 3/22	10-26	4/17		**3rd**
ITALIAN Monza 7.9.75	E. Fittipaldi	Ford V8 M23-DFV M23/10	1	1min 36.05sec 13/25	1min 33.08sec 3/26	1min 33.13sec 2/24	3-26	2/14		**2nd**
		Ford V8 M23-DFV M23/9	1T	1min 34.49sec 7/26						
	J. Mass	Ford V8 M23-DFV M23/6	2	1min 35.20sec 10/24	1min 33.46sec 4/26	1min 33.20sec 4/24	5-26		Lp 2 Accident damage	**4th**
USA Watkins Glen 5.10.75	E. Fittipaldi	Ford V8 M23-DFV M23/10	1	1min 42.99sec 2/18	1min 42.36sec 1/17	1min 42.92sec 3/18	2-20	2/10		**FL 2nd**
	J. Mass	Ford V8 M23-DFV M23/6	2	1min 45.08sec 11/18	1min43.10sec 4/17	1min 43.55sec 9/18	9-20	3/10		**3rd**

★ Some races ran four practices. A driver's best three results are counted.

Grand Prix team: not the fastest, but always up there.

During the close season a couple of events took a more than usually prominent place in the press. Unable to find a sponsor, the Hesketh team had closed its doors and pulled out of racing. Not everyone was sad at this loss, but they did make a fascinating addition to the Grand Prix world and for all their peculiarities, they were successful; their colourful team would be sorely missed. Their driver, golden boy James Hunt, was thus without a drive for 1976, though he had a few irons warming in the fire.

Simultaneously, and not completely independent of the Hesketh situation, Fittipaldi had not signed his contract with McLaren for 1976, though nobody worried unduly. Hunt had kept in touch with Teddy Mayer 'just in case' during the autumn, when he was informed by Emerson that he would not be re-signing with McLaren. This news broke out a couple of days later, and Hunt was signed to replace Emerson, who was going to drive for the Fittipaldi team.

James Hunt had matured markedly during 1975, being the only driver who seemed capable of keeping Lauda in view. A question mark hung over him though, and this concerned the Hesketh team. James Hunt had not really shone in the lower formulae and had only driven for Hesketh in Grand Prix, so it was just

possible that he was an average driver in a very good car – the very opposite of Ronnie Peterson's situation in 1975. The proof of the pudding is in the eating, and as a large part of the 'pudding' mixture remained essentially the same for Hunt as for Fittipaldi (the M23) so a judgement would soon be forthcoming.

The other event of that autumn virtually shook the world. Graham Hill, the 'Grandad' of the modern era, had finally hung up his gloves and helmet, or whatever ex-racing drivers hang up, and retired, at the Monaco Grand Prix. While not the most talented of drivers, he had a unique desire to succeed and, indeed, twice won the World Championship, driving for BRM and Lotus. He is still the only driver to have won the Indianapolis 500 and Le Mans 24-hour races as well. Above all though, Graham Hill was perhaps the most complete sportsman, let alone racing driver, in the eyes of the public, his popularity stemming from his unique, gentlemanly character. He was team manager of his own Embassy-Hill team, and it was when flying home from a test session in France that the plane, piloted by Hill, crashed with fatal consequences for all on board. Grand Prix racing thus lost its greatest ambassador, a young driver of talent in Tony Brise, and the rest of the Embassy-Hill team in one sad moment.

CHAPTER 5

Wine, Women, Song and the Championship

There were a few changes in the air for McLaren in 1976, James Hunt replacing Emerson Fittipaldi being the most public of these. Phil Kerr decided to return to New Zealand to start a business venture with Denny Hulme, later joined by Mike Hailwood. Jochen Mass remained, and although James Hunt had replaced Emerson Fittipaldi, the number one position was up for grabs, leaving all sorts of possibilities open.

It was intended to introduce Gordon Coppuck's M26 as early as possible, but he had not neglected the M23, revising the front suspension, paring 30lb (14kg) off its weight, and reverting to a lower wishbone rear suspension. By far the most interesting development was Alastair Caldwell's six-speed version of the Hewland gearbox. With this, the Cosworth engine could be kept revving within its relatively narrow power band, between 9,000–10,500rpm, and therefore be more effective, while Nicholson-McLaren naturally prepared the engines to suit. Any little advantage over their Cosworth-engined rivals, bringing them closer to the more powerful flat-12 cylindered Ferraris, would be needed.

Rival teams had not been idle during the winter either, most noteworthy being Tyrrell. They unveiled their innovative P34 six-wheeled car, with its four tiny front wheels, towards the end of 1975. With this revolutionary car, Tyrrell sought to gain a significant advantage through reducing the frontal area drag by taking the front wheels out of the airstream. Thus an improved top speed, with perhaps better front-end grip in the corners, was aimed for and Tyrrell being who they were, everyone had to take this development seriously.

Lotus introduced the Lotus 77 to replace the ageing 72 and failed 76. This retained certain all-adjustable characteristics of the 76 and contained a few aerodynamic secrets, but it flattered only to deceive, and put Lotus through more heartache before finally coming good.

Much was expected from the new Brabham BT45, which used the Alfa Romeo flat-12 engine. Having finished above McLaren in the 1975 Constructors' Championship, while retaining Pace and Reutemann as drivers, they posed a serious threat, especially if the Alfa engine was as powerful as proclaimed; but McLaren had experienced small Italian horses before!

If those were the major developments, things were not static at the other teams. The new Ligier team were to use the Matra V12 engine, first used in Grand Prix but finding fame in sports cars. Laffite had left Williams to become the driver of this all-French outfit, and while not expected to be front runners, at first, needed keeping an eye on. The Wolf-Williams team was backed by Canadian businessman Walter Wolf, with Ickx due to drive their first car, but much else had to be settled.

Penske had shown steady progress and, with Watson driving, this was likely to continue. The other American-founded team, Shadow, had suffered a major disaster when their sponsor, UOP, suddenly withdrew, leaving them severely under-financed. The rest of the field was made up of a reborn Hesketh team, Ensign

James Hunt

It is disconcerting to hear how often in recent years motor racing fans have called James Hunt 'lucky'. For enthusiasts who remember the years 1973–1978, Hunt and his apparent cavalier attitude were a throwback to the amateur days when motor racing was fun. Whatever he says in his often colourful television commentaries about 'professionalism' and 'driving for a finish', Hunt the driver was a 'charger'. The sight of Hunt in his patriotic-liveried Hesketh, or later the Marlboro-McLaren, scything through the field following another indifferent start, had the crowds sitting on the edge of their seats in excited admiration. There was no sitting back and watching a processional race brought to a clinical finish when Hunt was still in with a shout. It was only in the latter half of 1978, after half a season of near heroic effort, that Hunt finally seemed to throw in the towel and give in to fate.

By November 1975, when Hunt rather 'luckily' joined McLaren, he had long since left his accident-prone days behind. Mind you, over the next three years the underside of his Mclaren was not exactly an uncommon sight during a race. A year later, his flamboyant lifestyle, devil-may-care attitude, and particularly his exciting driving and ability to win against all odds, earned him the accolade 'Golden Boy' of British sport. He captured the public's imagination in a way other drivers such as Stewart or Prost never could.

Ten Grand Prix victories, though one of them was 'stolen' from him by the CSI, twelve pole positions and six fastest laps, along with three non-championship race wins, was the impressive haul from the 1976 and 1977 seasons. The following year, despite his M26 being well off the pace, he showed the old spirit with some tremendous drives in Spain and France, but thereafter seemed to lose motivation. This culminated with his replacement by Ronnie Peterson for 1979, and going off to rejoin his old Hesketh designer Dr Harvy Posthethwaite, at Wolf, for one last 'big whack'. It was no surprise when, after having failed to secure a single Championship point in the Wolf, he retired in mid-season.

When his car gave him a chance of success, Hunt was capable of outdriving anyone, but he was most definitely not cut out to drive around in the middle of the pack and wait for retirements to get him a points finish.

If seldom out of the sports pages as a driver, Hunt was never very far off the mark when it came to other newsworthy items, whether it was playing his trumpet to a packed Albert Hall, or thumping a Canadian marshall. Controversy followed him around and the politics of 1976 between McLaren, Ferrari and the CSI, were almost as absorbing as the racing. Apart from all the disqualifications, reinstatements, and fist-shaking of 1976, there was the visit to the Lotus pit to 'sort things out' with Andretti in Holland, refusal to attend the victory celebrations in Japan, and occasional accident of 1977. Finally in 1978, there was his brave rescuing of Ronnie Peterson from his burning Lotus in Italy. That he should just 'up and away' part-way through and not retire gracefully at the end of 1979, was entirely in keeping with his character and popular image.

Motor racing in general and Grand Prix racing in particular, are far more professional than ever before. The dedication and determination needed by everyone in McLaren to keep the team at the top is total, but is nearly matched by those struggling to find a place at the back of the grid. In short, it is perhaps just as well that drivers like James Hunt and Mike Hawthorn had their day when they did. If Hunt were driving the latest McLaren today alongside the current crop of drivers, there is little doubt that he would be winning just as he did in his heyday. Whether he would have had the dedication of Senna or Prost to develop the car to such performance in the first place is another matter.

For many motor racing enthusiasts, James Hunt is best remembered taking the chequered flag, both arms aloft, after yet another rousing drive from behind that brought the crowds to their feet. Everyone, except the Ferrari die-hards, went home happy and Hunt would usually show his affinity with the fans by celebrating with a beer, and possibly even a sponsor's cigarette.

with Chris Amon driving, and Surtees, with Alan Jones and Brett Lunger as drivers and a new car. March aimed to run two separate two-car teams, building on their success of 1975. With drivers Hans Stuck, Ernest Brambilla and others expected, they needed watching, especially as from South Africa they literally pulled an ace from up their sleeve. BRM showed up in Brazil, survived two laps, and that was it for the rest of the season.

McLaren's main opponents were again likely to be Ferrari. With Lauda and Regazzoni as drivers, the most powerful engine in Grand Prix and a new car on the way, there was never the slightest chance of underestimating them. They were, undoubtedly, the team to beat, and there were many occasions in 1975 when that looked impossible. With the largest budget in racing and their own test facilities, Ferrari were going to be difficult to dislodge.

THE HUNT IS ON

The Brazilian Grand Prix opened the season and after a frustrating practice, which included tailoring James Hunt into the car – a job which ought to have been done beforehand – Hunt made his mark by stealing the pole from Lauda near the end of the final practice session. This was significant, as it was James's first ever pole position and established his 'street cred' with his new team. It was also achieved with Fittipaldi's old car, M23–8/2, and at his home race; one in the eye for leaving McLaren. Jochen Mass was a second slower in sixth place, but it was Regazzoni who took the lead with one of his charging starts from the second row.

Lauda eventually slipped past Regazzoni, followed by Hunt. The latter's engine became a V7 when an injection trumpet broke, which caused the throttles to stick. Struggling to hold on to Lauda's shirt tails, Hunt was passed by Jarier, and then on lap 32, spun off when the throttles jammed open, leaving a trail of oil on the circuit. He had a lasting effect on events as Jarier crashed on this, and his Shadow teammate, Pryce, later lost second place to Depailler after running wide on Hunt's oil. Mass, after having to pit early on to fit a new nose cone, drove superbly to finish sixth and gain a well deserved point.

This race was the last for Peterson with Lotus, and he reappeared in the March factory team at the South African Grand Prix, Lotus now plumbing the depths. Hunt was happy enough, having out-qualified Lauda and kept pace with him in Brazil, and he positively looked forward to this race.

Prior to the South African Grand Prix itself, there was a tremendously exciting battle for grid positions. Hunt once again pipped Lauda for the pole, followed a smidgen later by Watson in the Penske, with Mass in fourth place. McLaren had a real chance to put one over on Ferrari, but as the green light flashed it was not to be. Hunt got off to another indifferent start and was swamped by Mass and a charging Brambilla, while Lauda roared off into the distance. Brambilla was not one to give up his position easily, and kept Hunt at bay by using some pretty ruthless tactics. If Hunt got his nose alongside Brambilla's on the inside of a corner, it was likely to be given a swift chop.

Hunt forced his way past on lap 5, outbraking Brambilla, but could do little about Lauda who had built up a nice lead. Lauda paced himself well, but then gradually the gap began to close. The Ferrari had a slow puncture and Hunt, driving furiously, came within 2 seconds of Lauda as the chequered flag came out. However, Lauda had now won three races on the trot, including the last race of 1975. Jochen Mass finished a worthy third, though some 40 seconds behind James Hunt.

There was a new race to follow this, the United States Grand Prix (West), held on the streets of Long Beach on the west coast of America. Hunt was fresh from a win in the non-championship Race of Champions, but was beaten off the front row of the grid by Regazzoni and Depailler, with Lauda next to him. Mass was a second slower in mid-grid, not a good place to be on a narrow, winding circuit.

Regazzoni put together a classic performance, leading Hunt, whose engine momentarily died, and Depailler got by; then on lap 3 the fireworks began. Hunt tried to pass Depailler on the inside of a hairpin, was forced to the outside on the straight, and was 'pushed' into the wall. For several laps afterwards, a furious Hunt stood out on the circuit waving

At the inaugural Long Beach Grand Prix, James Hunt ran in third place, before his accident with Depailler on lap 3. He did not have long to go, in this picture.

his fist at Depailler each time he passed. This only added to the Tyrrell driver's problem that was forcing him to brake early, but despite this he finished third behind Regazzoni, who was a massive 40 seconds ahead of Lauda. This made for five consecutive Ferrari victories. The Depailler/Hunt battle continued afterwards at the press conference, a fiery James Hunt not emerging in the best of lights. Jochen Mass, driving steadily, recorded his third points finish of the season, and led James Hunt in the Championship.

Hunt won his second race of the season, The International Trophy at Silverstone, taking pole and fastest lap to boot. This did not aid his Championship chances though, and as McLaren prepared for the Spanish Grand Prix there was every chance for Jochen Mass to establish himself as the number one. New car regulations

were introduced in Spain, incorporating additional safety features. The maximum dimensions for the cars had been drawn up around existing cars, so as not to make them obsolete overnight, the width being taken from the M23; this was to have far-reaching consequences by the end of the race.

Spain saw the introduction of the Ferrari 312–T2, while Andretti was back in a Lotus, alongside Gunnar Nilsson, to begin the long haul back after two successive back-of-the-grid starts. The major event was Depailler's debut in the six-wheeled Tyrrell P34. This was an historic moment, but Depailler promptly went and surprised everyone by qualifying third on the grid, one place ahead of Mass. Hunt rose to the challenges coming from both inside and outside McLaren, and claimed the pole position yet again, with Lauda, as ever, sitting alongside.

Once again Hunt failed to make the most of his grid position and Lauda, nursing broken ribs from a tractor accident, took the lead. After three pole positions, Hunt had failed to take the lead once, claiming that he started gently to preserve his clutch, although Lauda and the others did not seem unduly concerned or hampered by this. One wonders why he did not make a special effort to practise starts until he could make fast, clean get-aways.

Brambilla once again stormed through, barging past Depailler and Mass, but Hunt held him at bay this time. Depailler and Mass soon repassed the March to follow Hunt who, in turn, sat close to Lauda. Mass eventually found a way past the Tyrrell, which spun out with fading brakes. The McLarens now ran second and third, with both drivers keen to establish seniority. On lap 32 Hunt took the lead from Lauda, followed by Mass two laps later. They circulated nose to tail, though Mass was instructed not to pass Hunt. It was looking good for McLaren when, with ten laps to go, Mass's engine blew, leaving Hunt to record his first win for McLaren, beating Lauda by over 30 seconds. That was that, the duck was broken. Or was it?

Because of the new regulations, and to prove that the CSI (remember them?) actually existed beyond their Paris offices, a show was made at post-race scrutineering and, lo and behold, Hunt's M23, the very car on which the maximum width was based, was found to be too wide due to the bulge in the tyres. McLaren expected a fine but, after much arguing, Hunt was excluded from the results that evening. As can be imagined, the reactions within McLaren varied from disbelief to fury, but the fact was, however minor or indeed irrelevant, that they had broken a rule. This would probably not have been noticed at any previous race, but these were new regulations. Teddy Mayer, who you may remember was a trained lawyer, appealed on the grounds that the punishment did not fit the crime. As he was to put it: '. . . it's like hanging a man for a parking offence.'

Ferrari saw it differently though, as Lauda had just won again.

The season was becoming a bit unsavoury, particularly for Hunt and McLaren, and as for the extra width of the M23 not affecting performance, the next three races suggested differently. Both Tyrrell drivers appeared with the P34 at the Belgian Grand Prix, lining up fourth and seventh on the grid and, following on from Spain where Nilsson had finished third, the Lotus team continued their recovery. Lauda claimed his first pole of the season, ahead of Regazzoni, with Hunt in third place. Mass, however, was way back, some 2 seconds slower.

This time Hunt got into second place behind Lauda at the start, but he was holding up the others. Brambilla once again forced himself among the leaders, nearly spinning off for good measure, before a driveshaft cried for mercy and gave up on lap 6. Regazzoni, never one to hang around, was first past Hunt, then Laffite hustled his Ligier by. Depailler resumed their Long Beach battle, coming out on top, as did Scheckter after quite a fight. Something was clearly wrong with Hunt's car, and why was Mass so far back?

A seized transmission put Hunt out of his misery, while Mass finished a distant sixth. Lauda, meanwhile, strode on imperiously, leading Regazzoni home, with Laffite third and Scheckter fourth. The Championship seemed all over even now, with Lauda 27 points clear of Regazzoni and 36 ahead of Hunt.

Monaco brought even less cheer than usual for McLaren. The formerly fast M23 had in Hunt's words become 'evil' with its handling, and he was back on the seventh row of the grid, with Mass a row in front. Surely this was not due to a miserly ⅝ths of an inch (16mm) off the width of the car? If not, though, the team had little idea of what the problem might be. Lauda and Regazzoni sat majestically on the front of the grid, no doubt grinning like Cheshire cats.

As the green light came on Lauda was away, demonstrating the perfect start to Hunt, except

Hunt struggled manfully in Belgium, for little reward. It is lap 16 and Laffite is poised to overtake in the Ligier, with Depailler shadowing them in his P34 Tyrrell.

Mass leads Hunt during the early stages of the Monaco Grand Prix, in a distant tenth place.

108

Nobody's perfect. James Hunt spins during the Monaco Grand Prix and has already lost eleventh place to Jean-Pierre Jarier while Carlos Pace and Chris Amon are aiming for the gap he thoughtfully left. Hunt resumed in last place and failed to finish.

that Hunt was too far down the grid to see. Peterson, back in a March, squeezed ahead of Regazzoni, with the two Tyrrells behind. Hunt could not pass anyone and in frustration spun to the back on lap 8. It was a merciful release when his engine gave up later, while Mass doggedly kept up the chase, finishing a creditable fifth. Lauda won again in that demoralizing, dominating fashion, and Regazzoni was looking to make it another Ferrari 1–2 when he crashed near the end. So, the Tyrrells of Scheckter and Depailler finished next followed by Stuck, in a March.

After the first practice for the Swedish Grand Prix, with Hunt in mid-grid, McLaren, out of desperation, changed the M23 back to its settings in Spain, with the oil coolers remaining

under the rear wing instead of being along the side in front of the rear wheels. This made little difference, but Hunt moved up to eighth the next day, only three places behind Lauda! Jochen Mass was back in thirteenth position, two places behind Regazzoni. On the pole this time sat Scheckter, with Andretti still in a Lotus alongside and Amon third in the Ensign; something completely different.

The race was a triumph for the Tyrrell P34, though Andretti led for forty-six laps but was penalized a minute for jumping the start. Amon crashed while in third place at half distance when a front wishbone broke, and he was lucky to escape serious injury. Lauda moved into, and remained in, third position, but there was nothing he could do to stop Scheckter and Depailler stealing the limelight. Hunt came fifth, holding off a belated Regazzoni charge – a drive he was proud of as the car was so difficult to drive fast. To prove this point, Mass finished a lowly eleventh, miles back.

Any thought of the World Championship for Hunt seemed ridiculous now, while the M23 was still not right. Then, as a last resort and despite all logic, the oil coolers were moved less than an inch back, to their former position. While testing for the French Grand Prix, Hunt found that the handling problems were cured, but surely it was too late to think of beating Lauda in the Championship. There was no proof that the M23 was able to compete with the new Ferrari, and the M26 was still not ready – this was not really a Championship winning performance.

It did not take long to provide evidence of the M23's rehabilitation as a front-running car. Hunt claimed the pole ahead of Lauda, in France, after practice sessions which saw Pace, Peterson, Andretti and Watson in the top eight, with Mass a lowly fourteenth. McLaren were back at last. Then Hunt took a gamble. He spent an hour and a half 'scrubbing in' a set of tyres, to maintain their handling characteristics throughout the race; a far cry from today, when tyres often do not last the race distance. As ever, Lauda beat Hunt away at the start, his new tyres allowing him to pull steadily away, but Hunt was not unduly worried. Ferrari had already experienced engine problems in practice, and Hunt knew all was not well with his rival as he slid around on the oil and water coming out of Lauda's Ferrari. On lap 8 Lauda coasted to a halt, his engine blown, and Hunt won at his own pace, especially as Regazzoni's engine went the same way nine laps later, sending him into the catch fences – quite remarkable: two Ferrari engine failures.

Entertainment value was assured as a whole gaggle of drivers jockeyed for position behind Hunt, with both Tyrrells, Peterson, Watson and Pace – at last enjoying a decent race in the Brabham-Alfa – involved. After an exciting bat-

tle, Scheckter's engine went off the boil and Peterson dropped out of third position two laps from the end, when his fuel metering unit failed. He was having an unlucky year. Depailler claimed second with Watson promoted to third, but the action was not over yet!

The CSI decided to participate in the sport they purported to run and, as before, it was not advantageous. It had been an excitingly close-fought race so, for an encore, the CSI introduced their spectacular production, 'Post Race Scrutineering'. This is the game where all the names of the finishers of the first leg of the Grand Prix are put into a hat, and though James Hunt won and Patrick Neve finished eighteenth, nearly two laps adrift, these positions could quite easily be reversed after the all-important second leg.

And what a magnificent finale it was. Officials, scrutineers, team members, press, drivers, and quite probably programme sellers as well, enjoyed a multi-lingual slanging match, as cars were wheeled back and forth and measured with highly inventive instruments, the purpose of which remained obscure to all. Sadly, the scrutineers missed the 'big prize' and could not disqualify Hunt, but not to be outdone, they finally found a rear-wing side plate half an inch (13mm) too high on Watson's Penske. They could hardly conceal their delight as Watson was excluded from the results, thus ensuring that a third leg (the appeals section) of the race would be run at a later date. It was a little disappointing though; surely, after so much fuss, a few more disqualifications could have been found!

There was still the third leg of the Spanish Grand Prix to be run. This took place in Paris, and the field was decidedly thin. McLaren were appealing against the second leg exclusion of James Hunt, after he had won on the road. To recollect, the M23 was just over half an inch (13mm) too wide, and Teddy Mayer, with Colin Chapman there to give evidence on McLaren's behalf, claimed that the punishment did not fit the crime. The Court of Appeal agreed with Mayer and reinstated Hunt, fining

Did he, or didn't he? James Hunt on his way to his third victory of the season at Brands Hatch.

the team $3,000 instead. Everyone emerged from the hearing pleased, but in Italy a few dark comments were being made.

James Hunt was happy enough though, he now had 26 points, exactly half of Lauda's total, with half of the races run, and his home race, the British Grand Prix, was next. Any thoughts that this might run smoothly were tempered by memories of varying degrees of ill-luck, and incompetence, at the last three events. Lauda fought back to pip Hunt for the pole, with Andretti third, Regazzoni fourth, and Amon sixth. Brands Hatch was packed for the expected Hunt vs Lauda battle . . .

Off they went, towards Paddock Hill Bend. Regazzoni made another flying start, and tried to squeeze in in front of Lauda as he turned into the corner. The Ferraris collided, Regazzoni spun, and Hunt, dodging round the outside,

took off on impact. He could easily have turned over, which would have been a far more serious event than Warwick's crash at Monza in 1990, as the cars were less safe in 1976. Luck was on his side though, he crashed down, kept the engine running and, despite damaged steering, continued towards Druids Hill.

Suddenly, the race was stopped on the orders of the Safety Officer at Paddock Hill, in view of the chaos caused by Regazzoni. The great expected battle looked to be over when, in fact, it had only just begun. Seeing the red flags, Hunt made for the pits, without going round the full circuit, to restart in the spare car. Confusion then reigned. Allegations were made that the race was stopped because Hunt was involved and, as the dust died down, the circuit was relatively clear, while Lauda was miles away. The arguing continued unabated as the grid reformed, with Hunt, Regazzoni and Laffite in spare cars.

It was then announced that only those cars which had completed a full lap would be allowed to restart. Guess who this excluded? A large section of the crowd, many of whom had come to watch the race, and not a slanging match, began to demand to see what they paid their entrance fee for. They, in no uncertain terms, let it be known that a race with a full grid was wanted, and that petty officialdom could expect trouble if they did not deliver.

The rule books were consulted again, and interpreted differently. Yes you could restart if you were running, when the race was officially 'stopped', in your race car. Another arguing session followed, the wait more than keeping the crowd on their toes. But while all this had been going on, McLaren had repaired Hunt's race car. This was wheeled on to the grid, putting an end to the matter of spare cars, to the vocal approval of the paying customers. Incidentally, neither Regazzoni nor Laffite raced in their original race cars.

The restart got under way, with Lauda leading Hunt, and Regazzoni curbing his heroic instincts. Lauda pulled away as Hunt fought his tyre set-up, but as his fuel load lightened he reeled in the World Champion. The awaited battle now looked a certainty, but once Hunt passed Lauda, just after half-distance, he settled for a secure second place. Lauda's avoidance of a fight upset Hunt a bit, and the easy win took a little out of the occasion. Both Regazzoni and Laffite retired in their spare cars, and there were only ten well-spaced-out finishers. Hunt's victory, however, nicely rounded off the occasion.

Even as the awards were being made, Tyrrell, Fittipaldi and Ferrari were lodging official protests that Hunt had not been running when the first race was stopped. Track marshalls confirmed that Hunt was indeed running, if not racing, so Tyrrell and Fittipaldi withdrew their protests, but Ferrari did not. The results were allowed to stand, pending an appeal, and Hunt moved three points closer to Lauda. It was sig-

nificant that the very team whose driver had caused the accident in the first place, and who later raced in an illegal spare car, was the one to protest the result. So ended another British shambles.

Prior to the German Grand Prix at the Nürburgring, Hunt had been testing the M26, and declared it just about raceworthy. However, as the previous two races had shown, the M23 was still very competitive. What had transformed this car into a Ferrari-beater, after being so clearly outclassed by the end of 1975? Certainly Hunt's driving was a key factor, as Mass was often much slower in practice, and was in truth less of a support for Hunt than Regazzoni was for Lauda. Then again, Mass was not likely to get involved in an incident with his team leader. Also the new regulations, especially those concerning engine airboxes and wings, had kept the car competitive. Other teams, principally Tyrrell with their P34, were expected to challenge strongly, but other circumstances were to enter the equation to the M23's benefit.

With practice under way for the German Grand Prix, the RAC upheld the result of the British Grand Prix, but Ferrari decided to appeal further to the CSI. This did not stop Hunt claiming the pole again, with Lauda alongside for company, as usual. Lauda had been extremely vocal in his condemnation of the Nürgburgring prior to the race, based on the lack of safety features, taken for granted elsewhere. This was to be quite prophetic in a most bizarre way, shortly into the race.

Many drivers and team managers were concerned, as the 14-mile long circuit was wet in places, and dry in others. Twenty-five drivers started on wet-weather tyres, but Mass decided to gamble on dry tyres. Hunt also fancied these, but it was too much of a risk with everyone else on wet tyres. For once Lauda made a poor start, but with Regazzoni flying from the third row, Hunt still did not take the lead, at least until Regazzoni overdid it at one corner. Thus Hunt led, but Mass was keeping up and would not have to stop and change his tyres.

After one long lap Hunt went into the pits for dry tyres, allowing Peterson to take the lead and commit himself to another lap on wet tyres, followed by most of the other drivers. After two further laps, Hunt moved into second place, a full three-quarters of a minute behind Jochen Mass. This was quite a dilemma for McLaren: Hunt needed the points, but would Mass slow and allow him to pass in the German driver's home race; more to the point should he?

Subsequent events rendered this irrelevant as the race was stopped. Lauda had, inexplicably, endured a horrifying crash, the wreck being hit by two other cars and bursting into flames. His prophecies came true; there was insufficient assistance to either quell the fire, or get Lauda out of the car. Brett Lunger, Harald Ertl, Guy Edwards, and Arturo Merzario all rescued Lauda and saved his life. He was rushed to hospital and the race restarted to the original grid, minus six drivers; the news being that Lauda had suffered minor burns, but was conscious and had been talking to other drivers. Hunt controlled the restarted race from the front with Scheckter, Pace, Regazzoni, and Mass coming up behind. Then, with two laps to go, Regazzoni had yet another spin, clouting the barriers, and promoting Mass to third place, behind Scheckter. Hunt won his fourth race of the year and was only 14 points behind Lauda, but later that evening it was revealed just how serious Lauda's injuries were. For Lauda, the battle for life had replaced that for the World Championship.

It was at the Austrian Grand Prix that McLaren decided to put the M26 aside as far as Hunt was concerned, and to concentrate all efforts on the M23. Ferrari had not entered, ostensibly to protest over the Spanish and British results. Worse still, Ferrari then tried forcing the organizers to abandon the race altogether, inflaming matters still further. They may have had a point, but surely the place to prove it is on the race circuit? Not so, it seemed, in 1976. Despite an understandably small crowd, the meeting went ahead, with Hunt taking the pole again and Watson, Peterson, Nilsson, Laffite,

Pryce, Brambilla and the rest behind. How the status quo had changed.

In compensation, the race proved to be one of the most exciting of the season, at least in the early stages. Despite a smattering of rain, everyone started on dry tyres, and Hunt and Watson roared off neck and neck. Watson eased ahead, and as more rain fell Peterson got by into the lead. Scheckter also got past Hunt to challenge Peterson, then Watson joined in again, and finally Nilsson made it a four-way battle at the front.

As the rain stopped, Peterson fell back, while Scheckter crashed. Watson now led, with only Nilsson to worry about. Laffite moved up into second place, but a deranged front wing was causing Hunt handling problems, which accounted for him being off the pace. Though he nearly caught Nilsson, worried by falling oil pressure, Hunt had to settle for fourth place and only 3 points – a disappointment. However, John Watson and the Penske team were elated, as both took their respective maiden victories.

In no time at all everyone assembled for the Dutch Grand Prix, including Ferrari, whose threats of pulling out of racing altogether amounted to one race. Lauda was at home, fighting his way back to fitness despite the internal burns, and you could bet that Regazzoni, in the one entry, would be out to thwart Hunt. Mass gave the M26 its debut, and Shadow introduced the new DN8 for Pryce. With the Boro team making their debut, and Larry Perkins qualifying within two seconds of Peterson on the pole, a breath of fresh air swept through the grid.

Race day was very special for James Hunt as, apart from needing a win, it was his twenty-ninth birthday, and in celebration of this, so it seemed, another classic race was under way. Peterson led initially, and Watson squeezed ahead of Hunt who did not make the best of his front-row position, once again. Peterson struggled with understeer, and Watson began to look for a way past. Hunt was in third place, ahead of a marauding bunch of cars led by Andretti,

John Watson tried everything he knew to take the lead off James Hunt at the Dutch Grand Prix. Here Hunt hugs the inside line at the Tarzan hairpin, once again, to fend off another attack. Observe that neither driver is bouncing all over the kerbs, unlike some of the more unruly elements of today.

when after one of Watson's failed assaults on Peterson, he slipped through a gap into second. A few laps later Peterson ran wide and Hunt took the lead.

Shortly afterwards Watson overtook Peterson; this marked the prelude to the most exciting battle of the year. Hunt's car had a loose front brake duct, causing the car to understeer badly, and Watson was ready to pounce. At the end of the straight lies the Tarzan hairpin – the ideal place for overtaking – and a furious battle took place between the two Britons. Hunt kept a tight line into the hairpin, forcing Watson round the outside, the Ulsterman getting his Penske in front on occasions, but Hunt always emerged the better-placed to accelerate out of

the corner and retake the lead. This went on for lap after lap, with Watson being forced on to the sandy outside at times, in order to avoid Hunt as he cut across from the inside of the corner; Brambilla himself could not have been more ruthless. Watson then hung back a little, waiting to see if Hunt made a mistake, but before he could begin his next attack, his gearbox failed, to signal what was thought to be the end of the 'real' race.

Not a bit of it. Hunt and Watson had opened up a small lead, but with Watson gone Regazzoni, with Andretti in tow, charged after the McLaren, gradually closing the gap. Both the Ferrari and the Lotus were faster than the McLaren, but could Hunt hold out? They

James Hunt celebrates his fifth victory of the season in Holland, to close ever nearer to absent rival Niki Lauda.

closed to within striking distance and we now wondered if Regazzoni would try one of his suicide passing manoeuvres, maybe even taking Hunt out with him. There was little in it as they started the last lap, but Hunt upped the rating, benefited from Jones getting in the way, and did not let the Ferrari close enough to try anything. This well-deserved victory brought Hunt to within 2 points of Lauda, and he was now driving magnificently.

CHANGES

It is traditional for driver changes to be announced at the Italian Grand Prix, and Scheckter decided to leave Tyrrell, not being over-enamoured with their P34 car, to join the new Wolf team. Ferrari really pulled a fast one, giving their new driver, Reutemann, his debut, Stommelen taking his seat at Brabham. But the biggest surprise of this great occasion was the return of Lauda. Having looked death firmly in the eye, the great man made his comeback, and

at what better time and race. He could still fight Hunt for the title, from the front, and to prove this he qualified a stunning fifth, with Laffite in the Ligier on pole, and Scheckter beside him.

Where were Hunt and Mass though? 'Did not qualify' would have been the organizers' preference, but they just managed it and, with Watson, formed the last three cars on the grid; a staggering turnaround. This followed another of those crazy incidents in a year when the racing authorities finally went off their heads. The Italian press had instigated a 'hate' campaign against Hunt and McLaren, which was rather spicier than the English press are wont to do. They focused on why the McLaren team, with their outdated M23, were going so well. They had 'cheated' in Spain, so surely they must be cheating *per se*. Since McLaren had close ties with American racing, where alcohol is used in the fuel, they must surely be using 'dope' in their Grand Prix cars (it needed a 'dope' to believe this argument).

Bearing this in mind, fuel checks were a certainty, and so it proved. On the first day of

115

practice it rained, and times were consequently slower than expected. The scrutineers got to work measuring the height of the engine airbox orifices from the bottom of the chassis, finding that Peterson's and, horror of horros, Regazzoni's rear wings infringed regulations; out went their times.

Now, if the organizers were so concerned about the fuel being used, why were the fuel checks held over to the next day, when it happened to be dry, instead of being conducted on the first day? This ought to have been done immediately; or were the organizers thinking that the rain would nullify these times, if the next day was dry, and the cars thus faster? In this they were right.

These tests showed the petrol octane rating of the following teams to be: Ferrari 98.6, McLaren 101.6, and Penske 105.7 among others. The rules stated that fuel of one octane above that commercially available in a number of countries, including Britain, was permissible, which the organizers interpreted as being 101 octane, as 100 octane fuel was available in Italy, and they had a telex from the CSI to back their case. This involvement by the CSI once again illustrated their incompetence, because their interpretation was wrong, and they admitted as much three days later. The McLaren and Penske 'dry' qualifying results were disallowed on the Sunday morning, and as the organizers had no evidence of their 'cheating' in the first, wet, practice so those times could stand. Unfortunately both McLarens qualified, and Guy Edwards withdrew to allow Watson to start.

This 'misinterpretation' of the rules by the Italian organizers, backed by the CSI, was made worse because, in Britain at that time, Shell and BP five-star fuel was rated at 102 octane, and Esso's, though not published as such, was 104 octane, all available from many sites throughout the country. This left a taste in the mouth far worse than petrol itself.

In the fullness of time, as happened on several occasions during 1976, the memory of a good race was lost amidst all the controversy that surrounded the event. The on-circuit happenings seemed little more than a point around which all the arguing could swirl. Monza saw Scheckter lead Peterson, only to drop back, while Depailler then fought the flying Swede in another titanic battle, which ended as the Tyrrell driver fell back near the end. A final charge by Regazzoni completed the entertainment, but Peterson held on to win his first race in two years. Laffite finished third, and in fourth place came the real hero Lauda, but somehow all this seemed irrelevant.

The McLarens? Mass retired with ignition failure almost immediately, and Hunt got up to eleventh place when, during a challenge from Pryce, he ran off the road and out of the race on lap 12. Lauda now led Hunt by 5 points, with three races remaining.

One normally expects the Drivers' Championship points positions to alter *after* a race, but before the Canadian Grand Prix Lauda's lead over Hunt had increased to 17 points, yet only 9 are available for a win! 1976 was a special season in racing, and the third leg of the British Grand Prix had still to be run. This, as with the third leg of the Spanish Grand Prix, took place in Paris and, despite all the evidence to the contrary, Hunt was disqualified, it being claimed that he was not running when the race was stopped. Hunt certainly was still running, yet the CSI did not give any reason why they chose to reject the RAC report which was in favour of Hunt. Another CSI bungle, or was it deliberate? The British felt the latter; the Italians felt that justice had been done, especially after the Spanish events. The official records state that the 1976 British Grand Prix was won by Lauda, but all those present know who really won. This brought things nicely to the boil for the Canadian Grand Prix but Hunt's title chance had surely gone now. Relations between the two drivers degenerated amid all the rumours, adding a particularly fiery spice to the forthcoming race.

Hunt was on top form again, and he claimed the pole with Peterson alongside, while Brambilla, Depailler and Andretti separated him from

Lauda. In the race, Peterson beat Hunt at the start, but the latter followed closely behind. After a couple of attempts, Hunt took the lead on lap 9, but then came under pressure from Depailler. A re-run of the Dutch race was in the offing, with Depailler a little faster than Hunt, though still needing to get by. It was cut-and-thrust again, but Hunt used the backmarkers cleverly, keeping the Tyrrell at bay at the very place where Depailler might have been expecting to get through. Then, as the race entered its last phase and Depailler prepared his big challenge, he had to drop back as petrol had leaked into the cockpit, and was swilling all over the place. Hunt thus won comfortably, with Mass coming fifth, and chief rival Lauda eighth, despite a suspension breakage. After the race Hunt and Lauda had a 'clear the air' chat, emerging on good terms once again.

Unlike the previous few races, the days prior to the United States Grand Prix were controversy-free. The Championship battle had replaced the politics in the news, but was it a battle? Hunt was still 8 points behind Lauda, with only two races left. Prior to the race itself, it just poured down, but during a brief dry spell, Hunt managed to notch up another pole position, with Scheckter beside him, followed by the March trio of Peterson, Brambilla, and Stuck surrounding Lauda. Get out of that if you can! It proved to be very difficult indeed, and while Scheckter led Hunt away, Lauda was stuck (!) behind Peterson and Brambilla, a sure test of his nerve if ever he needed one. Gradually Lauda fought his way into third position, but was way behind the leading duo.

Out at the front, Scheckter held a small advantage over Hunt, who was not getting close

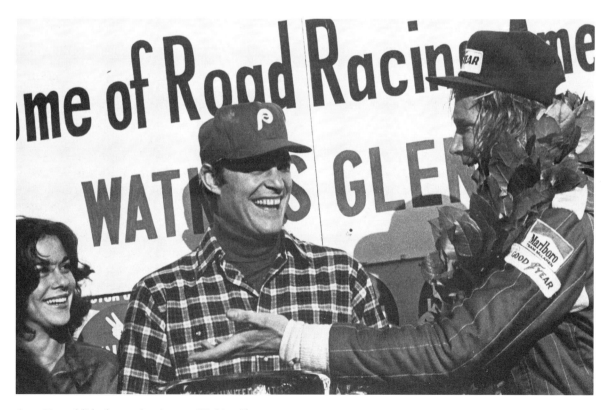

James Hunt, delighted at another victory at Watkins Glen.

enough to attack. Eventually, going into the chicane, Hunt got a lucky break as Scheckter was baulked by a backmarker, and he shot through. Three laps later Scheckter did likewise to Hunt, and re-took the lead. Now it was down to brass tacks; Hunt needed to win the race and he could not expect a repeat of his earlier lucky break, he just had to knuckle down and seek another way past. He caught up with Scheckter, hanging on grimly in case an over-taking opportunity arose, and squeezed through on the straight after the chicane, with a slingshot manoeuvre. Determined not to lose out again, Hunt kept up the pressure to record another victory, by 8 seconds.

Towards the end Lauda still held third place, but Mass was catching up, having fought his way through the field. Here was a real oppor-tunity for Mass to aid Hunt, but he failed by a mere car's length; another finely-timed race by the acknowledged master.

It was fitting that the sixteen-round fight for the World Championship should be concluded on the other side of the world, thousands of miles away from any previous race. The world press descended on Japan for their inaugural Grand Prix, and the locals must have wondered what all the fuss was about. Twenty-three drivers were to play bit parts in a race which focused solely on the Hunt vs Lauda battle, which Lauda now led by only 3 points. If Hunt won and there were no protests, he would be the Champion, as simple as that.

Practice sessions became tense affairs for drivers trying to learn the circuit, and get a good grid position. Andretti took the pole, but Hunt was alongside, with Lauda third. The biggest shock was local driver Masahiro Hasemi driving a locally built Kojima, with a Cosworth engine, who qualified tenth just over one second slower than Andretti, and ahead of Jochen.

Race day dawned wet and miserable. The circuit was awash, and every so often the clouds came down the mountains to enshroud the whole, grim scene. Tiny figures could be seen trying to sweep the water off the circuit, but it

Confident McLaren pits signals in Japan, while Hunt led Mass in the first two positions. Alastair Caldwell holds a clipboard, while Teddy Mayer looks out on to the circuit. The pit scene was less calm a bit later on.

was a forlorn hope. The drivers held a meeting to decide what to do, but were divided on whether to race or not. As they discussed this, the scheduled start-time came and went, with no decision forthcoming. Neither Hunt nor Lauda wanted to race, but were prepared to if necessary, although the conditions in which to stage the final round in this long, gruelling con-text were not acceptable, though, considering the way the season had developed, they were apt.

The officials then decided that the race would start after all, and the drivers went to their cars, fired up and formed the grid. If ever Hunt needed a good start, it was now, and as the race got under way he took the lead. Now he would have a clear road, while everyone else would be caught up in his, and each other's, spray. The race, and the Championship, lay in his own hands if only he could stay on the cir-cuit, and his car not fail.

The big showdown did not materialize, as a

As the track dries out in Japan, Hunt leads, while Mass closes in (both on wet tyres). Jochen looks more intent on taking the lead, rather than protecting James.

few drivers considered the track to be too treacherous to race on, and among them was Niki Lauda. After two laps he drove into his pits, got out of his car, and retired. Damaged eyelids from his accident had made it almost imposible for him to see with all the water about, and besides, he considered life to be more important than a second title. Under the circumstances this was a brave and sensible decision to take, as calm and calculating as any he had taken on the racing circuits of the world, and not a simple admission of defeat as was later portrayed.

Hunt was well in front, making the most of the clear road ahead, but then the rain eased off and the clouds drifted away. This caused a bit of a problem as all the drivers were on wet tyres, and these would wear much quicker without the cooling effects of the water. Hunt also had another problem to contend with: Brambilla was in his mirrors! With the 'mad March hare' around, absolutely anything was possible, not least that he might involve Hunt in one of his off-the-road excursions. All these fears suddenly erupted as Brambilla was alongside James when . . . he spun. For agonizing milli-seconds that seemed like hours, it looked as though Bram-

billa would take Hunt out, but luck was on his side and he carried on, with Mass now in his mirrors.

This ideal situation only lasted until half-distance when Mass crashed, leaving Hunt unprotected from Andretti and Depailler. He also had a slow puncture in his left rear tyre, while the left front was wearing badly under the strain of racing on the drying circuit. Hunt wanted Mayer to decide whether he ought to come in for a tyre change, while Mayer left the decision to Hunt, as he knew how the car was handling. The tension was growing visibly.

Depailler and Andretti went by, with eleven laps left, then the Tyrrell went in for new tyres, promoting Hunt back into second place. His rear tyre was now very soft, and the car bottomed out on all the bumps. Would it last? With five laps to go, luckily on the corner before the pits, fate took the decision out of his hands in an unexpected way. Suddenly, and dramatically, the tired and worn front left tyre blew apart. It could not have happened at a better place. A few seconds later and Hunt would have had to do another lap on a canvas shell. Instead he shot into the pits and the 'pitstop of the season' was under way. These days we are used to all four wheels being changed in around 6 seconds. This was not the case in 1976, and after being unable to fit the jack under the front due to the collapsed tyre (requiring a good heave-ho by the mechanics) 27 seconds elapsed before Hunt was ready to leave.

Hunt stormed out of the pits in a rage, thinking the title had slipped from his grasp. Throwing caution to the wind, he drove as fast as he could, in fifth position, passing Jones and Regazzoni battling for third place, on worn tyres, by simply driving round the outside of them at a slow corner. He was now third, but did not know it, or rather chose not to believe his pit signals, and continued as before. There were two cars ahead and Hunt was catching these fast. Coming out on to the straight once again, out came the chequered flag and Hunt did not have a chance to get past either of them. Instead, he drove round the slowing down lap at speed, and went straight into the pits to vent his wrath on Teddy Mayer. Luckily there were no punches thrown, but he took a good deal of convincing that he had finished third, Andretti coming first, with Depailler marginally ahead of Hunt, who was thus World Champion. But what about the protests? For once there were none, and the season finished on a happy note.

Honours were even, as Ferrari retained the Constructors' title, ahead of McLaren. This did not disappoint the Colnbrook team as, far from Hunt winning by stealth, he had, with seven unofficial victories, been a clear-cut, worthy Champion. Even if Lauda did miss two races, and Ferrari went 'off' a bit, the McLaren was not really competitive for three races after Spain, and then there was the Italian Fiasco. If Hunt had not been stripped, shamefully, of the British race, the winning margin would have been 13, and not 1, points.

The question remains, just how good was James Hunt? After his triumph, Teddy Mayer said that he was the most naturally talented of all the McLaren drivers, and that he was much quicker than Emerson Fittipaldi, though made

more mistakes. This is amply borne out by their comparative performances in the M23. Mayer also compared Hunt to the great, acknowledged master, Jackie Stewart, in his ability to win races in a car no better than the others, and in a more highly competitive era. Yet he had his flaws, especially when driving an uncompetitive car, or indeed in being able to help the team sort out serious problems, in the way that Lauda could. These were to come to the fore in the future.

Grand Prix racing does not stand still for long, and within three months Hunt would begin the defence of his title. This was one of the most hectic periods in his life, most of his time being devoted to sponsors, and he did not enjoy a long holiday. In between, there was the long-awaited M26 to develop into a race-winning car, but it was not a good winter, weather-wise, and development lagged behind schedule. Besides, the M23 was, in Hunt's hands, still setting competitive times which the new car did not improve upon. It is here that McLaren's future problems might be found to have germinated.

Was the M23 still highly competitive, or did Hunt's spirited driving make it appear so? Clearly the M26 was not going to take a quantum leap forward in performance, yet rival teams would introduce new cars, some of which could be expected to be significantly better than their predecessors, and thus present more than a serious challenge to the M26. McLaren would be caught with their trousers down, and a driver can only do so much. Hunt performed magnificently in 1976, winning consistently with a car no better than many others, but what could he do if one or more teams were to improve beyond the levels at McLaren?

Perhaps when evaluating the results of 1976 it might have been more relevant for McLaren to look closer at Jochen Mass's performances. Here was a good driver, consistently slower than Hunt, especially in practice, with by and large the same equipment, and yet often running in midfield. Ought this not to have told the team something about the car and its capabilities?

Grand Prix Results 1976

GRAND PRIX	DRIVER	CAR	NO	1ST PRACTICE★ Time/Posn	2ND PRACTICE★ Time/Posn	3RD PRACTICE★ Time/Posn	FINAL GRID POSN	FINAL PLACING	RETIRED CAUSE OF	HIGHEST POSN IN RACE
BRAZILIAN Interlagos 25.1.76	J. Hunt	Ford V8 M23-DFV M23/8	11	1min 33.87sec 4/22	1min 33.78sec 7/21	1min 32.50sec 1/22	Pole		Lp 32 Crash damage, oil	2nd
	J. Mass	Ford V8 M23-DFV M23/6	12	1min 34.58sec 5/22	1min 33.59sec 6/21	1min 34.74sec 9/22	6-22	6/14		6th
SOUTH AFRICAN Kyalami 6.3.76	J. Hunt	Ford V8 M23-DFV M23/8	11	1min 16.6sec 1/25	1min 16.59sec 1/24	1min 16.10sec 1/24	Pole	2/17		2nd
	J. Mass	Ford V8 M23-DFV M23/6	12	1min 17.61sec 7/25	1min 17.91sec 13/24	1min 16.45sec 4/24	4-25	3/17		3rd
USA (West) Long Beach 28.3.76	J. Hunt	Ford V8 M23-DFV M23/8	11	1min 25.22sec 2/26	1min 23.93sec 2/25	1min 23.42sec 3/26	3-20		Lp 4 Crash	2nd
	J. Mass	Ford V8 M23-DFV M23/6	12	1min 22.55sec 19/26	1min 25.00sec 7/25	1min 24.54sec 14/26	14-20	5/12		5th
SPANISH Jarama 2.5.76	J. Hunt	Ford V8 M23-DFV M23/8	11	1min 18.52sec 1/30	1min 19.19sec 1/28	1min 18.92sec 1/28	Pole	1/12 WINNER		1st
	J. Mass	Ford V8 M23-DFV M23/9	12	1min 19.36sec 7/30	1min 19.3sec 2/28	1min 19.14sec 2/28	4-24		Lp 66 Engine failure	FL 2nd
BELGIAN Zolder 16.5.76	J. Hunt	Ford V8 M23-DFV M28/8	11	1min 26.74sec 1/30	1min 27.87sec 7/28		3-26		Lp 36 Transmission failure	2nd
	J. Mass	Ford V8 M23-DFV M23/9	12	1min 29.92sec		1min 28.50sec 17/30	18-26	6/12		6th
MONACO Monte Carlo 23.5.76	J. Hunt	Ford V8 M23-DFV M23/8	11	1min 33.62sec 12/26	1min 31.88sec 6/24	1min 31.89sec 13/24	14-20		Lp 25 Engine failure	11th
	J. Mass	Ford V8 M23-DFV M23/9	12	1min 34.71sec 16/26	1min 33.40sec 15/24	1min 31.67sec 11/24	11-20	5/12		5th
SWEDISH Anderstorp 13.6.76	J. Hunt	Ford V8 M23-DFV M23/8	11	1min 28.67sec 19/28			8-26	5/14		5th
		Ford V8 M23-DFV M23/6	11T		1min 28.38sec 11/28	1min 26.96sec 8/28				
	J. Mass	Ford V8 M23-DFV M23/9	12	1min 29.60sec 19/28	1min 29.35sec 18/28	1min 27.57sec 13/28	13-26	11/14		11th
FRENCH Ricard-Castellet 4.7.76	J. Hunt	Ford V8 M23-DFV M23/8	11	1min 49.12sec 2/30	1min 47.89sec 1/29	1min 49.45sec 5/28	Pole	1/19 WINNER		1st
	J. Mass	Ford V8 M23-DFV M23/9	12	1min 50.91sec 13/30	1min 50.42sec 12/29	1min 50.10sec 11/28	14-26	18/19		18th

Race	Driver	Car	No.	Practice 1	Practice 2	Practice 3	Grid	Result	Retirement	Pos.
BRITISH Brands Hatch 18.7.76	J. Hunt	Ford V8 M23-DFV M23/8	11	1min 22.10sec 1/29	1min 20.39sec 1/31	1min 19.41sec 2/30	2-26	1/10 (Later disqualified)		**1st**
	J. Mass	Ford V8 M23-DFV M23/9	12	1min 23.46sec 8/29	1min 21.47sec 7/31	1min 20.61sec 12/30	12-26		Lp 3 Clutch	
GERMAN Nürburgring 1.8.76	J. Hunt	Ford V8 M23-DFV M23/8	11	7min 10.3sec 3/26	7min 6.5sec 1/28		Pole	1/15 WINNER		**1st**
	J. Mass	Ford V8 M23-DFV M23/9	12	7min 15.3sec 16/26	7min 13.0sec 9/28		9-26	3/15		**3rd**
AUSTRIAN Österreichring 15.8.76	J. Hunt	Ford V8 M23-DFV M23/8	11	1min 32.02sec 1/24		1min 56.65sec 9/23	Pole	4/12		**2nd**
	J. Mass	Ford V8 M23-DFV M23/9	12			1min 55.73sec 3/23	12-25	7/12		**7th**
DUTCH Zandvoort 29.8.76	J. Hunt	Ford V8 M23-DFV M23/8	11	1min 22.18sec 3/27	1min 21.57sec 1/27	1min 21.39sec 2/27	2-26	1/12 WINNER		**1st**
	J. Mass	Ford V8 M26-DFV M26/1	12	1min 23.69sec 12/27	1min 23.72sec 16/27	1min 22.48sec 12/27	15-26	9/12		**9th**
ITALIAN Monza 12.9.76	J. Hunt	Ford V8 M23-DFV M23/8	11		2min 08.76sec 5/24	1min 42.51sec 8/29 Time disallowed	24-26		Lp 12 Spun off	**12th**
	J. Mass	Ford V8 M26-DFV M26/1	12		2min 11.06sec 8/24	1min 42.68sec 10/29 Time disallowed	25-26		Lp 4 Ignition failure	
CANADIAN Mosport Park 3.10.76	J. Hunt	Ford V8 M23-DFV M23/8	11	1min 13.28sec 1/27	1min 13.44sec 2/26	1min 12.39sec 1/25	Pole	1/20 WINNER		**1st**
	J. Mass	Ford V8 M23-DFV M23/9	12	1min 15.1sec 8/27	1min 14.26sec 11/26	1min 13.44sec 11/25	11-24	5/20		**5th**
USA Watkins Glen 10.10.76	J. Hunt	Ford V8 M23-DFV M23/8	11	1min 59.73sec 11/26	1min 43.62sec 1/27		Pole	1/14 WINNER		**FL 1st**
	J. Mass	Ford V8 M23-DFV M23/9	12	1min 58.99sec 6/26	1min 46.07sec 17/27		17-26	4/14		**4th**
JAPANESE Mt Fuji 17.10.76	J. Hunt	Ford V8 M23-DFV M23/8	11	1min 13.76sec 1/26	1min 13.95sec 6/25	1min 12.80sec 2/25	2-25	3/11		**1st**
	J. Mass	Ford V8 M23-DFV M23/9	12	1min 14.07sec 5/26	1min 14.17sec 8/25	1min14.05sec 11/25	12-25		Lp 36 Crash	**2nd**

★ Some races ran four practices. A driver's best three results are counted.

In the US McLaren were still competitive. Johnny Rutherford had won the Indianapolis 500 again with the M16E, a car updated by young designer John Barnard, who was to re-enter the McLaren story at a later date. Gordon Coppuck had, you may remember, based the M23 on his M16 design, and now the new Indy car, the M24, came full circle, being based on the M23, complete with the turbocharged Cosworth DFX engine, developed from the Grand Prix DFV. This car was to take the team into the late 1970s.

THE MORNING AFTER

Before the 1977 season got under way there was the usual 'all change' among drivers, teams, and sponsors. Perhaps the most significant of these was the founding of the Walter Wolf Racing team. Canadian businessman Wolf had backed the Wolf-Williams team, but tired of the lack of success had set up his own outfit, with cars designed by Harvey Postlethwaite, from Hesketh. Their biggest coup though was in recruiting Scheckter from Tyrrell, happy to be back in a four-wheeled car once again and determined to remain at the front.

Regrettably, one front-running team, Penske, pulled out of Grand Prix, despite having won their first race. John Watson was quickly snapped up by Brabham, to replace Reutemann. As the merry-go-round gathered pace Regazzoni, dismissed by Ferrari, joined Ensign – a major coup for Mo Nunn's Walsall-based team. The two March teams were decimated by driver defections. Peterson went to Tyrrell for a more reliable car, Brambilla left to give the new Surtees car a thorough crash testing, and Stuck eventually ended up at Brabham, after Carlos Pace was killed.

Now running only two cars, March recruited Ian Scheckter, Jody's elder brother, and Alex Ribeiro, neither of whom were likely to set the world alight. However, March had a surprise in store. Robin Herd designed a car with four rear wheels, all driven, of standard front-wheel size. This was the March 771/240, defined more like a steam engine. Without taking the story too far forward, it was unfortunate that this became little more than an experiment and never raced, except on Scalextric toy circuits.

New or updated, cars were thus much in evidence at the re-instated Argentinian Grand Prix, though McLaren took the faithful M23 along to South America. This was not a time of technological striding forward though, except for the new, pretty Lotus 78. If ever the saying, 'If it looks right, it is right' was to be correct,

Jochen Mass

Nicknamed 'Hermann the German', Jochen was one of the most popular and happy drivers during his Grand Prix career. He replaced Hobbs in the Yardley car at the end of 1974, and became number two to Fittipaldi the following year. For the next two seasons he held that position to Hunt, though at first harbouring ambitions of ousting Hunt as number one.

It was in the role of a forceful number two that Mass excelled in Grand Prix racing. He was certainly a loyal and reliable driver, and would back up his team leader whenever possible. The three seasons he spent with McLaren were the best in his Grand Prix career, winning the shortened Spanish Grand Prix in 1975, and picking up many placings.

Though clearly not as fast as Hunt, Mass ran well throughout their two seasons together, but towards the end there were one or two incidents which resulted in Jochen's departure. The most publicized of these occurred when being lapped by Hunt, as he led the Canadian Grand Prix. The two collided, and Hunt was out. Mass continued to drive into the 1980s with a variety of mid/rearfield teams such as March, ATS and Arrows, performing as well as could be expected, given the machinery.

However, it was as a sports car driver that Mass shone, having won the European Touring Car Championship in 1972. During his McLaren years, he formed the most potent of partnerships with Jackie Ickx, driving works Porsches to many victories. Jochen's unhurried driving style, a little short of the top pace in Grand Prix, was ideally suited to long distance racing. Given a good car and co-driver, Mass was outstanding in this category. He has enjoyed a long and successful career in sports cars, and continues to race, and win, as a 'father' to the young charges in the Mercedes team.

Never one to be involved in all the 'hype' of racing, Jochen Mass's qualities, especially as number two, made him fairly unique among racing drivers. His reputation, and the respect in which he is held, have been justly deserved throughout his lengthy career.

here was its chance. But not quite yet. This sleek black and gold car was to usher in a completely new era in design, and herald the wing

James Hunt recorded his first win as reigning World Champion, appropriately, in his last race in his faithful M23/8–2. Here he leads Jody Scheckter in the Wolf, while chasing Mario Andretti's Lotus for the lead of the Race of Champions.

car. Colin Chapman was about to set the Grand Prix world alight once again.

In the humid heat of Buenos Aires, little seemed to have changed. James sat, M23 and all, on the pole and as the race set off Watson led away; *déjà vu?* On lap 10 Hunt, who had been pacing Watson, slipped by and built an ever increasing lead; 1976 continued, and there was no indication of anything clever from Lotus either. Mass was well up among the pack and all seemed rosy for McLaren. Then, on lap 32 with a huge lead, a bolt sheared in Hunt's M23 rear suspension, sending him off the road and into the catch fencing at the esses. The Brabhams of Watson and Pace now led, but Watson retired, when his car broke in half! Mass also retired and Scheckter stole past Pace to record a debut victory for Wolf. Reutemann brought the wayward Ferrari home third, Andretti the Lotus fifth, and Regazzoni turned in a fine performance, finishing sixth in his Ensign. It had been a freak accident for Hunt, and McLaren were confident enough.

A couple of weeks later in Brazil, the heat, cars, team, and drivers were all there as expected but, after a year's absence who should turn up again but BRM. Their new world beater was sitting at the back of the grid, and it was almost too painful to watch. Not that Hunt saw much of it, as he claimed the pole, with Mass fourth. This time local hero Pace got off to a flying start, followed by Reutemann and Hunt. On lap 3 Hunt passed the Ferrari, and three laps later Pace, who ran wide and clouted a McLaren back tyre, trying to close the gap. Hunt was struggling with mild understeer, exacerbated by the abrasive surface wearing his front tyres. His lead was never large, and Reutemann re-passed him on lap 23, Hunt stopping for fresh tyres two laps later. It was this delay in changing the tyres, not usually associated with Hunt, which might have cost him the race. He rejoined in fifth place, passing Lauda and Watson, to finish second, some 11 seconds behind Reutemann, whose tyres were almost shot. Perhaps if Hunt had come in for tyres when Reutemann had closed right up, and he was struggling with understeer, he would have had longer to come back and 'push' the Ferrari, maybe forcing Reutemann to wear his tyres too rapidly. Who knows, but it is much easier analysing these decisions fourteen years later at a typewriter, than behind the steering wheel, under intense pressure.

Jochen had quite an influence on the race results. Running in third place he was being pressed ever harder by Andretti, when on lap 12 at the corner following the straight, he had the mother and father of accidents. As he hit the catch fencing, this came back on to the track, collecting poor Regazzoni, and causing Depailler to spin on the debris, but he managed to restart. Peterson, in the second Tyrrell, came bounding over the brow of the hill and joined in the mêlée in front of him. It was, of course, Sod's Law that Depailler would later go off at the same corner, comprehensively wrecking Mass's car. Not a great start to the season for McLaren, but clearly the M23 was still competitive.

Before the South African Grand Prix, a significant change took place at Ferrari. Reutemann had undertaken most of the winter development work and, despite his win, the car was not all it should be, being difficult to handle. Lauda talked the team round to his way of thinking and then, as only he was able to do, systematically worked at comprehensively resorting the 312-T2's handling, after encouraging Reutemann to stay on in his South American homeland. This was to have an important effect on the rest of the season.

In pre-race testing Hunt had a big accident with the M26, and so it was back to the M23. This did not stop him claiming his third pole of the season though, and for once he led from the start. It did not last, and on lap 7 Lauda got through and simply sailed away to win. Hunt was later passed by Scheckter and Depailler to finish fourth, in front of Mass. The major event of the race was the awful death of Tom Pryce, when he hit a marshal crossing the circuit, the car continuing with Pryce already dead at the wheel, before crashing.

Hunt then won the only non-championship race of the season, at Brands Hatch, in an M23. It was at this race that the true potential of the Lotus 78 became apparent to the world at large, as Andretti led Hunt easily, until being sidelined near the end.

There was another absentee for the United States Grand Prix (West), as Brabham driver Carlos Pace had been killed in a flying accident. His place was taken by Hans Stuck, the ex-March driver. This time Hunt could only qualify eighth, with Mass a lowly fifteenth, but the M23 had never been particularly good on street circuits. Going into the first corner Reutemann braked too late, setting off a chain reaction which resulted in Hunt running over Watson's front tyre and taking off, an air display similar to that at the British Grand Prix.

Hunt went to the pits at the end of the lap for a quick check, and rejoined last. At the front Andretti was showing the Lotus off, winning by a second from Lauda, with Scheckter a good third; the Wolf team were certainly going to be a serious threat. Mass retired with transmission failure after having survived an earlier brush with Brambilla, and Hunt finished seventh, just behind Jarier in the ATS, using the old Penske cars. This was no heroic drive through the field though, as Hunt only passed three cars, and benefited from the numerous retirements.

Hunt had his first race with an M26 in Spain, with Mass still in an M23. It was not a particularly auspicious debut: Hunt qualified seventh, Mass ninth, while Andretti was so much faster than everyone else that it seemed to be a waste of time trying to keep up with him. Lauda, suffering from cracked ribs, agreed with this and despite a good start by Hunt into fourth, Andretti left everyone floundering around, and vanished. It seemed quite preposterous to even think that Andretti might not win, and he duly did so in masterly fashion. The Lotus was now demonstrably the car to beat. Hunt retired with an engine misfire on lap 10

Hunt gets away at the start of the Long Beach Grand Prix, leading Laffite and Peterson. Seconds later he was involved in another of his high flying acts.

After surviving one spectacular incident, Hunt keeps a close and wary eye on his running partner, 'Brambles' Brambilla.

126

Jochen Mass drove a very hard race in Monaco to finish a fine fourth. He was chased all the way by Mario Andretti who can be seen 'running as if on rails', behind Mass who has got slightly off line.

but Mass, dogged as ever, fought persistently hard. He finished fourth, just losing out to Scheckter; another valiant effort.

The Monaco Grand Prix exposed McLaren's dilemma. Hunt was supposed to be defending his title and after five races he only had 9 points, yet it was decided to leave the M26 back in England, as it was not considered ready for the rigours of the twisty circuit by the Mediterranean. Instead, both drivers used the M23, a car which had never really gone well on this circuit and, after its early season dash, was now no match for the Lotus or Ferrari. With the benefit of hindsight, it seems ridiculous that the bulk of winter testing was put into the M23, with the M26 fitted into the odd gap. The new car ought

to have been a step forward, and if not, the M23 would have still been reasonably competitive as a substitute. This very lack of development on the M26, when the opportunity was there, very probably cost Hunt the chance to have a real go at retaining his title.

As it happened, Hunt qualified a respectable seventh, with Mass ninth, ahead of the Lotuses. Cosworth had given McLaren, Lotus, and Tyrrell 'development' versions of the DFV engine, and it was the failure of this, when in fifth place, that ended Hunt's fine race. Jochen Mass, without such luxuries, fought on manfully driving to a good fourth place, the meat in a Reutemann/Andretti sandwich. The race was won by Jody Scheckter, just beating Lauda to the flag and

127

proving that his earlier win was no fluke. He also gave Cosworth's DFV engine its one hundredth Grand Prix win. Scheckter was now leading the World Championship to boot.

Hunt was back in an M26 for the Belgian Grand Prix but it made little difference as he qualified ninth, three places behind Mass in an M23. As if to emphasize the mountain McLaren had to climb with the M26, Andretti sat smiling on the pole, a full 1.5 seconds ahead of Watson. All was not lost though, as it was a wet race. Hunt, alone, started on dry tyres, hoping the circuit would soon dry out, but his gamble failed and he was back in twenty-fourth place by lap 2. With all the fun of the pitstops over by lap 25, it had indeed dried out; Lauda led Mass,

who then spun off after more rain. Hunt gamely drove on, steadily picking up places to finish seventh, while Nilsson, in a Lotus, passed Lauda to score his maiden victory. This again demonstrated how good the Lotus 78 was. Mind you, Brambilla kept on the circuit until the end, finishing fourth, so perhaps it was just a freak result after all!

Anderstorp, home of the Swedish Grand Prix, was also noted for its quirky results, so McLaren were quite happy to have Hunt in third place on the grid, in an M26, while Mass was ninth with an M23. Andretti, as during practice dominated the race, followed by Watson, with James running fourth. Luck was on his side though, and he moved up into second

Hunt tried a new nose cone on the M26 at the Paul Ricard circuit, in France.

Depailler, in his P34 Tyrrell, leads Hunt during their long battle in Sweden, during which James wore out his tyres while trying to keep up.

place by lap 30, well behind Andretti, as Watson and Scheckter eliminated each other. But the M26 was understeering badly again, and wore its tyres out due to a combination of this and Hunt hurling the car around to keep up the pace. He went into the pits for new tyres on lap 53, and finished a disappointed twelfth.

Out at the front Andretti was enjoying his little Sunday afternoon drive, and looking at him you would never have thought he was actually leading a Grand Prix. He drove to perfection and the car, in turn, never missed a beat, until lap 70 that is. With three laps left the engine coughed and spluttered, having used up all its fuel. Andretti darted into the pits, had a few gallons poured in, and set off again, but only finished sixth; a bitter disappointment. The fuel mixture control had vibrated from weak to rich and the petrol had been used too quickly.

True to its form the Swedish Grand Prix produced another odd result, with Laffite winning

his, and the Ligier team's first Grand Prix, while Mass finished a steady second and was now five points clear of Hunt.

INTO THE FRAY

By the French Grand Prix, Hunt was in a similar position to that of 1976. He had run well early on, and was then pegged back a bit; but this time there were three other Championship contenders, and not just Lauda. There was not much room for optimism as the M26 had still not looked like keeping tabs on the Lotus, and Lauda was busy collecting points as does a philatelist rare stamps, jealously guarding each one. Practice gave McLaren something to smile about as Hunt qualified second, behind Andretti, with Mass seventh still in an M23.

The lights turned green and Hunt shot into the lead. Could he repeat 1976? He was not

After a good start, Hunt leads the French Grand Prix on the opening lap, ahead of Watson, Laffite, Andretti, Nilsson, Reutemann, Mass, Scheckter, Brambilla and Jones. Watson took the lead in lap 4, while Andretti also passed Hunt on lap 17, who finally finished third.

pulling away though, and on lap 5 Watson went past, followed by Andretti twelve laps later. Hunt settled into third place, unable to do anything about the battle ahead. Watson spent nearly all the race fending off Andretti but, unlike Mass in Brazil, did not fall off the track. With victory seemingly assured, though Andretti was still only a cat's whisker behind, Watson's Brabham coughed on the last lap. Andretti came alongside but could not get past, then Watson's thirsty Alfa Romeo engine spluttered again, and Andretti was away round the last corner to win, as he had lost the previous race, with luck.

The media fanfare which preceded the Brit-

ish Grand Prix was mostly centred around whether the fortunes of Hunt, and McLaren, had turned the corner. Were we to see another dramatic charge for the Championship, or was it too late this time round? Indeed, was the M26 a serious Championship challenger, because though the Ferrari seemed to have been overcome, as far as a Ferrari and Lauda could be discarded, Watson in the Brabham was now looking good, perhaps too good for Hunt in his M26. All this came to the boil as practice got under way at Silverstone, but McLaren still had a few aces up their collective sleeves.

Jochen Mass was, at last, to race an M26, the car improving all the time. Also, a young Cana-

Canadian driver Gilles Villeneuve made his Grand Prix debut in Hunt's old M23/8–2 at Silverstone. During practice he had numerous spins, but qualified well and impressed throughout the meeting.

dian seen by Hunt the previous year, Gilles Villeneuve, was given a race, using Hunt's favourite car, M23/8–2. As Hunt gave the M26 its first pole position, Villeneuve spun his way, time and again, to qualify a creditable ninth, a popular grid position for a McLaren, two places ahead of Mass. Hunt was surrounded by his main challengers: Watson, Lauda, Scheckter, Nilsson, and Andretti, while further back history was created when Jean-Pierre Jabouille qualified the Renault turbo, the first time a turbocharged engined car had qualified for a Grand Prix.

The opening lap saw Hunt a sluggish fourth, with Villeneuve a spirited seventh, well ahead of Mass. Hunt was on top form, once under way, and was not going to disappoint the vast crowd which had turned up expecting a good result. His M26 was going exceptionally well, and the Lotuses were safely behind. The early entertainment focused on Watson leading, Hunt catching and then passing Scheckter, and the 'unknown' in car number 40, Villeneuve. He was comfortably holding his own, just behind the Lotus pair, but disappeared into the pits on lap 10. His temperature gauge was reading hot and, as he had run slightly off the circuit, he went to have it sorted out. Nothing wrong was found so, assuming that the gauge itself was faulty, he was sent out again, two laps down, and spent the rest of the race in front of, and holding pace with, the Scheckter-Andretti-Nilsson battle for fourth place – a most impressive debut.

This was only a sideline though, as Hunt was now catching Lauda. The wily Austrian realized he could not hold out for the whole race, and Hunt indeed passed him on lap 23. Now for Watson, and the lead. Hunt was really flying and quickly caught the Brabham. A long cut-and-thrust battle ensued, with Hunt trying to squeeze by at the Woodcote chicane, first on the inside, then the outside, for lap after lap. But Watson calmly kept him at bay, as with Andretti a couple of weeks earlier. It was a captivating duel, the reverse of their efforts at the 1976 Dutch Grand Prix. Then, it all happened. Watson's engine spluttered and Hunt shot past in a trice to take the lead. Great cheers erupted around the circuit while Watson headed for the pits and more fuel, but though he came out again, his race was over, leaving Lauda to in-

At last Hunt wins a Grand Prix in 1977. Appropriately, it was the British Grand Prix at Silverstone, and here he is delighted to accept the congratulations as he gives the M26 its first win.

herit second place. Hunt won emphatically, with Lauda way behind and Nilsson even further adrift. Mass finished fourth, and with neither Andretti nor Scheckter finishing in the points, it was a good all-round day for Hunt and McLaren. The Championship was still there to be won.

Of course, to achieve such a feat again Hunt and McLaren needed luck aplenty, with their rivals experiencing the reverse. For one rival in particular, the German Grand Prix was an extra special occasion; Lauda would never forget the race of 1976. This time around it was all very different as the challenging, yet dangerous, Nürburgring circuit was displaced by the featureless 'out and back' Hockenheimring, with its twisty stadium start/finish area. Certain journalists voiced their disapproval of this change of venue by referring to the forthcoming event as the German Formula 1 race, and not the German Grand Prix. For the actual teams and drivers it was another place of work though; yes, most missed the challenge of the Nürburgring, but few were happy with the safety arrangements, or lack of them. Wherever the race was

held there were more Championship points on offer, the pursuit of these being the motivating factor, not the circuit as such.

McLaren were back to their two-man team again, both in M26 cars, with Jochen Mass keen to perform well in his home race. Practice did not go as planned with Scheckter, Watson, and Lauda all in front of Hunt, and Mass back in seventeenth position. Hunt settled in third position from lap 8 to 33, but was slowed by a broken exhaust pipe and finally retired with a fuel pump failure; not the sort of result required. Worse still, Lauda won in fine style, clearly back at his best, and with Scheckter second and Reutemann fourth, Hunt was falling ever behind. Mass's race ended with a gearbox failure.

Races come thick and fast during the European season, and a fortnight later all the teams assembled for the Austrian Grand Prix. Hunt was fifth in the title race, 26 points behind Lauda, but he had overhauled a big deficit before, so there was everything to race for. The grid reflected the current competitive positions with Hunt next to Lauda, who took the pole, and Andretti, Watson and Reutemann up there,

Despite the wet and greasy track, Jochen Mass leads eventual winner Alan Jones, and Carlos Reutemann, on lap 6 of the Austrian Grand Prix, all three cars being on slick tyres. At this time, they were contesting ninth position.

with only Scheckter missing. Stuck, in the Brabham, was the joker in the pack, and Mass was in ninth position again.

There was a wet start, but most drivers were on dry tyres as the rain held off, and once things settled down Andretti took the lead. The circuit was wet in the early laps and one or two runners on wet-weather tyres came into the reckoning, while Lauda went backwards through the field. On lap 12 Andretti's engine gave up, leaving Hunt with a comfortable lead, from which he controlled the race. This looked to be the

renascence he needed, and with Jones second in the Shadow, Nilsson third, and Lauda fourth, things were looking up for McLaren. Then, on lap 40, Nilsson's engine blew up, moving Lauda up a place, and two laps later Tambay's went the same way, ending his skilful drive in the Ensign. Two laps further, with only ten to go, and Hunt sitting on a 20-second lead, his Cosworth development engine gave up, and he was out of the race, watching his Championship hopes fade. Jones deservedly won from a fortunate Lauda, with Mass trundling home a decidedly uncompetitive sixth. All was not quite dead and buried: the M26 was competitive and Hunt was driving as well as ever.

In no time at all everyone was at Zandvoort for the Dutch Grand Prix, with Lauda sitting on a 16-point lead, and double that over Hunt. But a win for the McLaren team leader − as he had achieved at the last two Dutch races − would mean that he was still in with a shout. Anything looked possible as Andretti lined up on the pole with Laffite alongside, and Hunt and Lauda occupying row 2; only Scheckter was out of the equation again. The lights turned green and Hunt made a storming start down the inside of Laffite and alongside Andretti, to sit it out with the American round the Tarzan hairpin, and take the lead. Laffite also slipped by in the kerfuffle, while Mass collided with Jones round the back of the pits, and copied his team leader by indulging in some aerobatics before ploughing into the catch fencing.

Andretti was soon past Laffite and started to haul in Hunt. Down the straight they went nose to tail, ending lap 4, Hunt hugging the inside line to the Tarzan bend, as with Watson in 1976. Andretti was a highly experienced USAC oval racer though, and he tried to drive round the outside of Hunt at the hairpin. Hunt held the charging American off, right round the circuit, until they completed lap 5. Down the straight they shot at 180mph (290kph) with James holding the middle of the road again, forcing Andretti on to the outside. This time Andretti was alongside going into the corner, and stayed on the outside all the way round. This was breathtaking stuff, but they looked too close. They were. Exiting the corner, on converging lines, and with the Lotus's right front wheel in between the two McLaren left-side ones, they touched. Hunt did another of his high-flying acts, landing on the kerb and smashing the water pump. Andretti spun, and then roared off, leaving Hunt enshrouded in steam, not all of it from the car!

Hunt set off for the Lotus pit to 'sort things out', and ended up quarrelling with Chapman,

and later Andretti when he returned after retiring. It all got a bit nasty, with Andretti referring to Hunt as 'the jerk' to the press, when the British driver apparently suggested that drivers do not overtake round the outside of corners in Grand Prix racing. It was not what one expects of modern professional sportsmen and the corporate image they represent, but it was good to see a bit of hot-blooded fervour from two drivers intent on winning, and not happy to just sit back and wait for the points to arrive. Mentioning which, Lauda won again after a one-sided duel with Laffite (knocking Hunt's title hopes on the head) though the Frenchman was only a couple of seconds behind. These two gave Brambilla another first for his encyclopaedia of accidents as, while lapping him, the air turbulence produced by their cars literally blew his Surtees off the road into a guard rail and demolished the front of the car. It certainly brought a new meaning to the term 'I just blew him away', but, as ever, Brambilla emerged unscathed.

With only four races remaining the title looked to be going to the Ferrari driver for the second time. Scheckter, Lauda's nearest challenger, had only gained points finishes in two of the last seven races, and only Andretti was left with a chance, 31 points behind Lauda, as one could not imagine team-mate Reutemann being allowed to pose a challenge.

For the Italian Grand Prix McLaren had a couple of surprises. One was local driver Bruno Giacomelli who was given an M23 to drive, and the second was that Hunt might not take part, because of a foot injury sustained while playing football. There was no keeping him down, even though his Championship had gone, and he set the fastest practice time ahead of Peterson, back at the front again at long last, Scheckter, Andretti, and Lauda, good racers all. Giacomelli was fifteenth, and Mass his customary ninth.

Scheckter beat Hunt away at the start, followed by Andretti, these three being stalked by Lauda. Hunt's car was not as well balanced as expected and Andretti slipped by on lap 2, to

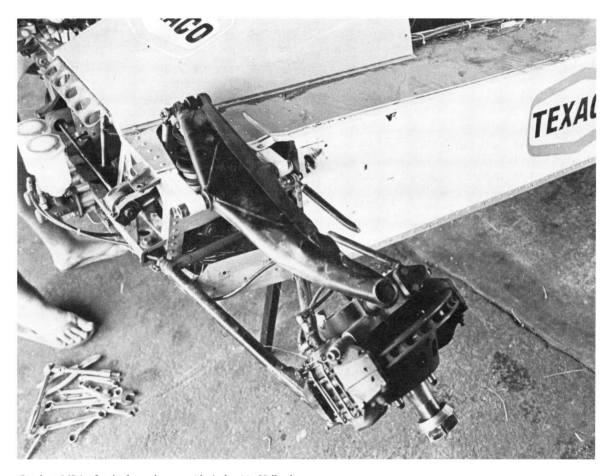

One bent M26, after the fun and games with Andretti in Holland.

dispose of Scheckter shortly afterwards. Hunt was third when, on lap 12, he spun off while lapping Jarier, under pressure from Reutemann. He rejoined in eighth place, passed Mass, and promptly spun off. Into the pits he went, did one final lap, and spun off yet again, this time to retire with braking and handling problems. Mass salvaged some joy for McLaren, coming fourth, while Giacomelli's engine failed.

Andretti duly won the race, but this was irrelevant as all Italy was to celebrate Lauda winning his second title, accompanied by Ferrari winning the Constructors' award. This was a first-rate achievement, and it is doubtful if any other contemporary driver could have claimed

the title, driving a Ferrari. He might not have won the most races, nor been the fastest or most spectacular driver, but he was the one to beat, and in the end, or indeed well before, Lauda beat his rivals more often than they managed to beat him.

The racing was far from over though, and Hunt claimed an emphatic pole position at the United States Grand Prix. The Brabhams were back in the picture, with Stuck and Watson next, and a less than happy Lauda well back, after announcing he was to join Brabham. His mechanic was dismissed on race day when he decided to follow Lauda, so there was an even thicker black cloud over the Ferrari pit than over the rest of the circuit, as the cars lined up for another wet race.

Stuck led Hunt away this time, but his clutch failed early on, and Hunt stalked him from just beyond the spray of his tyres. On lap 15 the German spun off, and Hunt led imperiously from Andretti, while Mass retired with drowned electrics. Even at this early stage the result looked cut and dried, but the circuit began to dry out. As the race neared its conclusion Hunt eased off and swooped around off the racing line, heading for the wet patches, to cool his rapidly deteriorating wet tyres. As the last lap approached Andretti was within striking distance, and everyone knew what these two out-and-out racers were capable of, but Hunt had the situation under control. He kept the hard-charging American a couple of seconds adrift all the way round, to record his second victory of the season. Brambilla finished the race in last place, after smashing the nose off his car. It looked more like a fairground go-kart than a Grand Prix car, and kept the spectators entertained.

When all the teams headed north for the Canadian Grand Prix there was one notable absentee. New World Champion Niki Lauda had opted out of the remaining two races of his Ferrari contract, ostensibly over the dismissal of his mechanic. This may have deprived the crowds of the great man's presence, but Ferrari raced Gilles Villeneuve, the Canadian who had earlier driven for McLaren, as their new number two, and thus guaranteed much local support.

The Mosport Park circuit did not meet the drivers' wholehearted approval with its poor surface and badly-secured guard rails and spectator nets. Once again threats of a boycott were raised, but efforts were made to improve things – though Ian Ashley had a very lucky escape when his Hesketh came off the road. The grid was as hotly contested as ever, and Andretti pipped Hunt for the pole, with Peterson and Nilsson ahead of Mass. This promised to be a real McLaren vs Lotus battle with both number twos closely involved.

It did not quite turn out that way, as Andretti snatched the lead, with Hunt on his tail, and Mass holding a comfortable third, but dropping back from the scorching pace of the two front runners. Andretti held all the aces this time, even though Hunt could probably have gone faster if he could have got past. Round and round they circulated in tandem until, on lap 59, they came up to lap Mass, still in third place. Here was Hunt's big chance, if Jochen could assist him. The three of them drove in line, astern for a whole lap, and then Andretti made his move at the hairpin. Mass did nothing to help the American who got a little crossed up, and Hunt nipped by to take the lead, still behind Mass. Perfect teamwork, and it looked like another victory was in the bag for McLaren.

Into lap 61 they went, towards the uphill right-hander beyond the pits, and Mass dutifully moved to the outside to let Hunt through. Unfortunately, Hunt was occupying the space so as to pass Jochen on the exit of the corner. The two McLarens touched and Hunt went head on into a wall, and was briefly trapped in the car by his feet. Mass spun, but was able to resume in fourth place with Andretti, probably laughing his head off, now leading by miles.

Hunt was not best pleased by this time and, as an unfortunate marshall tried to prevent him crossing the circuit to the pits, James thumped him and down he went. He then made angry gestures at Jochen each time he passed, the whole incident being viewed worldwide. It was not a scenario to be proud of, and once again the incidentals had overshadowed some marvellous driving.

Andretti now looked to be the one who had the race in the bag, leading by over a lap when, with two-and-a-half laps to go, the engine in the Lotus blew up and Scheckter was left with a very lucky win. Depailler brought the six-wheeled Tyrrell home second, for its best result of the season, and Mass finished a tail-between-his-legs third. Who says Grand Prix racing isn't fun?

So, the teams trekked half-way round the world for the final race, in Japan. Both Drivers' and Constructors' Championships were sewn up, and there was an 'end of term' air about events. Travelling so far was not ideal when there was still everything to race for, but with the Japanese Grand Prix having to stand on its own two feet, and with several absentees, enthusiasm was a bit low. Not within the McLaren team though, who were there to win, as were Lotus, Brabham, Wolf, Ferrari, Tyrrell, Shadow, and Ligier. Andretti once again pipped Hunt to the pole, with the Brabhams of Stuck and Watson behind, and Mass seventh. This time, Hunt beat Andretti into the first corner and simply drove into the distance, never to be challenged. On lap 6 Villeneuve contested Hunt's aerial reputation by braking late and ramming Peterson in the rear. Villeneuve somersaulted over the barriers and into a prohibited area, killing a marshall and a photographer, but escaped relatively unscathed himself.

A lap later Mass took second place off Scheckter, and the McLaren domination seemed complete; the M26 had, at last, come good. There was to be no happy ending to Jochen

Mass's McLaren career though, as his engine gave up on lap 28. Hunt was thus left to complete another imperious victory, with everyone else scraping around for the leftovers, a very long way behind indeed. But even now controversy raised its head once again. Hunt had done the business in emphatic fashion, and then blotted his copybook by dashing off to catch a plane home and, along with second-placed Reutemann, failed to appear on the winners' podium. Once again Hunt had done neither himself, McLaren, nor Grand Prix racing any favours. The fist waving, shouting, aerobatics, even the punching might all add a bit of spice to the sport, and at least shows some passion, but when you bite the hand that feeds you, you are on very shaky ground indeed.

Thus another exciting season closed, with McLaren back on top again. Jackie Stewart drove a number of Grand Prix cars that winter and confirmed that the M26 was definitely a winner. McLaren could look forward to 1978 with heart, but little did they realize what Colin Chapman had up his sleeve, and that five successful years were about to come to a fairly abrupt end.

Grand Prix Results 1977

GRAND PRIX	DRIVER	CAR	NO	1ST PRACTICE* Time/Posn	2ND PRACTICE* Time/Posn	3RD PRACTICE* Time/Posn	FINAL GRID POSN	FINAL PLACING	RETIRED CAUSE OF	HIGHEST POSN IN RACE
ARGENTINIAN Buenos Aires 9.1.77	J. Hunt	Ford V8 M23-DFV M23/8	1	1min 50.04sec 2/17	1min 48.48sec 1/14	1min 51.35sec 6/19	2-20		Lp 31 Broken suspension	FL 1st
	J. Mass	Ford V8 M23-DFV M23/9	2	1min 50.62sec 5/17	1min 49.81sec 4/14	1min 51.22sec 5/19	6-20		Lp 28 Engine cut out, spin	3rd
BRAZILIAN Interlagos 23.1.77	J. Hunt	Ford V8 M23-DFV M23/8	1	2min 31.64sec 3/21	2min 32.68sec 2/20	2min 30.11sec 1/21	Pole	2/7		FL 1st
	J. Mass	Ford V8 M23-DFV M23/9	2	2min 31.50sec 2/21	2min 32.68sec 7/20	2min 30.36sec 4/21	4-22		Lp 12 Accident	3rd
SOUTH AFRICAN Kyalami 5.3.77	J. Hunt	Ford V8 M23-DFV M23/11	1	1min 34.94sec 5/15	1min 16.23sec 1/21	1min 15.96sec 1/23	2-23	4/15		1st
	J. Mass	Ford V8 M23-DFV M23/6	2	1min 35.05sec 7/15	1min 17.06sec 12/21	1min16.99sec 13/23	14-23	5/15		3rd

	Driver	Car	No.							
USA (West) Long Beach 3.4.77	J. Hunt	Ford V8 M23-DFV M23/11	1	1min 23.83sec 7/22	1min 22.60sec 5/22	1min 22.53sec 7/22	7-22	7/11		7th
	J. Mass	Ford V8 M23-DFV M23/12	2	1min 23.98sec 10/22	1min 23.58sec 12/22	1min 23.23sec 15/22	16-22		Lp 39 Rear end vibration	10th
SPANISH Jarama 8.5.77	J. Hunt	Ford V8 M26-DFV M26/2	1	1min 20.18sec 7/22	1min 20.32 sec 4/24	1min 20.11sec 5/24	7-24		Lp 10 Engine	4th
	J. Mass	Ford V8 M23-DFV M23/12	2	1min 21.27sec 13/23	1min 20.41sec 5/24	1min 20.14sec 6/24	9-24	4/14		4th
	E. Villotta (Iberia Airlines)	Ford V8 M23-DFV M23/6	36	1min 21.97sec 20/22	1min 22.78sec 22/22	1min 22.48sec 22/24	22-24	13/14		10th
MONACO Monte Carlo 22.5.77	J. Hunt	Ford V8 M26-DFV M26/2	1	1min 32.56sec 10/16	2min 0.35sec 2/13	1min 30.85sec 6/18	7-20		Lp 25 Engine dropped valve	5th
	J. Mass	Ford V8 M23-DFV M23/12	2	1min 32.06sec 8/16		1min 31.36sec 10/18	9-20	4/12		4th
BELGIAN Zolder 5.6.77	J. Hunt	Ford V8 M26-DFV M26/2	1	1min 27.14sec 3/20			9-26	7/15		6th
	J. Mass	Ford V8 M23-DFV M23/12	2	1min 29.10sec 12/20		1min 26.81sec 5/22	6-26		Lp 39 Accident Spun off	1st
SWEDISH Anderstorp 19.6.77	J. Hunt	Ford V8 M26-DFV M26/2	1	1min 26.05sec 2/19	1min 26.09sec 3/19	1min 25.62sec 2/20	3-24	12/19		2nd
	J. Mass	Ford V8 M23-DFV M23/11	2	1min 28.38sec 20/29						
	J. Mass	Ford V8 M23-DFV M23/12	2	1min 27.94sec 13/19		1min 26.38sec 6/20	10-24	2/19		2nd
	B. Lunger (Chesterfield Racing)	Ford V8 M23-DFV M23/14	30	1min 28.68sec 17/19	1min 28.23sec 17/19	1min 28.21sec 17/20	21-24	11/19		10th
	E. Villotta (Iberia Airlines)	Ford V8 M23-DFV M23/6	36	1min 29.60sec 25/30	1min 29.14sec 22/29	1min 28.71sec 24/30	Did not qualify			
FRENCH Dijon- Prenois 3.7.77	J. Hunt	Ford V8 M26-DFV M26/2	1	1min 13.13sec 3/27	1min 13.12sec 4/20	1min 12.73sec 2/21	2-22	3/13		1st
	J. Mass	Ford V8 M23-DFV M23/12	2	1min 13.78sec 10/21	1min 13.92sec 12/20	1min 13.41sec 5/21	7-22	9/13		9th
	B. Lunger (Chesterfield Racing)	Ford V8 M23-DFV M23/14	30	1min 14.90sec 24/29	1min 14.83sec 23/29	1min 14.85sec 21/29	Did not qualify			
BRITISH Silverstone 16.7.77	J. Hunt	Ford V8 M26-DFV M26/2	1	1min 18.99sec 1/24	1min 18.49sec 1/24	1min 18.87sec 4/26	Pole	1/15 WINNER		FL 1st
		Ford V8 M26-DFV M23/12	2	1min 20.53sec 24/26						
	J. Mass	Ford V8 M26-DFV M26/1	2	1min 20.66sec 15/24		1min 19.55sec 11/26	11-26	4/15		4th

	Driver	Car	No.							
	B. Lunger (Chesterfield Racing)	Ford V8 M23-DFV M23/14	30	1min 20.42sec 14/24	1min 20.06sec 14/24	1min 20.39sec 21/26	19-26	13/15		13th
	E. Villotta (Iberia Airlines)	Ford V8 M23-DFV M23/6	36	1min 22.30sec 26/26		1min 21.53sec 30/30	Did not qualify 9-26			
	G. Villeneuve	Ford V8 M23-DFV M23/8	40	1min 20.07sec 8/24	1min 19.81sec 10/24	1min 19.32sec 7/26		11/15		7th
GERMAN Hockenheim-ring 31.7.77	J. Hunt	Ford V8 M26-DFV M26/2	1	1min 53.68sec 1/28	1min 56.57sec 13/21	1min 53.89sec 3/21	4-24		Lp 32 Mechanical fuel pump	3rd
		Ford V8 M23-DFV M23/12	1	1min 56.23sec 16/28						
	J. Mass	Ford V8 M26-DFV M26/1	2	1min 55.25sec 9/28	1min 57.44sec 10/21	1min 56.60sec 14/21	13-24		Lp 26 Gearbox	7th
	B. Lunger (Chesterfield Racing)	Ford V8 M23-DFV M23/14	30	1min 58.25sec 20/28	1min 57.92sec 20/21	1min 56.64sec 16/21	21-24		Lp 14 Damage Collision at start	20th
	E. Villotta (Iberia Airlines)	Ford V8 M23-DFV M23/6	36	1min 58.80sec 22/28	1min 57.75sec 21/23	1min 57.39sec 24/28	Practice only			
AUSTRIAN Österreichring 14.8.77	J. Hunt	Ford V8 M26-DFV M26/2	1	1min 39.69sec 1/30	1min 39.54sec 2/29	1min 39.45sec 1/28	2-25		Lp 43 Engine	1st
	J. Mass	Ford V8 M26-DFV M26/1	2	1min 41.23sec 7/30	1min 40.44sec 8/29	1min 41.55sec 10/28	9-25	6/17		5th
	B. Lunger (Chesterfield Racing)	Ford V8 M23-DFV M23/14	30	1min 42 62sec 16/30	1min 41.40sec 16/29	1min 41.90sec 15/28	17-25	10/17		10th
	E. Villotta (Ibria Airlines)	Ford V8 M23-DFV M23/6	36	1min 43.35sec 19/30	1min 43.21sec 26/29	1min 42.38sec 20/28	25-25	17/17		17th
DUTCH Zandvoort 28.8.77	J. Hunt	Ford V8 M26-DFV M26/2	1	1min 19.70sec 2/33	1min 19.72sec 1/31	1min 19.50sec 2/33	3-26		Lp 5 Accident	1st
	J. Mass	Ford V8 M26-DFV M26/1	2	1min 21.47sec 21/33	1min 21.30sec 16/31					
	J. Mass	Ford V8 M26-DFV M26/3	2		1min 20.76sec 10/18	1min 20.24sec 11/33	14-26		Lp 1 Accident	
	B. Lunger (Chesterfield Racing)	Ford V8 M23-DFV M23/14	30	1min 23.00sec 30/33	1min 21.77sec 16/31	1min 20.87sec 17/33	20-26	9/13		9th
ITALIAN Monza 11.9.77	J. Hunt	Ford V8 M26-DFV M26/2	1	1min 40.11sec 7/33		1min 38.08sec 1/33	Pole		Lp 26 Spun off braking problem	2nd
		Ford V8 M26-DFV M26/1	1	1min 43.26sec 28/33						
	J. Mass	Ford V8 M26-DFV M26/3Ford	2	1min 40.83sec 12/33	1min 40.77sec 10/32	1min 38.86sec 9/33	9-24	4/9	Lp 35 Engine	4th
	B. Giacomelli	V8 M23-DFV M23/8	14	1min 40.59sec 10/33	1min 41.27sec 17/32	1min 39.42sec 13/33	15-24		Lp 4 Engine	9th
	B. Lunger (Chesterfield Racing)	Ford V8 M23-DFV M23/14	30	1min 44.19sec 30/33		1min 40.26sec 31/33	20-24			18th

	E. Villotta (Iberia Airlines)	Ford V8 M23-DFV M23/6	36	1min 46.26sec 33/33	1min 44.43sec 31/32	1min 41.21sec 29/33	Did not qualify			
USA Watkins Glen 2.10.77	J. Hunt	Ford V8 M26-DFV M26/2	1	1min 41.41sec 1/25	1min 40.86sec 1/23	2min 14.54sec 6/22	Pole	1/19 WINNER		**1st**
	J. Mass	Ford V8 M26-DFV M26/3	2	1min 43.83sec 14/25	1min 43.24sec 13/23	2min 12.51sec 2/22	15-26		Lp 8 Fuel pump belt	**7th**
	B. Lunger (Chesterfield Racing)	Ford V8 M23-DFV M23/11	30	1min 43.70sec 13/25	1min 44.01sec 16/23	2min 24.47sec 18/22	17-26	10/19		**10th**
CANADIAN Mosport Park 9.10.77	J. Hunt	Ford V8 M26-DFV M26/2	1	1min 12.55sec 2/25	1min 11.94sec 2/25		2-25		Lp 61 Accident	**1st**
	J. Mass	Ford V8 M26-DFV M26/3	2	1min 13.48sec 3/25	1min 13.12sec 5/25		5-25	3/12		**3rd**
	B. Lunger (Chesterfield Racing)	Ford V8 M23-DFV M23/14	30	1min 14.93sec 14/25	1min 15.36sec 20/25		20-25	11/12		**9th**
JAPANESE Mt Fuji 23.10.77	J. Hunt	Ford V8 M26-DFV M26/3	1	1min 12.39sec 2/22		1min 12.67sec 3/22	2-23	1/12 WINNER		**1st**
	J. Mass	Ford V8 M26-DFV M26/1	2	1min 13.71sec 7/22		1min 13.37sec 8/23	8-23		Lp 28 Engine	**2nd**

★ Some races held four practices. A driver's best three results are counted

CHAPTER 6

Plumbing the Depths

It is difficult to assess chronologically McLaren's fortunes over the next three years, as the problems which manifested themselves in 1978 were to have a long term, on-going, and profound effect which resulted in drastic changes both within the team and Grand Prix racing itself. The leading teams of the 1970s; namely McLaren, Ferrari, Lotus, Tyrrell and Brabham were, by the end of 1980, with the exception of the last-named, virtual also-rans. Others, like Ligier, Williams and Renault, had taken their place, the latter having introduced a new source of power into the sports, the turbocharged engine.

Drivers as in all periods, come and go, but the personalities who packed the grids of the mid-1970s, such as Hunt, Lauda, Peterson, Scheckter, Andretti, Fittipaldi, Depailler, Regazzoni and Watson, all of whom were winners in any era, had departed the sport one way or another, or were in decline. Only Reutemann remained a winner, and others like Piquet, Villeneuve, Pironi, Jabouille, Arnoux, with Jones and Laffite having risen in stature, had taken their place. All within less than three years!

'GROUND EFFECTS'

These represented radical changes in the Grand Prix hierarchy but there was one further change, the catalyst for all this, which virtually transformed the sport and created conditions which nearly brought about its self-destruction. Almost inevitably this came from the ingenious mind of Colin Chapman, and took the title of 'ground effects'.

Racing cars had altered little since Chapman shook the world with his Lotus 72. True, they were faster, but even the M26 followed the basic design principles pioneered by Chapman. The Lotus 78 appeared in 1977, and the term 'wing car', entered racing terminology. This car's body acted as an upturned aircraft wing, being shaped to increase the loading, or downforce, on the tyres by controlling the airflow underneath, and creating a vacuum. Braking distances shortened and cornering speeds increased, with circuits being lapped faster. For 1978 Chapman took ground effects a step forward with his new car, rendering obsolete anything similar to the Lotus 72 – Ferrari excepted. Yet at that time Chapman was not aware of what he had started; for example, Peterson's pole position time at Brands Hatch was fully 3 seconds quicker than Lauda's of two years before, yet it would not have been good enough to scrape on to the back of the grid by 1980, such was the rate of progress. The consequences of ground effects were to turn Grand Prix racing upside down.

McLaren though, had little to worry about as the 1978 season approached, or so they thought. Race results, Jackie Stewart's driving impressions and their reputation for impeccable race preparation, suggested that the M26 would be the car to beat, or thereabouts. Furthermore, in James Hunt, they had the fastest and most aggressively skilled driver of the day, tipped by many as likely to become World Champion for the second time. Jochen Mass had been moved on, to be replaced by the promising Patrick Tambay who, apart from some good drives in the Ensign in the latter half of 1977, had swept

A close season practice session, with two of the likeliest Championship contenders for 1978, the M26, and a Lotus 78 – the latter winner of two races before being replaced by the incomparable Lotus 79 – being attended to.

the board in Can-Am, just like McLaren themselves used to. This was surely a good omen.

As ever, the opposition was not to be underrated. Tyrrell had designed a four-wheeled car, retained Depailler and recruited young Didier Pironi to replace Peterson. Ferrari looked weaker, with Lauda being replaced by the wild Gilles Villeneuve. Reutemann remained, but his abilities at sorting out the car were not in Lauda's class, and it was expected he would need all his undoubted driving skill for the team to retain the Constructors' Championship. But Ferrari held an ace up their sleeve. Michelin had entered Grand Prix with the Renault team in 1977, and Ferrari left the Goodyear camp in their favour. This was a major coup for the French tyre company, but would they be equal to the task?

Wolf, retaining Scheckter, Ligier, with

Laffite, and Renault were all worth keeping an eye on. Regazzoni had moved to Shadow, along with Stuck, but they were in all sorts of problems: most of the design staff, management, and mechanics had cleared off to form the Arrows team, with former Lotus driver Nilsson joining them, leaving Don Nichols with just a few cars lying around. In fact, as the dust settled, or rather did not as the ensuing legal battle carried on all season, Arrows even pinched Shadow's car design, just for good measure!

The main threat to McLaren was thus perceived as coming from Brabham and Lotus. Brabham had Niki Lauda as their new driver, with his renowned car-sorting abilities, alongside John Watson, one of the fastest drivers around. Naturally, it was expected that Gordon Murray would design something special to welcome Lauda, but it would still be powered by

142

the thirsty, inconsistent, and not particularly powerful, flat-12 Alfa Romeo engine. Unless this was to improve markedly there would be plenty of races where they would be totally out of contention.

Lotus, however, were a different kettle of fish. The Andretti/Chapman partnership was blossoming and Peterson was to return to the fold. Initially this was not to Andretti's liking, but once it was established that Peterson was to be number two, in every sense, harmony quickly returned. Chapman had designed a new car which, he said, would make the Lotus 78 'old hat'. This had been heard before about the Lotus 76 and 77, neither of which fulfilled that promise, but Chapman's record was unrivalled for revolutionary designs, and with Peterson as a number two Lotus were certainly one to watch.

Any shift in the status quo was not apparent at the two South American races. In Argentina none of the major teams had new cars, though Frank Williams had bounced back once again with the tidy FW06, driven by Alan Jones. The front of the grid could easily have been that of the year before, with Andretti on the pole, Hunt sixth, and Tambay ninth. Andretti strode off, in his inimitable super-smooth style, to win comfortably, but the circuit was suited to the Lotus, and this performance had been seen before. Watson retired with fourteen laps to go, and Lauda, Depailler and Hunt were all looking at second place, but finished in that order. Tambay came sixth, and the lightly modified M26s had not disgraced themselves, even if they were not out in front.

The Brazilian Grand Prix gave McLaren even less concern, as Hunt qualified on the front row, alongside Peterson, with Tambay fourth on the grid. Tyres were likely to be a problem though, and it was with these that an insight into the future was offered. Reutemann took an initial lead and proceeded to pull away. Though Hunt passed Peterson on lap 2 for second place, he was fully 6 seconds behind the Ferrari. By lap 7 Hunt was into the pits for new tyres, yet Reutemann carried on without any problems.

Michelin had clearly pulled a rabbit out of the hat for this race.

James Hunt rejoined the fray in twentieth position and made his way up to tenth, when he came up behind the new Arrows car, driven by Patrese. One lap later Hunt had spun off trying to pass the young Italian, the first of many drivers to be similarly troubled during the coming races. Tambay also spun off ten laps later, and Reutemann won easily, from Fittipaldi in the new Ralph Bellamy – (ex-Lotus and McLaren) designed family car. Regazzoni came fifth and Pironi sixth. James always regarded these early races as a bonus if points were scored, so 3 was not too disappointing.

The South African Grand Prix, as usual, was the scene of a few debuts. Martini and Theodore made their entries into Grand Prix racing, and Ensign were back again. More important was the introduction of the all-new Ferrari 312–T3 which, after the dominance of the old car in Brazil, made everyone sit up and take notice. Brabham also unveiled their BT46, which was intended to have the oil and water radiators mounted along the body surface, to improve the aerodynamics. This had not worked out so far, but with the combined brains of Lauda and Murray working on a solution, you could bet an answer would be found.

All was happy at McLaren as, despite Lauda and Andretti holding the front row, Hunt was third in practice, with Tambay sitting next to him. The race was a classic, but not for McLaren. Patrick burnt his clutch at the start, and got going in last place, while James was running fourth when his engine expired on lap 4. Tambay recovered to ninth place before spinning off, thus ending another encouraging drive.

Out at the front it was all very exciting. Lauda momentarily selected the wrong gear at the start, and Andretti led with impunity. Tyre wear caused him to fall back into the clutches of Scheckter, Lauda, Patrese, and Depailler; and on lap 27 Patrese sensationally took the lead from Scheckter, holding this until his engine expired with only fifteen laps to go. Patrese/ Arrows looked to be a driver/team combination with a future. Depailler then led from Andretti, with Peterson dutifully following his team leader, and when Andretti went into the pits for more fuel with only three laps to go, it looked as though Depailler was at last going to win a Grand Prix, in the new four-wheeled Tyrrell to boot.

Peterson thought otherwise and charged up behind Depailler, and they began the last lap nose to tail. Round the twisty back of the circuit they went, Peterson shadowing Depailler's every move. The Lotus feinted to one side and the Tyrrell parried it, so Peterson tried the other, only to be thwarted again. More slow corners ahead offered little opportunity for overtaking, but Peterson once more made to go

inside of the Tyrrell. Depailler moved over, only for the dashing Swede to dodge into the gap left by Depailler, and Peterson was away, with half a lap to spare. Poor old Depailler had lost out yet again, but what as magnificent finale to a really entertaining, hard-fought race.

The next two races on the calendar were not ones for Mclaren to get excited about. The United States Grand Prix (West), at Long Beach, saw the Ferraris dominate again. Hunt was seventh on the grid and Tambay eleventh – not too bad after a variety of practice problems and an accident. Villeneuve showed his potential by leading from the start, until indulging in James Hunt style aerobatics while trying to lap Regazzoni, which put him out. Reutemann then went on to win, chased by Jones, until his car's nose came loose; serving notice to the big

The start of the 1978 Long Beach Grand Prix with Reutemann just behind Watson who has been nudged by Villeneuve, while Lauda steers clear of trouble on the outside. Andretti leads Jones, with Peterson and Hunt contesting seventh place and Tambay two places further adrift.

144

By the time of the Monaco Grand Prix, in 1978, it was becoming clear that the M26 was not going to be as successful as had been expected. Patrick Tambay is reduced to battling away for seventh place, and worse was to come. The M26, even with skirts, was no match for the new Lotus 79.

guns. It was not a McLaren race though, and Hunt retired on lap 8, after clipping a wall while in sixth position, while Tambay came a distant twelfth.

Monaco offered little cheer for McLaren either, with James qualifying sixth, getting involved in a first lap fracas and spending the next forth-three laps wandering around at the back of the field, until the rear anti-roll bar broke and put him out of the race (and his misery). Patrick did well to come seventh after a big spin in Casino Square; adding to his stature.

There was much to take note of. Depailler finally broke his duck and won a Grand Prix, with both Brabhams, Scheckter and, initially, the Ferraris going well. Wolf debuted their 'Lotus 78' type WR5 car, Surtees the TS-20, and Ligier the JS9, and Lotus, briefly, the 79. There was much paddock debate as to whether it was more important for the air to pass smoothly over the car, supported by those such as McLaren, or under the car, as Chapman advocated. So far there had been little convincing evidence either way, and few could have expected the dramatic way Chapman was to settle the argument for all time.

It was at the Belgian Grand Prix that the way ahead was clearly pointed out to all and sundry. Andretti gave the Lotus 79 – a beautiful, sleek, black machine – its Grand Prix debut, and took the pole by miles. James Hunt was sixth on the grid, but over 1.5 seconds adrift of Mario

145

Patrick Tambay

Patrick Tambay is another of those drivers whose talent, for whatever reason, was not reflected in their results. Smooth, articulate, almost dapper, Patrick raised the intellectual level among Grand Prix drivers somewhat, and portrayed the image of the sophisticated Frenchman that he was.

His path to Grand Prix racing was a little unorthodox, coming third in the Formula 2 Championship in both 1975 and 1976, driving a Renault, and then racing in the Can-Am series the following year, becoming the distinguished Champion. This brought him to Mclaren's attention, and he replaced Mass as the number two to Hunt. It looked at the time as though he had come up trumps: McLaren were a top team, with a winning car, and possibly with the best contemporary driver – a very powerful looking unit indeed. Patrick's smooth driving, clearly of the highest class, had stood out like a sore thumb in the hurly-burly world of Can-Am; Teddy Mayer looked to have found a real golden nugget out in the west.

As we now know, Chapman was about to turn Grand Prix racing inside out and point it in a new direction once again. His ground effects Lotus 78 and 79 made the M26 obsolete, and while Hunt tried all he knew just to keep them in sight, Tambay smoothly brought his car home to enough finishes to eventually out-point his more illustrious team-mate, and gain many admirers on the way.

Watson was recruited for 1979 and, slowly, 'blue-eyed boy' Patrick was edged out of favour, as the M28 proved to be hopeless. Two mid-season 'did not qualify's' did Tambay's reputation no good at all, and he finished the season without scoring any points, his confidence seemingly shattered. No other Grand Prix team was interested in Tambay's services, though there is little doubt that his demise was more to do with McLaren than with his own ability.

Tambay made his way back to Can-Am for 1980, and fully rehabilitated his reputation by becoming the Champion again, with six victories. Still, there was no Grand Prix drive for 1981. Then Jabouille retired part-way into the season, and Tambay took over his drive at Ligier, putting up some good performances, only to be dispensed with at the season's end.

Fate was not kind to Tambay, but was even less so to Villeneuve, the Ferrari driver, who was killed practising for the 1982 Belgian Grand Prix. After a few races as a one-car team, it was Tambay who took over the no. 27 car, and he secured his first Grand Prix win in Germany, after team-mate Pironi was badly injured in practice. The following season saw Tambay joined by René Arnoux, and he surprised many by making his undoubtedly fast fellow-countryman look positively rustic, and by proving consistently not only the better, but faster, driver. In addition, he was maturing well as a test driver and was very popular with all the Ferrari team. Yet it was Patrick, and not Arnoux, who had to make way for Alboreto at the season's end.

Tambay spent the next two seasons with the rapidly declining Renault team, which did not enhance his reputation, and he finished off with a disappointing season with Haas-Lola. There, he showed progress, but the car was not worthy of his, nor fellow driver Jones's, ability. He thus retired with only two Grand Prix victories to his name, despite having driven for three top teams.

There have been few more cultured drivers than Patrick Tambay. Suggestions that he was not forceful enough to win were quashed in 1983 when, with a bit of luck, he might have won the World Championship. As it was, he seemed to arrive in the right team, at the wrong time, and thus the record books paint him as just another of the growing number of drivers who have won a Grand Prix race – a picture that completely hides his precise driving style and immense talent.

Andretti, with Bruno Giacomelli (replacing Patrick Tambay who had an injured leg) twenty-first. Andretti led from the start and won at his leisure, with Peterson, still in a Lotus 78, a fighting second after visiting the pits for tyres, and passing both Ferraris en route. Hunt had his second meeting of the season with young Patrese at the start, and was eliminated along with Lauda and Fittipaldi: quite a set of scalps for the Arrows driver.

If there were any doubting Thomases as to the effectiveness of Chapman's new car, the Spanish Grand Prix provided a comprehensive answer. Andretti and Peterson, both in 79s, sat calmly on the front row, having dominated practice. Chapman may have been smiling

For a few brief laps at the start of the Spanish Grand Prix, Hunt managed to lead from Andretti. Three years were to pass before a McLaren led a Grand Prix again.

away, but few rivals were. Hunt was not best pleased after a nasty accident, when local driver de Villota lost control and collided with him, wrecking his M26. It was a lucky escape for the Englishman, and probably for the Spaniard if James could have got hold of him. The fact remained that drivers without the necessary skill, were a liability in modern Grand Prix racing. Hunt, clearly wound up, qualified fourth and was certainly not going to let the Lotus pair have it all their own way.

Hunt started on soft tyres, knowing that they would be marginal in terms of longevity, and got inside of Andretti at the first corner, to lead for the first time that season. For five exuberant laps James used all his skill to stay ahead of the superior Lotus. It could not, and did not, last. On lap 6 Hunt slid marginally wide, Andretti drove through and was away. But Hunt was not finished, and he held second place until passed by Peterson on lap 53, which shows just how good a driver Andretti was. Three laps later Laffite and Lauda went by and Hunt went into

the pits for new tyres. It was unusual for him to wait so long before stopping for fresh tyres and perhaps, had he stopped just after half-distance, he might have finished higher; sixth place was a poor reward for such a tenacious drive. While not wanting to give too much away, this was the last time a McLaren was to lead a Grand Prix for over three years.

Sweden, as we have seen, seemed to have a knack for throwing up a freak result, and when the teams arrived, the air seemed charged with electricity. Andretti sat on the pole again, way ahead of Hunt, back in mid-grid with Tambay just behind, with Watson for company on the front row. It was the cars that Watson and Lauda were driving that caused all the fuss. Lotus had led the way with under-car aerodynamics, but Brabham's Gordon Murray had gone a stage further. The sides of the BT46 were sealed to the ground by sliding skirts, as per Lotus, but a big fan sat on the back of the car, supposedly to aid cooling. It also coincidentally, as Brabham would have everyone believe,

147

The Swedish Grand Prix had a reputation for producing freak results. The 1978 race was no different, with Niki Lauda winning in the only race in which the Brabham BT46 'fan' car was allowed to participate. Race leader Mario Andretti laps Patrick Tambay and Regazzoni, who finished fourth and fifth respectively, with Niki Lauda hot on his tail. In the background, Hunt has already been lapped.

sucked air from underneath the car, thus creating more downforce than even Chapman had managed to achieve. Protests flew back and forth, but the race took place, and on lap 38 Lauda 'out-Andrettied' Andretti, and disappeared.

Peterson had a fine drive through the field after a puncture, then got stuck behind Patrese, who employed some dreadful weaving tactics to keep the Lotus there. He was not making any friends in Grand Prix racing, but he finished second. Tambay finished a good fourth, with Hunt well out of it. Another first for Sweden.

There was quite a bit of falling out among the Grand Prix teams over the Brabham 'fan', and it was effectively banned, since it was decreed to

be a 'moving aerodynamic device', which was illegal. However, the Swedish result was allowed to stand. So, it was as if the Swedish incident had not occurred when the teams gathered for the French Grand Prix. John Watson sat on the pole ahead of Andretti, with James Hunt fourth, and Patrick Tambay sixth; it appeared that the M26 was competitive again, and Giacomelli was entered in a third car.

Watson took the lead, only to be passed by Andretti on the opening lap, who then, as expected, began to pull away. Peterson also passed the Brabham, and Hunt, driving his heart out, did likewise to take third place on lap 16. The Lotus 79 was far superior to the M26 but, using the long straight, Hunt forced Peterson to catch

Andretti. They circulated for lap after lap in close formation, the two Lotuses quite happy with the speed of the race, while Hunt was hanging on like grim death, driving flat out. Andretti began to pull away with that effortless ease synonymous with his driving for Lotus, but Hunt kept Peterson in sight, until he spun on the last lap, having been sick in his helmet. He kept it all going, though, to finish a fine third, having driven harder than for many of his victories. This was a sobering thought, as the Lotus drivers stepped out of their cars as fresh as daisies, and admitted as much. Unfortunately this was the last time the McLarens saw a Lotus in a race, so far back were they, and it was the last of James's heroic drives.

As far as McLaren were concerned the British Grand Prix came and went without notice. James tried the new M26-E, a sort of semi-Lotus copy, with side pods and sliding skirts, but he need not have bothered. The Lotus pair lined up on the front row, with Hunt a disappointing fourteenth, Giacomelli sixteenth, and Tambay twentieth. In a race in which both Lotuses retired, Reutemann beat Lauda to win, and Tambay picked up a point. Hunt's early retirement was not without notice, nor was the poor performance of the car.

The FOCA-organized German Grand Prix, at Hockenheimring, saw normal Lotus service resumed with both cars on the front row of the grid, and Andretti winning with impunity again, even if Peterson retired. Hunt, having qualified eighth, made the most of his inferior tools, driving manfully and with luck into fourth position by lap 12. Then a front tyre shredded way out on the circuit, and he lost three laps while driving gingerly back to the pits. He took a short-cut through the stadium and rejoined the race with new tyres, only to be disqualified for his keeness to get to his pits. Tambay also suffered a tyre failure, but he was pitched into the fencing, and that was his lot.

Following this race the Arrows team cars were banned by English courts, as the design belonged to the Shadow team, from whom they

emanated. They were prepared for such an eventuality and appeared in Austria with a new car. James Hunt qualified eighth again, with Patrick Tambay fourteenth. The Lotus pair were on the front row, as normal. There was a wet start and Andretti spun out on the first lap, leaving Peterson with a massive lead, and Hunt fifth. The race was stopped on lap 7, and Peterson won the restart easily enough, Hunt going out on the first lap, and Tambay spinning off on lap 34.

Holland was no better with Hunt seventh on the grid, 1.5 seconds behind the Lotus pair on the front row, a bit closer than in previous practices! Tambay was in mid-grid, with Giacomelli and Nelson Piquet being given another outing, further back. Andretti won again with Peterson only yards behind, but there was to be no battle with Hunt this year, as he finished a distant tenth.

McLaren had three works drivers again in Italy, plus the two B team entries, but the best that could be produced was tenth on the grid by Hunt. The week before it had been announced that James Hunt was to be replaced by Ronnie Peterson for 1979. James did not really want to go, but the team felt that he had not been giving his all, and that a fresh start was needed. A new ground effects car was on the drawing boards, and optimism ran high, especially since the recruitment of Peterson.

There remained the problem of the current dismal team performances. If Hunt really had been 'stroking it', as was claimed by Teddy Mayer, it had not been for long. James might not have impressed in Holland but, aside from the British Grand Prix, he had been well up the field in other races. Patrick was a talented driver, but got nowhere near James's qualifying times, and he seldom matched the latter's race speeds either. The M26 could not live with the Lotus 79 but, more worryingly, it was falling way behind other conventional cars, no matter how hard Hunt or Tambay tried. Finally, in view of the declining overall team performance, what on earth were McLaren doing running a third works car, as well as assisting with the so-called 'B' team? Did they think that by packing the grid with their cars they would get results through sheer volume? The fact was that James Hunt took the blame for the team's ills, an error of judgement repeated again in the near future.

The Italian Grand Prix was a catastrophe; there was a mix-up at the start, followed by a multiple accident. Ronnie Peterson, in a Lotus 78 and not a 79, bore the brunt of this and as his shattered car ground to a halt, it momentarily burst into flames. Hunt and Regazzoni, both being involved in the incident, bravely waded into the flames and dragged Peterson from his car. Brambilla also received serious injuries and was unable to race for a year, but it was the death of Peterson, the following morning, which shook the motor racing world. He had suffered severe leg injuries and died after a five-hour operation.

The recriminations as to who caused the accident flew all over the place. Fingers were pointed at Patrese, and he was subsequently refused entry at Watkins Glen at the instigation of certain drivers, one of whom was James Hunt. This was more a reaction to his unruly, occasionally dangerous driving than apportioning blame. The Starter, Reutemann, Scheckter and Hunt were all, at times, blamed by people with an axe to grind, but it seemed to be one of those tragedies peculiar to racing, where vulnerability is increased at a start. It was a sequence of events which all came together in the wrong way, at the wrong moment.

The restart was another bad joke as Ville-neuve jumped the lights; Andretti followed suit, and both were penalized a minute. Eventually Andretti 'won', after finally passing the Ferrari, to claim sixth place. Lauda, third on the road and a good way behind, was declared the 'official' winner.

Lotus and Andretti were dumbfounded by Peterson's death, but with Jarier deputizing, Andretti claimed the pole for the United States Grand Prix. James felt that the M26 was going better than at any time that season (a view not

shared by Patrick) but he was still two seconds slower than Andretti, in sixth place. Hunt was holding fifth position near the half-way stage, when he had to change his tyres. Reutemann won his fourth race of the year, with Jones a fine second, and the Renault fourth. Hunt recovered to finish seventh, behind Tambay.

Montreal's Ile Notre Dame island circuit was used for the final race of the year, the Canadian Grand Prix. It marked the end of three eventful seasons for James Hunt and McLaren, though with James qualifying nineteenth it ended on a low note. The race was no less of a disappointment for McLaren, Hunt spinning out at three-quarter distance, and Tambay coming a distant eighth. Jarier, in a Lotus 79, led the first forty-nine laps before retiring, leaving Villeneuve to record his first Frand Prix victory in his home race, and show Teddy Mayer just what he had allowed to slip through his fingers.

One suspects that the end of the season was greeted with a sigh of relief by most teams, since it offered them a chance to re-group, take stock, and see about ways to catch up with Lotus. Chapman's outfit had come back with a vengeance, winning eight races excluding the Italian Grand Prix, and having led four of the other seven. Brabham, despite achieving two lucky wins, had not really lived up to expectations, though Ferrari performed very well on the whole. Of the smaller teams Williams stood out, Frank finally achieving some reward for his years of persistence – which pleased everyone.

McLaren had provided the biggest surprise of all by their rate, and scale, of decline. It seems as though once they were falling behind, fingers were being pointed as to whose fault this was. Teddy Mayer and others accused James Hunt of giving up, and certainly by Austria the real 'tiger' had gone to a degree. This is a natural response when things are not going well. When with Hesketh, Hunt fought hard to achieve mid-grid positions, as this was a triumph at first. When he moved on to McLaren, his efforts brought the M23 and the team back to the top

Grand Prix Results 1978

GRAND PRIX	DRIVER	CAR	NO	1ST PRACTICE★ Time/Posn	2ND PRACTICE★ Time/Posn	3RD PRACTICE★ Time/Posn	FINAL GRID POSN	FINAL PLACING	RETIRED CAUSE OF	HIGHEST POSN IN RACE
ARGENTINIAN Buenos Aires 15.1.78	J. Hunt	Ford-DFV M26-DFV M26/4	7	1min 49.19sec 5/24	1min 49.29sec 5/24	1min 48.72sec 3/23	6-24	4/18		4th
	P. Tambay	Ford-DFV M26-DFV M26/3	8	1min 51.71sec 16/24	1min 49.47sec 6/24	1min 49.75sec 6/22	9-24	6/18		6th
	B. Lunger (Chesterfield/ Liggett)	Ford-DFV M23-DFV M23/14	30	1min 52.98sec 21/24	1min 52.27sec 18/24	1min 52.52sec 23/23	23-23	13/18		13th
BRAZILIAN Rio de Janeiro 29.1.78	J. Hunt	Ford-DFV M26-DFV M26/4	7	1min 41.59sec 2/23	1min 41.27sec 2/23	1min 40.53sec 2/22	2-22		Lp 25 Accident Spin off	2nd
	P. Tambay	Ford-DFV M26-DFV M26/3	8	1min 42.70sec 6/23	1min 42.51sec 8/23	1min 40.94sec 5/22	5-22		Lp 34 Accident Spin off	5th
	B. Lunger (Chesterfield/ Liggett	Ford-DFV M23-DFV M23/11	30	1min 45.56sec 17/23	1min 44.00sec 15/23	1min 42.65sec 13/22	14-22		Lp 11 Engine overheating	11th
SOUTH AFRICAN Kyalami 4.3.78	J. Hunt	Ford-DFV M26-DFV M26/4	7	1min 15.14sec 3/26	1min 15.65sec 4/26		3-26		Lp 5 Engine failure	4th
	P. Tambay	Ford-DFV M26-DFV M26/5	8	1min 15.30sec 4/26	1min 16.33sec 11/26 1min 17.83sec		4-26		Lp 56 Accident	8th
	B. Lunger (Chesterfield/ Liggett)	Ford-DFV M23-DFV M23/14	30	1min 17.30sec 22/26			19-26	11/12		11th
USA (West) Long Beach 2.4.78	J. Hunt	Ford-DFV M26-DFV M26/4	7	1min 22.36sec 10/21	1min 21.94sec 6/19		7-22		Lp 5 Accident Spun	7th
	P. Tambay	Ford-DFV M26-DFV M26/5	8	1min 23.69sec 17/21	1min 22.34sec 9/19		11-22	12/12		4th
	B. Lunger (Chesterfield/ Liggett)	Ford-DFV M23-DFV M23/11	30	1min 24.34sec 23/25	1min 23.80sec 20/21		Did not qualify			
MONACO Monte Carlo 7.5.78	J. Hunt	Ford-DFV M26-DFV M26/4	7	1min 30.39sec 6/20	1min 29.48sec 5/19	1min 29.22sec 5/20	5-20		Lp 43 Broken anti roll bar	14th
	P. Tambay	Ford-DFV M26-DFV M26/5	8	1min 32.41sec 18/20	1min 31.16sec 11/19	1min 30.09sec 11/20	12-20	7/11		7th
	B. Lunger (Chesterfield/ Liggett)	Ford-DFV M23-DFV M23/6	30	1min 39.11sec 31/32	1min 34.86sec 35/36		Did not qualify			
BELGIAN Zolder 21.5.78	J. Hunt	Ford-DFV M26-DFV M26/4	7	1min 23.16sec 5/22	1min 23.16sec 5/21	1min 22.50sec 5/17	6-24		Lp 1 Accident	
	P. Tambay	Ford-DFV M26-DFV	8	Did not attend						
	B. Lunger (Lark/Ligget Group)	Ford-DFV M26-DFV M26/6	30			1min 24.99sec 17/17	24-24	7/13		7th
	B. Giacomelli	Ford-DFV M26-DFV M26/7	33	1min 28.30sec 21/22	1min 25.47sec 18/21	1min 24.81sec 15/17	21-24	8/13		6th

Race	Driver	Car	No							
SPANISH Jarama 4.6.78	J. Hunt	Ford-DFV M26-DFV M26/3	7	1min 17.66sec 4/24	1min 19.43sec 10/23	1min 18.28sec 7/24	4-24	6/15		**1st**
	P. Tambay	Ford-DFV M26-DFV M26/5	8	1min 19.76sec 14/24	1min 20.17sec 12/23	1min 19.28sec 12/24	14-24			**12th**
	E. Villotta (Centro Asequrador)	Ford-DFV M23-DFV M23/7	28	1min 21.53sec 26/28	1min 22.41sec 27/27	1min 22.84sec 28/28	Did not qualify		Lp 16 Spin off Clutch	
	B. Lunger (Lark/Ligget Group)	Ford-DFV M26-DFV M26/6	30	1min 21.17sec 23/28	1min 22.07sec 26/27	1min 21.5sec 26/28	Did not qualify			
SWEDISH Anderstorp 16.7.78	J. Hunt	Ford-DFV M26-DFV M26/3	7	1min 29.95sec 10/24	1min 24.76sec 9/24	1min 25.59sec 16/24	14-24	8/15		**7th**
	P. Tambay	Ford-DFV M26-DFV M26/5	8	1min 25.43sec 8/24	1min 25.68sec 14/24	1min 24.98sec 14/24	15-24	4/15		**4th**
	B. Lunger (Lark/Ligget Group)	Ford-DFV M26-DFV M26/6	30	1min 28.39sec 25/27	1min 29.00sec 26/27	1min 28.50sec 27/27	Did not qualify			
FRENCH Ricard-Castellet 1.7.78	J. Hunt	Ford-DFV M26-DFV M26/3	7	1min 46.20sec 3/26	1min 45.32sec 7/26	1min 44.92sec 2/26	4-26	3/18		**3rd**
	P. Tambay	Ford-DFV M26-DFV M26/5	8	1min 47.06sec 6/26	1min 45.03sec 4/26	1min 46.15sec 8/26	6-26	9/18		**3rd**
	B. Lunger (Lark/Ligget Group)	Ford-DFV M23-DFV M23/6	30	1min 51.26sec 22/26	1min 49.65sec 22/26	1min 49.55sec 21/26	24-26		Lp 45 Engine	**12th**
	B. Giacomelli	Ford-DFV M26-DFV M26/7	33	1min 54.67sec 25/26	1min 50.77sec 25/26	1min 49.53sec 19/26	22-26		Lp 28 Engine	**13th**
BRITISH Brands Hatch 16.7.78	J. Hunt	Ford-DFV M26-DFV M26/3	7	1min 19.05sec 4/25	1min 19.23sec 9/26	1min 19.27sec 13/26	14-26		Lp 7 Accident	**9th**
	P. Tambay	Ford-DFV M26-DFV M26/5	8	1min 21.36sec 23/25	1min 20.14sec 14/26	1min 20.74sec 25/26	20-26	6/10		**6th**
	B. Lunger (Lark/Ligget Group)	Ford-DFV M23-DFV M23/6	30	1min 21.33sec 22/25	1min 21.38sec 25/26	1min 20.39sec 21/26	24-26	8/10		**8th**
	B. Giacomelli	Ford-DFV M26-DFV M26/7	33	1min 22.15sec 24/25	1min 20.91sec 23/26	1min 19.79sec 15/26	16-26	7/10		**7th**
	T. Trimmer (Melchester Racing)	Ford-DFV M23-DFV M23/14	40	1min 21.99sec 28/29	1min 22.03sec 28/30	1min 21.41sec 29/30	Did not qualify			
GERMAN Hockenheim-ring 30.7.78	J. Hunt	Ford-DFV M26-DFV M26/3	7	1min 54.28sec 7/23	1min 53.76sec 5/23	1min 53.54sec 6/22	8-24		Lp 34 Disqualified – taking shortcut to pits	**4th** / **9th**
	P. Tambay	Ford-DFV M26-DFV M26/5	8	1min 54.55sec 8/23	1min 54.71sec 11/23	1min 54.04sec 11/22	11-24		Lp 16 Accident Puncture	
AUSTRIAN Österreichring 13.8.78	J. Hunt	Ford-DFV M26-DFV M26/3	7	1min 39.10sec 6/25	1min 39.91sec 13/25	1min 40.84sec 8/24	8-26		Lp 1 (of restart) Accident	**5th**
	P. Tambay	Ford-DFV M26-DFV M26/5	8	1min 39.59sec 12/25	1min 39.62sec 10/25	1min 48.72sec 21/24	13-26		Lp 34 (of restart) Spun off	**7th**

Race	Driver	Car	No.							
	N. Piquet (BS Fabrications)	Ford-DFV M23-DFV M23/11	29	1min 41.15sec 17/25	1min 42.20sec 22/25		19-26		Lp 5 (in first race) Accident	**8th**
	B. Lunger (Ligget/BS Fabric)	Ford-DFV M26-DFV M26/6	30	1min 40.80sec 15/25	1min 41.11sec 16/25	1min 44.18sec 20/24	18-26	8/9		
	B. Giacomelli	Ford-DFV M26-DFV M26/7	33							
DUTCH Zandvoort 27.8.78	J. Hunt	Ford-DFV M26-DFV M26/3	7	1min 18.46sec 8/25	1min 18.28sec 8/25	1min 17.69sec 6/25	7-28	10/12		**9th**
	P. Tambay	Ford-DFV M26-DFV M26/5	8	1min 18.71sec 12/25	1min 19.10sec 14/25	1min 18.50sec 11/25	14-28	9/12		**9th**
	N. Piquet (BS Fabrications)	Ford-DFV M23-DFV M23/11	29	1min 20.64sec 21/25	1min 20.65sec 21/25	1min 20.64sec 27/25	27-28		Lp 16 Drive shaft	**16th**
	B. Lunger (Ligget/BS Fabric)	Ford-DFV M26-DFV M26/6	30	1min 20.94sec 23/25	1min 21.24sec 24/25	1min 20.03sec 17/25	26-28		Lp 35 Engine	**15th**
	B. Giacomelli	Ford-DFV M26-DFV M26/7	33	1min 19.83sec 17/25	1min 20.04sec 17/25	1min 20.16sec 19/25	19-28		Lp 60 Spun and stalled	**12th**
ITALIAN Monza 10.9.78	J. Hunt	Ford-DFV M26-DFV M26/1	7	1min 39.44sec 11/24	1min 39.66sec 7/24	1min 38.94sec 9/24	10-24		Lp 49 Distributor	**12th**
	P. Tambay	Ford-DFV M26-DFV M26/3	8	1min 40.24sec 16/24	1min 41.20sec 19/24	1min 40.16sec 17/24	19-24	5/14		**5th**
	N. Piquet (BS Fabrications)	Ford-DFV M23-DFV M23/11	29	1min 40.85sec 20/24	1min 41.55sec 22/24	1min 41.08sec 24/24	24-24	9/14		**9th**
	B. Lunger (Ligget/BS Fabric)	Ford-DFV M26-DFV M26/6	30	1min 52.16sec 24/24	1min 44.29sec 23/24	1min 40.30sec 20/24	21-24	Did not take part in restart		
	B. Giacomelli	Ford-DFV M26-DFV M26/7	33	1min 40.72sec 19/24	1min 41.48sec 21/24	1min 40.20sec 18/24	20-24	14/14		
USA Watkins Glen 1.10.78	J. Hunt	Ford-DFV M26-DFV M26/3	7	1min 40.32sec 6/26	1min 40.14sec 7/26	1min 39.99sec 3/25	6-26	7/16		**5th**
	P. Tambay	Ford-DFV M26-DFV M26/5	8	1min 41.97sec 14/20	1min 42.81sec 21/26	1min 42.04sec 15/25	18-26	6/16		**5th**
CANADIAN Montreal 8.10.78	J. Hunt	Ford-DFV M26-DFV M26/3	7	2min 11.60sec 18/22	2min 3.35sec 14/22	1min 40.97sec 11/22	19-22		Lp 51 Accident Spun off	**9th**
	P. Tambay	Ford-DFV M26-DFV M26/5	8	2min 9.03sec 11/22	2min 2.68sec 12/22	1min 40.67sec 17/22	17-22	8/12		**8th**

★ Some races ran four practices. A driver's best three results are counted.

again, and the heroic side of his driving flowered in maintaining this. This inspired piece of driving tends to wane when, despite giving everything, one cannot hope to live with the front runners, whose cars are much faster. Mid-grid placings do not generate the same enthusiasm, however professional one might claim to be, and Hunt's driving did seem to fade a little.

There were other problems though. Because of the rivalry with Michelin, softer qualifying tyres were being used, which allowed any driver to do a fast lap. This eroded the natural driving advantage of James's sheer speed − soft tyres being another limiting factor on driving skill. Another reason why McLaren were falling behind other teams with conventional cars was due to the engine. Nicholson-McLaren engines had lost their advantage and were no better than those provided off-the-shelf by Cosworth. Thus any small advantage associated with building one's own engines had been lost.

The M26 as a front-running car also needs to be put into perspective. At the Belgian Grand Prix in 1977, James Hunt had noted that the Lotus 78 had 'fantastic' front-end grip, this being its major advantage. A year later Andretti claimed that the main problem with the Lotus

79 was that its front-end grip was 'no better than a 78', but that rear-end grip was 'fantastic'. This illustrates just how far the M26 had fallen behind, by mid-1978, and perhaps offers a reason for Hunt's falling off in effort towards the end of the season.

McLaren had a new 'Lotus eater' ready for testing by late October. It would be an insult to Chapman to describe it as a Lotus copy, since the M28 was a fat, ugly, overweight car, totally unlike the graceful 79. Coppuck utilized the maximum dimensions permissible to create a large underbody area for ground effects. It had an aluminium honeycomb monocoque, but was really a conventional car, with side tunnels. At least it looked less like a Lotus than some of the

Gordon Coppuck's M28 'Lotus eater', driven by the luckless John Watson, during winter testing. The sheer bulk of the car makes it look as though it has indeed eaten a Lotus for breakfast.

other cars, and in winter testing it showed an improvement on the 1978 times.

There had been quite a merry-go-round among the drivers, as Reutemann left Ferrari to join Lotus, Scheckter joined Ferrari, Hunt took his place at Wolf, and John Watson joined Mclaren, being replaced at Brabham by McLaren B team occasional driver, Nelson Piquet. Piquet had completed a successful season in British Formula 3, and had the distinction of driving the last M23 in a Grand Prix, in Italy, five-and-a-half years after the car had made its debut.

Of the rivals, most trod the ground effects path. Ligier, Williams and Renault all succumbed to FOCA pressures and became two-car teams, with Depailler joining Ligier, Jarier going to Tyrrell, Regazzoni landing at Williams, and René Arnoux being recruited by Renault. Ligier, with their JS11 car, was the most radically changed team, the Matra V12 engine being replaced by the Cosworth unit – and what a transformation this was.

BACK TO SQUARE ONE

In South America, at both the Argentinian and Brazilian Grands Prix, Laffite took the pole, a second ahead of team-mate Depailler in second place in each case, and won both races. Lotus were competitive, but all was not well at McLaren. In Argentina John Watson was blamed by the organizers for a start-line crash, and fined £3,000 payable within two days, or he would not be allowed to start in Brazil; more on this later. Then, although he finished third in Argentina, he was 1.5 minutes behind Laffite, three miles at racing speeds!

The new M28 did not generate vast ground effects; it was slow in a straight line, its weight made acceleration leisurely and braking a lengthy operation. As to its cornering abilities, considerable structural flexing caused major traction problems, and both Tambay and Watson were scrabbling around trying to find grip.

Mid-grid was the best they could achieve in Brazil, along with Lauda, Hunt, and Fittipaldi, which made one think a bit.

Over the winter Jean-Marie Balestre had been elected President of the CSI (as a driver at that time, I do not remember being given a chance to 'elect' him), and this body in turn became FISA, charged by the FIA, the world governing body, to run Grand Prix racing. Balestre was determined to wrest control of the sport from FOCA, and a political battle was about to ensue. John Watson was the first victim of this, and FOCA paid his fine to enable him to race in Brazil.

Before the South African Grand Prix, FOCA offered the FIA an olive branch to work with FISA for the good of the sport, which included getting as much money as possible. This was rejected by the FIA, who reiterated that FISA were to run, and control, Grand Prix. Balestre himself, both unreasonably and unethically, wanted to control the finances of the sport and so, as with World War I, Grand Prix drifted into a conflict nobody wanted, and the trenches were dug. The very fact that the racing totally overshadowed the political ructions shows that a marvellous season was in store; and as far as this book is concerned, it was a pity that McLaren hardly featured in it, competitively.

The South African Grand Prix heralded the debut of the new Ferrari 312-T4, and the team swept to a comfortable 1–2 with Villeneuve leading home Scheckter. Watson retired with ignition problems, while Tambay came in tenth, three laps adrift.

Long Beach saw politics to the fore again. Villeneuve, who claimed the pole, three seconds faster than either McLaren, was fined £3,000 for overstepping the start-line, the cars having to go round for another lap. This did not prevent him from winning again, his talent benefitting from experience. McLaren's M28 was undergoing a variety of changes, none of which offered more than a little glimmer of hope at best, and the cars struggled throughout.

Watson retired from the Race of Champions

155

John Watson

Ulsterman John Watson was one of the most genuinely well liked and popular racing drivers of his era. Unfortunately, it often seemed as though the Fates had dealt him more than a rough hand.

In his early days, Watson proved to be a fast driver who, given the right car, could compete with anyone. This changed little throughout his career, even when he became an established front runner. He recorded his first victory, driving for the Penske team, in Austria 1976, and proved a strong opponent of Hunt's in several races during the latter half of the season.

When Penske pulled out, Watson moved on to Brabham and seemed certain to win a race, on several occasions, only for it to be snatched from him. Niki Lauda joined him for 1978, and with such a strong driver line-up and Lauda's undoubted car-sorting skills, much was expected from Brabham. However, 1978 was the last of the Lotus team's great years; Brabham were left behind with everyone else, and John did not record a victory.

Following the death of Ronnie Peterson, Watson was signed by McLaren for 1979. He had expected to race for one of the top teams in Grand Prix, and yet ill-luck caught him out again. The M28 car was a disaster, and the hasty replacement, the M29, little better. Watson struggled for two seasons along with Tambay, and then Prost, picking up places on driving skill alone.

When McLaren International was formed at the end of 1980, Alain Prost was to be retained, but sensibly at the time, he went off to Renault. Watson remained, and with the MP4 finally picked up his second victory, at the British Grand Prix, to put himself firmly back in the public eye. For 1982, Niki Lauda joined McLaren, and once again became John's team-mate. John Watson was never overawed by Lauda the driver, but there was much more in Lauda's armoury than driving ability. He was able to assist in the development of the MP4, and later the Tag/Porsche engine, though Watson's ability as a test driver has always been vastly underrated by the press, and much appreciated by his various teams. Then, at the end of 1983, misfortune struck again. Prost suddenly came on to the driver market, and Watson's contract expired at the end of the year, whereas Lauda still had a year to run. Prost was re-signed and that was it for John, except for one final race in 1985.

Lotus briefly enticed, then rejected, Watson at that time, and Toleman looked to be giving him a drive for 1985. This never materialized, and there were more than a few suggestions that Toleman, facing tyre supply problems, set this up as an underhand financial enticement, unbeknown to John.

Since that unhappy episode, Watson has raced sports cars, his best season being 1987 when he won three races driving for Jaguar. He raced in this category for Toyota in 1990, showing he still has all his ability, though mechanical unreliability let him down. Then at the end of 1990, he test drove the new Jordan Racing Grand Prix car at Silverstone, his eyes lighting up at the thought of being back behind the wheel of a beloved Grand Prix car again. Most of his time is now devoted to his John Watson Performance Driving Centre, based at Silverstone, where you can now book to be given a taste of what real driving is all about.

John Watson was very much an 'old style' racer, able to 'drive around' a problem and stay competitive. That, in three seasons as his team-mate, he was never overawed by Lauda, amply puts the Ulsterman's driving ability into perspective. If Lauda was able to sort his car a little better, that was no disgrace to Watson, as few other drivers could match the Austrian in this respect. However, John's abilities at this were far, far better than has been portrayed, as anyone who has worked with him will confirm.

at Brands Hatch, where Villeneuve notched up a hat trick of wins, and the M28 appeared in B form for the Spanish Grand Prix. The car was 50lb (23kg) lighter, 5in (127mm) shorter and featured many structural and suspension modifications. There was only one such car available, for John Watson. Lotus gave their sleek-looking 80 its debut, and Williams had two FWO7s,

one for Jones and one for Regazzoni. Neither of these were an immediate success, unlike the Ferrari, but nor were they three seconds adrift of the front-row Ligiers, like both McLarens. The race was little different from the South African Grand Prix either, Depailler's winning Ligier passing Tambay three times, as the latter crawled home thirteenth. Meanwhile, John

Despite its size and weight, the M28 was too flexible to cope with the downforce it generated. John Watson had one hell of a time trying to wrestle the car through races, let alone contest the lead with it. Here he practises for the Spanish Grand Prix, finally making eighteenth place on the grid, and has Jarier in his Tyrrell following.

Watson was running sixteenth when his engine expired. There was no apparent light at the end of the dark McLaren tunnel.

Trouble brewed again in the real battle of Grand Prix in 1979 – that between FISA and FOCA – before the Belgian Grand Prix, but sadly our brief is to concentrate on the trivia of the actual racing. While testing tyres before the meeting, John had destroyed his M28/B, and so another car was built up. It did not seem to help, as Watson still qualified over three seconds slower than the front-row Ligiers, while poor Patrick, back in an M26, failed to make the grid. Even Giacomelli in the new Alfa Romeo 177 was in front of Watson.

The race was a real humdinger, starting with Villeneuve getting into a minor kerfuffle on lap 1 and having to visit the pits. This presaged a classic drive back through the field to third place, which was cruelly snatched from him as he ran out of fuel on the last lap, finally coming seventh. Jones led most of the first forty laps, only to retire, followed by a succession of other drivers, with Scheckter running out the winner. This race also featured James Hunt in his best race to date in the not particularly competitive Wolf. He was in fourth place, really flying, and catching Scheckter rapidly, when he spun off on lap 41. Though not his last race, it was the last time Hunt featured on the leaders' board. Way behind all this, Watson struggled on gamely to finish in a lucky sixth place, an improved 1 minute 6 seconds adrift.

At Monaco, John had the M28/C which featured a revised body, sidepods and inboard front suspension. Patrick had an M28/B and, at this least favourite circuit for McLaren, failed to qualify again. Watson was nearer the back of the field than the front, but through persistency and retirements he finished fourth, and only 40 seconds behind the victorious Scheckter. By that time, this represented a distinct improvement. Regazzoni was second in the new Williams, but although Reutemann finished third, he did so in the old Lotus 79, the new 80 going much the same way as McLaren's M28.

All was not despondency in the McLaren team at this time, as a replacement for the M28 was on the drawing boards. This was based more on the Williams FW07 than on the Lotus, and as the former was showing race winning potential, there was hope in the team that their fortunes would soon change. For the French Grand Prix, however, John and Patrick were still in M28/Cs. Both qualified towards the wrong end of the grid and neither featured strongly in the race, but the race itself was worth travelling a long way to see.

Lotus were steadily 'doing a McLaren', slipping down the grid, and Tyrrell had not featured prominently so far; the same being true of Brabham. After an early season spurt, Ligier were being caught and had just lost Depailler, after a hang-gliding accident. He was replaced by Jackie Ickx; solid and reliable, rather than a genuine front runner anymore. Ferrari, with four victories shared equally between team leader Scheckter and the flying Villeneuve, were well to the fore, and Williams were coming along nicely. Perfectly timed for their home race, Renault were truly competitive with their turbo-engined car, without the advantage of height above sea level. The season, which was looking so promising, was about to 'deliver' in unforgettable fashion.

The Renaults held the front row, with the Ferraris and Brabhams taking the next four places. When was the last time that a Cosworth-engined car did not feature so high up the grid? Villeneuve did one of his flying starts, which were fast becoming a speciality, to lead the two Renaults. He steadily pulled away from the field, but there was to be no denying Jabouille, who took over the lead to record an historic

victory, in front of an ecstatic home crowd. With only a couple of laps to go Arnoux, in the second Renault, came up behind Villeneuve and passed the Ferrari; an emphatic Renault 1–2 looked on the cards, but we were about to witness the racing spirit of the Canadian driver.

The two enthusiastic fighters seemed unaware of the 1970s tradition of racing becoming more like a pensioners' club, and their ensuing performance made people's hair stand on end. At the end of the long straight, they entered the twisty section side by side. Banging wheels continually, first one then the other got his nose in front, each succeeding corner seeing the two pixilated drivers more determined than ever. These were not your local stock cars up to their tricks, but racing cars going at about four times that speed, and one could only marvel at the skill being exhibited. Inevitably, one slid a little wide at a corner, and Villeneuve nipped through the gap to win by the 'comfortable' margin of nearly a quarter of a second. It was fantastic racing, through some 'old women' were muttering words such as: 'dangerous . . . irresponsible . . . punishment . . .'; I suspect there was a good deal of jealousy about.

Not before time as far as McLaren were concerned, the M29 made its debut at the British Grand Prix, in John's hands. The M29 looked like the Ligier/Williams/Lotus 79 cars, and weighed 125lb (57kg) less than its ugly sister. Official practice showed up the difference between the two cars, with John seventh on the grid and Patrick eighteenth. The race was a straight fight between the Williams and Renault teams, with both leading drivers retiring, leaving good old Regazzoni to record the first ever victory for Frank Williams, after ten long years of trying. Watson came in a popular fourth, in front of Scheckter. He was still lapped by the leaders, but he was back in the points again.

For the German Grand Prix Lotus were even further back on the grid than were McLaren, with Patrick Tambay now in an M29. Having tasted victory, the Williams team wanted more and Jones swept home to lead an emphatic 1–2

Sensibly, rather than throw more money down the drain, McLaren built the M29 as a Williams/
Lotus copy, stop-gap car. It was far better than the M28, but still not a front runner. John
Watson practises at Silverstone for the British Grand Prix debut for the new car.

During the British Grand Prix, John Watson got the M29 going well, and here he leads Keke
Rosberg's Wolf, en route to a confidence-boosting fourth place.

for them, after overcoming the early challenge of Renault. Watson came fifth, still over 1.5 minutes behind. The M29 may have looked like a Williams, but it was not performing like one.

Austria saw little change, with Renault and Williams at the front and Lauda and Villeneuve among them; both McLarens were 2.5 seconds adrift, nearer the back than the front. Jones got ahead of the Renault at the start, but from the third row a red streak of lightning burst through to take the lead; it could only have been Villeneuve. Jones dislodged the Ferrari on lap 3 to lead it home, and this was only the appetizer for things to come.

The McLarens were mid-grid cannon fodder in Holland; both suffered an engine misfire in the race, both retired with engine problems and, no doubt, both drivers were grateful for an early bath. Were this book not about McLaren, neither would have warranted a mention, since all the major events were happening out of their sight, at the front of the grid. Williams, Renault and Ferrari cars made up the front three rows, though a six-way dice was out of the question, as Arnoux and Regazzoni eliminated each other in a start-line fracas, which reduced the innocent Scheckter to 'tail-end Charlie'. This left Jones leading Villeneuve until lap 11, when the Ferrari went through. Villeneuve drew away for a while, demonstrating his maturity, but into the second half of the race Jones was stalking the Ferrari once again.

On lap 47 Villeneuve spun right in front of Jones and displayed his mastery by keeping the car going; while the Australian demonstrated his skill by not hitting the pirouetting Ferrari, waiting for a gap, and going through – no fuss, no mess, just two fine drivers hard at it. Villeneuve had a slow puncture in a rear tyre, but thought the change in handling was due to the tyres going 'off'. There was no holding him, and he set off after the Williams as fast as ever. James Hunt may have retired, but here was his spiritual replacement.

Past the pits at 180mph shot Villeneuve when a loud bang resounded: the rear tyre had had enough. Another display of the unique Villeneuve car control was on view. Going into the Tarzan hairpin on only three wheels, at a speed that does not bear thinking about, Villeneuve kept his wits about him in the wildly spinning car, so that when it stopped he was ready to get on his way again. He had to drive round the circuit to get to his pits, with the rubber flailing at the bodywork and suspension, and he was not hanging around either; Boudicca at full cry in her chariot could not have offered a more awe-inspiring sight. The rear suspension could not take the hammering and bits fell off *en route*, so that Villeneuve was left trailing round on two wheels, with a front one in the air, to retire. This gave plenty of ammunition for the old fuddy duddies to have a moan about, while Jones achieved a hat-trick of victories, with Scheckter coming a fighting second.

The Italian Grand Prix was, in many respects, similar to the Dutch affair. The front six cars were the same, and both McLarens were finding that suspension revisions only made matters worse. Their race was just as dismal: Patrick Tambay retired with an engine failure on lap 4, and John Watson ran off into the sand ten laps later. At the front, both Renaults (and Jones) retired, leaving Scheckter to lead Villeneuve home by fractions of a second, the Canadian sticking rigidly to team orders and not challenging Scheckter. Regazzoni was not going to let Ferrari have it all their own way, and with two laps to go he was 2 seconds behind, and closing fast. His final assault was spoiled when he ran short of fuel and had to back off.

It was a great result for all Italy: Scheckter had become the new World Champion; Ferrari had taken the Constructors' title; Villeneuve had thrilled the world, and the old favourite, Regazzoni, had come third. The cheering went on for many hours that night.

Before the Canadian Grand Prix there was a non-championship event at the Imola circuit, which Lauda won in the Brabham BT48, with Tambay light-years behind in an M28. Then in

Canada, the meeting looked as if it was to be overshadowed by other events. Lauda, after trying the new Cosworth-engined BT49, went back to his hotel and retired, as simple as that. He claimed a loss of motivation, and in all truth it had been a frustrating season with an unreliable, though occasionally fast, car, and young Piquet giving him a good run for his money.

Lauda received a lot of criticism for this, especially as the team had worked miracles to get the new car ready, but few of us have looked death straight between the eyes and come back for more, as he had done. Two good drivers had thus departed during the season, but with the emergence of Villeneuve, Jones, Arnoux and Piquet they were not going to be missed for long.

Jones and Villeneuve did not intend being upstaged by Lauda and sat on the front of the grid, while Piquet was fourth with the new Brabham. The two McLarens were in what was fast becoming their accepted place, the rear end of the grid, making little progress.

It was Villeneuve who took the lead, and with Jones sitting back, giving the occasional jab just to let the Ferrari know he was still around, the crowd were happy, Then Jones moved closer, and another battle royal began. After a couple of dummy runs, Jones sat it out side by side with Villeneuve into the hairpin, neither driver giving an inch, nor doing anything silly. This time, Villeneuve came off second best, but he did not give up, chasing Jones all the way to the flag.

If the Australian had erred once, Villeneuve was ready to take advantage, but Jones was a cool, tough, customer, probably the only one capable of resisting the Canadian at that time. Their respective team-mates finished well adrift, and Watson picked up the last point on offer, two laps down, having had to pit for more petrol.

A classic season drew to a close with the United States Grand Prix. Villeneuve astounded everyone with his car control during the soaking wet first practice, while Piquet got between

him and Jones after the dry second session. While Tambay was nearly last, Watson was nicely in mid-grid, which looked as if McLaren were making progress, until you realized that Watson was 3.5 seconds behind Jones!

The race started in the wet and Piquet, on dry tyres, ensured another Jones/Villeneuve affair, the Ferrari building an initial advantage. Then the rain stopped and Jones caught and passed Villeneuve. For once, there was little the Ferrari driver could do about it. Jones glided away while Villeneuve called at his pits for dry tyres. Following what was then a rapid pitstop of fully 20 seconds, Villeneuve re-entered the race without a hope of challenging Jones, but then Jones went for his tyre change. Off he set, little knowing that a rear wheel was not tightened properly. The wheel fell off, and that was that. Villeneuve won a race with a high rate of attrition, but even so Watson could only manage sixth place, lapped yet again.

What had been a terrific year for Grand Prix racing, with even the posturing in the political arena remaining a distant sideshow, was another calamitous one for McLaren, and they were not out of the woods yet. After all the optimism of a new car/new driver line-up, the results were meagre in the extreme: seventh place in the Constructors' Championship, 98 points behind Ferrari; John Watson ninth in the Drivers' Championship, while Patrick Tambay did not even achieve a single points' finish. The M28 'Lotus eater', which by its sheer size looked as though it had actually swallowed a Lotus, was a disaster, and the M29 'Williams copy' (though 'reject' might have been more accurate) was no panacea. No wonder the team members felt somewhat bewildered by events.

This lack of competitiveness had a dramatic effect on the drivers. John Watson, never known as a great one for setting up a car, but an undoubted fast driver, felt his confidence shaken after a year of grappling with cars which nobody seemed to understand. Patrick Tambay, a smooth, cultured driver with talent to spare, looked almost impotent at times. His confi-

161

Grand Prix Results 1979

GRAND PRIX	DRIVER	CAR	NO	1ST PRACTICE Time/Posn	2ND PRACTICE Time/Posn	3RD PRACTICE Time/Posn	FINAL GRID POSN	FINAL PLACING	RETIRED CAUSE OF	HIGHEST POSN IN RACE
ARGENTINIAN Buenos Aires 21.1.79	J. Watson	Ford-DFV M28/2	7	1min 46.49sec 5/26	1min 46.73sec 6/25	1min 45.76sec 3/24	6–24	3/11		2nd
	P. Tambay	Ford-DFV M28/1	8	1min 48.34sec 14/26	1min 47.79sec 8/25	1min 46.56sec 8/24	9–24			
BRAZILIAN Interlagos 30.1.79	J. Watson	Ford-DFV M28/2	7	2min 28.66sec 12/24	2min 29.35sec 15/23	2min 27.82sec 10/25	14–23	8/15		11th
	P. Tambay	Ford-DFV M26/5	8			2min 29.39sec 14/25	17–23		Lp 7 Accident	3rd
SOUTH AFRICAN Kyalami 3.3.79	J. Watson	Ford-DFV M28/2	7	1min 14.44sec 12/26	1min 16.10sec 11/23	1min 14.55sec 14/25	14–24		Lp 61 Ignition	11th
	P. Tambay	Ford-DFV M28/1	8	1min 14.58sec 14/26	1min 15.39sec 9/23	1min 16.22sec 22/25	18–24	10/13		3rd
USA (West) Long Beach 8.4.79	J. Watson	Ford-DFV M28/2	7	1min 23.73sec 23/25	1min 21.30sec 18/25		18–24		Lp 62 Injection unit	12th
	P. Tambay	Ford-DFV M28/3	8	1min 22.57sec 19/25	1min 21.41sec 19/25		19–24		Lp 1 Accident	
SPANISH Jarama 29.4.79	J. Watson	Ford-DFV M28/1	7	1min 17/11sec 12/26	1min 17.60sec 20/26		18–24		Lp 21 Engine	14th
	P. Tambay	Ford-DFV M28/3	8	1min 18.60sec 16/26	1min 17.45sec 19/26		20–24	13/14		13th
BELGIAN Zolder 13.5.79	J. Watson	Ford-DFV M28/2	7	1min 26.60sec 13/28	1min 24.47sec 19/28		19–24	6/11		6th
	P. Tambay	Ford-DFV M28/7	8	1min 29.57sec 26/28	1min 25.69sec 26/28		Did not qualify			
MONACO Monte Carlo 27.5.79	J. Watson	Ford-DFV M28/3	7	1min 28.89sec 10/24	1min 28.23sec 9/24		14–20	4/6		4th
	P. Tambay	Ford-DFV M28/2	8	1min 30.68sec 21/24	1min 29.53sec 22/24		Did not qualify			
FRENCH Dijon-Prenois 1.7.79	J. Watson	Ford-DFV M28/3	7	1min 09.97sec 12/27	1min 11.56sec 17/27	1min 11.04sec 19/27	18–24	11/18		11th
	P. Tambay	Ford-DFV M28/2	8	1min 11.10sec 17/27	1min 10.92sec 15/23	1min 11.40sec 22/27	20–24	10/18		10th
BRITISH Silverstone 14.7.79	J. Watson	Ford-DFV M29/1	7	1min 14.65sec 9/26	1min 13.57sec 6/26		7–24	4/14		4th
	P. Tambay	Ford-DFV M28/2	8	1min 16.23sec 19/26	1min 15.69sec 16/26		18–24	7/14		7th
GERMAN Hockenheim-ring 29.7.79	J. Watson	Ford-DFV M29/1	7	1min 51.17sec 11/25	1min 50.86sec 11/25		12–24	5/12		5th
	P. Tambay	Ford-DFV M29/2	8	1min 52.93sec 15/25	1min 51.47sec 16/25		15–24		Lp 30 Broken rear suspension	9th
AUSTRIAN Österreichring 12.8.79	J. Watson	Ford-DFV M29/1	7	1min 37.16sec 10/26	1min 39.80sec 23/26		16–24	9/10		9th
	P. Tambay	Ford-DFV M29/2	8	1min 37.87sec 14/26	1min 36.72sec 14/26		14–24	10/10		10th
DUTCH Zandvoort 26.8.79	J. Watson	Ford-DFV M29/3	7	1min 21.80sec 22/26	1min 17.75sec 11/25		12–24		Lp 22 Engine	6th
	P. Tambay	Ford-DFV M29/2	8	1min 21.89sec 23/26	1min 18.15sec 14/25		14–24		Lp 6 Engine	10th

Race	Driver	Car	No						Pos
ITALIAN Monza 9.9.79	J. Watson	Ford-DFV M29/3	7	1min 38.77sec 17/27	1min 38.09sec 19/28	19-24		Lp 13 Accident	**9th**
	P. Tambay	Ford-DFV M29/2	8	1min 37.32sec 11/27	1min 37.23sec 14/28	14-24		Lp 3 Engine	**13th**
CANADIAN Montreal 30.9.79	J. Watson	Ford-DFV M29/3	7	1min 35.56sec 27/27	1min 33.36sec 16/28	17-24	7/10		**7th**
	P. Tambay	Ford-DFV M29/2	8	1min 33.60sec 11/27	1min 34.40sec 22/28	20-24		Lp 19 Engine	**13th**
USA Watkins Glen 7.10.79	J. Watson	Ford-DFV M29/3	7		1min 39.23sec 13/30	13-24	6/7		**6th**
	P. Tambay	Ford-DFV M29/2	8		1min 40.73sec 22/30	22-24		Lp 20 Engine	**11th**

dence had its foundations whipped away, and he barely looked the potential race winner he ought to have been. Patrick was thus dispensed with, to be replaced by young French Formula 3 Champion, Alain Prost. How long would it take McLaren to undermine him?

Considering the time it had taken from the decision to abandon the M28, to building the first M29, the latter car had not done too badly. McLaren were no longer front runners, but progress was being made, albeit slowly, and Gordon Coppuck, John Baldwin and Teddy Mayer were working flat out to improve the car; they felt they were now heading in the right direction. As an aside to this, Marlboro, McLaren's main sponsors, were concerned at their decline and suggested a link-up with the Project Four Formula 2 team they also sponsored. Teddy Mayer managed to pursuade them, however, that McLaren were capable of doing the job.

McLaren were not struggling in the dark alone. Lotus, the previous seasons' standard setters, were in a similar position. Chapman may have begun the ground effects revolution but, as with the Russian proletariat in 1917, events soon overtook him. There were many similarities to the introduction of wings a decade before, in that it was all a bit of a black art. Few people really seemed to understand *exactly* what they were doing, and why, which probably explains why Ligier fell from grace while Williams rose in stature. Tyrrell never really got to grips

with the problem all season, and Brabham only offered a challenge in short-lived bursts. How the mighty had fallen!

Of the new teams, Alfa Romeo made quiet progress, while Arrows had taken a step or two backwards. Renault – not really too concerned with aerodynamic wizardry, more with their turbo engine – become a real force in the second half of the season. The lack of consistent front-running performances from all these teams left the door open for Ferrari to deservedly take both Championships. This was thanks to a combination of power and reliability from the cars, and consistency and sheer brilliance from the drivers. There was much to look foward to, and the prospect of Villeneuve, Jones, Piquet and Arnoux battling away held much expectation in store. Hunt and Lauda, who were they?

RING OUT THE OLD, RING IN THE NEW

The world of Grand Prix is seldom inactive, and if you sit back and close your eyes for long, you will have missed something. In the annual drivers' lottery, new faces appeared in new places, though many could see which side their bread was buttered and chose to stay put. Others, such as Patrick Tambay, were cast aside to seek work in the lesser formulae wherever they could find it, but with the

163

retirement of Hunt and Lauda, the rate of attrition was relatively low.

Perhaps the most surprising change involved the release of Regazzoni by Williams, who returned to Ensign. Williams claimed that they wanted a number two who would back Jones for a Championship challenge, by claiming points off potential rivals. Regazzoni's win, two second places, and two thirds in the last nine races, was deemed insufficient, and Reutemann, unhappy at Lotus, was signed as a replacement. Reutemann, an undoubted winner, but not always the most highly motivated of drivers, was in the middle of a contractual wrangle with Lotus, who wanted de Angelis as his replacement, from a reluctant Shadow team. All looked to be at an impasse, but Frank Williams made his move and presumably he knew best, though it was unfortunate for Regazzoni.

There were, of course, other driver changes, but the move of Depailler to Alfa Romeo (his place at Ligier being taken by Pironi, and Irishman Derek Daly replacing the latter at Tyrrell) was the most significant. Rosberg, who replaced Hunt in the Wolf, joined Fittipaldi when Walter Wolf sold up his team, lock, stock and barrel to the Brazilian outfit. Finally an Italian team, Osella, arrived on the scene, with young Eddie Cheever as their driver.

The two South American races, as ever, seemed to be a carry-over from the previous season, with Jones winning in Argentina and Arnoux opening his account in Brazil. New McLaren driver Alain Prost established himself in mid-grid, while in Brazil John Watson was fully 6 seconds behind Jabouille on the pole; already Alain's showing was better than his supposed team leader! While neither McLaren featured in either race, except as also-rans, Villeneuve produced another mercurial start in Brazil and forced his Ferrari inbetween Jabouille and Pironi to briefly lead the race, before being forced back with handling problems. Prost claimed distant points finishes in both races, while the biggest surprise was de Angelis's second place, driving a Lotus, in Brazil.

As usual the South African Grand Prix saw the introduction of some new cars: Tyrrell with two 010s, ATS with a new D4, and McLaren with an M29/C for Prost, reflecting his newfound esteem. The M29/C had a new front suspension, revised bodywork and a greater rearward bias to the weight distribution. It had shown up reasonably well in testing, but at Kyalami the front suspension broke and Prost crashed heavily. For official practice Prost used an M29/B and, at nearly the same spot, the rear suspension broke and he hit a wall, this time injuring his wrist. He was out of the race and the one following! With Watson's poor grid position he had no chance, and the turbo Renaults overwhelmed everyone. Arnoux duly won and Watson was lapped twice, in a soul-destroying race.

At Long Beach for the United States Grand Prix (West), Stephen South, a promising British driver who had undertaken quite a bit of testing for McLaren, replaced Alain Prost. He failed to qualify, but Marlboro were at least back towards the front of the grid again. This was not thanks to John Watson, who was 3 seconds adrift of poleman Piquet, in twenty-first position, but Giacomelli in the Alfa Romeo team, sponsored by McLaren's backers, the Italian cars ominously wearing a very similar colour scheme.

There was a high rate of attrition in the race, and this helped Fittipaldi (who started last on the grid) and Watson to claim third and fourth places, though John was again lapped. The worst accident happened to Regazzoni who crashed heavily in his Ensign, seriously injuring his legs and spine. He was never to race again and, indeed, is virtually tied to a wheelchair.

The Williams, Ligiers, and Renaults held the front of the grid in Belgium with, depressingly, the Lotus, Tyrrell and fast-fading Ferrari teams holding the middle ground, the McLarens near the back, and Fittipaldi last of all again. The Grand Prix world had certainly been turned upside down.

Prior to the race, a little incident occurred which acted as a trigger to a near catastrophic

The year 1980 was best forgotten by all those involved with McLaren. There was never any let-up in effort though, typified by John Watson's drive through the rain at the Belgian Grand Prix, while contesting a mid-field position. The difficulties of following a car closely, in such conditions, are obvious from this picture.

explosion. Yes, our old friend politics had been simmering away nicely, and now the lid was blown off the pan. Fourteen drivers, some of their own volition, others egged on by their teams, failed to attend post-practice briefing. The steam did not rise immediately, but the delay was not long.

A few modifications to the brakes and suspension of the M29/Cs made little difference. Both Prost and Watson were way off the pace and neither finished. Pironi won his first race, with both Williams drivers showing up well.

Once again Monaco proved to be an unlucky circuit for McLaren, with Watson failing to qualify and being clearly unsettled, while Prost made a satisfactory tenth on the grid. Out at the front it was the usual Williams/Ligier/Piquet line-up, with Villeneuve up there as the wild card. The race got off to a spectacular start with Daly taking to the sky, as a means of overtaking on this very difficult circuit. Unfortunately, after leaping over several cars, he landed on his team-mate Jarier, and Prost was also eliminated in the ensuing *brouhaha*, leaving the Alfas as

Marlboro's representatives once again. Reutemann won from Laffite with a drive of measured brilliance, and former McLaren men Piquet, Mass, Villeneuve and Fittipaldi, took the other points positions, presumably glad they were no longer driving a McLaren car.

Spain was to be the venue for a titanic contest, one which certainly went down in the annals of motor racing, yet did not take place on the circuit. It was, of course, the battle of the year and featured those two contestants for the *control* of Grand Prix racing: FISA vs FOCA. Both sides claimed right to be on their side, yet events showed this to be more a rough house than an honourable duel. The events of the Belgian weigh-in now began to take on their real meaning. The fourteen 'naughty' drivers were all fined for not attending the briefing session; none of whom paid and so their licences were withdrawn. Though the drivers were probably little more than pawns in the whole incident, the reaction of FISA was that of the spoiled brat.

Anxious not to incur the wrath of the governing body, mainly because their motor racing involvement stretched beyond Grand Prix racing, the Ferrari, Renault and Alfa teams did not enter the Spanish Grand Prix. With the exception of Renault, this made little difference to the grid, and practice was as hard fought as usual. Prost suffered a nasty accident courtesy of another mechanical failure, and was lucky to escape serious injuries. He was not entirely happy with McLaren's famed reliability, which appeared to be deteriorating, along with the team's performance. However, he qualified seventh, with Watson twelfth, but neither finished the race. The race was won by Jones after Reutemann and Laffite, jousting for the lead, had crashed out on lap 36 while lapping de Vilotta. (Remember him, the cause of a practice accident involving James Hunt two years previously?) Later on, following the licence appeals hearing, FISA declared the race 'illegal', and Championship points were not awarded. Jones still won a Grand Prix though, whatever the bureaucrats had to say later.

Naturally, all sorts of fun and games ensued, but the fines were eventually paid, and the threatened boycott of the French Grand Prix did not take place. The front of the grid only featured the Renaults from the 'FISA' teams, but Prost was seventh, showing real progress at only 2 seconds down, while Watson was an encouraging twelfth. Lotus and Tyrrell still occupied mid-grid positions, but Ferrari had now sunk beyond them almost out of sight. Villeneuve, as ever, had other ideas and by lap 2 had jumped from seventeenth to eighth, as only he could, but there progress was halted.

This was only the hors-d'oeuvre for the main course, which was a delicious helping of Jones, Pironi, Laffite, Piquet and Arnoux battling away for the lead in spirited fashion. Whatever venom the politicians might spew out was kept well in its place by the sight of these fine racing drivers giving their all. Prost and Watson would undoubtedly have loved to be involved with that scrap as well, but the M29s were not up to it, and Alain retired, disappointed, while John finished a lapped seventh.

Ligier were out to avenge Jones's victory in France and were really on song at Brands Hatch, with both cars on the front row of the grid. Pironi's pole position time was over 5 seconds faster than Peterson's of 1978, which itself was outstanding. Such was the increase in speeds created by the ground effects revolution that Peterson would not even have qualified for the 1980 race. This puts McLaren's steady drift down the grid into perspective, because Prost was seventh-fastest, over 1.5 seconds slower than Pironi, with a time far faster than any M26 could have managed. McLaren were going backwards in relation to everyone else, while still improving markedly on what they had done before.

Both M29/Cs featured a smoother underside, the benefit of work done by Robin Herd of March, and strengthened rear suspension, particularly welcomed by Alain Prost. Both McLarens ran around in mid-field, and while Watson retired with an engine failure, Prost

166

demonstrated his potential with a smooth drive into sixth position. At the front, both Ligiers led Jones and Piquet, and looked devastatingly fast through the corners. However, both eventually retired with tyre failures, leaving Jones to record another hat-trick of wins, and Williams their fourth win in a row. The reception from the crowd was nearly equal to that greeting Hunt's victory four years before, so popular was the hard-charging Aussie.

Driving changes were in the air at the German Grand Prix, following the death during pre-race testing of Patrick Depailler, while World Champion Jody Scheckter announced his retirement. He had clearly had enough of trailing around at the back of the field in his uncompetitive Ferrari while still giving his all. Even his promising team-mate, Villeneuve, had achieved little, despite never once letting up; this was one of Ferrari's worst years ever.

The grid had the familiar Williams/Renault/Ligier/Piquet look about it at the front, with both McLarens back in their more customary mid/rear-grid positions. Jabouille led Jones for over half of the race, until Jones took over and it looked like another win for the Australian driver. Then, with five laps to go, his front tyre deflated and he shot into the pits. Laffite went by to win from Reutemann, reversing the recent fortunes of the Ligier team, with Jones coming in third. Prost finished eleventh, but Watson had been running a good sixth when his engine failed on lap 40.

There was little change at the Austrian Grand Prix, a week later. The Renault, Williams, and Ligier drivers occupied the front of the grid, with Prost in mid-field and Watson near the back again. Prost was now regarded by all and sundry as the senior McLaren driver, and Watson looked either 'lost', or had given up, depending on your point of view. By Alain's own admission, he was better at setting the car up than John, and could therefore drive it faster, and Teddy Mayer suggested that John was not particularly good when it came to diagnosing a problem. Because of this, solutions were given

to the wrong problems, which left the team all at sea, John with a car that performed worse than that of his team-mates, and which led to a lack of confidence between driver and team alike. Yet changes were afoot, and were soon to make themselves known.

Watson again retired with an engine failure, and Prost ran consistently, though well behind the leaders, to finish seventh; nothing had changed. Out at the front, the Renaults led early on, though Arnoux later retired, leaving Jabouille to at last record another well deserved victory ahead of Jones. Another drive of note, which failed to last the distance, was that of Nigel Mansell on his Grand Prix debut, in a Lotus. He performed well enough, though few people would ever suspect the role he was to play in the McLaren story in the years to come, without ever driving for the team.

Then, for the Dutch Grand Prix, came the moment McLaren had been waiting for: the introduction of their new ground-effects car, Coppuck's M30. It was 50 per cent stiffer than the M29, and much improved all round, but was, in the words of Alain Prost, who had undertaken the development driving, 'dangerously fragile'. The M30 did not have a particularly auspicious debut either, with Prost back in eighteenth place on the grid, and Watson, in an M29, up in ninth, despite a very lucky escape after his brakes failed as he went into the Tarzan hairpin; Prost noted this.

Jones led from the Renaults but ran wide, damaging his car's skirts, necessitating a three-and-a-half-lap pitstop. This was the presage for a stirring, forceful drive through the field, without a realistic hope of gaining points, to finish eleventh – a shining example to all drivers. Thereafter, Piquet won at ease, while Watson, driving with more brio than for a long time, climbed up to eighth before an engine failure put him out once again. Prost meanwhile demonstrated his smooth driving abilities, and was rewarded with sixth place, despite the car being well off the pace.

Before the Italian Grand Prix, an even bigger

167

change was announced at McLaren. The old Team McLaren had ceased to exist as such, having merged with the Formula 2 outfit, Project Four, to form McLaren International. Project Four boss Ron Dennis became joint Managing Director with Teddy Mayer, and Gordon Coppuck was effectively sacked and replaced by John Barnard, also from Project Four.

It is quite clear that Marlboro, sponsors of both McLaren and Project Four, were the instigators of the merger, and they deserve a great deal of credit for their actions. After all, Marlboro only put vast sums of money into motor racing in order to promote the sales of their product. Despite the money they spread around all levels of motor sport, they are not benefactors. When the team they sponsor does not deliver the goods, it would be far easier for Marlboro to do the same as Camel did at the end of 1990, and take their backing to another team. Such was the money Marlboro put forward, they would not have been short of takers among the leading teams. Instead, they showed great loyalty, and did something positive. Perhaps it would have been difficult for McLaren to refuse the merger, but it went ahead and offered much promise for the future.

This promise did not manifest itself from the word go: for the Italian Grand Prix, at the Imola circuit and not Monza, John Watson was in mid-grid in the M29, while Alain Prost only just made last place, in the M30. At the front of the grid the Renault and Williams cars sat in place, with Piquet up there in his Brabham. Giacomelli had boosted local spirits with a fine fourth place, while Ferrari demonstrated their new 126 turbo engine and Alfa also announced that they had a new turbo V8 under development.

Once again the Renaults led, only to fall away, leaving Piquet to win comfortably and pose a serious threat to Jones in the Drivers' Championship. Watson ran a distant seventh, before going out with a suspension failure this time, and Prost was a well-adrift seventh once more.

John Barnard had begun to modify the M29 and M30 before the Canadian Grand Prix. Prost qualified twelfth, but Watson was really forcing his way back into the picture, in seventh place on the grid. The race was a real title contender between Piquet and Jones, and these two collided at the start, necessitating a re-run. Though Williams had already won the Constructors' title, Jones was clearly rattled by Piquet's late charge in the Drivers' Championship.

Jones led again, but Piquet took the lead on lap 2 and proceeded to pull away. It was exciting stuff, demanding all the attention of the crowd, but if you could drag your eyes away, at about one-third distance, you would have seen two Marlboro-sponsored cars running well. 'But both Alfas retired earlier on', you might have thought, then on close inspection you would realize that Watson was fourth, and Prost was battling it out with Reutemann and Laffite, not far behind. The Championship was settled on lap 24 when Piquet's engine failed, leaving Jones out in front of the race and heading the Championship, with Watson third and Prost closing in.

This was just like days of yore, only spoiled when Prost spun out with a suspension failure and Watson spun out of third place while lapping Mass, but managed to finish fourth. Unfortunately though, Jabouille's Renault had an awful accident, of such force that his legs were shattered and he was lucky to survive. Unbeknown to McLaren, this was to have important consequences for the newly formed team.

The final race, the United States Grand Prix at Watkins Glen, did indeed see a Marlboro-liveried car on the pole, but this time it really was an Alfa, driven by Giacomelli – the first time in twenty-nine years an Alfa had been placed so high. The drivers' title might have been decided, but there was still a race to win, and Piquet, Reutemann, Jones, and Arnoux, as ever, were out to do so. Watson qualified ninth, but Prost destroyed the sole M30 in a crash caused by another suspension failure. He was knocked out and damaged a wrist, tried to drive the next day but was not up to it, and did not race. In fact, his faith in the McLaren team had gone, and caused his eventual departure.

Giacomelli dominated the race while Jones, after sliding off the track when second and resuming twelfth, kept the event alive with a storming drive back to second place. Then the Alfa's engine cried enough, with Giacomelli well ahead, and Jones rounded off the season with his sixth win, or fifth if you follow the FISA results. Watson ran behind the leaders, still going well though, but a shock absorber failed, and he endured a lengthy pitstop and was not classified a finisher.

ASSESSMENT TIME

A season of disappointment, frustration, bewilderment, and finally realistic hope for the future, had come to an end for McLaren, but their plans did not go ahead as they wished. Prost was definitely being kept on as a driver, but Watson's position was far from secure. Teddy Mayer was not entirely convinced of the Ulsterman's efforts yet, unusually in motor racing, Alain spoke up in his team-mate's favour. He let it be known that he valued John's experience, which he had generously shared, despite being overshadowed by the young Frenchman. Prost's confidence in the team had been badly shaken, mainly as a result of the mechanical failures he had suffered, and he wanted to leave. Problems!

As for John Watson, he never felt that he was going to be dropped from the team, although we now know that if Alain had stayed with McLaren, he might well have been. But John was glad that the season was over. In two short years, Watson had gone from being the 'blue-eyed boy', to a virtual outcast, and was now on the way back into favour again. John makes this strange situation very clear:

'When I arrived at McLaren, Patrick Tambay was the established "golden boy", and was,

during 1979, relegated into oblivion. Then, in 1980, I too went the same way, and Alain became the favourite. For three-quarters of the season I was subjected to very unreasonable treatment by the team, then with Alain failing to perform with the M30, and saying it was "crap", suddenly I was back in favour again.'

McLaren were technically in a disarray and were clutching at straws. When Alain performed well, he was the bee's knees, when he became increasingly critical of the team, so the pendulum swung back towards John. It was a sign of desperation.

McLaren's three-year decline, which resulted in the formation of the McLaren International team, stemmed from the onset of ground effects. McLaren were a very practical, hugely experienced, mechanical engineering team, one of the very best, but ground effects demanded a totally different technological, theoretically based approach. McLaren were using an engineering solution to aerodynamic problems, and probably never grasped this fact. The more the design engineers failed to come to terms with the new problems, the more Teddy Mayer became involved in the cars, and he was not even a qualified engineer, though possessed immense experience.

There was no way out. The M28 flexed badly, and then put on too much weight to counter this. The M29, completed in such a short time, was never more than an interim car and could not be expected to compete with the Williams, Ligier, or Brabham cars, which had been fully developed. Though tested in the Lockheed wind-tunnel in Georgia, as was the M28, they used full-size cars, not scale models, and as a result the wrong set of results were obtained, and were interpreted wrongly; that engineering approach to an eaerodynamic problem!

John Watson felt that aerodynamics were the root-cause of the problem, but when Alain Prost came along and did better with the M29, so John's became very much a voice in the wil-

169

Grand Prix Results 1980

GRAND PRIX	DRIVER	CAR	NO	1ST PRACTICE Time/Posn	2ND PRACTICE Time/Posn	3RD PRACTICE Time/Posn	FINAL GRID POSN	FINAL PLACING	RETIRED CAUSE OF	HIGHEST POSN IN RACE
ARGENTINIAN Buenos Aires 13.1.80	J. Watson	Ford-DFV M29/2	7	1min 47.70sec 16/28	1min 48.06sec 15/28		18-24		Lp 5 Gearbox oil leak	12th
	A. Prost	Ford-DFV M29/1	8	1min 46.75sec 10/28	1min 46.81sec 8/28		11-24	6/7		6th
BRAZILIAN Interlagos 27.1.80	J. Watson	Ford-DFV M29/2B	7	2min 28.82sec 22/28	2min 27.29sec 20/25		23-24	11/16		9th
	A. Prost	Ford-DFV M29/1B	8	2min 24.95sec 13/28	2min 26.21sec 16/28		13-24	5/16		5th
SOUTH AFRICAN Kyalami 1.3.80	J. Watson	Ford-DFV M29/1B	7	1min 14.04sec 25/27	1min 13.61sec 22/26		21-24	11/13		11th
	A. Prost	Ford-DFV M29/3C	8	1min 13.76sec 21/27			Did not start, Crashed, injured wrist during practice			
USA (West) Long Beach 30.3.80	J. Watson	Ford-DFV M29/2C	7	1min 22.22sec 20/25	1min 20.87sec 18/24		22-24	4/10		4th
	S. South	Ford-DFV M29/4C	8	1min 24.90sec 25/25	1min 24.12sec 24/24		Did not qualify			
BELGIAN Zolder 4.5.80	J. Watson	Ford-DFV M29/2C	7	1min 22.57sec 19/25	1min 30.64sec 3/21		20-24		Lp 61 Running not classified	13th
	A. Prost	Ford-DFV M29/4C	8	1min 22.26sec 18/25	1min 31.01sec 6/21		19-24		Lp 29 Transmission	
MONACO Monte Carlo 18.5.80	J. Watson	Ford-DFV M29/2C	7	1min 48.11sec 9/27	1min 27.73sec 19/27		Did not qualify	9/20		
	A. Prost	Ford-DFV M29/4C	8	1min 49.78sec 19/27	1min 26.83sec 10/27				Lp 1 Accident	
SPANISH Jarama 1.6.80	J. Watson	Ford-DFV M29/2C	7	1min 14.58sec 9/21	1min 14.69sec 12/22		11-22		Lp 48 Accident	5th
	A. Prost	Ford-DFV M29/4C	8	1min 14.04sec 6/21	1min 13.63sec 3/22		5-22		Lp 5 Engine	13th
FRENCH Ricard-Castellet 29.6.80	J. Watson	Ford-DFV M29/2C	7	1min 41.63sec 11/22	1min 41.81sec 14/27		14-24	7/14		7th
	A. Prost	Ford-DFV M29/4C	8	1min 40.73sec 8/27	1min 40.63sec 7/27		8-24		Lp 6 Transmission	6th
BRITISH Brands Hatch 13.7.80	J. Watson	Ford-DFV M29/2C	7	1min 13.72sec 7/27	1min 13.92sec 13/27		11-24	8/13		7th
	A. Prost	Ford-DFV M29/4C	8	1min 12.76sec 5/27	1min 12.63sec 7/27		8-24	6/13		6th
GERMAN Hockenheim-ring 10.8.80	J. Watson	Ford-DFV M29/2C	7	2min 04.47sec 15/26	1min 49.26sec 20/26		19-24		Lp 39 Engine	6th
	A. Prost	Ford-DFV M29/5C	8	2min 04.57sec 14/26	1min 48.75sec 14/26		13-24	11/16		11th
AUSTRIAN Österreichring 17.8.80	J. Watson	Ford-DFV M29/3C	7	1min 35.56sec 11/25	1min 36.32sec 25/25		21-24		Lp 35 Engine failure	8th
	A. Prost	Ford-DFV M29/5C	8	1min 34.50sec 8/25	1min 34.35sec 12/25		12-24	7/16		

DUTCH Zandvoort 31.8.80	J. Watson	Ford-DFV M29/2	7	1min 23.49sec 28/28	1min 18.53sec 7/28	9-24		Lp 19 Engine	**7th**
	A. Prost	Ford-DFV M30/1	8	1min 19.07sec 13/28	1min 19.68sec 22/28	18-24	6/11		
ITALIAN Monza 14.9.80	J. Watson	Ford-DFV M29/2	7	1min 37.39sec 16/26	1min 36.45sec 15/20	14-24		Lp 21 Hub bearing failure	**6th**
	A. Prost	Ford-DFV M30/1	8	1min 37.28sec 15/26	1min 37.54sec 22/28	24-24	7/12		
CANADIAN Montreal 29.9.80	J. Watson	Ford-DFV M29/2	7	1min 31.88sec 4/25	1min 28.76sec 7/28	7-24	4/12	Lp 42 Front sump failure	**3rd**
	A. Prost	Ford-DFV M30/1	8	1min 33.99sec 10/27	1min 29.50sec	12-24			**4th**
USA Watkins Glen 5.10.80	J. Watson	Ford-DFV M29/2	7	1min 35.33sec 5/27	1min 35.20sec 6/24	9-24	12/13		**5th**
	A. Prost	Ford-DFV M30/1	8	1min 35.99sec 10/27		Did not start			

derness. It did not take long for Prost to be regarded as the number one driver, thus getting the better equipment and more attention. Even Prost was cross at the treatment meted out to Watson, and told the team as much. The team empathized more with Alain and his findings, because the latter tended to fit in more with their ideas, whereas John's seemed to come from fairyland.

Robin Herd's input, mid-season, into the underside of the car, using carbon fibre materials and radial, rather than angular, corners, improved performance, as did John Barnard's aerodynamic alterations for the North American races. John Watson's performances sud-denly improved, and there was some talk of him trying harder as it was 'contract renewal time'. These were great insults to the driver. He had always driven hard, but the car was much better than hitherto and, with Alain in the M30, John drove the latest M29 and was able to demonstrate the improvements. John Barnard was more in touch with Watson's way of thinking than either the outgoing Coppuck, or Teddy Mayer had been, and it showed; he was back.

Nevertheless, the wealthy Italian, Project Four Formula 2 driver, Andrea de Cesaris, was being lined up to join the Grand Prix team, when unexpected events took place.

CHAPTER 7

Born-Again Racers

History has a habit of bestowing labels on to specific timespans, ostensibly to aid identification. For example, we have the 'roaring twenties', or the 1978/79 British 'winter of discontent'. These are only very broad, sweeping generalizations at best; one would not find the twenties very 'roaring' if one were a coal miner, shipbuilder, farmworker, etc. It might, however, be pertinent to describe the 1980/81 close season as Grand Prix racing's own winter of discontent. Even with the benefit of a decade's breathing space, it is still very difficult to evaluate, or justify, the events which so nearly tore Grand Prix racing asunder.

We have earlier referred to Jean-Marie Balestre, the President of FISA, who was determined to wrest control of Grand Prix racing back from FOCA to the FIA, through its delegated body, FISA. Laudable though this may have been at the time, especially in view of the 'closed shop' mentality of certain FOCA luminaries, the loss of control by the FIA was a direct result of their ineptitude and unsuitability to govern Grand Prix racing. In their place, with the occasional muscle-flexing exercise to keep the FIA at bay, FOCA had put together a package guaranteeing full grids, close racing, television, undreamt of commercial opportunities, more races, and even improved the 'safety' aspects of the sport.

In short, FOCA provided a worldwide show of nine months' duration with a high entertainment level, which still encouraged technical innovation for the participating teams, and spin-offs for the motor trade in its widest sense. There were faults, of course, and it might have been time for a change of direction, but the route chosen by Balestre – a path, moreover, which gave more than enough evidence to accuse the man of seeking personal power – was not one of fair-minded consensus, but of bullheaded confrontation.

Let us keep one thing clear through all the mud that was thrown around, by all sides. The issue at stake was the *control* of Grand Prix racing. There seemed to be so many side isues that one could be forgiven for assuming that Grand Prix racing had entered into a fight for the sheer hell of it. Balestre, whose other FISA council members seemed to have abdicated any opinions they might have held, fired the first shots in the war by banning the sliding skirts on Grand Prix cars. To justify such a sweeping change, and one given at short notice, our old friend safety was resurrected. Cars were cornering so fast that spectators were in danger if a car came off the road. There was a physical limit as to how much a circuit could be altered to slow cars down yet still provide a worthwhile driving challenge, and keep safety levels constant for both drivers and spectators. Banning skirts was one way of cutting down the cornering speed of the cars, a way approved of by the FISA-courted teams of Renault, Ferrari, Alfa Romeo, Osella, and Ligier, all of whom either had, or intended to introduce, turbo engines. Might not a reduction in tyre widths have served the same purpose, without giving the FISA-aligned teams an advantage?

When a racing team has spent hundreds of thousands of pounds developing a new car for the coming season, only to find that arbitrary rule changes make it obsolete, then reactions are likely to be hostile. If that team is one of a group of fifteen who have suffered likewise, then they are not going to sit down and write off the time, effort, and money that have been wasted. They are likely to resist.

The FOCA teams threatened to set up their own series, to which FISA, under the influence of Balestre, responded that circuit owners, national clubs, etc. that aided this, would be banned from official FIA-sanctioned events, thus restricting their activities to the annual FOCA race. FISA would continue to run the Grand Prix World Championship as before.

There was a serious and very real threat of FOCA being forced to break away. Heels were dug in on both sides, but rather than reach a compromise, Balestre was prepared to wreck Grand Prix racing, and return it to the 'good old days' of the 1950s, when grids were made up of ten to fifteen cars, most of which were unlikel to challenge for the lead of a race, rather than see FOCA have any semblance of control.

That FOCA were capable of putting on their own events was shown at the South African Grand Prix, while we had to wait a full year before we could see what FISA would have offered, at the laughable 1982 San Marino Grand Prix. It took Renault, faced with the commercial realities of selling cars in America, to bang a few FISA heads together and get them talking to FOCA, to bring Grand Prix racing to its senses – and even that did not last long.

One result of all the winter bickering was the withdrawal of Goodyear from the scene. This had a far-reaching effect, not only because of the loss of their tyres, but also telling Grand Prix racing that if it did not sort itself out soon, other sponsors would be taking their money elsewhere. Marlboro were keener than most to get things moving, since they had a foot in either camp – they sponsored both Alfa and McLaren. McLaren, as we have seen, had re-grouped, but were an unproven outfit, what-ever their potential. Even this potential was lim-ited, as their first-choice driver, Alain Prost, had upped and away to Renault, a change facilitated by Jabouille moving to Ligier.

McLaren, and Teddy Mayer in particular, were not happy about this, as Alain had signed a two-year contract. Mayer, with his legal train-ing, made things very difficult indeed for Prost, who needed the Renault legal department to help him out of his predicament, and the Renault team were not entirely happy with the episode. There was certainly nothing honour-able about Alain's decision to welch on his con-tract, though nothing to compare with the shenanigans of Alesi in 1990. Following Hunt, Tambay and Watson, he was the fourth driver to lose confidence, or faith, in the team and its ability to provide not only race winning, but in Prost's case, 'safe' cars. In short, his belief in the team had evaporated, and he wanted to get out before he was pushed, like Tambay.

CRASHING THEIR WAY BACK

All things considered, 1981 did not look too enticing for either Grand Prix racing or McLaren. Promising former Project Four driver Andrea de Cesaris, who enjoyed a dual reputa-tion of being both fast and a bit wild, was hastily recruited as a condition of Marlboro's continu-ing support, and John Watson retained his seat. A new, revolutionary car was underway as well, designed by John Barnard, but in the meantime Barnard had also modified the old M29/C as a stopgap, in case there was any racing before the new car was ready.

As the new season approached FISA and FOCA were still miles apart, but as a pirate series had not been set up by FOCA, a compro-mise was possible, though FISA were adamant about the skirt ban. The FISA Grand Prix cal-endar was fixed, but then they informed South Africa that their race could not be run, and gave them a later date. The South Africans, grateful for any international sport at that time, replied that arrangements were too far advanced, and that they could not accept the revised date, over which they had not been consulted, true to FISA form. This gave the opening the FOCA teams were looking for, and they informed the South Africans that they would run a race on the original date if required. Their hands were snapped off.

Most teams retained their 1980 cars and, since only Renault and Ligier of the FISA-aligned teams were serious front runners, there was little change. Emerson Fittipaldi had retired after a long and mostly fruitless battle, driving his family team cars, and became their team manager, with Brazilian Chicco Serra taking his place alongside Rosberg. Lotus had lost Andretti to Alfa, but retained de Angelis and Mansell to drive their 81s, and former McLaren driver, Jochen Mass, had left Arrows, replaced by Siegfried Stohr. March had returned to the fray, with Daly and Salazar in 811s, while Theodore's TR2 was really a Shadow DN12, driven by Geoff Lees. Tyrrell had recruited Eddie Cheever, and South African Mrs Desire Wilson, who had driven well in Britain's own Formula 1 series, but that line-up was hardly equal to those of old.

Because Goodyear had withdrawn and Michelin had sided with the FISA teams, tyres were Goodyear from the British Formula 1 series, and proved an adequate substitute. Practice had not been kind to Watson, for while de Cesaris had qualified in mid-grid in the revised M29/C, John was down in fifteenth place. The front of the grid was the usual Williams/ Brabham/Lotus/Arrows mix, but there was a wild card: it was wet at the start of the race.

Cars set off on a mixture of wet or dry tyres, but those on 'wets' soon had an advantage, as the other cars slithered all over the place and fell back. Piquet led easily, but what was this? A McLaren in second place! Sure enough, John Watson was taking advantage of the rain and his own smooth driving to elevate himself. He actually led for a couple of laps when Piquet went in for dry tyres; the first time a McLaren had headed the field since Spain, nearly three years before.

Yes, it was a lucky lead through fortuitous circumstances, and no, it could not last, but

1981 was McLaren International's first season, and the old M29 cars, to 'C' and 'F' specification, were in use for six races. Here is a naked, full frontal view of the soon to be replaced car.

after coming in for dry tyres himself, Watson made a strong challenge for fourth place, only losing out to Rosberg at the end. Reutemann, running non-stop on dry tyres, won from Piquet, but was unlikely to be awarded Championship points. De Cesaris spun off on lap 55, having shown himself to be more than a capable driver and, given a good car, one to watch for the future.

Thanks mainly to Renault, FISA and FOCA got together to thrash out the 'Concorde Agreement'. FOCA accepted the ban on skirts, while FISA, and Balestre in particular, allowed FOCA to deal with the financial arrangements, including television, for the races. It was, shall we say, an uneasy alliance with the two sides'

This is the rear end view of the same car. The mechanic carries on working, ignoring the attention of the photographer.

public protagonists, Balestre and Ecclestone, working together for the benefit of Grand Prix racing. How long the 'marriage' would last was a moot point, but there is no doubt that the two sides did need each other.

Thus, the door was ajar for the United States (West) Grand Prix to go ahead, at Long Beach. Michelin agreed to supply all the teams with tyres and, more impressively, treat each team equally, whether contracted or not. McLaren hoped to give their new car, designated MP4, its debut, but it was not used.

The new MP4 was quite revolutionary.

Though it used the standard Cosworth engine/ Hewland gearbox package, it was built – if that is the right word – entirely out of carbon fibre, except for certain items, such as the suspension. The monocoques were manufactured to John Barnard's specification by Hercules Incorporated, an American company, hence the desire to have a car ready for Long Beach. These monocoques were shipped to the new McLaren headquarters at Woking for assembly. The car had been developed using extensive wind-tunnel tests and, unlike many competitors' cars, kept the front half of the normally redundant

175

Andrea de Cesaris

Quite apart from having the worst results of any regular McLaren driver, alongside Gethin, de Cesaris has the unenviable record of being the most unsuccessful Grand Prix driver of all time, having failed to secure a single victory in 150 races to the end of 1990. This does not tell the whole story though. It is the regularity with which he has managed to crash, spin, or get involved in any number of incidents, that has earned him the nickname 'de Crasharis'. Despite this, he has driven for many mid-field/lower order teams during his ten-year career. This speaks volumes about the importance of money in motor sport.

Yet it could all have been so very different. De Cesaris was one of the leading runners in Formula 3 in 1979, and following this with a reasonably successful season with Ron Dennis's Project Four Formula 2 outfit. He was undoubtedly quick, and suggested great things for the future, but these seasons were punctuated by a variety of incidents, many of his own making.

Following the Project Four/McLaren merger and the departure of Prost, the recruiting of de Cesaris to partner Watson, given other driver availability, was a logical move. Apart from the money he brought along, de Cesaris, at that time, was a fast, promising driver who, with experience, was a potential World Champion, and a good long-term prospect.

Instead, the 1981 season turned into a personal disaster for de Cesaris. Seemingly attempting to sprint before he could walk, de Cesaris launched himself on the Grand Prix world with two crashes in his first two races. He finished the season having entered sixteen races; being withdrawn from one as he smashed up the only chassis available to him in practice; gained one Championship point and five other placings; had seven crashes; and retired twice through mechanical failure. In all, de Cesaris had fourteen crashes, two spins causing retirement/ checking of the car, and one crash with little damage, during official practice/races that season. McLaren could not afford that rate of attrition, so he had to go. Perhaps his greatest contribution to the team was that he thoroughly 'crash tested' the carbon fibre MP4 car, not really an outstanding testimonial for a racing driver.

Since then, de Cesaris has managed to keep himself employed driving in Grand Prix. He averages a Championship point every three-and-a-half races, and has seldom looked like a front-running driver, though the same could be said of many of the teams he has driven for. The passing of the years has seen de Cesaris experiencing fewer incidents, though never quite managing to keep out of trouble. Regrettably, the flame that flickered so brightly in the lesser formulae has dimmed somewhat, and one no longer really expects to see de Cesaris running at the front anymore.

---

sidepods to encourage over-body downforce. Independently, Colin Chapman (who else?) had been designing the twin chassis Lotus 88, using a weave of carbon fibre for stiffness, and kevlar for its impact-absorbing qualities. Two completely new cars destined in their own different ways to set Grand Prix racing alight again. True to form Chapman, at the press debut of the Lotus, referred to the MP4 as being '. . . a little bit out of date, I'm afraid . . .' He may well have been right, but events were not going to give him a chance to prove the case.

The major change among the FISA teams concerned Ferrari. Retaining Villeneuve, they recruited Pironi from Ligier, a driver who had gained an 'ice cool' reputation for clinical high-speed driving. The big change there was the introduction of the 126CX V6 turbo-engined car. Renault's turbo engine had proved to be more powerful than any of the normally aspirated 3-litre engines, and the equivalence ratio of 2:1 in swept volume was clearly advantageous to the 1.5-litre turbo engine. That the complete turbo engine, with all its attendant ancillaries, was less aerodynamically adaptable and weighed more than a 3-litre engine was almost irrelevant because, if the extra horsepower could not overcome this, then FISA, by keeping the minimum weight limit artificially high and by banning skirts, could be relied on to back 'their' teams. Ferrari thus followed the turbo road and from the outset their engine, as expected, was not lacking in horsepower, even if the car itself was nothing special.

Emerson Fittipaldi in the Texaco-Marlboro liveried M23, during his Championship-winning year of 1974.

James Hunt's 1976 Championship-winning M23-8/2, with Alastair Caldwell leaning on it, at Colnbrook, during that momentous season.

'Bottoms up'. Mechanics attend to de Cesaris's M29/F at Long Beach. His race ended on lap 1, but a year later Andrea took the pole, in a Marlboro-liveried Alfa Romeo.

It was a while before Andrea de Cesaris was allowed an MP4 car, but when he was, things initially looked up for him. His poor Grand Prix record does not mean that he is a bad driver per se, just that he has not really managed to meet the incredibly high standard required to succeed, or even compete, at this level. He looks neat enough here, but look at the wear on the right front tyre.

For John Watson the last year of Team McLaren, 1980, was not the happiest of his career. Yet despite all the problems, caused mainly by the team, he had the good grace not to go whingeing about his ills to everyone and anyone, and was to bounce back pretty convincingly.

Getting into, or out of, a Grand Prix car, or any single-seater for that matter, is not the easiest task around. For instance, a driver cannot fasten his own safety harness, and Niki Lauda makes sure that he does not get entangled in this before he sits down.

Andrea de Cesaris leads a Ligier, John Watson, and the rest, during a 1981 race.

John Watson and Andrea de Cesaris take off at the start of the 1981 British Grand Prix. This was the race which saw McLaren back at the top of the results sheet, after three-and-a-half years, and was John's first win in nearly five years.

Another McLaren pit scene. Everyone appears to be standing around, but in reality they are all primed and ready to go.

Niki Lauda is busy explaining a handling imbalance.

Britain's last World Champion, James Hunt, now one half of the BBC's renowned Grand Prix commentating team.

A youthful looking Alain Prost during his first season of Grand Prix racing, with McLaren. He was undoubtedly good, but nobody expected the young tyro to become that *good, at the time.*

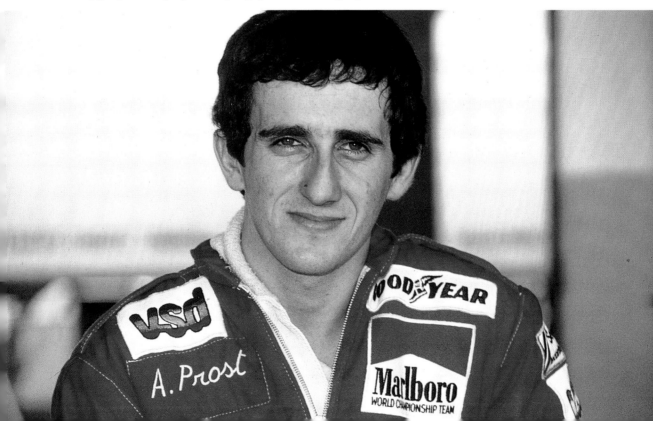

1981 was McLaren International's first season of racing, though at a quick glance the cars looked the same as before, thanks to Marlboro. John Watson might have been lucky to keep his drive, but soon showed his new bosses that they had made the right decision.

The start of the 1982 Long Beach Grand Prix. De Cesaris leads Niki Lauda away, followed by a Renault, Alfa, and the rest; John Watson is back in eleventh position. This was the race in which Niki Lauda announced his intent, on his return to the sport, with a very impressive victory.

John Barnard's MP4 was a revolutionary car, with the monocoque being built entirely of a carbon fibre composite structure. Though scorned by sceptics at first, this method soon ousted the traditional aluminium used for Grand Prix cars, and is even beginning to make its appearance on road cars today.

The grid assembles for the start of the 1982 British Grand Prix, at Brands Hatch. Behind the two Brabhams Niki Lauda is in fourth place, while pole position driver Rosberg has to start from the back of the grid.

With all the protective clothing worn by drivers these days, this could be almost anyone. However, as with knights of old, the helmet design will tell you that it is John Watson, at Silverstone, in 1983.

The year 1982 marked Niki Lauda's comeback, and many were the debates as to whether it would be a success or not. This was resolved by the third race of the season, the Long Beach Grand Prix, which Lauda won virtually unchallenged. He won his second race of that season at Brands Hatch, at the British Grand Prix.

(Overleaf)   The start of the awfully wet Portuguese Grand Prix in 1985 shows just how difficult racing in the rain is. Here, Alain Prost leads Alboreto, Warwick, Tyrrell, Tambay (Renault), Piquet (No. 7), Johansson (Ferrari), Patrese (No. 22) and the rest.

Work goes on inside the McLaren pit during a test session, at Brands Hatch. Away from all the glamour and razzmatazz of the races, this is where all the real work is done.

Niki Lauda and John Barnard, at a Silverstone test session. These two forged a working relationship, which ultimately took Niki to his third title.

Niki Lauda practising in his MP4-1/C for the 1983 British Grand Prix, for which his Cosworth-engined car could only gain a mid-grid position. In the race, Lauda managed to finish in the points, overcoming several, more powerful, turbo-engined cars with his unique race-craft.

Much is said and written about the splendour of Monaco, and despite the growth of modern concrete monstrosities, there are still scenes worth travelling to see. Casino Square is one such place, and Andrea de Cesaris leads John Watson in this lovely scene.

The 1985 Portuguese swimming gala. Lauda's powerful breast stroke takes him past a Renault.

McLaren's mechanics, and other team members, have long been immaculately turned out at races, and are, in effect, mobile advertising hoardings. Niki Lauda is being attended to amidst the onlookers.

McLaren are often accused of being a humourless team, but John Watson, Niki Lauda, Ron Dennis (back to the camera), and others are obviously enjoying themselves.

Alain Prost in an MP4-2B, on his way to fourth place in the European Grand Prix, at Brands Hatch. This drive secured him his first World Championship, though not in the manner either he, or Ron Dennis, wanted, with a victory.

Championship rivals for most of 1985, Alain Prost leads Michele Alboreto. Despite Prost's emphatic victory in the Championship, it was only at the Dutch Grand Prix that he finally overhauled the Italian in the title race.

Ayrton Senna and Gerhard Berger at the launch of the 1990 MP4/5B.

In practice at Long Beach neither McLaren driver shone with their outdated, though up-rated, M29/Fs, featuring revised suspension, bodywork, and aerodynamics. Out of twenty-four cars on the grid, de Cesaris was twenty-second, with Watson a place behind, fully 5 yawning seconds slower than Patrese on pole. This was more than could be said for Chapman's state-of-the-art Lotus 88, which did not get past the scrutineers, thanks to numerous protests about the secondary chassis forming a movable aerodynamic structure.

Once Patrese had his little thrill leading the race, after another meteoric start by Villeneuve, the race turned into a Williams benefit, as Jones led Reutemann home comfortably, followed by Piquet, and Andretti in the Alfa Romeo. Poor old Andrea de Cesaris did not even complete a single lap, colliding with Prost, in the Renault, and Rebaque in a Brabham. John Watson lasted fourteen more laps, before an engine misfire drove him into retirement.

In Brazil, there were a few changes among the 'rent-a-driver' positions. This time the Lotus 88 passed scrutineering, only to be re-jected the next day. Watson and de Cesaris had to struggle on with the M29/F, but the most interesting car was the Brabham BT49-C. To enforce the sliding skirt ban, cars had to have a clearance of at least 6 centimetres (2.3 inches) between the bodywork and the ground, and were checked for this after coming off the cir-cuit. Gordon Murray, the ingenious Brabham designer, had been looking at ways around this, and his new invention, more of which shortly, was to create another furore and yet, ultimately, show up FISA and especially Balestre in very dark colours indeed.

Practice placed the Williams pair, Piquet, and Patrese at the front, with Prost and Giacomelli for company. De Cesaris, who must have been dizzy so often did he spin, was in mid-grid, while Watson was near the back, having been plagued by understeer. Once again there was a wet start, and Piquet, quite astonishingly, though perhaps thinking of Reutemann in South Africa, started on dry tyres. He promptly made his way backwards as the Williams drivers roared off, and de Cesaris retired early on, with electrical problems.

Watson fought on gamely, getting into fifth position before spinning and falling back to finish eighth. At the front, Reutemann was comfortably leading his team leader and, as neither of them was being challenged, a pit board was hung out instructing Reutemann to slow and let Jones past to win. Reutemann re-sponded by going faster, while Jones also upped his rating, but got no closer. Out went the pit board again and again and again, but Reutemann still did not slow down. Jones was charging away, while the Argentinian simply kept his distance. Then out came the chequered flag a lap early: the two-hour rule was invoked, due to the wet start, and Reutemann won from an unhappy Jones. Reutemann said he was goint to let Jones pass on the last lap, but this was denied him. I wonder what excuse he would have used had the race not been stopped a lap short!

John Watson gave the MP4 its debut in Ar-gentina, while Andrea de Cesaris continued in an M29/F. The Lotus 88 was excluded once again, and a furious Chapman did not watch the race, the first time for twenty-two years. MP4, 'a little bit out of date'? At least it was racing. The Williams, Renaults and Brabhams formed the front of the grid, while John and Andrea reversed their Brazilian practice positions, ex-cept that Andrea kept on spinning around. But it was not as simple as that. Brabham were using a hydro-pneumatic system which raised the car body above the 6-centimetre clearance re-quired, and lowered this to the ground when moving at speed. This effectively allowed the cars to create downforce as before, while the lack of suspension movement, necessary to keep the body touching the circuit as sliding skirts were banned, made the cars very stiff indeed.

Despite protests the car was allowed to race, and a measure of its impact was not so much the way in which Piquet won with ease, but the fact that his number two, Rebaque, passed Reutemann for second place on lap 15. Again, protests were raised against the car at the end of the race, but the car was cleared, and the events concerning Brabham and Lotus completely overshadowed the MP4's debut, which saw John Watson up to sixth, before retiring.

Following the Argentinian Grand Prix Chapman issued a statement which suggested there had been an official collusion against the Lotus 88. Balestre immediately fined Lotus $100,000, and thirteen teams issued a statement criticizing him over his heavy-handed and unnecessary actions. Fortunately, the FIA rescinded the fine ten days later, and summarily carpeted Balestre for his unilateral decision. There were people with backbones in Paris after all.

A new event came next; the San Marino Grand Prix, not held in that nominally independent, mountainous Italian principality, but at the Imola circuit, scene of the last Italian Grand Prix. Would France try to pull a fast one to gain a second race with an Andorran Grand Prix, or perhaps Britain, with a Welsh Grand Prix? Certainly the new race made an idealistic mark, only to be bitten by the sharp teeth of reality. The week before, an FIA tribunal had banned the Lotus 88, so they did not enter, having no competitive cars. The scrutineers, mindful of the nit-picking which had accompanied all the protests of the Lotus, played tit for tat on the teams, and promptly disqualified all except Renault, Talbot-Ligier, and new boys Toleman, for having movable aerodynamic devices on their cars. As these were mostly only flexible body panels, they were easily replaced by aluminium. However, a point was made that it was easy to find nearly all cars to be illegal.

Meanwhile, Tyrrell, Williams, Osella, Fittipaldi and Arrows all had hydro-pneumatic, 'artful dodger' suspension systems, à la Brabham. When asked what these systems actually did, the scrutineers received mumbled replies. So, five observers were positioned at strategic points around the circuit, and the teams were told that if any car was found to be close to, or touching,

the circuit at all five points, then it would be disqualified. This would stop the foul play! Unfortunately for the scrutineers, the five observers reported that *every* car was cheating! Reality struck back with a vengeance.

At least Villeneuve on the pole was a relief for the Italians, while Watson was seventh, only an encouraging 1.5 seconds adrift. De Cesaris was in mid-grid, still with an M29/F, though he had two accidents. It was Watson, while jousting for fifth place, who ruined his own chances at the beginning of the race, knocking off his front wing and spending two laps in the pits. He ran well thereafter, even going faster than the leaders, but was of course well down. De Cesaris, on the other hand, had a splendid race, coming sixth after a steady drive, which suggested that he was learning. None of this was relevant to Piquet, Patrese, and Reutemann, who took the leading positions, while Rebaque came fourth in the second Brabham, ahead of the first 'FISA' car of Pironi.

Lotus returned for the Belgian Grand Prix, but controversy was not far away again. The reformed drivers' union, the GPDA, only wanted twenty-six cars on the grid and threatened to disrupt the start, while the mechanics were not happy with the crowded pits and all the hangers on who clog things up. One could certainly sympathize with them, but the organizers, smelling a whiff of disruption in the air said that the scheduled start would be kept, come what may.

While this little witches' brew was simmering nicely, a little light entertainment was duly provided by Laffite. Coming in from practice, he was approaching the scrutineering area where the 6-centimetre ground clearance was checked, when his engine failed. Unfortunately, the Ligier used the Matra V12 engine to work its hydro-pneumatic 'artful dodger' system, and the car came in scraping along the ground, its sidepods giving it a very hangdog look. Abiding strictly by the rules, Laffite's times were excluded, and Jacques did not quite see the funny side of it.

Andrea de Cesaris scored his only point in a season's racing for McLaren, at the 1981 San Marino Grand Prix. Here, in the obsolescent M29/F, he drove well in the rain, and for once kept the car on the circuit to finish sixth.

Most teams now used these 'artful dodger' systems to cheat on the 6-centimetre rule, though not McLaren. On the face of it you would expect FISA to do something about this quickly. Once out on the circuit, the cars cornered almost as fast as with skirts, yet had little or no suspension movement. This rigidity made them more like high-speed go-karts than racing cars. They were difficult to drive, unforgiving, and very tiring on the driver.

In short, the cars were far more dangerous than before. Yet Balestre, having banned the use of skirts in the name of safety, now sanctioned the use of the more dangerous cars; cars moreover, which in all probability, broke more rules than the banned Lotus 88! A contradiction which indicates that Balestre's shameful tactics over the banning of skirts, was merely a step towards his own ambitions, namely controlling

Grand Prix racing through FISA, which he dominated.

For a change, McLaren raised a few eyebrows in practice, as Watson qualified fifth, ahead of Jones, in the MP4. De Cesaris, still in an M29/F, only just made the race, showing the yawning gap not only in driving ability, but in the cars. There was an awful incident during practice which further backed the mechanics' complaints, when one of the Osella mechanics stepped into the path of Reutemann, in the pitlane, receiving injuries which later claimed his life.

The threatened drivers' strike began on the grid – when about a dozen got out of their cars – but did not last long. This incident may have unsettled officials, because when the cars arrived back in a disorderly group after a lap of the circuit, the red light unexpectedly came on, followed by the green. In the confusion Patrese stalled and, not expecting the race to start, a mechanic went to his aid. As the cars sped away, Stohr ran into the back of his stationary teammate, crushing the mechanic, who received leg injuries for his trouble.

Neither Arrows took part in the restart, and Jones and Piquet led away. This did not last long; Jones pushed Piquet off, elevating Watson to fifth place. This turned into fourth a few laps later, when Jones ran off the circuit and out of the race, when his car jumped out of gear. Watson's car began to suffer similar trouble, and he slowly drifted back to finish seventh, while de Cesaris retired with more terminal gearbox problems. Reutemann consolidated his position at the top of the drivers' table, with another smooth victory, while Laffite restored the smile to his face, by coming second.

There was much head scratching at McLaren before allowing de Cesaris to have an MP4 for the Monaco Grand Prix. The cars were tried with an 'artful dodger' system, but Watson did not like it and his was removed. De Cesaris suffered another practice accident, but both qualified in mid-grid, so honours were shared.

A fire in a hotel above the tunnel, with water dripping on to the circuit, rendered this a no-overtaking area for the race, but de Cesaris was determined to do something about Prost before he arrived there. It did not quite work out and he really put Marlboro back in the news, as he landed on Andretti's Marlboro-sponsored Alfa, eliminating both cars. Piquet and Jones resumed their personal feud at the front, while Watson had moved steadily into fifth by half-distance. He got into fourth position, before retiring with a blown engine, and just after this Piquet crashed while lapping Tambay. Near the end Jones, leading comfortably, began suffering fuel-feed problems, and shot into the pits for more petrol. This did not cure matters and Villeneuve closed in, taking the lead near the end, to give Ferrari their first turbo victory.

Villeneuve's classic victory in Spain rather eclipsed some very solid progress by McLaren.

Watson had qualified in fourth place, while de Cesaris was again in mid-grid, very promising. Unfortunately, Andrea rather blotted his copybook again, after a bit of argy-bargy with Rebaque, and retired on lap 10. Earlier, Villeneuve had produced another of his electric starts to take second place, but Jones was way ahead in the lead.

Uncharacteristically, Jones ran wide at a corner on lap 14, went off the circuit and out of the race. This left Villeneuve, in the ill-handling but powerful Ferrari, leading Reutemann, and possibly the most exciting race in modern times was well and truly on. For lap after lap the Williams was virtually pushing the Ferrari around the twisty back of the circuit, while along the straight Villeneuve pulled out a few lengths' breathing space for the next lap. On and on they went, Reutemann probing here and there, but unable to find a way through, while Villeneuve's sheer brilliance kept the Ferrari on the road. By half-distance Watson was up into third place and, though passed by Laffite, both were closing on the leading pair. On lap 60 Laffite and Watson both passed Reutemann and began to threaten Villeneuve. Five laps later de Angelis made it five in a row, with the Ferrari clearly holding everyone up, but using those vital few car lengths gained on the straight to his advantage.

With twenty laps left, these five cars ran in each other's pockets, but ahead they were closing on Giacomelli's Alfa. Fully aware of the situation, Villeneuve slowed ever so gently to the pace of Giacomelli, yet still held the others at bay, thus not spoiling his rhythm and denying his followers a potential overtaking opportunity. Surely though, no driver could resist such intense pressure, Villeneuve just had to make a mistake. It says much for the genius of the man, to say nothing of his pure racing instincts, that he took the chequered flag, with four cars following nose to tail, and Watson was third at the death. A brilliant drive, great race, and McLaren's best result for over two years; the politics seemed to fade into insignificance.

TYRED OUT

Not for long though, as Chapman had re-designed his Lotus 88 into an 88B, with an inner and outer sprung structure. He had invited the RAC to scrutineer this as though presented at a race, and it had been passed. Now Chapman was determined to use the car again.

Goodyear returned to the scene in France, though only supplied the Williams and Brabham teams. Michelin responded by putting their efforts into their originally contracted teams, leaving the rest, including McLaren, to make do with standard covers. This did not make too much of a difference because, behind Arnoux, Watson was second and, more impressively, de Cesaris was fifth.

Piquet flew into the lead and disappeared, while Villeneuve climbed six places into fifth, at the start. Watson held second place, while de Cesaris was fourth, both slipping back a little thereafter, with Watson running a comfortable third. But fate was to take a hand. It began to rain, intermittently at first, then heavier, and the race was stopped after lap 58. As three-quarters' distance had not been run, the results could not stand, so a short twenty-two lap race was organized, with the two times to be added together to achieve a final result.

This may have seemed a fair and safe way of arranging matters, but it was to have a very unsatisfactory outcome. The Goodyear teams did not have any soft, short-life tyres, unlike the Michelin teams, and they could not compete. Prost won the short race in the Renault, with Watson second, and they took the two leading positions. Piquet, who had dominated the first race, was way back, thanks to his tyres, and wound up third. An unsatisfactory set of results, and not the best of ways for Prost to achieve his first Grand Prix win. De Cesaris suffered badly; when it began to rain he went into the pits early for wet tyres, only for the race to be stopped a couple of laps later.

Silverstone played host to the British Grand Prix with its delightful garden fête atmosphere still prevalent at that time. After two good results, McLaren hopes were high and were bolstered when both cars qualified on the third row of the grid, and reflected the expectant mood of the large crowd. Since James Hunt had retired, there had been little for British fans to cheer, and they had eagerly forged a loyal bond with Alan Jones, the forceful Australian driver. But deep down, a British driver to cheer was wanted more than anything, if only to counter the rapid growth of French drivers. John Watson was about to fill that void.

Before this, there was the inevitable political pantomime. As promised, the Lotus 88B was presented at scrutineering, passed, and took part in the first practice. Some of us naïve onlookers assumed that the national organizing body, the RAC, ran its own Grand Prix, but we received a rude awakening. FISA's representative got in touch with Paris, and the RAC was informed that since the Lotus 88B was derived from the banned Lotus 88, it too was illegal, and its qualifying times were to be scratched. Moreover, there were veiled threats that if the RAC did not comply and allowed the car to continue, pending an appeal – surely a fair approach, considering that the scrutineers on the spot thought the car legal – then the British Grand Prix would lose its World Championship status. The whole episode reflected badly on the sport, and left many wondering just what sort of people ran FISA in Paris.

Andrea de Cesaris indulged in some over-exuberant antics during the warm-up, keeping his mechanics on their toes, and the furrows on Ron Dennis and Teddy Mayer's foreheads nice and deep. The Renaults and Ferraris took an early lead, but on lap 4 Villeneuve, thanks to a combination of rock-hard suspension and soft tyres, got crossed up at Woodcote and was hit by Jones. Andrea arrived at the wrong moment, got involved, and ended up in the catch fencing. John was more fortunate, as he stood on his brakes, closed his eyes, opened them when almost at a standstill, miraculously found himself still on the circuit, and set off again.

Watson was not to be denied and he drove forcefully, benefitting from others' misfortune, like Piquet's nasty accident, and determinedly overhauled Reutemann. By lap 17 he was second but a long way behind Arnoux, and the race became a bit processional, with many leading drivers already out. Little changed, but by two-thirds' distance, the exhaust note on Arnoux's car suggested something was amiss. Watson was too far back to notice, but he responded to pit signals, and very likely the encouraging signs from the vast crowd, to reel Arnoux in. It all seemed a bit unreal at first, but ten laps later, going into Becketts, we held our breath, and pinched ourselves to make sure we had not fallen asleep and were dreaming, as John Watson took the lead. Naturally, that inborn British pessimism came to the fore, and the prophets of impending doom made their predictions, but even if the MP4 had faltered, I think the crowd would have willed it to the chequered flag. To say it was a popular victory was modest in the extreme . . . and to think that McLaren had nearly dispensed with Watson's services!

Euphoria over a victory does not last long during the European season. It may have been the first McLaren victory in nearly four years and the first for McLaren International, to say nothing of John Watson's first for five years, but it was only a stepping stone to the future. Just over a week later in the German Grand Prix, at the Hockenheimring, if you did not have a turbo engine, you were in trouble. McLaren were further troubled as the MP4's flexed badly over the bumpy circuit, thanks to the lack of suspension movement and the sudden removal of downforce. Both drivers spun in practice and lined up in mid-grid.

Jones was determined that lack of a turbo engine in his Williams was not going to be a handicap, and eventually took the lead. Before this, de Cesaris's had tangled with Tambay and was eliminated early on, while Watson did his best in mid-field. Jones was at his fighting best and nobody, turbo car or not, was going to stand in his way. It took a faltering engine to

eliminate him and give Piquet a lucky victory, while Watson came a providential, and lapped, sixth.

The dramatic Österreichring is as challenging a circuit as they come, but proved another haven for the turbo cars, with three of them at the front of the grid. Watson, still battling with an understeering, flexing MP4, qualified in mid-field, while de Cesaris had another practice crash, further enhancing his 'de Crasharis' nickname, and was not allowed out in the spare car by Ron Dennis. He was nearer the back, than the front of the grid.

As expected, the turbo cars of Villeneuve, Prost and Arnoux took off, only for the first two to drop back and retire, and then for Laffite to finally pass Arnoux to win. This was the third consecutive race in which the Renaults had taken the front row of the grid and failed to secure a victory. Neither McLaren featured strongly, as expected, but Watson came sixth for his fifth consecutive finish in the points, while de Cesaris was two places back.

CHALLENGES

On the Saturday afternoon of the Dutch Grand Prix meeting, McLaren were in a quandary. De Cesaris had crashed once again and wrecked his car beyond immediate repair. Ron Dennis and Teddy Mayer decided that he could not use the spare car, and so, despite qualifying in mid-grid, the entry was withdrawn. Andrea was a fast, talented driver, but seldom did a meeting go by without him giving his hard-pressed mechanics even more to do. He had not been free of incidents in the lower formulae by any means, but worst of all, he did not seem to learn from his mistakes. Finally, McLaren could take no more, and Andrea de Cesaris was not only out of the Dutch Grand Prix, but was to be released at the end of the season.

The race developed into a battle between Prost and Jones, and exciting it was too, while Laffite took himself and Reutemann out with a rare error, while disputing third place. All this left Watson in fourth place, until sidelined by his electrics. Jones's tyres went off and he fell back, leaving Prost to secure another victory for Renault, ahead of Piquet, who was fast closing on Reutemann in the Drivers' Championship.

After his disciplining at Zandvoort, you would have thought that Andrea de Cesaris would have, at last, learnt his lesson, but no. During unofficial practice for the Italian Grand Prix, Andrea crashed once again. There were dark mutterings among his mechanics that this was his nineteenth crash of the season, and there was no rush to repair the car. The pit lane was also alight with driver speculation. Alan Jones had announced his intention to retire at the end of the season, and the word was out that Niki Lauda was considering a comeback. Hot stuff indeed.

Overshadowing this was the Drivers' Championship contest between Piquet and Reutemann. Practice saw Arnoux give Renault their sixth consecutive pole position, ahead of Reutemann, with Piquet sixth, Watson just behind him, and de Cesaris in mid-grid, while Henton qualified a Toleman for the first time. It was not a classic race, and Prost won from Jones and Reutemann, with Piquet taking a lucky sixth place from de Cesaris, when the latter slid off on oil on the last lap. Watson had been running well when, on lap 20, he misjudged one of the Lesmo corners and slammed into the barriers, the car tearing in two before being thrown back across the track. It was a nasty accident, but proved, even more than de Cesaris' numerous efforts, the strength of the carbon fibre monocoque, as John Watson was able to walk away virtually unscathed.

During September Niki Lauda tried out an MP4 at Donnington Park, a circuit he was not familiar with, but it was enough to make him decide he could rise to the challenge of a comeback. It was just a matter of deciding which team to join. The Canadian Grand Prix put an end to this idle speculation though, especially as Piquet claimed the pole, with Reutemann right

there beside him. Jones was third, but Reutemann could expect no help from him, so if he wanted the title – and he was the favourite – it was down to him. Watson was in ninth place with, for once, an accident-free de Cesaris four places behind.

Insurance problems nearly caused the race to be cancelled, and then the start was delayed, thanks to rain. Once underway, there were plenty of treats in store. Local hero Villeneuve collided with Arnoux on lap 1, and continued with a disintegrating front aerofoil, until it finally fell off. Even this did not stop him, and one wondered why the cars had these aerofoils if Villeneuve could keep going in such appalling conditions. Other drivers were less keen to go flat out, Reutemann among them, and Watson extracted the most from this. Driving as tidily as ever, given the conditions, he followed Laffite home for second place, having come through from ninth. De Cesaris came off second best while challenging Piquet for fifth place near the end, and spun off.

The title challenge went to the final race of the season, the United States Grand Prix, held in a car park at Las Vegas. That such a venue should be used showed both FOCA and FISA in a bad light. Compared to great circuits of the past, such as Spa and the Nürburgring, or contemporary ones, like the Österreichring or Silverstone, it was a sick joke, little more than a poor go-kart track, and hardly a serious challenge to Grand Prix drivers.

Being professionals, the drivers did their best, and after a practice tangle with Piquet, Reutemann claimed the pole, Piquet was fourth, Watson sixth and de Cesaris in mid-field. Jones vanished at the green light and drove a masterful race around the concrete walls, while Reutemann, with a poor-handling car, lost all heart and drifted backwards. De Cesaris got into a tangle with Tambay (who must have thought that McLaren were still haunting him), but continued, with bent steering. Watson was troubled with poor handling, but finished seventh, while Piquet, despite extreme fatigue,

Grand Prix Results 1981

GRAND PRIX	DRIVER	CAR	NO	1ST PRACTICE Time/Posn	2ND PRACTICE Time/Posn	3RD PRACTICE Time/Posn	FINAL GRID POSN	FINAL PLACING	RETIRED CAUSE OF	HIGHEST POSN IN RACE
SOUTH AFRICAN Kyalami 7.2.81	J. Watson	Ford-DFV M29/4C	7	1min 15.25sec 13/18	1min 15.85sec 12/15		15-19	5/11		5th
	A. de Cesaris	Ford-DFV M29/5C	8	1min 14.91sec 8/18	1min 14.39sec 7/15		9-19		Lp 54 Spun off	9th
USA (West) Long Beach 15.3.81	J. Watson	Ford-DFV M29/4C	7	1min 26.42sec 28/30	1min 22.18sec 21/30		23-24		Lp 16 Accident	20th
	A. de Cesaris	Ford-DFV M29/5F	8	1min 22.73sec 24/30	1min 22.03sec 20/30		22-24		Lp 1 Accident	
BRAZILIAN Rio de Janeiro 29.3.81	J. Watson	Ford-DFV M29/4C	7	1min 45.02sec 9/27	1min 45.20sec 9/28		11-24		Lp 35 Gearbox	5th
	A. de Cesaris	Ford-DFV M29/5F	8	1min 46.39sec 17/27	1min 46.60sec 18/28		18-24	11/13		12th
ARGENTINIAN Buenos Aires 12.4.81	J. Watson	Ford-DFV MP4/1	7	1min 40.06sec 21/28	1min 38.26sec 12/28		15-24	8/14		6th
	A. de Cesaris	Ford-DFV M29/5F	8	1min 39.41sec 20/28	1min 38.78sec 18/28		20-24		Lp 10 Electric trouble	12th
SAN-MARINO Imola 3.5.81	J. Watson	Ford-DFV MP4/2	7	1min 37.64sec 11/30	1min 36.24sec 6/29		7-23	10/14		6th
	A. de Cesaris	Ford-DFV M29/4F	8	1min 38.02sec 12/30	1min 37.38sec 13/29		14-23	6/14		6th
BELGIAN Zolder 17.5.81	J. Watson	Ford-DFV MP4/1	7	1min 23.73sec 4/29	1min 30.92sec 4/30		5-24	7/13		4th
	A. de Cesaris	Ford-DFV M29/4F	8	1min 26.95sec 23/29	1min 30.99sec 5/30		23-24		Lp 12 Gearbox failure	19th
MONACO Monte Carlo 31.5.81	J. Watson	Ford-DFV MP4/2	7	1min 28.14sec 9/24	1min 27.06sec 9/25		10-20		Lp 53 Engine	5th
	A. de Cesaris	Ford-DFV MP4/1	8	1min 28.97sec 15/24	1min 27.12sec 10/25		11-20		Lp 1 Accident	
SPANISH Jarama 21.6.81	J. Watson	Ford-DFV MP4/2	7	1min 15.09sec 5/29	1min 15.66sec 4/29		4-23	3/17		3rd
	A. de Cesaris	Ford-DFV MP4/1	8	1min 16.21sec 10/29	1min 15.85sec 14/29		13-23		Lp 10 Off track	15th
FRENCH Dijon-Prenois 5.7.81	J. Watson	Ford-DFV MP4/2	7	1min 07.05sec 1/27	1min 06.36sec 2/26		2-24	2/17		2nd
	A. de Cesaris	Ford-DFV MP4/1	8	1min 08.83sec 8/27	1min 07.03sec 5/26		5-24	11/17		4th
BRITISH Silverstone 18.7.81	J. Watson	Ford-DFV MP4/2	7	1min 13.37sec 5/30	1min 12.71sec 5/30		5-24	1/11 WINNER		1st
	A. de Cesaris	Ford-DFV MP4/1	8	1min 13.98sec 7/30	1min 12.73sec 6/30		6-24		Lp 3 Accident	8th
GERMAN Hockenheim-ring 2.8.81	J. Watson	Ford-DFV MP4/2	7	1min 49.52sec 7/30	1min 50.36sec 10/30		9-24	6/16		6th
	A. de Cesaris	Ford-DFV MP4/1	8	1min 50.07sec 9/30	1min 49.58sec 6/30		10-24		Lp 5 Accident	8th
AUSTRIAN Österreichring 16.8.81	J. Watson	Ford-DFV MP4/3	7	1min 36.01sec 11/28	1min 35.98sec 12/27		12-23	6/11		6th
	A. de Cesaris	Ford-DFV MP4/1	8	1min 36.66sec 15/29			17-23	8/11		8th

DUTCH Zandvoort 30.8.81	J. Watson	Ford-DFV MP4/3	7	1min 19.31sec 6/29	1min 19.65sec 8/30	8-25		Lp 51 Electrical failure	**4th**
	A. de Cesaris	Ford-DFV MP4/1	8	1min 20.65sec 11/29	1min 20.38sec 13/30	13-25	Did not start. Practice crash, no chassis left		
ITALIAN Monza 13.9.81	J. Watson	Ford-DFV MP4/3	7	1min 35.80sec 6/29	1min 35.56sec 7/30	7-24		Lp 20 Crash	**7th**
	A. de Cesaris	Ford-DFV MP4/1	8		1min 37.02sec 15/30	10-24		Lp 52 Tyre failure	**7th**
CANADIAN Montreal 27.9.81	J. Watson	Ford-DFV MP4/4	7	1min 31.62sec 7/30	1min 30.57sec 9/30	9-24	2/14		**FL 2nd**
	A. de Cesaris	Ford-DFV MP4/1	8	1min 32.28sec 14/30	1min 31.51sec 13/30	13-24	13/14		**6th**
USA Las Vegas 17.10.81	J. Watson	Ford-DFV MP4/4	7	1min 19.98sec 13/30	1min 18.61sec 4/29	6-24	7/14		**5th**
	A. de Cesaris	Ford-DFV MP4/1	8	1min 19.34sec 7/30	1min 19.21sec 12/29	14-24	12/14		**10th**

just scraped home in fifth place to become the new World Champion, pipping a very disgruntled Reutemann by one point.

The year 1981 had not been a vintage one, and no one driver particularly stood out, though Jones was as determined as ever and Villeneuve irrepressible. It was argued that Reutemann had thrown away the World Championship, and there was uncertainty as to whether he would carry on, but Piquet was a worthy Champion with a great future in front of him. The same applied for Prost, who demonstrated a sure-footed approach at Renault, without really hinting at the greatness to come. Above all, Watson had thoroughly rehabilitated himself in the top flight again, though he never thought he had left. He was probably right, because McLaren International, at last, gave him the tools to prove himself.

Perhaps McLaren's one failure had been to make significant progress with de Cesaris. His speed was greater than his ability, and the damage he caused overstretched the team. They were continually patching up his handiwork, rather than trying out new ideas, and this came at a crucial time in the new team's existence. Once Niki Lauda had been recruited, de Cesaris was dispensed with, but what of Watson? Lauda had teamed up with him before at Brabham, and it was Watson who had left after one season. Frank Williams was no doubt aware of this when he made Watson an offer to replace Jones, but Watson, knowing that a turbocharged engine was on the cards, knew where his best options lay and stayed put.

LAUDA RETURNS

The recruitment of Niki Lauda was a real coup for Ron Dennis, but it was also a huge risk. In any sport few former champions make a successful comeback, and in Grand Prix racing the speed increase of the cars in the intervening years would make this doubly difficult for Niki. There was also wild speculation that James Hunt and Jackie Stewart too were considering lucrative offers to come back, the latter even being quoted as saying that the return of this triumvirate would '. . . be the best thing that could happen to Grand Prix racing'. There is modesty for you. It all came to nought for the two British drivers, but for Lauda the challenge of making a successful comeback was very real. He was in.

Sponsors, led by Marlboro and Renault, had voiced concern during the season at the political strife, a sure enough warning to all concerned

Niki Lauda and Stirling Moss, Brands Hatch 1984. Who knows what they're saying, but the meeting of two 'greats' is certainly a momentous occasion.

Niki Lauda

Austrian driver Niki Lauda's achievements in Grand Prix racing were legendary even before his premature retirement during practice for the USA Grand Prix, in 1979. Starting out initially in the March team, and then with the BRM outfit, he moved on to Ferrari for 1974, and thereafter became the most successful and dominant driver during the 1970s – a period when Grand Prix was at its most 'open' and competitive. Initially a fast driver with his Ferrari, he quickly became the standard-setter in race tactics, doing just enough to win, or salvage as many points as possible from the situation. Lauda also took car testing and setting up to new heights, proving to be the most complete driver of his era.

World Champion in 1975, and again in 1977, while runner-up to Hunt in the thrilling 1976 season, Lauda and his Ferrari became the arch enemy of the McLaren fans. However, Niki won everyone's heart following his remarkable recovery and singly determined return to racing, following his awful accident at the Nürburgring in 1976. His esteem was never in doubt thereafter.

Lauda moved on to Brabham for 1978, alongside Watson, recording a victory in the BT46 'for car's' only race. His retirement came following a singularly unsuccessful season, in which he was occasionally upstaged by young team-mate Nelson Piquet, and he 'lost the motivation' to continue.

In the mean time Niki founded his own airline, Laudair, in which he was also a pilot. It was thus a major coup for Ron Dennis to entice Lauda back into a racing car, for 1982. After a short settling-in period, Lauda quickly began to work with the team to get the best out of the MP4. Watson looked his equal as a driver, but it was Lauda who did most of the test driving.

For 1984 Prost joined McLaren, and with Porsche/Tag power, they dominated Grand Prix racing. Prost won more races than Lauda, but it was the later's racecraft and eye on the Championship table that secured his third title, by a mere half-point. This in itself typified the man, not always the fastest driver, but the one most likely to be there at the finish.

The following season was a Prost *tour de force*, and Lauda only recorded one victory. Towards the end there was a bit of 'parting of the ways' with Ron Dennis, and Lauda retired at the end of the season. One feels sure though that the two seasons alongside Niki Lauda were vital in the transformation of Alain Prost into the 'master's' successor.

Niki was a true 'great' as a driver, and the best of his era. That he was able to return and to win with all his old wily skills only served to enhance his claim as perhaps the most complete driver of all time.

that if they did not get their house in order, the furnishings would be quickly removed. This very real threat may well have encouraged FISA and FOCA to work together a bit more, and to agree to the banning of the hydro-pneumatic 'artful dodger' systems on the cars, and a reduction of the minimum weight limit to 580kg (1,279lb).

After a quiet winter, harmony between the two sides seemed to prevail, but at the South African Grand Prix, war erupted again. The problem this time concerned the drivers, led by Lauda, who objected to the 'super licences' FISA expected them to sign. One of the clauses, it was feared, would tie drivers to teams and allow the introduction of soccer-type transfer fees. This had come about, ironically, following Prost's move to Renault, mid-contract, from McLaren, and the teams wanted to retain control over their drivers.

An effectively unanimous strike by the drivers ensued. They locked themselves in a hotel room, to prevent intimidation by the teams or race organizers, while negotiations were started. The previous autumn, Balestre had been elected for another term as the President of FISA, and vowed to carry on 'as before', in other words, in an autocratic fashion. The fact that, in certain cases, incomplete 'super licence' forms were sent out to be signed and returned, smacks of deceit from the governing body. Perhaps the drivers reacted hastily, but a point was made, even if they were later fined $5,000 each, with those involved in the Belgian fracas being fined a further $5,000.

Eventually, the drivers returned to work, and there were a few changes to be seen. Andretti, like Jones, had left the Grand Prix scene, though he continued to race in America. His place in the Alfa team was taken by none other than de Cesaris, facilitated by Marlboro money, of course. Rosberg had woken one morning to find his fairy godmother sitting by his bed, and he was lifted from the shambles of the Fittipaldi team to join Reutemann at Williams – a real rags-to-riches story. Brabham had recruited

Patrese to support Piquet, and they had a new car, the BT50, complete with BMW 4-cylinder turbocharged engine. Tyrrell had young Italian Alboreto and Abba drummer Borgudd, while Arrows had ex-Toleman Brian Henton and Baldi driving and ex-McLaren driver Jochen Mass made a return to Grand Prix racing with March. Significantly the Lotus, Renault and Ferrari teams were unchanged, with the latter having the new 126C2, Harvey Postlethwaite-designed cars, a major improvement over the previous one.

McLaren had built a new MP4 for Watson to 'B' specification, while Lauda had an older one uprated. These retained their push-rod operated, inboard, front suspension, unlike many other teams, who had copied Brabham's pull-rod system, and were tidied up aerodynamically. It was an evolution based on the experience of the previous season, and was to good effect, as we shall see.

The high-altitude South African circuit proved to the advantage of the turbo-engined cars, which dominated the front of the grid, with Watson ninth, and Lauda thirteenth. The race, as expected, began as a turbo benefit but Reutemann, in contrast to his dispirited drive at Las Vegas, moved himself up into third place, with Watson fifth, and Lauda sixth. The Argentinian was back at his imperious best, though Lauda was matching him, having passed both Watson and Rosberg to claim fourth place.

Race leader Prost then got a puncture and made for the pits. He followed this with a fine drive to eventually retake the lead and win, while Reutemann passed Arnoux, and Lauda came fourth. He was not back to his best, but this was quite a return, as he finished two places up on Watson, who arrived back with tales of woe, and earned himself the nickname 'John Whatswrong' from the mechanics. As a finale, all the drivers had their licences suspended, pending FISA enquiries, and fines; nice to know that racing does not claim all the limelight.

Since the Argentinian race had been cancelled,

the Brazilian Grand Prix was next, and there were some changes to be seen with the cars. Brabham had reverted back to their BT49/D, while Alfa debuted their 182 with V12 power, the V8 turbo engine still not being ready. Lotus also introduced their new 81, though it did not break new ground and looked very much an interim design.

As at the South American races of 1981, a new technical problem, which bent the rules, was thrust at the scrutineers in Brazil. There was a minimum weight limit of 580kg (1,279lb) which the turbo-engined cars, with all their pipework, could reach, but which the Cosworth-powered cars could easily undercut, thus reducing the power advantage of the turbocharged engines. This rule was introduced to ensure that all the necessary safety measures were built into the racing cars, and that they were not lightweight at the expense of strength. The need for a minimum weight limit was thus essential in the 1970s, but with the increasing use of materials, such as carbon fibre, kevlar and titanium, which are both very strong and light, there was no longer a valid reason for the rule, especially in the top level, forcing ground of motor racing.

A rule is a rule though, and the scrutineers are bound by these, so certain FOCA teams seized on a technical loophole and installed bags, ostensibly to carry water to cool the brakes. This was nothing new, and had been used before, but some teams carried as much as 100lb (45kg)'s worth of water. Needless to say, this water ballast was quickly drained from the tanks once out on the circuit, and the cars ran underweight. This may have been cheating, but if a law can no longer be justified, it is there to be broken and it is up to the governing body, whether it be Parliament or FISA, to rescind the law.

Lauda qualified a fine fifth behind Rosberg, with Watson in mid-grid, but McLaren had high hopes for the race. The heat was bound to affect the drivers, and give those from South America a marginal advantage. Villeneuve

stormed off into an early lead, while Reutemann eliminated Lauda and Arnoux, in two separate incidents, putting himself out into the bargain. Meanwhile, Piquet and Rosberg were battling away for second place, and they began to put pressure on Villeneuve. It must have been the heat that affected Villeneuve, for he succumbed and spun off, just when it looked as though there might be a repeat of the Spanish race.

Piquet then began to pull away from Rosberg, both drivers being exhausted, and in the closing laps the relatively frail Brazilian was taking corners with his head resting on the opposite side of the cockpit. He kept going, though, to record a brave, well fought victory ahead of Rosberg. Watson had driven a fine, determined race to finish fourth, behind Prost, a well deserved result which was shortly to provide unexpected dividends. Piquet virtually collapsed on the winners' podium from the exertions of the afternoon, but the local scrutineers were to prove unbiased in their interpretation of the rules, by disqualifying both Piquet and Rosberg, on the grounds that their cars were underweight, thus Watson took second place. A later FISA Court of Appeal upheld the decision, though we all knew who the real, moral winner of the race was.

Prior to the United States (West) Grand Prix, at Long Beach, Reutemann decided to retire, leaving Williams in a pickle, and Grand Prix racing to mourn the loss of three of its best drivers. Reutemann had never been the World Champion, and could be very inconsistent, but there was no doubt that when in the mood, he had the smooth ability to beat anyone, almost irrespective of the car.

BENDING THE RULES

Despite the disqualifications of Brazil, some FOCA teams' cars had water tanks fitted which could hold 12 gallons (54 litres) of water! Andretti was signed as a one-off to drive for

188

Niki Lauda celebrates the first victory of his comeback: the 1982 United States (West) Grand Prix, at Long Beach. On the podium with him are Keke Rosberg and Gilles Villeneuve, both of whom drove for McLaren in Grand Prix racing.

Williams, while still racing at a CART meeting. Turbo power was not the be–all and end–all on this street circuit, and handling agility came well to the fore. As a result, Villeneuve's Ferrari wore a twin rear-wing arrangement, whose legality came under careful scrutiny. This did not make much difference to their practice fortunes, as Lauda was a magnificent second on the grid, while de Cesaris in the Alfa sat on the pole, presumably 'cocking a snook' at his former employers. Watson qualified eleventh, but had suffered a variety of problems in both practice sessions.

The race proved, again, the potential of the MP4, and the improvement in car preparation since the formation of McLaren International. Watson immediately began making his way up the field, and by lap 20 he was third, but he had worn his tyres and had to stop for more, winding up seventh. Up at the front Lauda was giving the young 'hot shoes' a lesson in race craft. On lap 6, in a deft move while under pressure for third place from Giacomelli, he made room for the Alfa to pass, only for the latter to find his way blocked by Arnoux, in second. The two collided and retired, and now Lauda only had de Cesaris in front.

The former McLaren driver's reputation suggested that he would not last the distance, and after being stalked by Lauda, de Cesaris lost out while lapping a back-marker, shaking a fist at him just when it was needed to change gear! Lauda took over the lead, which he never lost. It was a cool, crisp, no frills display, giving more than enough evidence that his comeback was very serious indeed. After that effort, and with the relatively limited driving talent at that time, it would be a foolish man who would bet against Niki taking a third world title.

McLaren were cock-a-hoop with this victory, as Lauda had engineered victory in his own way; but then again he did not have to race Jones or Reutemann. It was thus understandable that opinions were divided as to whether or not to race at the San Marino Grand Prix. Following the FISA Court of Appeal ruling on the Brazilian results, the FOCA teams boycotted the event, citing their cars as being underweight and therefore illegal.

The event was little more than a farce. Only fourteen cars took part, including two Tyrrells, acting as troubleshooters for FOCA, and two other FOCA cars. Pironi may well have ignored team orders to beat Villeneuve, but victories do not come any more hollow. Sadly, it was to be Villeneuve's last race, and Marlboro and Elf threatened to reduce their level of financial involvement if Grand Prix racing was disrupted again. Both FISA and FOCA needed to heed this warning and, to counter the arbitrary actions of Balestre and FISA, a forceful response was needed. Grand Prix racing was in a no-win situation. As an aside, Balestre and FISA had been carpeted by the FIA for their handling of the drivers' strike and the fines, while modified drivers' licence forms were issued.

That shambles over, normality returned in Belgium, but just before the end of the final qualifying hour, a calamitous accident occurred. Villeneuve, going flat out, came up behind Mass who was making his way along much more slowly. Mass's car acted as a launching ramp, and Villeneuve became airborne, crashed down and cartwheeled along the circuit, the car disintegrating around him. He died later in hospital, so bad were his internal injuries.

This raised the whole question of only allowing cars eight tyres for use in qualifying. There used to be two sets of tyres per car, but another recent arbitrary rule-change by Balestre and FISA had altered this to eight tyres, in the knowledge that Williams had been testing a six-wheeled car; another example of an unbiased governing body? The real problem in qualifying was the use of super grippy, short-life tyres which only lasted a couple of laps. Thus drivers had to go all out and try to steer clear of other cars on their one fast lap. It was often a tall order and, finally, a fatality occurred. It was nobody's fault really, just an unfortunate set of circumstances caused by the qualifying regulations.

At the meeting, Williams introduced two new FW08 cars and Derek Daly as a regular driver. Rosberg qualified third, just ahead of Lauda, while Watson was back in tenth place, both MP4s being fitted with weight-saving carbon fibre brakes, for the second time. The race began under a bit of a cloud, and once the leading Renaults had faltered, Rosberg led from de Cesaris and Lauda. All three drivers looked comfortable, but charging through the field came Watson, making his way up to fourth place.

Just after half-distance, de Cesaris went out with gearbox trouble, while Watson, consistent as ever, closed up on Lauda, whose tyres were going off. Watson did not linger, soon passing his team-mate, and set off after Rosberg, who was well ahead. The Williams began to slow a little, though Watson was not in sight of him, but his pit kept him informed of events. Then, there by the roadside was a crashed Williams and John therefore eased off, thinking he was in command of the race. But it was a mistake: Daly had crashed, and Rosberg was still in front. Driving as smoothly as ever, Watson got his head down again, to remorselessly close on the Williams, but the finish was not far away. Even if Watson caught Rosberg, he still had to get past, and that would be no easy task.

Once Watson had the Williams in his sights, he seemed to go even faster, swooping through the bends like a bird in flight, not bouncing all over the kerbs like some unruly drivers, and in one sweet manoeuvre was through into the lead on the penultimate lap. Another McLaren victory, in consecutive races, and with Lauda third, all looked good. That is until the cars were weighed and Niki's was 2lb (1kg) under the limit, not enough to give any advantage whatsoever, but it transgressed the rules, and he was excluded from the results. McLaren still led the Constructors' Championship though, for the first time in years.

An occurrence in Belgium showed the new team spirit within McLaren. Watson, whose car was looked after by Teddy Mayer, tried out and decided to use a different tyre combination for the race, if it was warm. He advised Lauda to do likewise, but as he had not tried them, the Austrian decided not to. John won the race of course, while Niki was slowed by his tyres, but he was man enough to admit as much afterwards and accept his error. This was Lauda all over, a man who knows his own mind, but who can acknowledge he has been bettered.

For a variety of reasons, mostly because the suspension settings were difficult to calculate due to the Michelin tyres, neither Watson nor Lauda featured strongly at Monaco. Both qualified, and ran, in mid-field and both retired. Patrese scored a lucky maiden victory in the BT49/D, when Prost crashed two laps from the end, as it began to rain. De Angelis did well to finish third, and a rousing drive from Mansell netted Lotus fourth.

The United States Grand Prix, in Detroit, provided another example of how FISA just flouted or ignored rules as it pleased them. Before a circuit could host a Grand Prix, it had to have held a race meeting, to prove itself, as much as anything. This little matter was waived, as it had been at Las Vegas, though the Detroit circuit was a little more imaginative. As expected then, practice was full of problems; safety measures needed sorting out, and the track broke up in places. World Champion Piquet even failed to qualify, as it rained during the second practice, while de Cesaris was an impressive second on the grid. Here was another driver who appeared to be doing better away from McLaren.

Neither McLaren showed up particularly well, and as Prost shot off to lead the race, not too much was expected from them. The race was stopped on lap 6 after an accident involving de Angelis and Surer blocked the circuit. Before the restart, involving only eighteen cars, Watson had different tyres fitted to counter the excessive understeer which had troubled him. This worked a treat.

Prost led away again but did not shake off Rosberg. Meanwhile, Watson settled into his stride before making any moves, then began his charge, while keeping well clear of the menacing concrete walls. By lap 24, John was up behind Niki in fifth place on the road and then put in an astonishing lap. Under braking for three separate corners, involving no driver errors, Watson passed Lauda, Cheever, and Pironi, to take second place in a brilliant driving display.

He was not finished yet, Rosberg was out in front and Watson wanted the lead badly. Six laps later, he passed the ragged, hard-charging Rosberg as he had done the others, while Lauda made his way up to third place. Lauda caught Rosberg and, four laps later, as he looked set to take second place, made a hash of the overtaking manoeuvre and ended up in the guard rails. Watson was going as smoothly as ever, looking very assured, and on lap 38 took the overall lead and went on to record a triumphant victory. He may have needed the lucky break of the race being stopped, but over the years Lady Luck has never really smiled kindly on him. John's drive thoroughly deserved a victory, nothing less, and he was now leading the Drivers' Championship.

The teams moved on to Montreal for the Canadian Grand Prix, and the Ile Notre Dame circuit was renamed after Gilles Villeneuve. Watson qualified a creditable sixth with Lauda in mid-grid, but the race got off to a disastrous start. Pironi stalled his Ferrari on the grid, and

Palletti hit him at about 100mph, and died. This was going to be a very difficult season for Grand Prix racing.

It was 6.30 p.m. before the race restarted, and it proved a turbo event at the front. Lauda retired early on with a fuel-pump failure, while Watson kept going and was rewarded with a fortuitous third place, thanks to a high rate of attrition, with only five cars running at the finish. Piquet, in the BMW-engined BT50 and Patrese in the Cosworth-engined BT49 gave Brabham a 1–2, but had it been cricket, bad light would have stopped play rather earlier.

The Dutch Grand Prix had been dropped from the initial FISA calendar, but was hastily restored, though not in its usual slot. As a result, there was little spectator interest but, as ever, the teams were going flat out. Patrese had a BT50, while Moreno replaced an ill Mansell at Lotus. McLaren tried out a shallower rear wing to minimize drag on the straight, and also gave their carbon fibre brakes another airing. But the big news was that Tambay would drive for Ferrari, using Villeneuve's number 27. Ferrari were thus back as a two-car team. Toleman had also re-entered the fray and were to make quite an impression.

With a long straight, the turbo-engined cars took the front places on the grid, with Lauda fifth and Watson back in mid-field this time. Prost and Arnoux led early on but fell by the wayside, leaving Pironi to beat Piquet to the flag, while Lauda took a distant fourth place behind Rosberg, with Watson a lapped ninth. Not a really satisfactory event nor result for McLaren.

Brands Hatch is not a discriminatory circuit, and if a chassis handles well, whether powered by a turbo engine or not, anything is possible. So it proved, as Rosberg sat proudly in pole position, beaming like a Cheshire cat. This smile was sadly wiped off his face when his car refused to start for the parade lap and he had to start from the back of the grid. Lauda had also qualified well, in fifth place, with Watson disappointingly back in mid-field.

Race day was hot, and the sun was clearly smiling on Niki. With Rosberg out of the way, as such, the other front-row car of Patrese stalled and was rammed by Arnoux, eliminating both. Piquet led at first, amid rumours that he intended to make a pitstop for more fuel and tyres, and while Watson retired on lap 3, Lauda was perfectly poised in second place. As for the Brabham pitstop, it had to wait for another day, as Piquet's engine failed on lap 10, and with Lauda in the lead the race was as good as over. Warwick delighted the crowd, in the Toleman, taking second place off Pironi before retiring, and Lauda controlled events from the front, as in days of old. The Ferrari pair of Pironi and Tambay followed Lauda home at a respectful distance; how he must have enjoyed that win.

The Paul Ricard circuit in France with its long straight most certainly did favour the turbo-engined cars, and while the Renault, Ferrari and Brabham teams clogged the front of the grid, Lauda was the fastest Cosworth engine qualifier, in ninth place, while Watson was two places back. Once again Brabham intended to make a pitstop, but both cars, each having led, retired early on.

Watson retired with a rough sounding engine, while Lauda could make no impression on the leading cars and finished eighth. Arnoux made it a joyous month for Renault (since Bernard Hinault had won the *Tour de France* on a Renault bicycle), but there were repercussions. Arnoux had agreed to allow Prost to win and boost his Championship challenge if they were in a 1–2 situation. While this sort of jiggery-pokery is anathema to most racing enthusiasts, it is desirable for a team. However, as Arnoux did not object, and Prost would have understood had Arnoux done so, Prost did not challenge Arnoux and a 20-second gap built up. When Arnoux disobeyed the pit signals, it was too late for Prost to do anything about it; he was not best pleased!

Disaster continued to plague Ferrari, and at the German Grand Prix Pironi, having already claimed pole position, crashed heavily into the back of Prost in pouring rain. It was a needless accident, decidedly unlucky, and Pironi, though finally recovering enough to race power boats, never raced a Grand Prix car again.

Lauda did not race either after injuring a wrist in practice. The long straights at Hockenheim meant that Watson could only qualify tenth. The race was the expected turbo walkover, and also featured a fisticuffs between race leader Piquet and Salazar, after they eliminated each other. Thanks again to some disciplined, skilled driving and benefitting from retirements, Watson made his way up to third place, only for the front suspension to fail a few laps from the end. Tambay gave Ferrari something to cheer, as he scored a maiden victory – one much deserved by the former McLaren driver.

The Österreichring was too fast a circuit to expect a home victory for Niki, and he qualified in tenth position. John, struggling with understeer, was way back, 5.5 seconds off Piquet's pole time, and with even less likelihood of closing the gap on Pironi's Championship lead. The Brabhams led early on and Piquet finally came into the pits for the much vaunted pitstop, but it was ten laps too early, so clearly all was not well. The Williams mechanics rigged their pits up as though a pitstop would be made, but this was either a practical joke, or just a distraction. Whatever, Patrese came in on time, and resumed racing still in the lead, only to retire a few laps later.

Prost took over the lead, with Lauda running fifth and Watson two places behind, only to retire with a blown engine. It looked all sewn up for Prost, but he retired on lap 49, leaving de Angelis out in front in the Lotus. Rosberg, sensing victory, began to charge, catching de Angelis and they set out on the last lap nose to tail. There was no unruly blocking or silly overtaking manoeuvres, but de Angelis used the advantage of leading to good effect. The last corner before the finishing line was the crucial one and, as the Lotus spluttered, so Rosberg closed to within touching distance. In they went, Rosberg initially aiming at the outside

while de Angelis hugged the kerb, and they accelerated hard out of it with Rosberg coming alongside the Lotus, but not past. De Angelis won by a couple of feet to record the Cosworth engine's 150th Grand Prix victory, his own maiden win, and the first for Lotus in four long years. No wonder Colin Chapman was smiling that broad grin of his; after all the traumas he, more than anyone, deserved success again. Amidst all this, Tambay's neat and tidy passing of Lauda to steal fifth place went unnoticed, but it further enhanced Ferrari's lead in the Constructors' Championship.

A new World Championship event, the Swiss Grand Prix, came next. It was held at Dijon in France because the Swiss had banned motor racing back in 1955. Arnoux had signed for Ferrari in 1983, but more ill-luck fell on the Maranello team when Tambay hurt his back and could not race, despite qualifying. There were no red cars in the race. Watson had an unfortunate practice again, but Lauda qualified fourth.

The Renaults led early on but Arnoux retired, leaving Prost on his own, while Lauda ran a confident third. Watson meanwhile blotted his copybook. He damaged a skirt by running over a kerb and having it replaced cost him three laps. Rosberg chased hard after Prost, and got past to record his first ever victory, and more importantly, usurp Pironi at the head of the Drivers' Championship, while Niki's third place drew him level with his luckless teammate.

The Italian Grand Prix will not be fondly remembered by Lauda for, having qualified with Watson in mid-grid, his car's poor handling forced him to give up. Andretti make another one-off appearance, this time for Ferrari, and he sensationally took the pole position. The race was a turbo car benefit, but Watson kept his flickering Championship hopes alive with a steady fourth position, his first points in seven races. This was the result of Teddy Mayer's vast race experience, for he substantially reduced the downforce on the car before the race and it, in

Grand Prix Results 1982

GRAND PRIX	DRIVER	CAR	NO	1ST PRACTICE Time/Posn	2ND PRACTICE Time/Posn	3RD PRACTICE Time/Posn	FINAL GRID POSN	FINAL PLACING	RETIRED CAUSE OF	HIGHEST POSN IN RACE
SOUTH AFRICAN Kyalami 23.1.82	J. Watson	Ford-DFV MP4/5	7		1min 09.74sec 9/29		9–26	4/18		5th
	N. Lauda	Ford-DFV MP4/4	8		1min 10.68sec 13/29		13–26	6/18		4th
BRAZILIAN Rio de Janeiro 21.3.82	J. Watson	Ford-DFV MP4/5	7	1min 31.91sec 11/30	1min 32.15sec 12/29		12–26	4/12		4th
	N. Lauda	Ford-DFV MP4/4	8	1min 30.72sec 7/30	1min 30.15sec 12/29		5–26		Lp 23 Accident suspension damage	7th
USA (West) Long Beach 4.4.82	J. Watson	Ford-DFV MP4/2	7	1min 32.90sec 26/31	1min 28.89sec 10/31		11–26	7/11		4th
	N. Lauda	Ford-DFV MP4/4	8	1min 28.79sec 2/31	1min 27.44sec 2/31		2–26	1/11 WINNER		FL 1st
SAN-MARINO Imola 25.4.82		Team entries withdrawn								
BELGIAN Zolder 9.5.82	J. Watson	Ford-DFV MP4/2	7	1min 18.64sec 12/32	1min 17.14sec 10/32		10–26	1/10 WINNER		FL 1st
	N. Lauda	Ford-DFV MP4/6	8	1min 17.58sec 6/32	1min 16.05sec 4/32		4–26	(3/10) Disqualified – car underweight		2nd
MONACO Monte Carlo 23.5.82	J. Watson	Ford-DFV MP4/2	7	1min 27.32sec 12/30	1min 25.58sec 10/31		10–20		Lp 36 Ignition	8th
	N. Lauda	Ford-DFV MP4/6	8	1min 25.84sec 7/30	1min 26.02sec 12/31		12–20		Lp 57 Engine	8th
DETROIT, USA 6.6.82	J. Watson	Ford-DFV MP4/5	7	1min 51.87sec 17/28	2min 11.38sec 3/21		17–25	1/12 WINNER		1st
	N. Lauda	Ford-DFV MP4/6	8	1min 51.03sec 7/30	2min 09.12sec 1/21		10–25		Lp 41 Accident	3rd
CANADIAN Montreal 13.6.82	J. Watson	Ford-DFV MP4/5	7	1min 35.03sec 17/28	1min 28.82sec 5/29		6–23	3/12		3rd
	N. Lauda	Ford-DFV MP4/6	8	1min 32.25sec 9/28	1min 29.54sec 11/29		11–23		Lp 18 Clutch failure	10th
DUTCH Zandvoort 3.7.82	J. Watson	Ford-DFV MP4/5	7	1min 16.70sec 11/31	1min 18.15sec 10/29		11–26	9/15		9th
	N. Lauda	Ford-DFV MP4/6	8	1min 15.83sec 5/31	1min 17.65sec 7/29		5–26	4/15		4th
BRITISH Brands Hatch 18.7.82	J. Watson	Ford-DFV MP4/5	7	1min 11.56sec 10/30	1min 11.42sec 11/30		12–26		Lp 3 Spun, stalled	15th
	N. Lauda	Ford-DFV MP4/6	8	1min 11.30sec 7/30	1min 10.64sec 5/30		5–26	1/11 WINNER		1st
FRENCH Ricard-Castellet 25.7.82	J. Watson	Ford-DFV MP4/7	7	1min 35.94sec 10/30	1min 39.15sec 11/30		12–26		Lp 14 Electrical connections	9th
	N. Lauda	Ford-DFV MP4/6	8	1min 37.78sec 5/30	1min 38.03sec 9/26		9–26	8/16		6th
GERMAN Hockenheim-ring 8.8.82	J. Watson	Ford-DFV MP4/7	7	1min 53.07sec 11/30	2min 07.82sec 6/29		9–25		Lp 37 Broken suspension	3rd
	N. Lauda	Ford-DFV MP4/6	8	1min 52.68sec 8/30		Did not start. Injured wrist				

AUSTRIAN Österreichring 15.8.82	J. Watson	Ford-DFV MP4/5	7	1min 34.67sec 18/29	1min 34.16sec 17/29	18-26		Lp 45 Engine	**7th**
	N. Lauda	Ford-DFV MP4/6	8	1min 33.01sec 8/29	1min 32.13sec 9/29	10-26	5/7		**5th**
SWISS Dijon-Prenois, France 29.8.82	J. Watson	Ford-DFV MP4/5	7	1min 04.00sec 10/29	1min 04.71sec 7/26	10-25	13/16		**6th**
	N. Lauda	Ford-DFV MP4/70	8	1min 02.98sec 3/29		4-25	3/16		**3rd**
ITALIAN Monza 12.9.82	J. Watson	Ford-DFV MP4/5	7	1min 34.73sec 19/30	1min 33.19sec 12/30	12-26	4/13		**4th**
	N. Lauda	Ford-DFV MP4/2	8	1min 33.57sec 11/30	1min 32.78sec 10/30	10-26		Lp 22 Handling gave up	**9th**
USA Las Vegas 25.9.82	J. Watson	Ford-DFV MP4/5	7	1min 19.32sec 10/30	1min 17.99sec 9/30	8-24	2/14		**2nd**
	N. Lauda	Ford-DFV MP4/7	8	1min 19.17sec 6/30	1min 18.33sec 13/30	12-24		Lp 54 Engine	**6th**

Watson's words 'came alive'. The Italian crowd rejoiced, well almost, in Arnoux's victory, for although he drove a Renault, he would drive a Ferrari in 1983. Tambay and Andretti occupied the next two places and assured Ferrari of the Constructors' Championship, a fitting reward for what had been a heart-breaking year for them.

Once again the Drivers' title was decided in a Las Vegas car park, which says it all! To win the title, John had to win the race without Rosberg scoring any points; it was a slim chance, but better than none. He qualified indifferently yet again, but drove a magnificent race, only to lose out to the eleventh different race winner of the season, and the fifth taking his debut victory. Alboreto won in the Tyrrell, giving that team their first win in over four years, while Rosberg clinched the title by finishing fifth.

The loss of drivers such as Andretti, Pironi, Jones, Reutemann and Villeneuve, with only Lauda coming in at that level, was a terrific blow to Grand Prix racing. However, Rosberg was a worthy Champion; he never gave up all season, and extracted all he could out of the non-turbocharged Williams cars. If Watson had qualified better, or perhaps, as Teddy Mayer was to suggest, if a little more effort had been directed his way by the team, then he ought to

have taken the title. The string of races in mid-season where he did not score any points proved his undoing, but the Championship lasts a season, and over the season it was Rosberg who performed best; and remember, he lost the six points for the second place in Brazil. John Watson was never to come so close again.

On the 3rd of November 1982, FISA introduced new regulations, banning side skirts and insisting that cars should have flat bottoms. These two changes, along with a few less contentious ones, virtually eliminated ground effects from the vocabulary of Grand Prix racing, the cars having to rely on the downforce provided by the wings and over-body airflow. A good argument could certainly be made for the need to reduce cornering speedds, a dispute which seemed to rage from season to season, with the safety of both spectators and drivers to the fore.

On these grounds alone, a ban on ground effects made sense, but what about limiting the ever-rising power output of the turbocharged engines? Cars powered by these were arriving at corners, even after quite modcst straights, 20mph (30kph) faster than those with normally-aspirated engines. Brakes and tyres suffered heavy punishment and the higher the speed, the greater the danger. But, rather than reduce the size of the turbo engines, say to 1 litre, or limiting the boost pressure, a 250-litre (55-gallon) fuel limit was imposed which, after the experience gained in the 1982 World Sportscar Championship, suggested that there would be a few Grand Prix economy-run races, to add a little variety.

Considering these abrupt changes, it was not surprising that many teams, particularly those using Cosworth engines, were not happy. True, the minimum weight limit had been reduced to 540kg (1,190lb), a move in the right direction, but the loss of ground effects took away any lingering hopes of Cosworth-powered cars seriously challenging the turbo teams. Because the cornering speed equation would now be dominated by the wings (and the bigger the wing, generally, the higher the cornering speed and greater the drag), the higher-powered turbo engines were obviously at an advantage. Thus, apart from being able to outrun a Cosworth-powered car along the straights, a turbo car would probably corner faster as well. Game, set and match.

Brabham and Williams were less pleased with these rule changes than most; the former had to drop their new BT51 car which could not be made to conform to the new regulations, while a ban was imposed on six-wheeled cars. Williams had built and been testing for over a year a six-wheeled car which, unlike the Tyrrell P34 of 1976–1977, had four wheels, the same size as the standard front wheel, at the back. Now all that money and time were wasted thanks to more arbitrary rule changes, limiting the competitiveness not of the FISA teams, though Osella and Ligier would suffer, but aimed at the FOCA teams, even though many were now looking at turbo engines.

An even greater shock hit motor racing in December, with the death of Colin Chapman. He had been working on the new Renault turbo-powered Lotus 93T when motor racing was robbed of its most gifted and successful designer. Naturally, as the cars became more complex, his individual contribution to each new car lessened, but he oversaw the projects, often

initiated new ideas, and still ran the team and Lotus Cars. In Grand Prix racing alone his achievements were legion, not just in the titles won, but in the innovative designs. He had a major say in the design of the Vanwall; his Lotus 25 broke new ground with its monocoque chassis, while the 33 built on this. The 49, designed for the Cosworth engine, used this chassis as a stressed member of the car, while the 72 introduced the modern era. Finally, exploring ground effects with the 77 and 78, he again took Grand Prix racing by storm with the 79, and who knows how good the banned 88 might have been. Other designers equalled, or occasionally surpassed his efforts but nobody even came near his level of ingenuity, and there was no more a charismatic leader.

Following the introduction of these new regulations, the teams and their personnel proved their dependability, devotion to the job and considerable expertise by getting the new cars ready to race in Brazil. Gordon Murray, fast filling Chapman's shoes, once again came up with an original design, the BT52, owing more to the slimline look of the late 1960s than the wide-bodied cars of recent years. Others followed a similar route, though the turbo teams, excluding Brabham of course, tended to use a wider-bodied car.

A further innovation in Murray's thinking concerned the use of pitstops. He felt these to be beneficial, so rather than have a car running with a half-filled fuel tank at the beginning of the race, the BT52 had a reduced fuel capacity. This enabled the car to be smaller, nimble and, unlike the other turbo-engined cars, at least initially got right down to the 540kg (1,190lb) limit. As with Chapman, where Murray led, others followed.

Not John Barnard though. The wide-bodied MP4 had been well proven with five wins in two seasons; it looked right, had a good lift/drag ratio, and the large plan body could still generate some over-body downforce. On top of all this, there was another consideration: a turbocharged engine. In 1981 it was clear that

John Barnard

It did not take long for John Barnard's talent to blossom as he rose to become one of the most gifted car designers in Grand Prix racing. Like many great designers before him, for example Ferdinand Porsche, or Sir Nigel Gresley in the steam locomotive field, Barnard craved both responsibility of and recognition for his design work, perhaps to the point of vanity.

After a spell at GEC designing machines to make lightbulbs, Barnard landed himself in the Lola drawing office, in 1968. He was responsible for several successful designs before leaving in 1972 to join McLaren, as a sort of 'number two' to Gordon Coppuck. Barnard came to dislike McLaren's 'design by committee' tradition, and after designing the unused M25 F5000 car and the USAC M16/E Indycar, he left in mid-1975 for the American-based Parnelli-Jones team, and later Jim Hall's outfit. It was at the latter, where he received scant recognition for his Lotus 78-based ground effects USAC car, that Barnard really came into his own as a designer and, frustrated by his 'man behind the scenes' image, he left.

Ron Dennis recruited John Barnard in 1979 to research and design a new Grand Prix car for Project 4, and this eventually became the revolutionary MP4, introduced in 1981, by which time Project 4 had merged with McLaren to form McLaren International. Barnard became a director of the new company and took sole responsibility, and therefore credit, for the car, while at the same time laying down the parameters for the projected Tag/Porsche engine. The MP4 was Barnard's car, and he did not intend having his design compromised merely to accept an engine.

With each passing season McLaren grew in stature, and Barnard was always on top of the job in hand; but there were problems. When Niki Lauda announced his retirement at the Austrian Grand Prix in 1985, Ron Dennis credited Lauda's success in large part to Barnard, and yet a year later, after the same race, Barnard had gone.

Barnard joined Ferrari for 1987 and stayed there until 1989, leaving for Benetton as Alain Prost was about to join. Though Barnard's Ferrari and Benetton cars have all won races, they have not been the best around, a fact which ultimately leads to question whether Niki Lauda and Alain Prost made the MP4/2 series look better than it was. After all, when Prost arrived at Ferrari for 1990, he virtually transformed the team, after Barnard had left.

It is said that John Barnard is stubborn and not always receptive to new ideas, especially if they are not his own. He undoubtedly, at least at one stage, craved recognition and credit for his designs; those years 'behind the scenes' clearly leaving their mark. In his favour though, all his designs have been deserving of the highest praise. Motor racing is usually a team effort, and who can blame the car designer for not leaving all the credit to the drivers?

---

unless FISA had a major shake-up, the 3-litre engined cars would soon be doomed, as far as being truly competitive was concerned. FOCA had fought the turbo engines, and especially the restriction on aerodynamic ground effects, but once Brabham, whose owner Bernie Ecclestone was the leading light in FOCA, got the BMW turbo engine, the writing was on the wall in large clear letters.

John Barnard and Ron Dennis most certainly did not lack foresight and began looking for a turbo engine in 1981. They did not want a compromise engine ('here, try and fit this into your car'), and Ron optimistically approached Porsche, who had perhaps the greatest turbo

engine experience at that time. The idea was for Porsche to design and build, as contractors, a turbo engine whose outside dimensions were decided by McLaren. Ron Dennis would raise the finance, and the engine would belong to McLaren. A contract to design the engine was signed, leaving Ron to find a backer to provide the money to build the engine.

This all reads nice and easily enough and with hindsight, well, you or I could have done it, but Ron took one hell of a risk in initiating this project. If securing the finance to build this engine was all he achieved with McLaren, Ron Dennis would have earned himself a proud place in the history of Grand Prix racing. He has achieved just a little more. After trying several options, Techniques d'Avant Garde, co-sponsors of rivals Williams, came forth with the money, mainly as a result of the enthusiasm of the owner's son, Mansour Ojjeh, and the building contract with Porsche was signed in December 1982. It was initially hoped that the new engine would be ready for the Belgian Grand Prix, but in the meantime, the MP4 was updated to 'C' specification.

Another change took place at McLaren during the close season. McLaren and Project Four, the teams which had merged to form McLaren International, had fused together successfully, but Teddy Mayer and Tyler Alexander decided that the time was right to go their separate ways. There were no recriminations, no public rows, just a feeling that it was time to move on to something else, leaving the aspiring talents of Ron Dennis and John Barnard to develop in their own direction. Teddy Mayer and Tyler Alexander were now very much the old guard, and had seen it all before. It was time to give the new boys the chance to do things their own way, having successfully played with a straight bat through the transition period.

Certainly Teddy Mayer would be missed by John Watson. Mayer had looked after John's car in 1982, something the McLaren driver initially was less than keen on. After a rough time in 1980, John felt the full benefit of Teddy's immense race experience, in this respect perhaps greater than John Barnard's, as Teddy Mayer was able to set up the car more to John's driving style. Niki Lauda may well have suffered in that Barnard was too inflexible and too theoretical about the car's optimum settings, whereas Watson's was more race forgiving. This may have had something to do with the fact that Niki regularly out-qualified John, whereas John often performed better once in the race.

The downside to this was that whenever Teddy Mayer did something good to Watson's car, he stuck it up Barnard's nose, not exactly conducive to a harmonious working relationship. Mayer and Alexander's contribution to McLaren and to Grand Prix racing cannot be overstated, and though they had latterly suffered some pretty lean years, McLaren had enjoyed enormous success, in America as well as in Grand Prix, under their skilful, often colourful leadership.

TIGER AND TURBOS

In Brazil for the opening race of 1983, the regulations ensured that new cars abounded, and the MP4/C was one of the few to be almost indistinguishable, on the surface, from the previous season. Major changes included Alfa Romeo's withdrawal from competition as a factory team though Euroracing, sponsored by Marlboro, ran the whole operation, their occasional shambolic team performance making one think there had been no change at all. They did have, at last, the V8 turbo engine installed in their new 183T cars, which threatened to literally boost their performance. ATS ran a single car, complete with BMW turbo engine, which certainly offered them the opportunity to run with the 'big boys'. Ligier, after a disastrous year, had lost their Talbot sponsorship and mythological turbo engine, and returned to the Cosworth fold once again. Perhaps the most interesting and potentially successful change concerned Lotus, who had, for one car initially, Renault turbo power. It was a pity that Chapman would not be there to direct his team into this new, exciting phase.

In Brazil, fiendishly hot and sunny as ever, it was Rosberg in the Cosworth-powered Williams who sat proudly on the pole. His new team-mate, Laffite, was towards the back with most of the Cosworth-engined runners, which included John Watson, but Niki Lauda was tucked up behind the leading turbo cars in ninth place. Rosberg led initially until Piquet took over on lap 5, never to be headed. Piquet fooled everybody by delaying his pitstop until two-thirds distance had been run, and he rejoined, still in the lead.

John Watson gave a good account of himself in the MP4/1–C during 1983, and never gave up. The Brabham, with BMW turbo power, might be the faster car, but Watson did his best to keep in touch whenever possible.

Watson, fighting from his lowly grid position, had a marvellous race. He got the bit between his teeth right from the start and passed Lauda, Warwick, Baldi, Cheever (Renault), Arnoux (Ferrari), Tambay, Patrese, and Prost to take third place on lap 17. Some of his overtaking manoeuvres were as incisive as a surgeon with his knife, making room where none existed with a variety of feints and twists of which George Best would have been proud. Twelve laps later he was second, as Rosberg went in for a pitstop, with as forceful, smooth and controlled a drive as one could wish to see, only to be so cruelly rewarded when his engine failed at half-distance.

Lauda was no slouch either, steadily progressing into fourth place just before Watson retired, having overtaken six cars *en route*. He was to relieve Prost of second place a little later, only to lose it in turn to a flying Rosberg. Two fine

drives, and the MP4/Cs looked very competitive, to begin the season, with the turbo engine on its way.

Lest the racing did not quite satisfy everyone, the officials got into the act at the end, disqualifying Rosberg once more from his well-earned second place for receiving a push-start following a flash fire during his pitstop. In case that was not enough, de Angelis was disqualified from thirteenth place, for racing a Cosworth-, and not Renault-powered car, even though he had practised both!

The United States (West) Grand Prix at Long Beach followed. The circuit was altered this year, but was none the worse for it. Due to the escalating costs of staging the race, especially the cost of air freighting the teams and their vast amounts of equipment, this was to be the last Grand Prix to run there. American CART racing was scheduled for the following three years, and there was to be no return for the Grand Prix fraternity.

On the credit side Alan Jones, the 1980 World Champion, made a one-off drive with Arrows in an attempt to entice a big money sponsor to the team, who would then provide him with a competitive drive, or so it was hoped. It was like using a spratt to catch a mackerel, but rumours spread that he was to replace John Watson at McLaren. This was denied by the team and after the actual race, could not have been further from anyone's mind.

Practice was a disaster for both Lauda and Watson. The new section of the circuit contained a bump which had the engineers agonizing over ride heights; it was, however, a problem common to all teams. McLaren also had enormous trouble getting their Michelin tyres to warm up thoroughly, and therefore to offer enough grip. That Watson and Lauda lined up in twenty-second and twenty-third places respectively puts Rosberg and Laffite's performances in the Williams FW08/Cs, with third and fourth places, into perspective. It would be safe to say that nobody at McLaren was expecting too much on race day.

Race morning warm-up, running softer compound tyres, showed McLaren in a different light, but they were surely too far back on the grid to make an impression. Watson gained two places on the opening lap, but was then displaced by Lauda, whom he proceeded to follow for half the race. Both cars were clearly working their tyres much better, and the red and white pair began to make dramatic progress through the field. At first they passed cars they ought to have preceeded in the first place, though these included Piquet, a lowly twentieth at the start, and Giacomelli, now in the Toleman.

Progress was initially noteworthy rather than startling. The leaders still pulled away, having a clear road in front, but when lapping the tailenders, they slowed, and thanks to a few retirements, the McLaren pair began to close. Then came a spate of pitstops, and suddenly Niki and

John were in the points, the Ulsterman now looking hard for a way past his team-mate. Lauda, wise and canny as ever, knew that he could not resist for long and let Watson through to chase Patrese, while towing Niki along.

Then ahead there remained only Laffite, driving exceptionally well in the Williams, and showing that he had lost none of his flair, and was not coasting into retirement. Like the other Goodyear and Pirelli runners though, Laffite was in tyre trouble and Watson, running confidently and supremely smoothly, cut into his lead like a hot knife into butter, shot past, and was away. Lauda did likewise, and though there were still over thirty laps to run, only a mechanical failure could stop a McLaren 1–2, since neither driver looked even close to making an error, and nor was anybody left running likely to have a hope in hell of relieving Niki of second place.

While not getting carried away by the record-breaking victory, from such a lowly grid position, it was the second race in succession in which the McLaren pair, and John Watson in particular, had come through the field in fine style. Watson had passed twelve drivers *en route* to his victory, and though the list of those conquored was not as impressive, though lengthier, than in Brazil, the likes of Piquet, Giacomelli, Arnoux, Laffite and Lauda were certainly not slouches.

Thereafter, as was expected with a Cosworth engine, momentum was lost a bit. In an attempt to remain competitive, Cosworth had introduced their short-stroke DFY derivative of the ageing DFV, giving about 30bhp more. McLaren used these at the unusually early French Grand Prix, but Watson's let him down after only four laps. Lauda did not last the distance either, both starting in mid-grid, with Lauda as the fastest Cosworth runner. It was a turbo walkover with Prost winning from Piquet, though both Williams drivers finished in the points.

The San Marino Grand Prix was little different. John qualified in twenty-fourth position,

The final Long Beach Grand Prix took place in 1983; a circuit enjoyed by most drivers. As an apt finale, John Watson wrote himself into the record books by winning, after starting from twenty-second place on the grid. Here he is in thirteenth position on lap 17, leading Guerrero, de Angelis (who is about to stop at the pits), and Cecotto.

5½ seconds behind Tambay on the pole, proof, if one was needed, of the gulf that now existed between the two types of engines. This was no circuit for miracles, unlike Long Beach, but through a combination of smooth, skilful driving and a few retirements, Watson claimed fifth place though lapped, as Tambay, Prost and Arnoux took the major honours.

Then at Monaco, that least successful of circuits for McLaren down the years, the team plumbed new depths. Neither driver qualified for the race, though a certain amount of bad luck was involved. The MP4s' inability to heat up their tyres, due in part to the lessened downforce, wasted the first practice, while rain during the second qualifying session ruled out any chance of getting on to the grid. Instead, they had to sit and watch Rosberg at his magnificent best beat all the turbo cars and win from the front.

A shortened, but nevertheless challenging Spa circuit hosted the Belgian Grand Prix for the first time since 1970. The Porsche engine was nowhere near ready, and on this fast, demanding circuit Lauda and Watson had little chance, and qualified towards the rear of the grid. Neither ran particularly well and Watson retired after colliding with Jarier's Ligier. Lauda lasted longer, until his engine failed, but his efforts were no more effective than Watson's. Prost drove a masterly race, underlining his Championship potential, to win from Tambay and Cheever, though both Rosberg and Laffite finished in the points again.

Organization for the Detroit Grand Prix was much improved this time around, though one would still barely class it a Grand Prix circuit. Nevertheless, it was to be the scene for a very historic occasion, unbeknown to everyone at the time. Michelin, at last, gave McLaren tyres

201

more suited to the MP4, which demonstrated that the recent lack of competitiveness was not entirely due to the car.

There was a certain irony in that the problem was related to the reduced minimum weight for the cars. The virtual elimination of ground effects greatly reduced the downforce on the tyres, which did not heat up to the required temperature and offered less grip. This was not helped by the otherwise welcomed weight reduction. The turbo cars, such as Renault, solved this by using huge or multi wings to generate extra downforce, but of course the extra power of the engines could drag these through the air easily enough. A Cosworth engine, giving away a considerable bhp advantage, would prove ridiculously slow on the straights, if it had to pull a wing of such a size along. The new tyres at least allowed the MP4 to generate extra grip, and results improved.

Osella had an Alfa V12 engine for Ghinzani, replacing a Cosworth unit, but this made little difference. Both Lauda and Watson were still near the wrong end of the grid, with the turbo cars at the front again, but there was to be no fairy tale result for McLaren this time. Lauda in fact got nowhere fast. He finally gave up after fifty laps with a failed damper, having got no higher than eleventh. Watson, however, was having a real 'go'.

Piquet led early on before a puncture let him down, but the turbo cars were not having it all their own way. Watson once again blended smooth driving with the occasional splash of aggression, and while others fell by the wayside through a combination of unruly driving and lack of mechanical sympathy, John's potion began to pay dividends. Even when going flat out, Watson seldom looked to be going really fast. You needed to keep an eye fixed on the stopwatch to make sure that he was not just cruising round. Unlike other more flamboyant drivers who hung the tail out, or those less refined who bounced off kerbs, walls, other like-minded drivers, and anything else which happened to be around, Watson was always tidy, and on circuits

like Detroit, this was likely to reward him.

Watson's progress through the field was steady rather than meteoric, but he still wound up in third place at the end. Alboretto won in the Tyrrell, and this was the 155th, and final, Grand Prix victory for the Cosworth engine, albeit in DFY form. With Rosberg taking second place, all three places on the podium were occupied by drivers of Cosworth-powered cars, a convincing and entirely fitting way to end a sixteen-year winning run.

A week later in Canada, it was back to the turbo circuits, and Watson and Lauda could only qualify towards the back of the grid again. McLaren were seemingly treading water, awaiting their own turbocharged engine, and Lauda, to a certain extent, gave the impression that it was hardly worth competing when there was little chance of success. He spun and stalled, and that was that, but Watson – his car sporting his newly awarded MBE insignia – carried on as gamely as ever for a respectable sixth, after another of his measured performances. Arnoux won from Cheever and Tambay, but in fourth place was the effervescent Rosberg, another Cosworth-powered driver, who would not simply give in.

Silverstone, using the title 'The Fastest Grand Prix Circuit in the World', was likely to offer the Cosworth runners few crumbs of comfort. Practice confirmed this with Arnoux, Tambay and Prost all exceeding the 150mph (240kph) average lap speed. Can you imagine *averaging* 150mph around a circuit with four corners, three curves, a chicane, and only two moderate straights! And remember that ground effects were drastically reduced from the previous seasons – those engines must have been producing some large horses.

Lauda qualified in mid-grid, while Watson disappointed once again, back in twenty-fourth position. Two events pleased the crowds, though. Honda gave their turbo engine its Grand Prix debut, driven by Johansson from the Spirit team, and Mansell at last had a Renault turbo engine in his Lotus. As expected, the race was a turbo benefit, kept alive by the pitstops (in which even McLaren indulged for once), the battle at the front, and Mansell's good showing in coming fourth. Prost defeated Piquet and Tambay to open up a lead in the Championship, while Lauda put up a spirited performance for sixth place. Watson, having no magical formula this time, was well back, in ninth place.

At the end of the race Tyrrell protested against the Renault and Ferrari teams for injecting water into the fuel/air mixture. This was ostensibly done for cooling purposes, but evidence was later produced to show that this also affected the octane rating of the fuel. The protest was dismissed, but it was interesting to speculate why Lotus, who also used Renault engines, were not included in the protest. Surely it had nothing to do with them being part of the FOCA family?

There was still no Tag/Porsche engine for the German Grand Prix, though tests were now underway. As far as the Cosworth runners were concerned, they had no chance against the turbo cars, and poor old John Watson was twenty-third on the grid, 8½ seconds slower than Tambay on the pole, with Lauda five places in front.

As far as the Championship was concerned, it was developing into a three-horse race between Prost, Piquet and the revelation of the year, Tambay. The latter had regained all the confidence knocked out of him after two uncompetitive years with McLaren and being replaced at Ligier, and had lost none of his smooth, cultured, driving ability. He returned to Grand Prix racing in the hottest seat going, the Ferrari number 27 of the late Gilles Villeneuve. Few if any drivers could have taken over such a car/number combination so successfully and with such dignity. Here he sat on the pole at Hockenheim a year after his first victory, a serious Championship challenger and, perhaps most surprisingly, having comfortably outdriven his hard-charging though untidy teammate Arnoux throughout the season.

The race was a turbo walkover, of course, but Watson, up to twentieth by the end of lap 1, then followed in Lauda's wheeltracks all the way to the end, so that they finished fifth and sixth. Once again, there were no heroics from either driver, just a supreme exhibition of racecraft, allied to consistent, skilful driving and the ability to benefit from others' misfortune or incompetence. Not the way either would really *want* to race, but a near-perfect demonstration of making the best of the situation. I say 'near-perfect', because Lauda overshot his pit during the refuelling stop, had to reverse slightly, and was subsequently disqualified. Watson thus inherited fifth place, while Arnoux won, and only Prost of the Championship contenders added to his points, finishing in fourth place.

Austria, Niki's home race, was to be the last one before McLaren introduced their turbo car. Tambay took the pole while Mansell, clearly enjoying Renault turbo power, had the Lotus in third place. Lauda was keen to do as well as possible; he was the fastest Cosworth qualifier, though only in fourteenth place on the grid. John was three places behind, yet 6 seconds slower than Tambay!

From the start the battle for the lead featured the three Championship contenders, plus Arnoux, who soon took the lead off Tambay. There was no let up, except that Tambay's engine failed, and the race finished off with Prost furiously chasing Arnoux. Prost hounded the Ferrari mercilessly until it gave best, and he extended his lead with another fine victory.

Further back Lauda, as wily and tenacious as ever, picked up places whenever and however he could, finishing his last drive in an MP4/C with a well-earned sixth place. He was lapped twice, but given the right car/engine, there were few people who doubted his ability to be right at the front again. Watson was quickly into the pits, having damaged his front wings at the start. Yet he too finished only two laps down, in ninth place, with yet another accomplished, steady drive back up the field.

McLaren's great day finally came at the

It was a long time coming, but here is the Tag/Porsche engine as fitted into Niki Lauda's MP4/1–E at the Dutch Grand Prix meeting.

Dutch Grand Prix when the Tag/Porsche engine was given its debut, driven by Niki Lauda. The engine was installed in an MP4/1E modified car, though a new car was due for 1984. As one would expect on the debut of a new car/ engine, there were numerous problems and Lauda qualified down in nineteenth place. It may have been sixteen years to the race, since the Cosworth engine scored a victory on its debut, but the competition was hotter in 1983, and the Tab/Porsche engine just a little more complicated.

John Watson had to continue with his usual Cosworth-engined car, which sparked off rumours again about his future with McLaren. Whether this had any bearing on the race was

difficult to say, but on a circuit suited to turbo cars because of its long straight, John, once again, demonstrated his tenacious race abilities. While Lauda, after a quiet race, retired on lap 26 with brake trouble, Watson was in the groove, passing Cosworth and turbo cars alike as he advanced up the field. Never putting a wheel out of place – unlike Prost who, when challenging Piquet for the lead, made a rare but genuine error and took both cars out of the race – Watson made his way up into second place before his pitstop, on lap 42. He resumed in third place and never lost it, finishing a mere 44 seconds behind a lucky Arnoux and Tambay, and ahead of several turbo cars.

His reward was an MP4/1E for the Italian

John Watson's first race with the Tag turbo-engined MP4/1–E was in the Italian Grand Prix, and he outqualified Niki Lauda to boot. Watson ran well, and his practice performances, as seen here, showed there was still plenty of fire in his belly.

Grand Prix, and both cars were up with the best along the straights, though both were in mid-grid, with Watson 5½ seconds adrift of Patrese on the pole; plenty of room for improvement! Overnight, befoe the race, a few of the leading grid places were decorated with some not so well chosen words about the cars/drivers, while those of Tambay and Arnoux were graced with words of encouragement. The Italian organizers joined in the fun by having the offensive comments erased, yet leaving the complimentary ones, for the Ferraris, in place. Who ever said they were biased?

John Watson might well have wished he still had his old car, as he retired with electrical problems as early as lap 14, though he was already in seventh place. Niki was even worse off, having to visit the pits to sort out an engine misfire. This was all to no avail as he too retired, right outside the Brabham pit, and he was unceremoniously pushed out of the way to make room for the race leader, Piquet, who was due in. As Piquet had won all too easily from Arnoux, and as Prost failed to score points again, the Championship was coming nicely to the boil.

The discarded title 'Grand Prix of Europe' was used to justify Brands Hatch holding a race in place of the cancelled event in New York. It may have been arranged at short notice, but one would never have known. Both McLarens sported large rear wings like the other turbo teams, and for once Watson out-qualified Lauda, though both were still only in mid-grid. Mansell raised local hopes, qualifying third, and all was set for a real battle.

This did not take long to materialize; from the green light de Angelis was chasing Patrese for the lead, and made a passing manoeuvre on lap 11 which resulted in both cars spinning off. Fortunately neither retired, but Piquet took the lead and drove another mature race to win, ahead of Prost, and move closer to the Frenchman with only one race remaining. Both McLarens ran well initially, but Lauda retired with an engine failure while Watson seriously contemplated the value of the new-style rear wing, as it began to break up. He rushed into the pits and was sent out for a couple of laps while a new wing was made ready. Meanwhile, the old wing broke up completely and, the next thing John knew, he was heading for the catch

205

John Watson tailed Niki Lauda for ten laps at the European Grand Prix, held at Brands Hatch, before finally relieving him of tenth place. Here they go round Druids, with Watson feeling the pressure of reigning World Champion Keke ('never say die') Rosberg, from behind, in the Finn's last race in the Cosworth-engined Williams.

John Watson has passed Niki Lauda at last during the European Grand Prix, at Brands Hatch. Now it is Lauda's turn to fend off the flying Finn.

fences at some god awful speed he would rather not think about. Fortunately, he emerged from the tangle of wood and netting unscathed. What a way to finish your 150th Grand Prix race, though.

So, the Drivers' Championship was down to the last race, in South Africa, though Prost was a clear favourite. Williams brought their FW09 Honda-powered cars (the Spirit team having been dropped by Honda), while Tambay was to make way for Alboretto at Ferrari, a poor reward for a good season. He made up for it by claiming the pole yet again, with both Brabhams before Arnoux, who was ahead of

Prost. The McLarens had not gone well in practice, and with both ending up in mid-grid, there was still work to be done. Then, on pre-race warm up, Lauda was the fastest of all the drivers – a good omen for the race.

Not for Watson, however. His car would not start on the grid and, instead of starting from the back, he re-took his original place after the warm-up lap and was disqualified! Lauda was determined that the Tag/Porsche-engined car would claim some points before the season was out, and drove with great gusto. He picked his way through the field, not waiting for cars to retire and, despite a lengthy pitstop, drove his

Lap 2 of the South African Grand Prix, the final race of 1983, and Niki Lauda, in tenth position, leads Warwick, Cheever, Mansell and John Watson, while Laffite is about to retire his Williams. Anyone thinking that those at the back of the field are poor drivers, not really trying, can forget it. The three cars battling it out, three abreast in the distance, are contesting twenty-second place, and are trying just as hard as those at the front.

Grand Prix Results 1983

GRAND PRIX	DRIVER	CAR	NO	1ST PRACTICE Time/Posn	2ND PRACTICE Time/Posn	3RD PRACTICE Time/Posn	FINAL GRID POSN	FINAL PLACING	RETIRED CAUSE OF	HIGHEST POSN IN RACE
BRAZILIAN Jacarepagua 13.3.83	J. Watson	Ford-DFV MP4/1C-6	7	1min 37.84sec 14/27	1min 36.98sec 14/27		15-26		Lp 35 Engine seizure	2nd
	N. Lauda	Ford-DFV MP4/1C-7	8	1min 36.05sec 8/27	1min 36.90sec 13/27		9-26	3/17		2nd
USA (West) Long Beach 27.3.83	J. Watson	Ford-DFV MP4/1C-6	7	1min 32.44sec 22/26	1min 30.10sec 21/28		22-26	1/12 WINNER		1st
	N. Lauda	Ford-DFV MP4/1C-7	8	1min 30.26sec 11/26	1min 30.19sec 22/28		23-26	2/12		FL 2nd
FRENCH Ricard Castellet 7.4.83	J. Watson	Ford-DFY MP4/1C-6	7	1min 41.84sec 12/29	1min 42.45sec 14/29		12-26		Lp 4 Engine failure	25th
	N. Lauda	Ford-DFV MP4/1C-7	8	1min 41.07sec 9/29	1min 41.49sec 10/29		14-26		Lp 30 Seized transmission	6th
SAN MARINO Imola 30.4.83	J. Watson	Ford-DFY MP4/1C-6	7	1min 37.85sec 22/28	1min 36.65sec 22/27		23-26	5/12		5th
	N. Lauda	Ford-DFY MP4/1C-7	8	1min 38.09sec 25/28	1min 36.10sec 16/27		17-26		Lp 12 Accident	9th
MONACO Monte Carlo 15.5.83	J. Watson	Ford-DFY MP4/1C-8	7	1min 30.28sec 23/26	1min 53.77sec 7/19		Did not qualify	Did not qualify		
	N. Lauda	Ford-DFY MP4/1C-7	8	1min 29.90sec 22/26	1min 54.45sec 4/19					
BELGIAN Spa-Fran-corchamps 22.5.83	J. Watson	Ford-DFY MP4/1C-8	7	2min 10.32sec 20/28			20-26		Lp 9 Collision	
	N. Lauda	Ford-DFY MP4/1C-7	8	2min 09.48sec 15/28	3min 00.36sec 18/22		15-26		Lp 34 Engine failure	
DETROIT, USA 5.6.83	J. Watson	Ford-DFY MP4/1C-8	7	2min 10.63sec 11/27	1min 49.25sec 21/27		21-26	3/12		FL 3rd
	N. Lauda	Ford-DFY MP4/1C-7	8	2min 09.02sec 9/27	1min 48.99sec 17/27		18-26		Lp 50 Driver gave up	11th
CANADIAN Montreal 12.6.83	J. Watson	Ford-DFY MP4/1C-8	7	1min 34.81sec 18/28	1min 33.71sec 19/28		20-26	6/11		6th
	N. Lauda	Ford-DFY MP4/1C-7	8	1min 34.45sec 20/28	1min 33.67sec 18/28		19-26		Lp 12 Spun and stalled	14th
BRITISH Silverstone 16.6.83	J. Watson	Ford-DFY MP4/1C-8	7	1min 15.61sec 23/28	1min 16.09sec 21/28		24-26	9/17		9th
	N. Lauda	Ford-DFY MP4/1C-7	8	1min 14.27sec 14/28	1min 15.12sec 15/28		15-26	6/17		5th
GERMAN Hockenheim-ring 7.8.83	J. Watson	Ford-DFY MP4/1C-2	7	1min 57.78sec 24/29			23-26	6/13		6th
	N. Lauda	Ford-DFY MP4/1C-7	8	1min 56.73sec 19/29			18-26	5/13		5th
AUSTRIAN Österreichring 11.8.83	J. Watson	Ford-DFY MP4/1C-2	7	1min 36.52sec 15/29	1min 36.14sec 17/29		17-26	9/13		9th
	N. Lauda	Ford-DFY MP4/1C-7	8	1min 33.75sec 10/29	1min 36.60sec 21/29		14-26	6/13		6th
DUTCH Zandvoort 2.8.83	J. Watson	Ford-DFY MP4/1C-2	7	1min 21.01sec 21/29	1min 17.79sec 11/29		15-26	3/14		3rd
	N. Lauda	McLaren-TAG MP4/1E-6	8	1min 20.17sec 16/29	1min 21.05sec 28/29		19-26		Lp 26 Brake failure	12th

ITALIAN Monza 11.9.83	J. Watson	McLaren-TAG 7 MP4/1E-5 8	1min 35.93sec 15/29	1min 34.71sec 16/28	10-26		Lp 14 Electrics failure Lp 25 No reason given	**7th** **14th**
	N. Lauda	McLaren-TAG MP4/1E-6	1min 33.19sec 10/29	1min 33.13sec 13/28	13-26			
EUROPEAN Brands Hatch 25.9.83	Watson	McLaren-TAG 7 MP4/1E-5	1min 14.30sec 10/29	1min 13.78sec 9/29	10-26		Lp 37 Accident	**10th**
	N. Lauda	McLaren-TAG 8 MP4/1E-6	1min 15.27sec 15/29	1min 13.92sec 11/29	13-26		Lp 26 Engine failure	**10th**
SOUTH AFRICAN Kyalami 15.10.83	J. Watson	McLaren-TAG 7 MP4/1E-7	1min 08.33sec 13/26	1min 10.64sec 17/25	15-26		Lp 19 Disqualified	**11th**
	N. Lauda	McLaren-TAG 8 MP4/1E-6	1min 07.97sec 9/26	1min 08.59sec 14/25	12-26	11/13		**2nd**

way up to second place, after Piquet had eased back, knowing Prost had retired. Patrese was leading, but Lauda systematically closed the gap until, with less than five laps remaining, his engine spluttered to a halt, leaving de Cesaris second and Piquet third with a couple of points to spare over Prost. The new World Champion had deservedly taken his second title, over the whole season, and celebrated as McLaren were busy packing away. They knew their time had yet to come, though for John Watson it was not to be.

CHAPTER 8

To the Top and no Going Back

This book is essentially about the events of McLaren's involvement in Grand Prix racing, both within the team and the sport. What has happened, if not the how or why, is common knowledge now, and the events of 1984 have since been surpassed. Yet, at the time of the pre-season testing in Rio de Janeiro, if anybody had tried to predict the coming season's events, as they eventually transpired, that person would have soon been left talking to himself. 'Idiot', 'pie in the sky', 'dreamer' would have been just some of the more respectable adjectives using by racing journalists, as they departed our mythical soothsayer.

Looking back on the statistical records of 1984 one still tends to say 'Wow' when considering the enormity of McLaren's success. They were the Constructors' Champions with a record 143½ points; while their drivers occupied the top two positions in their Championship. Out of sixteen Grands Prix, McLaren won twelve; a ratio of 75 per cent, exceeding anything since Mercedes in 1955, when the competition was inferior in both quantity and quality. Furthermore, their record of four 1–2 victories had not been bettered since 1952, while they also won seven consecutive races, another record not even approached since the Ferrari walkover of the Formula 2 Grand Prix era of 1952–1953. This was domination of the highest order – even Lotus had not reached such heights – and on paper it seems so simple, yet reality is always missing from any bland statistical assessment. What then had caused this sudden, dramatic transformation?

As ever with any monumental change of fortune, there is a multitude of reasons, though to read some sections of the press at the time, you would have thought this was all down to one simple answer: the Tag/Porsche engine. For those keeping an eye on such matters, Niki Lauda's performance in the South African Grand Prix at the end of 1983 offered a portent for the future. It was there that the Tag/Porsche engine was seen to be more than capable of running with the Renault, Ferrari and BMW turbo engines installed in a car which was little more than a modified version of the previous Cosworth-powered variants.

However, at the aforementioned early season testing in Brazil, the same combination proved almost disastrous, thanks to the Bosch-designed electronic management system not being up to the job. To their immense credit, the Bosch engineers, suitably chastened, thoroughly re-examined their whole system during the next few weeks and there were no mistakes on the next visit to Brazil.

We have mentioned earlier the subtle yet vitally important difference in approach which enabled McLaren to entice Porsche, the world leaders at that time in racing turbo-engine technology, to build an engine for them. They were not customers of Porsche, fitting an engine into the McLaren chassis as best they could, like many other Grand Prix teams. Porsche engineers, led by Hans Mezger, might have had a fairly free hand as to the internal design of the engine, but John Barnard exercized strict control over the external shape and dimensions. He

'Who says three heads are better than one, Ron? We'll do it my way.' Niki Lauda makes his point to Ron Dennis and Alain Prost during a Brands testing session, in 1984.

would not accept any engineering solution which would compromise the aerodynamics of the car, taking shape in his mind. The engine was to power the car, not the car be a mere vehicle for an engine. This attitude proved to be a considerable eye-opener for Porsche. For once their engineers did not know best and, as contractors, they had to fulfill McLaren's requirements to the letter.

Again, though, the engine did not just 'happen', the idea may have been conceived by John Barnard and Ron Dennis, but it was the latter who then had to find the builder and the finance. The initial design contracts with Porsche were signed without financial backing for the project and, having outfoxed the Grand Prix fraternity by getting Porsche to undertake

the work, Dennis now pulled another fast one.

TAG were, at that time, co-sponsors of the rival Williams team and, audacious or just downright desperate, Ron Dennis contacted the owners and met with a favourable response. Negotiations got underway yet, though secret, there were no underhand dealings. Frank Williams was informed of progress and was offered use of the embryonic engine – after McLaren, of course. This he refused, having already opened negotiations with Honda, and TAG were later to cease their sponsorship of Williams. However, this was another event which underlined the emergence of McLaren International as a real force. The engine was thus an amalgam of Porsche and Bosch technical expertise, TAG marketing ambitions, and

211

Alain Prost

The greatest racing driver of all time, or just plain lucky? These are two opinions about Alain Prost, held by many seasoned observers of Grand Prix racing. His record suggests the former, but does luck follow him around, or does Prost simply make his own luck happen?

Prost is a diminutive figure, yet a giant of a driver. He was the man to beat throughout the 1980s, and continues in this role into the 1990s. World Champion in 1985, 1986 and 1989, and runner-up in 1983, 1984, 1988 and 1990, Prost's record is second to none. In addition, he has won more Grand Prix races than any other driver, and his winning ratio of under one-in-four is up with the best.

Prost entered Grand Prix racing with McLaren in 1980. It was a difficult season, labouring with the M29, and he left to join Renault in 1981. There, with a competitive car, Prost was very often right at the front of the pack, and yet failed to clinch the World Championship. This ultimately led to his dismissal at the end of 1983, and he re-joined McLaren alongside the master tactician, Niki Lauda.

The two years spent driving side by side were perhaps the most important factor in the transformation of Alain Prost from just another fast driver, into the 'master' he is. Lauda pipped Prost to the 1984 Championship by a mere half-point, and taught his team-mate a good deal about race tactics. Thereafter, the Prost/McLaren relationship matured into the equal of any other in the past, to name but Clark/Lotus and Stewart/Tyrrell. McLaren simply became Prost's team.

Then in 1988 Senna joined McLaren, and Prost had a real challenge on his hands. Senna won the Championship that year, but Prost got his revenge in 1989. Unfortunately, the Prost/Mclaren relationship turned sour, and they parted on acrimonious terms. Prost then went off to Ferrari to drive alongside Mansell, and almost single-handedly, like Lauda before him, whipped the Italian outfit into shape. Prost's ability to know what is needed, and to get it, was proven in such a determined fashion that his British team-mate was rather 'pushed out' of things at Maranello, and given a driving lesson or two. No wonder Prost has the nickname of 'Professor'.

As a driver, Prost is undoubtedly fast, but he is also exceptionally smooth, in the Lauda/Stewart mould. He is not the fastest qualifier, but once the race is underway his progress through the field, though seldom spectacular, always has a certain inevitability about it. His precise, diligent use of tactics could hardly be bettered by Lauda himself, and his car control is brilliant.

How about the 'luck' that Prost seems to enjoy? Well, as the old racing maxim goes: 'To finish first, you must first finish!' and if Prost has been left behind, only for the leader to retire, then Prost has had to be ahead of the rest in order to notch up another victory. In any case, winning against drivers of the calibre of Piquet, Lauda, Senna and Mansell, all in competitive cars, shows that Prost has real class.

Prost shares with Fangio the ability to choose the right team, at the right time. He is also a master of race tactics. All this rolled into one person suggests that at the very least, he will go down as the greatest driver of his era, and possibly the greatest of all time.

McLaren oversight and planning; a truly international co-operative plan, which helped achieve outstanding results.

It cannot be emphasized too strongly that the Tag/Porsche engine was only one, albeit major, part of the successful equation. John Barnard designed a brand new car for 1984, the MP4/2, which not only looked very similar to the earlier versions but, like all good things, incorporated the best qualities of the previous series. The MP4 had always been a very stable, fine-handling car, suited to most circuits, qualities that were attributed to the suspension, stiff monocoque, and body shape.

Though totally new, the MP4/2 retained a similar suspension layout, that at the rear incorporated into a new rear-end body shape which hugged the turbo engine, adding curvacious looks to its improved aerodynamic credentials. The sidepods were also shortened, to a length similar to those on the new Brabham car, unlike many teams who had copied the super-short sidepods used by Brabham in 1983. When the McLaren preparation was taken into account, these cars, when they appeared virtually untried at the Brazilian Grand Prix, looked like winners.

However, even the best designed or prepared car, with the best engine, needs to be driven. If you or I had sat in that car at the start of practice for the Brazilian Grand Prix, even after some extensive testing beforehand, we would have had to dream up some highly original and inventive stories to explain to Ron Dennis how we had failed to qualify for the race, by a mile. I doubt very much if he would have been very impressed with the damage we, almost certainly, would have caused either. You, as the reader, would not by now expect Ron Dennis to overlook such a matter, and you would be quite right. Niki Lauda, that great tactician of the race circuits, was firmly encamped in the McLaren team and, so he thought, was John Watson.

John, by the end of 1983, had not signed a contract for the new year but thought little of it at the time. He was after all too busy racing, and

there had been no serious rumours linking other drivers with McLaren or, indeed, linking him elsewhere. The time for such matters would come at the end of the season and there did not seem to be any serious threat from without. After all, had he not held position alongside the legendary Niki Lauda?

Events were to move quickly following Alain Prost's failure to land the Championship in South Africa. Mindful of the fact that motor racing was only a means of selling cars, to the vast, nationalized Renault combine, the team management made him the scapegoat for failure; better to blame him than accept responsibility themselves. Suddenly Prost was without a drive, but not without hope. Ron Dennis had earlier approached him with a view to renewing his relationship with McLaren, but nothing had emerged and, in any case, there was no vacancy. Thanks to Renault, the situation had changed, and Ron now held all the aces. Nevertheless, Prost was too good a driver to miss, even if the odd doubt remained as to whether Renault had made Alain Prost, or vice versa, and he rejoined McLaren.

The problem of three drivers remained, and you could be sure that there was no way Niki Lauda was going to be put out to grass – and no chance of McLaren becoming a three-car team. It was long-standing loyal servant John Watson who was to go just when, quite understandably, he had assumed it was about time to begin discussing the next contract. He was expendable, at a time when all the other top vacancies were filled!

John Watson's dismissal, as that is what it amounted to, was a sad affair and did not reflect well on McLaren, although they were awkwardly placed in a no-win situation. John had raced for McLaren over five seasons, having gone there with a high reputation, only to find the team established on a very long and slippery slope down. By mid-1980 his reputation was almost in tatters, thanks mainly to some decidedly uncompetitive machinery, and a not entirely supportive team, a situation which young Alain Prost found insulting to his then team-mate.

Luck smiled on John Watson at the end of that season and he retained his place in the new McLaren International team. In addition, given the MP4, he studiously and victoriously rebuilt his career. He was not overawed by Niki Lauda, indeed the great man's arrival and good friendship spurred him on to even greater heights, to the point where he was at least the equal of the Austrian once the green light shone. Then, as a reward for seventy-three races, and two where he failed to qualify, and after refusing advances from Williams and other teams, he was out. Worst of all, there was nowhere for him to go. It was not a very dignified end to the Grand Prix career of one of the most genuinely well-liked of drivers, and more importantly, a very fast, skilful, and highly polished exponent of the art of race driving.

What were McLaren to do though? Pass up the chance of obtaining the services of perhaps the fastest contemporary driver; one who was young and hungry enough to want to win the World Championship, and with the talent to more than match his ambition? Furthermore, Alain Prost had a proven record as a good test driver, a facet that John Watson never really shone at and, although Niki Lauda's contract virtually gave him exclusive testing rights, Prost and Lauda were soon to work together as a team, forming a unique relationship. It was an agonizing, difficult decision for Ron Dennis, but in the long term the correct one. Prost was just too good a driver to be allowed to walk away from under their noses, and nobody in their right mind would have dismissed Niki Lauda. But, for an enticing 'what if?' to ponder those long winter nights, how about Alain Prost and John Watson driving the MP4/2 with TAG/Porsche engine in 1984/85 and perhaps thereafter? Could Ron Dennis have let the wrong man go?

BREAKING THE RECORDS

So, the mouth-watering ingredients of car, en-gine, drivers and unrivalled preparation – mixed together by the most professional team in racing and backed by loyal, supportive sponsors Marlboro, TAG, Boss, SAIMA and Unipart – a combination that could not fail. Or could it?

What about the opposition? When Brabham's Gordon Murray designed a new car, only a fool would fail to take notice. Murray was as near to Colin Chapman, as a designer, as anyone in Grand Prix racing. Like the former Lotus boss, Murray's designs had the right elements of ingenuity, originality, and fallibility, but never for a moment could you accuse him of following where others led.

The new BT53 was going to be straight out of the box at the opening Brazilian Grand Prix, just like the MP4/2, but this circumstance did not prevent Piquet winning the opening round in 1983. Still powered by the beefy BMW engine and driven by Piquet, as fast and thoughtful a driver as they come, this combination was a very serious contender. The only way in which the team could not measure up to McLaren was on the driving front. Once again Brabham employed a number two, Teo Fabi, who was just that and, because he was contesting in the American CART series, Fabi could not even race a full season.

Then there was Renault, backed by a bottomless pit of money or so it seemed. They certainly had the car, the engine and the driver, in 1983, to sweep all before them, and yet, once again, they failed. Alain Prost was nearly exasperated by the team's inability to maintain their competitiveness throughout the season, and this was the root to all their problems, not the drivers. Instead, they had a new car, the RE50 and a new engine, the EF4, which promised as much power as any rival. Patrick Tambay and Derek Warwick, drivers of proven quality and outstanding potential, completed the equation.

Ferrari, with Arnoux and Alboreto, had a similar combination of driving talent as Renault and McLaren. They had a new car, the 126C4, and a very powerful engine; never to be overlooked. Lotus retained both Mansell and de

Niki Lauda trying his hardest during practice, for the British Grand Prix in 1984. He still qualified one place behind Alain Prost.

Angelis as drivers (both more top class number two's than real winners) and had their new 95T car, with Renault power. Ligier were in a similar situation – their JS23 car also had a Renault engine. The now much improved de Cesaris led their team, with the latest racing driver off the French production line, François Hesnault, as number two. Tyrrell, with their two debutant drivers Martin Brundle and Danny Sullivan and Cosworth-powered 012 car, had now slipped in among the also-rans, and could no longer expect to challenge for race wins.

The Spirit, RAM, Osella, and Arrows teams comprised the expected tail-end Charlies, but do not for one minute think that they were incompetent. If any of the 'big boys' should slip up, these would jump into their shoes and be worthy of their place. Euroracing, using the Alfa Romeo engine and team, did not quite fall into this category, with Patrese and Cheever as drivers; nor did Toleman, with ex-motorbike racer Johnny Cecotto and promising newcomer Ayrton Senna as drivers.

Last of all, though, was possibly the team most fancied to scale the heights: Williams. Patrick Head had produced the FW09 for the Honda engine and it looked a formidable package, despite the car having to be built round the engine, unlike the MP4/2. The Williams team could match McLaren stroke for stroke in terms of preparation and professionalism, and in Frank Williams himself, were led by a man in as complete control as Ron Dennis. With Rosberg and Laffite as drivers, perhaps Williams gave just a little to the McLaren pair, but Rosberg was a fighter to the end and never a man to give in lightly.

If the opposition did not look as redoubtable, with any number of new, untried cars, McLaren were hardly a proven package either. Besides, a battle between Piquet, Rosberg, Arnoux, Tambay, Lauda, and Prost, all in turbo cars, would be enough to make anybody's hair stand on end. And it would be a brave man who would have bet a week's wages on the outcome.

So, how did McLaren just walk over the

215

opposition? The fuel load was cut from 250 to 220 litres (55 to 48.5 gallons) and refuelling was no longer permitted. This caused a few races to turn into economy runs. The fuel gauge usurped the rev-counter as the most important instrument for the driver, and the Tag/Porsche engine quickly took a lead in this respect. Tyre stops were still permitted though, and with Goodyear running radial-ply tyres for the first time and Pirelli making progress, competition was likely to be fierce. Michelin had the practical experience of running radial-ply compounds, and proved another consistent factor in the increasingly dominant McLaren equation.

Consistency and reliability were the keys to McLaren's success over the sixteen-race season. During official practices Piquet, de Angelis, Warwick, and Alain Prost fought a season-long battle for the leading positions, but once BMW started to provide special qualifying engines, Piquet claimed the pole position as his own (he recorded nine altogether). Lauda would usually be among the next half-dozen qualifiers, ahead

of the pack in mid-field, but off the pace of the hares.

THE HARE AND THE TORTOISE

In many respects, the races followed Aesop's mythical contest between the hare and the tortoise, as indeed did the Drivers' Championship battle. Take the final round, the Portuguese Grand Prix, as an example. This race was revived after a twenty-year absence, and Lauda led Prost in the Drivers' Championship by 3½ points. To date, Alain had won six races, mostly leading from the front, while Niki had won five, coming through from a lesser grid position with that unique blend of speed, patience, forcefulness and unrivalled racecraft, to outfox everyone. It had happened too often over the years for the performance to be based on luck alone.

In Portugal the objectives were clear for all to see. Prost needed to finish 4 points clear of

The two pace makers of 1984, Alain Prost and Nelson Piquet, battling it out again, at Brands Hatch. Once again though, the 'hares' were to lose out to the 'tortoise' Niki Lauda.

216

The 'master' makes his move. Having taken second place off Piquet, in the background, the lap before, Niki Lauda laps Ghinzani's Osella during his pursuit of Alain Prost, at Brands Hatch in 1984. Nine laps later Prost's gearbox failed, and Lauda went on to win his third British Grand Prix.

Lauda to win the Championship which, given McLaren's equality and reliability of equipment, meant that the Frenchman had to win. Lauda had other options, needing only to finish second to ensure his third title, while Prost needed no reminding that he was up against the greatest tactician of them all.

When practice was over, Prost sat on the front row of the grid, once again giving best to Piquet, but Lauda was back in eleventh position. After race morning warm-up though, it was pretty clear that Lauda was equal to the best, as usual, but had he left himself too much to do on this occasion? The cars lined up on the grid and, as the red light came on, the tension was electric. What it must have been like for the main contestants, heaven knows, but all this faded away when the green light shone and Rosberg shot into the lead, ahead of Prost. For

seven laps the fiery Finn headed the field, then Prost edged past and took control. Prost knew that he had to win, and did that from the front.

Piquet had spun to the back of the field on the opening lap, and with both Renaults conquered, Lauda's task was no longer so daunting for such a master. Once his fuel load lightened, Niki began his moves. Steadily increasing his speed, having conserved his tyres, he began his move up the field – and you can be sure that rival team managers had informed their drivers of this fact so that they knew what to expect. Quite ruthlessly, Johansson, Alboreto, Rosberg and Senna were all passed, while de Angelis slowed a little, offering no resistance. Now only Mansell sat between Lauda and Prost, and it was not the best of places to be for the British driver in his last race for Lotus.

Mansell seemed to be holding his own, and

217

although Lauda was closing in, it was not enough. The wily fox would surely have had something up his sleeve, and Mansell's position in the last few laps would have been untenable, with Lauda determined to secure the Championship. As luck would have it, Mansell's bacon was saved when, with seventeen laps to go, his brakes failed and he spun off. Lauda was now second, and Prost was soon notified of this. What could he do? To his credit Alain did not mope and curse his luck. Instead, he went faster, trying to force Niki to maybe, just maybe, make a mistake, or even break his car. Lauda was too wise for all this. He knew that the Championship was won, and continued just fast enough to keep Senna at bay. Prost, mindful that Lauda had not taken his bait, and that he might be the one to make a mistake and forfeit the race, slowed again, and in due course McLaren recorded their fourth 1–2 triumph.

This was virtually the story of the season, Prost leading most of the way and Lauda coming from behind. It sounds easy on paper, but the reality was not quite that simple; neither was the opposition always breaking down. On the contrary, Lauda's sheer mastery was demonstrated in a race where perhaps no other driver would have finished, let alone won, in Lauda's car.

Fittingly, Niki's *tour de force* came at the Austrian Grand Prix. Initially, there was nothing special about the race. Piquet, as usual, sat on the pole; with Prost beside him and Lauda in fourth place. There was a bit of fun and games, as the first start was aborted thanks to a couple of stalled cars, but off they went at the second attempt. Out at the front Prost led Piquet briefly, then the Brabham got ahead, and these two fought a furious battle for the lead. Lauda began steadily, running sixth, before picking up places, and once he had passed Tambay for third place, the hares at the front were no longer pulling away. It is when this happens that you sit up and take notice.

Almost from the start, Prost had been holding the gear lever in place when in fourth gear. This makes steering your road car difficult, and that

factor is monumentally increased in a Grand Prix car. It does not inspire confidence either, because you know that something is amiss, with the likelihood that it will get worse. In this instance, the worst did not happen. Just after half-distance, with Piquet, Prost, and Lauda equally spaced out, de Angelis retired, spilling oil on to the circuit. No oil flags were out, and as Piquet arrived on the scene, he nearly lost control. Prost came next, holding his car in fourth gear, and promptly spun out. Lauda got through easily enough and continued the pursuit of Piquet.

With this, the first showing of the Lauda genius began to pay dividends. Piquet, during his battle with Prost, had worn his tyres, while Lauda had calmly sat back and nursed his when the fuel load was heavy. The Austrian had already been closing on the two leaders, and with Prost gone, Lauda remorselessly hauled Piquet in. On lap 40 Lauda took the lead and Piquet eased off to save his tyres. It looked like all was over; Niki had done it yet again.

For a few spectators, and anybody in the pits who happened to be watching a television monitor closely – and it appears that few were – there was a sign that all was not well, as Lauda threw an arm skywards. Amidst all the usual noise and cacophony emitted from the back of his car, Lauda heard a loud 'bang', lost the drive to the wheels and, thinking that the engine had blown, expected to retire. Trying other gears to see if he could avoid the long walk back to the pits, Lauda discovered that the car was fine except for there being no fourth gear, and so he continued. In fact, a gear had broken up, and Niki's race could have ended at any minute, but driving with the velvet touch synonymous with a true ace, Lauda took the McLaren to the chequered flag, at a barely diminished speed, to win comfortably; another example of the Lauda 'genius'.

Piquet knew that Lauda had slowed a little, but assumed that this was simply to save both tyres and car. His Brabham was in no condition to challenge a healthy McLaren, but he was unaware that the McLaren was in trouble, and that it would fail on the slowing-down lap. Yes, Lauda was lucky to complete the race, but there was no other contemporary driver capable of nursing the stricken car home, and probably not another in the history of Grand Prix racing who could have so outfoxed the opposition, that there was no hint of the trouble he was in. Lauda's season-long display of race tactics enabled him to overcome the opposition and to deservedly claim his third World Championship.

Piquet was the main threat to the McLaren supremacy, and though he often led the merry dance, the BMW engines let him down on too many occasions. When he did run well, as when winning the Canadian and the United States Grands Prix, held in Detroit, even the McLaren pair could do nothing to stop him, but mostly they did not need to. Renault also showed good potential, especially early on, but managed to snatch defeat from the jaws of certain victory on a couple of occasions. Rosberg fought like a tiger all season and his victory at Dallas, when just about everyone else fell off the crumbling circuit, was a testimony to his superb car control. The Honda engines were all-or-nothing in terms of power, very difficult to control and unreliable, but their time would come. Ferrari, with Alboreto, also picked up a victory, in Belgium, but though front runners, were never to offer a serious challenge to McLaren. The same could also be said of Lotus, only they failed to win a race of any sort.

One or two younger drivers impressed when the circumstances allowed. These included Boutsen, in an Arrows; Senna, with several top-class performances in a Toleman; and the Tyrrell pair of Brundle and Bellof. This latter pair, battling with Cosworth-powered cars, came to the fore on several occasions during the first half of the season, culminating with an excellent second place for Brundle in Detroit. Thereafter, Tyrrell's season collapsed spectacularly, with Brundle badly breaking his legs in Dallas and – just in case you had been thinking politics had

kept clear of the seasons events – a FISA decision to ban Tyrrell from all races from the British Grand Prix onwards!

This was another FISA 'first' and the whole incident reflected badly on Grand Prix racing, not just because Tyrrell had been accused of cheating, but also because an FIA court later upheld the ban amidst some disgraceful proceedings. Now, Ken Tyrrell was not the most popular of team owners, with his crusade against the turbocharged engine, over the years. One by one, the other FOCA teams had used turbo engines, thus weakening the Tyrrell argument, until Tyrrell were one of the few teams still using the Cosworth engine.

WATER FIGHTS

During 1984 Tyrrell cars had been pulling into the pits towards the end of some races, to take on a water ballast, the popular inference being that the cars were running under the minimum weight limit during the race. Following the examination of this water container, in Detroit, lead balls were found inside, and the water showed evidence of performance additives. It was from this that FISA took their cue to ban Tyrrell.

Tyrrell obtained a court injunction which allowed them to take part in the British Grand Prix (though being unable to score World Championship points) before the FIA court hearing, which upheld the FISA decision. Scientific analysis of the water had been wrongly interpreted by FISA, and the evidence showed that no effective additives were present. The court also ignored the rather obvious fact that, had the cars been carrying additives which would improve performance, they would go slower after their pitstop to, allegedly, have the system flushed out, and not faster, as they invariably did.

As for the ballast, the rules state that it must require a tool to remove it, and that a scrutineers' tag can be fixed if necessary. This was usually interpreted as meaning that the ballast must be fixed to the car. In fact, the lead balls required a special tool to remove them from the water container, and a scrutineers' tag could be attached to the opening. Finally the court, against legal procedure, brought another charge during the hearing, concerning two holes in the base of the car. These were undoubtedly illegal, and were used as a means of pressure relief. However, Ken Tyrrell produced statements from other designers, including John Barnard, saying that these offered no performance advantage at all. It goes without saying that this 'kangaroo court' ignored such affidavits, in a hearing which, had it been a criminal court, would have brought government intervention. But in motor racing, it seemed, anything goes.

The Grand Prix racing fraternity are a hardy lot, and get on with their work under circumstances which, in any other industry, would discourage even the most resilient and have them scream in despair. Those doing the real work in Grand Prix, not the vast multitude of hangers-on who purport to be working in this field, are not above such emotional displays, but they then get on with the work in hand. With the court battles between Tyrrell and FISA/FIA, and the cancellation of the scheduled 1985 season opener, in Dallas, most people would have simply thrown their hands in the air. Not the Grand Prix teams though; they spent the long winter break preparing for the new season, and would be ready to race in Brazil, South Africa, Timbuctoo, or wherever the first race was held.

For most teams, McLaren were the target to aim for and surpass; that is the standard, now go ahead and meet it. The situation was entirely different for McLaren: they were there to be shot down. Of course, they would meet the challenge from a position of strength, but there would be a problem with motivation – a 'We've done it all before' attitude. Ron Dennis had to pre-empt any complacency creeping into the team, and this very situation was to be the sternest test to date for his management philosophy.

Ron Dennis believes that attention to detail is the key to success. This ranges from the obvious, such as ensuring the cars are thoroughly prepared – a time-honoured McLaren tradition – right down to the cleanliness of the Woking factory. Everything, but everything, if it is worth doing, must be done right, and that means that every job within the team is important and requires the total commitment of the employees to their specific job, whether it be a racing driver or a tea boy. It is the duty of management to ensure that these efforts are not wasted, or perceived to be, and that the best is always forthcoming.

Of course, any amount of motivation is wasted if there is no direction offered. There were few personnel changes, though Alan Jenkins, Prost's race engineer, left, and both McLaren drivers were delighted to stay on. Lauda and Prost were easily the strongest pairing of drivers in Grand Prix, and that part of the package was right. The car's reliability and performance had been outstanding, so there was no reason to make major changes to a winning machine. It was evolved into the MP4/2B through a logical programme of development. The car received all-new bodywork, while the monocoque was revised to incorporate a new footbox, and the little 'winglets' on the rear wing were removed – both latter modifications due to rule changes. The front suspension was modified, but at the rear John Barnard opted for a completely new layout. The rocker-arm system was replaced by a push-rod design similar to that used by most other teams, following Brabham's lead. This was sleeker than the previous layout and, with an improved airflow helped by the new bodywork, was, as one would expect, a significant improvement on the old system.

A number of teams at this time suggested that if they too had the TAG engine, they could have 'done a McLaren'; regrettably, quite a few people believed such stories as well. That the TAG engine was excellent, there was no doubt, but it was neither the most powerful, nor

Perhaps it was the unaesthetic surroundings of the circuit at the New Nürburgring, but Alain Prost appears to be the only person who was enthusiastic about his sixth win of 1984, at the European Grand Prix.

entirely trouble-free. It was undoubtedly the best all-round race engine, and there was no let-up in the development work on it. Over the winter, Porsche had squeezed out more power and cured the mysterious water leaks, which had caused a few problems. Similarly, Bosch, the engine management manufacturers, refined their Motronic system to cure any misfires, and also to measure the fuel accurately, so that the barest minimum was carried in a race. On the debit side, however, a new gearbox was not ready and, as it had become increasingly marginal, with the power of the TAG engine, so the likelihood of a failure grew.

All this sounds easy and straightforward, but it took thousands of man-hours to achieve. The days when the mechanics could tinker around with the engine to gain a few horsepower or rivit a bit of aluminium on to the car to reduce drag, were long gone. Any attempt at a modification was thoroughly researched, to ensure that the optimum use-value was gained, and only when proven was it incorporated into the design. After all, why change for change's sake?

To contradict this, Ron Dennis, though perfectly happy with the Michelin tyres, signed a money-spinning contract with Goodyear. Initially, the new tyres did not perform as well as had the Michelins; was this a punishment for making an unnecessary change? On the contrary, as events turned out, that decision was full of good fortune. While the ink was drying on McLaren's secret Goodyear contract, Michelin announced that they were to pull out of Grand

221

Grand Prix Results 1984

GRAND PRIX	DRIVER	CAR	NO	1ST PRACTICE Time/Posn	2ND PRACTICE Time/Posn	3RD PRACTICE Time/Posn	FINAL GRID POSN	FINAL PLACING	RETIRED CAUSE OF	HIGHEST POSN IN RACE
BRAZILIAN Jacarepagua 25.3.84	A. Prost	McLaren-TAG MP4/2-2	7	1min 29.82sec 3/27	1min 29.33sec 4/27		4–26	1/9 WINNER		FL 1st
	N. Lauda	McLaren-TAG MP4/2-1	8	1min 29.95sec 5/27	1min 29.85sec 5/27		6–26		Lp 39 Electrical trouble	1st
SOUTH AFRICAN Kyalami 7.4.84	A. Prost	McLaren-TAG MP4/2-3	7	1min 06.58sec 8/25	1min 05.35sec 5/27		5–26	2/13		2nd
	N. Lauda	McLaren-TAG MP4/2-1	8	1min 06.24sec 6/25	1min 06.04sec 7/27		8–26	1/13 WINNER		1st
BELGIAN Zolder 29.4.84	A. Prost	McLaren-TAG MP4/2-2	7	1min 16.59sec 2/27	1min 16.60sec 7/27		8–26		Lp 6 Electrical failure, fire	8th
	N. Lauda	McLaren-TAG MP4/2-1	8	1min 18.83sec 14/27	1min 18.07sec 13/27		14–26		Lp 36 Engine failure	7th
SAN MARINO Imola 6.5.84	A. Prost	McLaren-TAG MP4/2-3	7	1min 35.69sec 1/27	1min 28.63sec 2/29		2–26	1/11 WINNER		1st
	N. Lauda	McLaren-TAG MP4/2-1	8	1min 38.02sec 8/27	1min 30.33sec 5/29		5–26		Lp 16 Engine failure	4th
FRENCH Dijon-Prenois 20.5.84	A. Prost	McLaren-TAG MP4/2-2	7	1min 2.99sec 5/27			5–26	7/14		FL 2nd
	N. Lauda	McLaren-TAG MP4/2-1	8	1min 4.42sec 9/27			9–26	1/14 WINNER		1st
MONACO Monte Carlo 3.6.84	A. Prost	McLaren-TAG MP4/2-2	7	1min 23.94sec 3/27	1min 22.66sec 1/27		Pole	1/9 WINNER		1st
	N. Lauda	McLaren-TAG MP4/2-1	8	1min 24.51sec 5/27	1min 23.89sec 8/27		8–20		Lp 24 Spun and stalled	2nd
CANADIAN Montreal 17.6.84	A. Prost	McLaren-TAG MP4/2-2	7	1min 26.48sec 1/26	1min 26.20sec 2/26		2–26	3/12		2nd
	N. Lauda	McLaren-TAG MP4/2-1	8	1min 28.55sec 3/26	1min 27.39sec 8/26		8–26	2/12		2nd
DETROIT, USA 24.6.84	A. Prost	McLaren-TAG MP4/2-2	7	1min 45.72sec 3/26	1min 41.64sec 2/27		2–25	5/6		2nd
	N. Lauda	McLaren-TAG MP4/2-1	8	(disqualified–rear aerofoil)	1min 43.48sec 10/27		10–25		Lp 34 Engine failure	6th
DALLAS, USA 8.7.84	A. Prost	McLaren-TAG MP4/2-2	7	1min 38.54sec 5/27	1min 41.34sec 9/20		6–25		Lp 57 Crashed	1st
	N. Lauda	McLaren-TAG MP4/2-1	8	1min 37.99sec 4/27	1min 41.84sec 10/20		4–25		Lp 61 Crashed	3rd
BRITISH Brands Hatch 22.7.84	A. Prost	McLaren-TAG MP4/2-2	7	1min 11.49sec 1/29	1min 11.08sec 2/29		2–27		Lp 38 Gearbox	1st
	N. Lauda	McLaren-TAG MP4/2-1	8	1min 11.60sec 2/29	1min 11.34sec 3/29		3–27	1/13 WINNER		FL 1st
GERMAN Hockenheim-ring 5.8.84	A. Prost	McLaren-TAG MP4/2-3	7	1min 49.44sec 6/28	1min 47.01sec 1/28		Pole	1/10 WINNER		1st
	N. Lauda	McLaren-TAG MP4/2-1	8	1min 48.91sec 4/28	1min 49.00sec 7/28		7–26	2/10		2nd
AUSTRIAN Österreichring 19.8.84	A. Prost	McLaren-TAG MP4/2-2	7	1min 26.20sec 1/30	1min 27.10sec 3/28		2–25		Lp 29 Spun off	2nd
	N. Lauda	McLaren-TAG MP4/2-1	8	1min 26.72sec 2/30	1min 27.31sec 6/28		4–25	1/11 WINNER		FL 1st

DUTCH Zandvoort 26.8.84	A. Prost	McLaren-TAG 7 MP4/2-2	1min 14.95sec 7/28	1min 13.57sec 1/28	Pole	1/12 WINNER	**1st**
	N. Lauda	McLaren-TAG 8 MP4/2-1	1min 15.56sec 6/28	1min 14.87sec 6/28	6-27	2/12	**2nd**
ITALIAN Monza 9.9.84	A. Prost	McLaren-TAG 7 MP4/2-3	1min 30.14sec 7/29	1min 26.67sec 7/29	2-25	Lp 4 Engine failure	**2nd**
	N. Lauda	McLaren-TAG 8 MP4/2-1	1min 37.19sec 26/29	1min 28.53sec 21/29	11-25	1/8 WINNER	**FL 1st**
EUROPEAN Ersatz- Nürburgring 7.10.84	A. Prost	McLaren-TAG 7 MP4/2-2	1min 19.18sec 2/27	1min 40.69sec 3/25	2-26	1/10 WINNER	**1st**
	N. Lauda	McLaren-TAG 8 MP4/2-1	1min 22.64sec 15/27	1min 40.39sec 2/25	15-26	4/10	**4th**
PORTUGUESE Estoril 21.10.84	A. Prost	McLaren-TAG 7 MP4/2-2	1min 28.28sec 1/27	1min 21.77sec 2/28	2-27	1/17 WINNER	**1st**
	N. Lauda	McLaren-TAG 8 MP4/2-1	1min 28.84sec 3/27	1min 23.18sec 10/28	11-27	2/17	**FL 2nd**

Facial studies at a triumphant occasion for McLaren International. On the left a placid, calm-looking John Barnard hides the obvious joy he must have felt, as his MP4/2 had won three-quarters of the 1984 Grands Prix. Ron Dennis, the mastermind behind the phenomenal success of McLaren International, cannot hide the pride he feels at being top of the motor racing world for the first time. A pensive Alain Prost is probably reflecting on how, despite winning seven races, he has lost out in the World Championship for the second year running; while Niki Lauda does not attempt to conceal his delight at winning his third title, and signals as much to all and sundry.

Prix racing. Nobody would suggest that McLaren could find themsleves in the same position as Toleman, up the creek without a paddle, or rather unable to race, because Goodyear could not cope with any more teams, but you could bet that their coffers would have been less full.

TOUGH AT THE TOP

McLaren had thus pulled together their operation, and were ready to defend their two titles in 1985. They had done all that was possible during the winter, but what had the opposition been up to? As ever, Brabham were expected to lead the challenge with a new car, the BT54, and the BMW 4-cylinder engine. This had let the side down on a great many occasions in 1984, and had undergone a rigorous development programme to improve its reliability. Furthermore, BMW had substantially increased the power output, especially for the high-boost qualifying engines, which promised much for the coming season.

In addition, Bernie Ecclestone had signed a tyre contract with Pirelli – Pirelli's first major team – and the individual attention bestowed on Brabham was expected to outweigh the tyre outfit's lack of experience alongside Goodyear. With Piquet behind the wheel for his seventh season with Brabham, McLaren would certainly know they had a fight on their hands, though once again Piquet's partner, Hesnault, would not offer much support.

Renault had a new car, the RE60, and a new engine was due by mid-season, while they retained Tambay and Warwick as drivers, The ingredients looked promising, but somehow one did not expect too much from them. Rightly or wrongly, they seemed to be on the downward slope despite their abundant talent, and needed to turn the corner before mounting a serious challenge from the front.

Ferrari knew all about bouncing back, and with the Postlethwaite – designed 156/85 car

complete with revised engine, could not be overlooked. Alboreto and Arnoux were to remain as drivers, though after just one race the little Frenchman was to be 'rested' for the season. The depth of the Ferrari challenge would depend, as much as anything, on the Italian temperament when the going got rough, and McLaren were certainly not going to make it easy for them.

On the other hand, Lotus looked distinctly promising. For a start their new car, the 97T, was better than the old, and the Renault engine was certainly going to be powerful enough. If this package could be made to last a race, then who knows what might happen. But it was on the driving front that the main interest and, indeed, possibilities were to be found. Mansell had moved on, never having really fulfilled his initial promise but still with much untapped talent. De Angelis remained as the number one, to be joined by Senna, from Toleman – a move which might have been aided by Chapman's celestial hand. Senna had much to learn but talent aplenty, and looked to be the brightest prospect for several years. It was a shrewd move by Lotus, and they might have pulled a gem out of the hat from under everyone else's nose.

All things considered, the biggest challenge to McLaren was expected from their long-time sparring partners, Williams. Patrick Head had designed the new FW10 and if, as was expected, Honda could tame their engine's vast output, everyone had better watch out, especially with Rosberg at the wheel.

The only cloud on their horizon concerned the recruitment of Mansell as the number two. Here was a talented fighter of a driver, but one who really ought to have done better after four seasons in Grand Prix. The main problem was that Rosberg felt considerably less than enthusiastic about his new team-mate; an opinion based, mainly, on the word of others. This was unlikely to produce a harmonious team atmosphere, and whereas a bit of healthy internal competition can be beneficial, hostile rivalry is seldom so. When up against the comprehensive

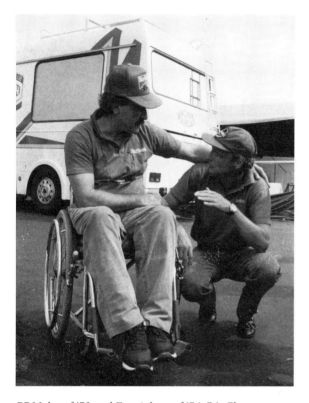

BRM class of '73, and Ferrari classes of '74–76. Clay Regazzoni and Niki Lauda in Austria 1985.

team effort of McLaren, you need to match them stroke for stroke in every department, or else you can forget about beating them.

In addition to these heavyweights, there was the supporting cast of teams like RAM, Osella, Minardi, Zakspeed, Spirit, and Euroracing, the old Alfa set-up; good teams all, but unlikely to pose a threat to McLaren. Toleman were in an even less threatening position. They had Watson and Johansson signed to drive but, with the withdrawal of Michelin, were without tyres. They had departed the Pirelli fold amid much rancour in 1984, so would hardly be welcomed back, and Goodyear had enough teams to service, thank you. So, no tyres, no racing.

This still left Ligier, with de Cesaris and Laffite, who returned to the fold after a couple of years at Williams. With a new car and the

Renault engine, they could not be neglected, especially since both drivers were capable of running at the front, given the chance. Then there was the Arrows team, with their new A8 car, specifically designed for the very powerful BMW turbo engine while, in Boutsen and Berger, they had a promising young pair of drivers.

If you have been reading carefully, you will have noted the absence of Tyrrell. You may remember that they were banned by FISA for the last races of 1984, an unjust ruling which Ken Tyrrell would not let go unchallenged. Quite rightly, Tyrrell sought to fight the FIA rulings in a civil court. Once action was set in motion, FISA had a change of heart and abruptly did an unashamed about-turn to allow Tyrrell back into Grand Prix racing, if the court actions were dropped!

Now some people seem to write, and think, that Ken is an out-and-out trouble-maker, but that he is not. He does stand up for what he believes is right though, and was unlikely to be browbeaten by the grey men of FISA. The FISA/FIA rulings against Tyrrell were a disgrace, a thinly disguised attempt at bully-boy tactics, and the people responsible, all along the line, ought to have been punished for their craven actions.

Ken Tyrrell is driven by the urge to race, not to cause trouble, and so the court actions were dropped and his team were back; on the whole a sensible decision. They had a new car due, the 014, with Brundle and Bellof (the new World Sportscar Champion) as drivers and, wait for it, Renault turbo engines. Just in case you think that was a misprint, I will repeat it, Renault turbo engines. Yes, the very same Renault who had turned Tyrrell away a year before, and against whom Tyrrell regularly protested for a wide variety of reasons. Now, if Renault were so keen not to supply Tyrrell with engines, and quite understandably so considering how difficult Tyrrell made life for them, why the sudden volte-face? Surely, this had nothing to do with pressure from FISA as a little sweetener to encourage the court actions to be dropped, perish the thought.

Teddy Mayer and Tyler Alexander reappeared on the scene to run the Team Haas, which used a Lola car and Hart engine. Nothing much could be expected from them, but you could not fail to ignore their experience, nor their driver, none other than Alan Jones. They might not be winning straight out of the box, but could certainly not be overlooked.

DEFENCE OF THE REALM

To Brazil then, and McLaren began the defence of their two titles. Alboreto shocked everyone by stealing the pole, while the MP4/2Bs performed commendably, virtually 'off the shelf', with Prost sixth and Lauda ninth on the grid. The first lap was interesting for the Williams team. Rosberg went into the lead while Mansell, after a little *brouhaha* with Alboreto, went into the fencing! Prost quickly mastered the situation, showing how he had benefited from a year with the master tactician, and ten laps after Rosberg's turbo failed on lap 9, slipped by Alboreto to cruise to a nicely judged 3-second victory, McLaren's eighth on the trot. Lauda was not so lucky. Having moved into third place when Rosberg retired, another 'Lauda

Lap 11 of the San Marino 'economy drive' Grand Prix. Alboreto has just nipped inside of de Angelis, the eventual winner (who never actually led the race), to take second place. A lap later Prost would get past the Lotus, in pursuit of the Ferrari, and Senna. The crowd still display loyalty to their late hero, Gilles Villeneuve.

*Lap 23 of the 1985 San Marino Grand Prix, and Prost has just taken second place off Alboreto.
There, in the background, Lauda will have noted how Prost executed the manoeuvre, as he closes
on the Ferrari.*

special' looked in the offing, but his fuel-metering unit began to play up, and he retired at one-third distance.

Lauda's problem excepted, the McLaren performance in Brazil gave little encouragement to the opposition, but the Portuguese Grand Prix was different. In atrocious conditions Prost crashed on the flooded straight while Lauda, in third place, retired with an engine failure. This was the race which confirmed Senna's immense potential, as he won brilliantly despite some heart-stopping moments, putting Lotus back in the winners' circle once again.

The San Marino Grand Prix saw the Euro-racing team introduce their new 185T cars, but once again the McLarens were ousted from the front of the grid. Prost qualified sixth two places in front of Lauda, with Piquet still not among the front runners. The race was something else though, and has come to represent all that is wrong with a fuel capacity limited formula.

Senna led at the start, tracked by Prost, who later slowed to conserve his fuel. Senna was seemingly oblivious to this requirement, he raced away in the lead until he ran out of fuel with four laps to go. Johansson then briefly led in the Ferrari – he had been released by the *hors de combat* Toleman team to replace Arnoux – until he ran out of fuel, a lap later. Prost, who had studiously obeyed his fuel read-out, took the chequered flag, but also ran out of fuel on his slowing down lap; another McLaren victory,

227

in bizarre circumstances. Prost had played and won by the rules in force, and would not have dropped back from Senna in the first place had he not used up too much fuel at that stage.

Unfortunately, a spanner was thrown into the works. Prost's car was weighed and found to be 2kg (4lb) under the minimum weight limit of 540kg (1,190lb). Ron Dennis was informed of this and new scales were brought, tested, and used, but still the weight was 538kg (1,186lb). Thus, Prost was disqualified from the results and de Angelis was declared the winner, despite having never actually led the race.

Yes, Prost's car was illegal when weighed, but had he stopped just after the finishing line, there was a chance that the remaining fuel, possibly around half a gallon (2 litres), would have been enough to have passed the scrutineers. At no stage during the race was the car below the minimum weight, bearing in mind tyre and brake wear, and petrol, oil and water used. McLaren accepted the disqualification, but one wonders what Teddy Mayer's reaction might have been.

On the credit side, Lauda finished a splendid fourth, despite a spin when the car jumped out of gear. During that spin, Lauda not only kept the whole thing going, but lost little time, a demonstration of sheer class. He later lost fifth gear and had to hold fourth gear in position, making the result even more meritorious, though showing how marginal the gearbox had become.

Lotus looked to be a serious threat to McLaren, with de Angelis leading the Championship, but the next five races saw a resurgent Ferrari help Alboreto challenge Prost, while Lauda's hopes for a fourth title vanished.

This close-up of Alain Prost, on his way to third place in the Canadian Grand Prix, shows the immaculate presentation of the McLaren International cars.

Alain Prost on his way to third place, in the 1985 French Grand Prix.

McLaren's well nigh legendary reliability took a bit of a knock as Lauda retired through a different failure on his car in four of these races, and spun out on debris in the first. Prost was luckier in this respect, suffering only one car failure when the carbon fibre brakes let him down at Detroit, but he recorded victories in Monaco and England. Alboreto, Piquet and Rosberg all won a race, and with Senna and Mansell looking ominously competitive in the Williams and running at the front, McLaren were not having it all their own way this time around.

The pattern of the races had changed somewhat as well. Neither Prost nor Lauda were among the hares during qualifying, because the Tag/Porsche engine could not match the qualifying boost of the Honda, Renault, Ferrari and BMW engines. Once in race trim though, the Bosch engine management system allowed the Tag/Porsche engine to run competitively within the fuel restrictions. If Prost appeared to be outdriven, as by Senna at Silverstone, this was usually because he obeyed the fuel gauge, while Senna carried on oblivious to this and promptly ran out of fuel. However, despite the increasing depth of the serious competition, only Alboreto emerged to challenge Prost.

McLaren were to bounce back from this trough in their performances. The carbon fibre brakes proved problematic on the twisty circuits of Monaco, Detroit and Montreal, but worked well on the faster circuits. However, the major contribution to the improvement in Alain's, if not Niki's results, came with the revised front suspension geometry used at the French Grand

It did not take Niki Lauda long to realize that Alain Prost was the faster driver, but the 'master' was still capable of giving his 'pupil' a lesson or two. Here, in the French Grand Prix, Niki leads Alain, in third place, before retiring with gearbox problems.

Prix. Prior to this the cars tended to oversteer into, and understeer out of, corners. Both Lauda and Prost preferred a touch of understeer, and this unpredictability (though making little difference to your road car) undermines confidence at full-blown race speeds. Suddenly, they looked competitive again.

In fact, it was the five races from Silverstone onwards which all but secured Alain Prost his first World Championship. He won three himself – while Lauda at last chalked up a victory and Alboreto won one race – before Ferrari, at the Italian Grand Prix of all places, hopelessly

lost their way. Alboreto increased his lead over Prost to 5 points by beating him into second place at the German Grand Prix, held at the new Nürburgring circuit, but Prost then drew level by winning in Austria. It was at Niki's home race that Lauda stole into view again.

Having endured what seemed to be the traditional bad luck of the reigning World Champion, Lauda came back with a bang. After a disrupted first start, which he led, Niki steadfastly kept pace with Alain, in the spare car, who led the restarted race until he stopped for fresh tyres, on lap 25. Now Lauda led by 30

230

seconds from Prost, who halved the lead in the next fifteen laps. This in itself was good enough to win, but he would have had to pass Lauda first. He did not get the chance, however, as a turbo failed on Niki's car, on lap 40, and the Austrian was out again. Prost duly slaughtered the rest of the opposition, but Lauda stole the limelight.

Despite a few 'ifs and buts' over whether to sign for Williams, Niki Lauda chose to announce his second retirement in Austria, and the incident sparked off a distinct cooling of the relationship between himself and Ron Dennis. As ever with these things, it was the result of a misunderstanding. Ron Dennis rather overdid the part John Barnard played in making the Lauda/McLaren equation such a success. Niki felt rather affronted by this, and the matter was not really satisfactorily resolved until he had left the team. Considering the usually immaculate professionalism of McLaren International in all matters, this was something of a slip-up. Whether this unnecessary storm in a tea cup was the catalyst for Lauda's performance in the Dutch Grand Prix, I do not know, but it certainly offered a posible answer as to whether

The adoring Austrian crowds watch Niki Lauda lead his home Grand Prix.

Lauda leading his last home race in Austria. Once again he was to suffer a mechanical failure – this time his engine gave out.

231

Pole position, fastest lap, and victory. Prost shows his delight after vanquishing Senna and Alboreto, in Austria, for his fourth win of the season.

Prost would have got past Lauda, had the latter not retired.

Prior to the Dutch Grand Prix it was announced that Keke Rosberg, the ebullient and resolute Williams driver, would be Niki Lauda's replacement for 1986, his place at Williams being taken by Piquet. It was the latter driver who pipped Rosberg for the pole in Holland, with Prost third and Lauda back in tenth place. But this was far from the end of the matter.

Piquet promptly stalled at the start and Rosberg opened up a decent lead, until the Honda engine let him down once again, on lap 20.

Prost now took over, while Lauda headed for the pits for new tyres, to resume in eighth position. We did not know it at the time, but Niki Lauda was stamping his authority on the race in his inimitable style.

Ten laps later Lauda moved into third place and, with Alboreto and then Prost stopping for fresh tyres, took over the lead on lap 33. It was all beginning to look rather ominous, and Prost spent nearly 20 seconds in the pits when a wheel nut jammed. Resuming in third place and driving as economically as ever, the Frenchman overhauled Senna, then closed on his team-mate at the rate of a second a lap, as in Austria. Lauda responded by upping the rating, but Prost seemed to have that little extra up his sleeve. As he came within Lauda's slipstream, some people mistakenly thought it was all over; the two Mclarens had at last enjoyed a trouble-free, no-holds-barred battle and Prost had won hands down.

It was known that Niki Lauda would give best to an opponent if he thought there was little to be gained by fighting; remember how he allowed James Hunt to pull away at the 1976 British Grand Prix. He did not become one of the greatest drivers by giving way whenever challenged, though. As Prost closed in, Lauda noted that they were gaining on Piquet, and rather than get embroiled with a tail-end Charlie, if ever Piquet could be so described, he slowed down. How many drivers deal with a rival coming up fast by reducing speed?

Prost is no fool and he could see Lauda's game-plan, but countering it proved more difficult. Zandvoort has the Tarzan hairpin at the end of its straight, ideal for overtaking, and Prost used this to the full. Ducking and diving, feinting first one side, then the other, charging forward, then falling back, Prost sought to find a chink in Lauda's armour, but Lauda neatly and ruthlessly parried each succeeding thrust. Time and again they charged along the straight, with

The 1985 season was dreadfully unlucky for Lauda, suffering one mechanical failure after another. In between these, he proved he could still show a clean pair of heels to his rivals. He has just taken the lead off the newest Grand Prix star, Ayrton Senna, at the Dutch Grand Prix.

233

*The final 'heavyweight' battle. Lauda and Prost slug it out during the final laps of the Dutch
Grand Prix. The true width of Lauda's car, as seen by Prost, is not apparent in this picture, as it
seemed to double in size whenever the Frenchman tried to find a way past.*

Alain in Niki's wheel-tracks before pulling out
to seek a way through at the hairpin. But, without recourse to dangerous, unruly tactics, Lauda
left Prost nowhere to go.

The last couple of laps saw Alain launch the
most fearful assault, but Niki met fire with fire,
right the way to the final corner, as the two red-
and-white cars emerged apparently side by side,
in the dash for the chequered flag. Throughout
their titanic battle, Lauda had had the situation
under control, and he crossed the line with
room to spare. He had done just enough to win,
yet again, and given Prost a lesson to boot, a
display of track craft at its very best.

Both drivers thoroughly enjoyed their battle
and, as a consolation, Alain Prost took the lead
off Alboreto in the Championship, for the first
time since the opening race of the season. Niki
Lauda commented afterwards, 'I'll help Alain

win the World Championship later in the year;
he doesn't need any help from me, just yet.'
With Prost's victory in Italy, and with Ferrari
and thus Alboreto in disarray Alain was not
going to need his team-mate's help.

That was it for McLaren as far as victories
were concerned, in the face of the increasingly
fast and reliable Williams team. The re-run
Belgian Grand Prix, on a wet track, saw Prost
settle for a points finish after Alboreto had retired early on, a decision Ron Dennis found
hard to comprehend, but in the light of Alain's
recent Championship challenges, perfectly understandable. A bird in the hand is worth two in
the bush, and why risk spinning off when you
are already secure in third place, thus extending
your Championship lead?

Lauda injured a wrist during practice in
Belgium, and missed that race and the following

European Grand Prix, at Brands Hatch. He was replaced by John Watson, back in a Grand Prix car after a two-year absence, except for a couple of outings with Toleman. Moreover, Watson had only undertaken a few sports car races during the intervening period, and was thus not race fit. The opposition had the benefit of a season's racing and experience of their turbo cars, which were considerably faster than the Cosworth-powered cars with which Watson was familiar. Still, this was an opportunity to return to where his heart lay and where he belonged, Grand Prix racing, and it was too good a chance to refuse.

McLaren went to Donnington Park, and Prost set a benchmark for Watson, which the latter struggled to match. Then it was on to Brands Hatch and the real thing this time. Unable to make the best of his qualifying tyres, Watson qualified near the back, while Prost could only make sixth place on the grid. The race was truly memorable; Mansell, at last, secured his first, long-overdue Grand Prix win, a feat that was wildly appreciated by everyone present. Perhaps of greater significance, though, was Prost's tenacious drive into fourth place, which secured him his first World Championship. There is a sad irony in that he lost the Championship in 1984, by winning the deciding race, yet won the title in 1985 by finishing fourth!

John Watson had his final Grand Prix race, in Niki Lauda's car, and after a spoiled start, having to dodge on to the grass, drove with increasing confidence and speed to finish seventh. The circumstances weighed too heavily against John, and even a driver of his ability could not overcome a two-year lay-off.

Niki Lauda resumed racing in South Africa and continued his sequence of retirements, while Alain Prost gathered more points, and Mansell continued in his winning ways, the Williams now clearly being faster than the McLaren. The inaugural Australian Grand Prix, held on the streets of Adelaide, was the final race of the year and was important for McLaren because they had not won the Constructors' Championship. It was also to be the last race for the Renault team, after eight-and-a-half seasons in the sport; local driver Alan Jones's 100th Grand Prix, and Niki Lauda's last race. With Senna, the Williams pair, Prost, Alboreto, and Surer (in a Brabham) at the front, the grid wore a familiar face, though Lauda was in sixteenth place.

The race was far from a gentle end-of-season outing; Mansell tangled with Senna while the rest chased Rosberg, before tyre stops took their toll. Prost's engine failed on lap 27 but ominously, despite the huffing and puffing of the hard chargers, Lauda was already in fourth place. Here he was again, in his last race, demonstrating his unique skills. Thirty laps later, Lauda out-braked Senna on the back straight to take the lead, with Rosberg in third place, after two pitstops for tyres. But it only lasted a couple of laps, as Lauda had been having to pump his brakes for quite a while, and on lap 58 the car locked a rear wheel and got away from him, and he retired for good.

Despite failing to score any points in Australia, McLaren International duly won their second Constructors' World Championship. Rosberg's victory confirmed that Williams were the team of the moment, and also that McLaren's new driver was on top form. It was McLaren's established tenets of preparation, thorough ongoing development and consistency over the whole season which had seen them through. Other teams produced faster cars at varying times, but none were able to maintain the essential level of competitiveness throughout. The thorough professionalism of each and every team member, rivalled but never bettered, had seen McLaren through to the top once again.

It had not been plain sailing this time. Most obviously, the Tag/Porsche engine was no match for its rivals during qualifying. Moreover, Niki Lauda retired on four occasions with engine-related failures, and twice more with electrical malfunctions, whilst Alain Prost

Grand Prix Results 1985

GRAND PRIX	DRIVER	CAR	NO	1ST PRACTICE Time/Posn	2ND PRACTICE Time/Posn	3RD PRACTICE Time/Posn	FINAL GRID POSN	FINAL PLACING	RETIRED CAUSE OF	HIGHEST POSN IN RACE
BRAZILIAN Jacarepagua 7.4.85	N. Lauda	McLaren-TAG MP4/2B-4	1	1min 30.72sec 5/25	1min 29.98sec 7/23		9-25		Lp 28 Electrical fault	3rd
	A. Prost	McLaren-TAG MP4/2B-5	2	1min 30.25sec 3/25	1min 29.12sec 5/23		6-25	1/13 WINNER		FL 1st
PORTUGUESE Estoril 21.4.85	N. Lauda	McLaren-TAG MP4/2B-4	1	1min 23.67sec 3/24	1min 23.29sec 8/24		7-26		Lp 49 Engine failure	FL 5th
	A. Prost	McLaren-TAG MP4/2B-5	2	1min 23.89sec 5/24	1min 21.42sec 2/24		2-26		Lp 30 Accident	3rd
SAN MARINO Imola 5.5.85	N. Lauda	McLaren-TAG MP4/2B-4	1	1min 29.41sec 7/25	1min 28.91sec 7/25		8-25	4/10		3rd
	A. Prost	McLaren-TAG MP4/2B-5	2	1min 28.60sec 4/25	1min 28.10sec 5/25		6-25	(1/10)	Disqualified	1st
MONACO Monte Carlo 19.5.85	N. Lauda	McLaren-TAG MP4/2B-4	1	1min 22.90sec 7/26	1min 21.91sec 14/25		14-20		Lp 18 Off track stalled	8th
	A. Prost	McLaren-TAG MP4/2B-5	2	1min 22.27sec 4/26	1min 20.89sec 5/25		5-20	1/11 WINNER		1st
CANADIAN Montreal 16.6.85	N. Lauda	McLaren-TAG MP4/2B-4	1	1min 28.13sec 12/25	1min 28.13sec 18/25		17-25		Lp 38 Engine failure	8th
	A. Prost	McLaren-TAG MP4/2B-5	2	1min 25.98sec 3/25	1min 25.56sec 11/25		5-25	3/18		2nd
DETROIT, USA 23.6.85	N. Lauda	McLaren-TAG MP4/2B-4	1	1min 46.27sec 12/25			12-25		Lp 11 Brakes	9th
	A. Prost	McLaren-TAG MP4/2B-5	2	1min 44.09sec 4/25			4-25		Lp 20 Crashed	7th
FRENCH Ricard-Castellet 7.7.85	N. Lauda	McLaren-TAG MP4/2B-4	1	1min 33.86sec 4/26	1min 34.17sec 6/25		6-25		Lp 31 Gearbox	3rd
	A. Prost	McLaren-TAG MP4/2B-5	2	1min 33.55sec 3/26	1min 33.34sec 3/25		4-25	3/15		2nd
BRITISH Silverstone 21.7.85	N. Lauda	McLaren-TAG MP4/2B-4	1	1min 07.74sec 7/26	1min 09.00sec 16/25		10-26		Lp 58 Electronics	3rd
	A. Prost	McLaren-TAG MP4/2B-2	2	1min 06.31sec 2/26	1min 08.53sec 11/25		3-26	1/11 WINNER		FL 1st
GERMAN Nürburgring 4.8.85	N. Lauda	McLaren-TAG MP4/2B-4	1	1min 19.65sec 12/26	1min 44.33sec 13/21		12-27	5/10		FL 5th
	A. Prost	McLaren-TAG MP4/2B-2	2	1min 18.73sec 3/26	1min 43.09sec 12/21		3-27	2/10		2nd
AUSTRIAN Österreichring 18.8.85	N. Lauda	McLaren-TAG MP4/2B-4	1	1min 26.25sec 2/25	1min 26.73sec 3/22		3-25		Lp 40 Engine failure	1st
	A. Prost	McLaren-TAG MP4/2B-3	2	1min 25.49sec 1/25			Pole	1/9 WINNER		FL 1st
DUTCH Zandvoort 25.8.85	N. Lauda	McLaren-TAG MP4/2B-4	1	1min 13.06sec 10/27			10-26	1/11 WINNER		1st
	A. Prost	McLaren-TAG MP4/2B-3	2	1min 11.80sec 3/27	1min 29.51sec 2/13		3-26	2/11		FL 2nd
ITALIAN Monza 8.9.85	N. Lauda	McLaren-TAG MP4/2B-4	1	1min 28.47sec 12/27	1min 28.50sec 15/27		16-26		Lp 34 Engine failure	3rd
	A. Prost	McLaren-TAG MP4/2B-5	2	1min 27.58sec 7/27	1min 25.78sec 5/27		5-26	1/11 WINNER		1st

BELGIAN Spa-Fran-corchamps 15.9.85	N. Lauda	McLaren-TAG 1 MP4/2B-4	Withdrew injured					
	A. Prost	McLaren-TAG 2 MP4/2B-5	1min 56.56sec 1/24	1min 55.31sec 1/24	Pole	3/11		FL 2nd
EUROPEAN Brands Hatch 6.10.85	J. Watson	McLaren-TAG 1 MP4/2B-4	1min 12.50sec 17/27	1min 12.52sec 21/27	21–26	7/12		7th
	A. Prost	McLaren-TAG 2 MP4/2B-2	1min 10.35sec 6/27	1min 09.43sec 4/27	6–26	4/12		3rd
SOUTH AFRICAN Kyalami 19.10.85	N. Lauda	McLaren-TAG 1 MP4/2B-4	1min 05.36sec 8/21	1min 04.28sec 8/21	8–20		Lp 38 Turbo failure	2nd
	A. Prost	McLaren-TAG 2 MP4/2B-6	1min 05.76sec 11/21	1min 04.38sec 9/21	9–20	3/7		2nd
AUSTRALIAN Adelaide 3.11.85	N. Lauda	McLaren-TAG 1 MP4/2B-4	1min 24.69sec 13/25	1min 23.94sec 14/23	16–25		Lp 58 Crashed	1st
	A. Prost	McLaren-TAG 2 MP4/2B-6	1min 23.94sec 7/25	1min 21.89sec 4/23	4–25		Lp 27 Engine failure	3rd

suffered one engine failure. These incidents suggest that, with two of the smoothest, mechanically sympathetic drivers of any era, the engine was working harder to keep pace with the rivals. On the other hand, the modified gearbox had improved reliability, though Lauda retired three times thanks to this component. The same could not be said of McLaren's own carbon fibre brakes. Lauda retired twice with brake-related problems, and Prost once. The increased speeds of 1985 had severely marginalized the brakes' performance, and the reward for all the effort of manufacturing their own brakes was negligible.

Perhaps the most surprising statistic of the season was that Niki retired in eleven out of fourteen races. Alain failed to finish only three out of sixteen races and was only twice let down by his car. The McLaren response to this is that it was down to luck, and Niki's had run out. Prost needed this reliability – and Ferrari's inability to provide Alboreto with a decent car, for the all-important run-in to the season's end – to secure the title. In the five races after the Dutch Grand Prix, when Prost took over the lead of the Drivers' Championship from Alboreto, the Italian failed to secure a single points finish, and this, as much as anything, gave Prost the final walkover.

PROST RETAINS THE CHAMPIONSHIP

For 1986 McLaren were faced with a different set of problems. Thanks to the all-round development of Alain Prost as a driver, the retirement of Niki Lauda was not the disaster it might have been. In fact, part of Niki's unique contribution to Grand Prix racing was his role in the education of Alain, particularly as regards race tactics and car testing, a bestowal freely admitted by Alain. With Lauda's retirement, one of the most harmonious and productive of driver relationships was broken up. The assimilation of Keke Rosberg into the team would be no easy task, because here was a driver very much his own man, who was undoubtedly fast, and yet had a very different driving style to Prost or Lauda.

Team motivation was going to be one of McLaren's biggest hurdles for 1986. As with all things, when one has achieved a goal, that initial drive is not there in quite the same way. When one has repeated that achievement, there is a danger of complacency setting in. Keeping drivers motivated is not so easy in Grand Prix racing, because the more important one's role is within the team, the less scope there is of having reserves sitting in the wings – since they would want to exercise their talent elsewhere. Further-more, as the opposition was looking distinctly competitive by the end of 1985, the prospect of challenging for the left-overs, instead of the real prize, is not guaranteed to bring out the best, when one is used to leading from the front. The solution to this problem lies at the very heart of Ron Dennis's management philosophy, and this was expected to be sorely tested during the coming season.

Keke Rosberg would have no such motiva-tional problems, however. He wanted to be the World Champion again. His presence in the team as an equal number one driver would en-sure that Prost kept well and truly on his toes, and not be blighted by the reigning Champion's traditional slackening off. Prost expected Rosberg to be a handful and to be out-qualified by him, but he knew that he had certain advant-ages, such as experience with the car, and that

his style was more suited to McLaren than that of the rustic, hard-charging methods of Keke Rosberg. McLaren did not expect too many problems on the account of their drivers.

John Barnard thoroughly re-designed the car and made the most of the reduced fuel capacity, to 195 litres (43 gallons). This loss of 27 litres (6 gallons), allowed the driver to sit in a more reclined position than hitherto, and this oppor-tunity to substantially lower the car and im-prove the aerodynamic package was taken. The main gain was the higher top speed, aided by an increase in power from the Tag/Porsche en-gine. This, in turn, had its turbos repositioned to improve the air inflow and make room for the fitting of the latest state-of-the-art Bosch engine management system. By measuring the actual mass of air, instead of the volume, and mixing the exact amount of fuel required, this system promised to optimize the use of the fuel

Keke Rosberg

My first sight of Keke in Formula 1 was at the very wet International Trophy, in 1978. Rain is often regarded as a great equalizing factor, and Rosberg kept his slow and heavy Theodore on the island (or lake!) to win, while most of the illustrious competitors took to the scenery.

A robust, often rustic driver, Rosberg suffered the indignities of driving the Theodore, and later ATS cars for the rest of 1978. The following year, after Hunt's sudden retirement, he landed the Wolf drive; if anything, Rosberg's battle with this car served to show that Hunt had taken the right decision. The following two seasons saw Rosberg in yet another uncompetitive car, the Fittipaldi, but his forceful driving and 'never say die' attitude drew attention to him.

Then, in 1982, Rosberg joined the Williams team and became World Champion, equalling Mike Hawthorn's feat of achieving this despite winning only one race during the season. Over the next three years at Williams, Rosberg's hard-charging, often spectacular driving left nobody in any doubt that he was among the top contemporary drivers, though he only won four more Grand Prix races.

Rosberg replaced Niki Lauda at McLaren in 1986 and many enthusiasts looked forward to the prospect of Prost being pushed to the limit by Rosberg in an equal car. It did not work out like that, and Rosberg retired after just one season, realizing he was in a team very much dedicated to Prost and his economical style of driving – the car was not really suited to Keke's more aggressive style. He did not have much luck either, though there were occasions when he showed that he was still up with the best. A good example of this was at the Australian Grand Prix when he ran everyone ragged, only to be sidelined near the end, his eighth retirement of the season.

Despite the 'hard-charging' image, Keke Rosberg was very much a professional racing driver in the modern sense. He devoted his considerable energies to his sponsors as he raced, giving 100 per cent at all times. Rosberg also enjoyed the fruits of his success, and the image of the Finn standing by his aeroplane, briefcase in hand, is nearly as strong as that of Rosberg wrestling an uncompetitive car into a position it did not deserve. Perhaps the season at McLaren was not a fitting finale to a fine racing career, but he came out of retirement in 1991 to race the new Peugeot sports car. Keke will not go unnoticed for long in the more leisurely world of sports car racing.

during a race, so that not a drop would be wasted.

The higher top speeds meant that the brakes were in for a caning, but another McLaren-built component, the gearbox, was modified to include a sixth gear. As speeds had increased, so the gaps between the gears had become wider, causing the engine to fall out of its narrow peak operating band, further limiting its competitiveness. The extra gear closed up these gaps and eliminated the problem. So, with a re-designed rear suspension and four new MP4/2C tubs moulded at Woking, and not by Hercules, McLaren were ready to take on all-comers, in what was to prove a dramatic season.

The last four races of 1985 had finally eradicated any doubts that lingered about the Honda engine. Indeed, Rosberg confirmed that, at the top end of its rev range, it was considerably more powerful than the Tag/Porsche, despite the latter's recent 50bhp increase. Williams, with their new FW11 and teamwork equal to McLaren, were going to fight every inch of the way. Mansell had grown in confidence and stature as a driver, but it was the recruitment of Piquet which held the greatest threat to McLaren. Twice World Champion, Piquet was still probably the fastest driver in Grand Prix racing and, given a fully competitive car – and Williams promised nothing less – was a man to watch.

Lotus were expected to offer less of a challenge, at least as far as the Constructors' Championship was concerned. Senna, the undoubted up-and-coming man, remained, and was expected to mount a serious title challenge, but therein lay a major problem. The team wanted Warwick to partner Senna, as de Angelis had left, but Senna threatened to join Brabham if Warwick were recruited, because Senna felt that Lotus could not cope with two top drivers. After one season there, saying this about the second most successful team in Grand Prix racing seemed a mixture of arrogance and flying scared of any direct competition. It would have been interesting had the Lotus management

called Senna's bluff; look what happened to Brabham. However, Lotus had a new car, the 98T, with the powerful Renault engine, and experience in depth.

To howls of derision from all sides, Lotus capitulated to Senna and recruited a talented Scottish driver, Johnny Dumfries, though not the next Clark or Stewart. In so doing, Lotus virtually surrendered their challenge for the Constructors' Championship to back Senna. Yet, history has suggested that Senna was probably right, and that Lotus were not as good a team as seemed apparent at that time. It was his method of displaying this which caused concern.

It is foolish to brush aside Ferrari before a new season begins, and McLaren certainly did not underrate the Maranello team. Postlethwaite's F1/86 was again driven by Alboreto and Johansson, two good drivers, but not really in the top class. However, a Ferrari is all about its engine; yet even here there were signs that they could not match Honda. To be fully competitive, they would need to wring a few extra horses out of their V6, or beef them up somewhat.

Brabham offered the most interesting situation; they had lost Piquet, but gained de Angelis and Patrese – a curious mix. Murray's BT54 was a good car, badly let down by its Pirelli tyres, and he had a new design for 1986, the startlingly low BT55. This sleek projectile was again powered by the BMW engine, producing 1,050bhp in qualifying trim, mated to a seven-speed gearbox. The package looked promising, but seemed marginally lacking in the cockpit; and one wondered whether they could mount a season-long challenge.

Those were the leading contenders, but some of the lesser lights were capable of having the odd good day. Ligier, once one of the better teams, had teamed up Arnoux (sacked by Ferrari early in 1985) with Laffite. Both were not the youngest of drivers, but had been winners in the past. With a new car, the JS27, and the Renault engine, they might just come up trumps. The Haas-Lola team were expected to do well. With Tambay and Jones as their drivers, a new car, the THL-2, and the new Ford-Cosworth turbocharged engine, when it was ready, hopes were high. Former McLaren chief Teddy Mayer ran the outfit, assisted by Tyler Alexander, so all the ingredients were there; it just needed the right mix.

That Tyrrell could no longer be considered one of the top teams was a warning to all of the fickle nature of Grand Prix racing. A new car – the 014, powered by the Renault engine – might just work, but one could hardly see drivers Brundle and Strieff causing many upsets. The same could be said about Arrows, with Boutsen (who had not progressed as expected) and Surer at the wheel of the BMW-engined A8 cars. At least the engine had oodles of power. Perhaps the joker in the pack might just be Benetton, who had bought the Toleman team, lock, stock and barrel. The Italian clothing team had Teo Fabi and the highly promising Gerhard Berger as drivers. Their B186 chassis, actually designed as a Toleman,

was mated to the BMW engine, and might just have the qualities to mount a challenge if Pirelli caught up with their tyres.

The season opened in Brazil, but there was to be no dream start in McLaren's defence of the two Championships. For the second race in succession, neither car finished, but it was Mansell and Senna who stole the headlines. The Englishman tangled with the Brazilian at the first corner, eliminating himself, and Piquet came through to win the pipe owner. 'Aha,' some of the cynical press thought, 'will Mansell never learn, trying to win the race at the first corner. Piquet will put him in his place.'

In Spain, Mansell was to put right the wrongs of Brazil. Rosberg showed his true colours here as well, holding third place until lap 30, and leading Prost for a further four laps. He then fell back, his tyres fed up of his hard-driving style; Rosberg certainly had a problem with the understeering McLaren chassis.

Prost came through from fifth position to within striking distance of the lead, but then Mansell, with a deflating rear tyre, shot into the

Alain Prost, as smooth and precise as ever, practises for an eventual fourth place on the grid for the Spanish Grand Prix.

240

Sometimes Grand Prix racing can be dull for the drivers. A featureless circuit, uninteresting landscape and hot weather call for more professionalism than inspiration. Prost could be almost anywhere in the world here, but in fact is practising for the 1986 Spanish Grand Prix. At least the weather was not too hot in April.

pits with ten laps to go. With a deficit to Senna of over 20 seconds, Mansell took second place off Prost, with four laps left, and tore after Lotus, shattering all times set for the new circuit in the process. Mansell drove like a man possessed, and on the last lap he was not even put off by Senna's weaving. Exiting the last corner he came out from behind Senna to snatch the lead just before the finishing line, and elatedly completed his victory lap.

Then the awful news was broken, Senna had won, by a matter of inches. Overnight, the organizers had moved the finishing line about 30 yards towards the last corner, and not informed the teams. This was indeed bad organization, but the position of the timing equipment and finishing gantry for the flag ought to have given the Williams team some clues, and they could have informed Mansell of this over the radio. You could not imagine McLaren making such an error.

What was fast getting a reputation for the annual economy run, the San Marino Grand Prix came next; and it promised even more fun and games than usual with the reduced fuel capacity for 1986. The Haas-Lola team debuted

Photographs can lie! Alain Prost is actually leading Keke Rosberg, in the Spanish Grand Prix, by almost a full lap. Rosberg's front left tyre does not appear to be wearing too well, with Prost's showing similar deterioration.

the Ford-Cosworth turbo engine, though as with the old DFV engine, there was to be no dream debut, because Jones actually qualified way behind Tambay with the Hart-engined car.

Senna claimed the pole again, but Prost and Rosberg were in the top five, Keke hurling the car round in wild abandon, the car obviously not handling to his liking. Piquet led easily at first, until the tyre stops, when Rosberg took over, only to lose out when he took his foot off the brake as a rear wheel was being tightened, with near disastrous consequences. Prost now led and gradually pulled away from Rosberg, while Piquet was touring in third place, obeying his fuel read-out. It looked to be another dull walkover, until Piquet's computer gave him the go-ahead, and then he charged. With two laps to go Piquet closed on Rosberg, who was confident of holding him off, the computer on the McLaren informing him that there was enough fuel left, when . . . splutter, splutter, he was out.

Prost began his last lap with just enough fuel

left, but he had seen Rosberg's car parked by the track side, and guessed what had happened. All was well until a mile from the end, when the engine cut out. Weaving desperately, as if out of control, Prost swished some fuel into the engine and it barked into life again. A few hundred yards later, the same thing happened and Prost repeated his act; meanwhile Piquet was gaining hand over fist. Then the McLaren spluttered into life, giving Prost enough momentum to carry him to the chequered flag – his 30-second lead being whittled down to a mere 5½ seconds – I suppose a fuel economy race can make for exciting finishes. Unlike in 1985, there were no problems with Alain's car, and he was declared the official winner. Keke was not exactly convinced of the Bosch engine management system's reliability, though, and clearly he was using more fuel than Alain.

Monaco proved nothing else but an Alain Prost walkover; pole position, leading from the front except while in the pits for tyres, and set-

Pole position at Monaco is more important than at any other circuit, and the advantage to Prost is seen clearly here. He leads the way round the old Station hairpin from Senna, Mansell, Alboreto, Rosberg (up from ninth place), Berger, Patrese, Brundle, Tambay and Piquet.

Keke Rosberg had his best result of 1986 at Monaco, finishing in second place and recording the only McLaren 1–2 victory of the season. He is just leaving the tunnel, after having lapped Arnoux in fifth place.

ting fastest lap. If not exactly spectacular to watch it was another example of his genius. Rosberg made up for this with an, at times, thrilling drive from ninth place on the grid to a distant second at the finish.

McLaren had begun to note that when Rosberg said that the car understeered too much, he was not talking about minute adjustments *à la* Prost and Lauda, no, a major change was required. John Barnard was reluctant to make wholesale handling changes to his beloved creations; all his work towards a built-in life for each component would go out of the window, as parts for the car would no longer be interchangeable. Furthermore, problems would arise over the setting up of the spare car. John Barnard felt that Rosberg would have to alter his driving style, while Rosberg naturally felt that if McLaren hired him, knowing how he had always driven, then they ought to accommodate that style. This may have contributed

Prost and Rosberg enjoy giving everyone a champagne shower after their Monaco victory. This act has become very familiar to Alain Prost over the years.

243

to John Barnard's growing unease within the team.

Alain Prost now led the Drivers' Championship, while McLaren did likewise with the Constructors'. It did not last, because Williams came on the boil, winning eight of the next ten races. Prior to the Belgian Grand Prix, FISA made a hasty, but welcome decision, to curb the power of the turbo engines for 1987, with an intention to eliminate them as soon as practicable – a bit unfortunate on Ford. A series of deaths involving rally drivers and spectators, a Formula 3 driver, and finally Elio de Angelis, while testing his Brabham at Paul Ricard, caused a worried FISA to act before matters got out of control and governments began to interfere. This decision, wisely taken with some urgency, also gave encouraging noises about the need for consultation. Although the latter was not allowed to delay the decision-making process, it seemed that FISA at last understood that the days of their dictats were numbered.

Alain Prost was mixed up in a first-lap contretemps in Belgium, but recovered from second-last place, and a pitstop to have a new front wing fitted, to finish a splendid sixth, the fastest driver on the demanding Spa circuit. Mansell won his first race of the season, while Rosberg retired on lap 6, with a failed engine.

Mansell continued his winning run in Canada, taking the pole and leading all the way, except for the routine tyre stops. Rosberg ran well for much of the race, leading Prost, before having to pay the price for really racing, by easing off in the closing laps to conserve fuel. He finished fourth, though once again, he was far from happy with the handling of his car. Prost showed his class again. After a wheel nut jammed in his pitstop, he managed with a smooth drive to gain second place. The driving styles of the McLaren drivers made a stark contrast.

Senna interrupted the Williams victory trail by winning the United States Grand Prix, in Detroit, and taking over the lead of the Championship. This heightened the folly of running only one top driver, as Lotus languished well

behind Williams and McLaren in the Constructors' contest. Prost was pipped for second place by Laffite, the Ligiers improving at every race, while Rosberg retired early on with a transmission failure.

Mansell resumed his winning ways in France, and then Britain; Prost picking up second and third places, but otherwise being outclassed by the Englishman on the rampage. Rosberg's plight worsened: the car was still far from suitable for his driving, and he was plainly no challenge for Prost.

Piquet, to much surprise, had been comprehensively outdriven by Mansell, and the two disliked each other. However, the Brazilian pulled up his socks and hit back, winning first in Germany, and then at the inaugural Hungarian

Lap 1 of the 1986 German Grand Prix, at the Hockenheimring. Senna leads Berger, Rosberg, Piquet, Prost, Mansell and Patrese.

244

Alain Prost led in Germany though is seen here in third place, inside the stadium section of the Hockenheimring. Alain eventually finished sixth, after running out of fuel on the last lap. He proceeded to push his car towards the finish, as a protest at the fuel limit for the cars.

Alain Prost is the most precise of the modern crop of Grand Prix drivers, yet when he is really trying, he can 'kerb-hop' like the rest. Fourth place on the grid, in Australia, was the best he could wring from this effort.

245

Grand Prix. Rosberg announced his retirement in Germany where, ironically, for the first time Mclaren had got the car to handle to his liking. He led the race on three occasions, and looked to be heading for a good second place when he ran out of fuel on the last lap. The same fate befell Prost, but he stuttered into the stadium area before finally grinding to a halt. His subsequent attempt to push the car to the line was done in a mixture of anger and protest at the silly state to which Grand Prix racing had sunk.

TROUBLES AHEAD

Following the Austrian Grand Prix matters came to a head in the McLaren camp. Things were not helped by Alain Prost's impressive victory there, which the engine management system nearly prevented, on the last lap again. John Barnard had earlier sold his share in McLaren International, and his attitude had seemed to change with his new status as an employee. Right from the word 'go' Barnard had not seen eye to eye with Rosberg, at least as far as the cars were concerned. Rosberg's naturally forceful, flamboyant driving was not suited to the MP4/2C, which had been fashioned for Prost and Lauda. Rosberg did not want to change his driving, and probably could not, while Barnard felt that since the cars were successful, they ought not be altered to the wide degree that Keke demanded.

During practice for the Austrian Grand Prix, John Barnard had wanted to lower the car and fit a Lotus-type of skid plate. This proved to be inconclusive in terms of speed, but Alain disliked the stiffly sprung car and had it set up as before, virtually behind John's back. This situation was decidedly unhealthy.

On top of this, relations between John Barnard and Ron Dennis deteriorated when the former began discussing contracts with other teams, in particular Ferrari, and when Barnard was perceived as letting standards fall. It was clear that the partnership was breaking up and,

though Rosberg was leaving at the end of the season, the day after the Austrian race Ron Dennis invited John Barnard to take his hook and sling it elsewhere, which he did. Race engineers Steve Nichol and Tim Wright promptly stepped forward into the breach, but the following Italian and Portuguese Grand Prix still went to the Williams drivers.

With two races left, Prost was 11 points behind Mansell, while Williams had already taken the Constructors' Championship. To compound McLaren's problems, Benetton had steadily improved to the point where Fabi claimed the pole in both Austria and Italy, while Berger won in Mexico, thanks to his Pirelli tyres lasting the race. Mansell muffed his start and had to drive through from the back of the pack, but Prost paced himself and then steadfastly trounced all the Goodyear runners who, like himself, had to change tyres. Thus a final showdown was set for the Australian Grand Prix, with Mansell still 6 points clear of Prost.

The preliminaries went Mansell's way; he set the fastest time in both practice sessions, with Prost back in fourth place. But on race morning, as on so many occasions, Prost was again the fastest on the circuit, if only by a couple of cats' whiskers, but he had to win the race – in which case Mansell only needed to finish third. The vagaries of the points scoring system, where a driver's best eleven results counted, dictated that Prost would lose one point from those scored in Australia, while Mansell would lose two. On the credit side, Rosberg was going to do all he could to help Prost win, whereas Piquet, Mansell's team-mate, could not similarly be relied on.

If 1985 had seen Mansell come of age as a driver, in 1986 he matured into a top class exponent of the art. In Brazil he threw away his chances at the opening corner, but confirmed his graduation in Australia.

Mansell led at the start, but backed off at the first corner rather than get embroiled with Senna and Piquet, who were going at it hammer and tongs. At the end of lap 1 Mansell led

*Lap 10 of the 1986 Australian Grand Prix, and Prost is lining up to relieve Mansell, the
Championship favourite, of third place.*

*A lap later, and Prost has done it, but there is an awful long way to go, and one hell of a lot of
water to pass under the bridge.*

247

*Rosberg, meanwhile, was not messing around either. In his last Grand Prix he wanted to finish
on the top, and to help Prost retain the Championship. He is leading and has positioned his hand
to get maximum lock for the next bend. His last race ended with a blown rear tyre.*

Prost, and then contentedly spent much of the
race either just in front, or just behind, the
McLaren, knowing that the Championship was
in the bag. One could not have imagined such
restraint from him, earlier in the season.

Prost knew what he had to do and, as un-
obtrusively as ever, got on with the job in hand.
By lap 23 the McLaren's were 1–2 again, as in
the good old days, only it was Rosberg, going
out with a bang, who was leading, and
majestically so at that. This was no problem to
Prost, as Rosberg had promised to pull over and
let Prost win, if he could still win the Championship by so doing, but Mansell was still comfortably tracking Prost; stalemate.

Goodyear, unsure of the projected rate of
tyre wear, and doubly wary after Pirelli pulled a
fast one on them in Mexico, had advised for
their cars to prepare for one pitstop during the
race. However, fate took a hand. Prost, normally the most precise of drivers, clipped a kerb
while lapping Berger and had to change his

tyres on lap 32. On inspecting these, Goodyear
announced that, punctures aside, they would
last the race, and the drivers were informed accordingly. This looked like a double blow for
Alain, as he was now back in fourth place, and
the other drivers need not stop for fresh tyres, as
had been budgeted for.

Prost shadowed the second place duel between Mansell and Piquet and, as Piquet was
allowed through, made his move. Mansell was
unperturbed and did not give in, holding off
Prost without recourse to unruly tactics. Prost
then tried a fresh approach and dropped back,
leaving Mansell isolated in third place; his time
spent partnering Lauda was not wasted. Then,
after imperceptibly closing the gap, Prost
charged at Mansell as the Williams car was exiting a corner and, driving at the very limit of his
ability, pulled alongside. Just as he edged his
nose in front, there was Keke, out of his car and
gesturing his sorrow to Alain, who was now
second.

248

A rear tyre on Rosberg's car had given out and, fearing that the rumbling was that of his engine about to blow, he promptly retired. That was on lap 63, and before Goodyear really knew that a tyre had shredded itself through wear, it was too late. In the next lap, Mansell, safely in third position, was coming up to lap Alliot at around 180mph (290kph). He had run the most mature, sensible race of his life, concerned only with winning the Championship; Lauda himself could not have controlled events better.

Then, with terrifying force, Mansell's left rear tyre blew up and his race for the title was instantaneously replaced by the fight for life. The three-wheeled car, trailing a firework display, was thrust first one way, then the other, repeatedly along the straight and anything could happen at those speeds. Mansell fought to keep the car straight and brought his car to a standstill gently against a wall, his race run and, more than probably, the Championship lost.

Piquet now led the race, and if he won, he would be the Champion. However, he too was on his original tyres, like Mansell. Once Goodyear and Williams knew what had happened, only one sane decision could be taken, bearing in mind that Prost, on new tyres, could hound Piquet: Piquet had to change his tyres. It was an awful decision to make, but using the on-car radio, Piquet was quickly called in to give him as long a run as possible against Prost.

There were sixteen laps to go and Piquet tore out of the pits after Prost. The gap appeared to be too great, and Prost was unlikely to blow his chances at this stage. Still Piquet pressed on, bringing back memories of those lightning-quick qualifying laps of his Brabham days, and gained on Prost, but it did not seem enough. Prost looked as though he had the race in the bag, but only he knew how tenuous was his grip on the title. His dratted computer indicated a gallon of fuel short of that needed to finish the race. Yes, it had been wrong before, but try and believe that with everything at stake. Yet Prost just had to slow down to save fuel, while Piquet was going like a bat out of hell!

Prost's mentor, Niki Lauda, would have coped with the situation, and now Alain was tested. Prost eased back, knowing that Piquet was gaining fast, and then, with the computer giving him no hope at all, it was down to the last lap. There was nothing for it but to go for broke. If he pussy-footed any longer, Piquet would catch him; so he gave it his all. Piquet charged as hard as ever and still gained; if Prost's car coughed now, it would be all over. With Piquet in his mirrors, Prost entered the final bend, losing sight of Piquet. It was a straight run to the line, and the engine never missed a beat. The chequered flag went by in a blur, and Prost had retained his Championship by a mere 4 seconds, his delight unconcealed as he leapt from his car. Magnanimous as ever, he offered his sincerest commiserations to Mansell, twice having lost the Championship himself at the last gasp. This time, Prost won without having the best car.

Alain Prost had been the first driver to retain the title since Jack Brabham in 1960. McLaren had been unable to emulate Ferrari's three Constructors titles of the 1970s, though, being soundly beaten by Williams. Unquestionably, the awards had gone to the right people. Alain Prost was clearly the best all-round driver and, as Rosberg readily acknowledged, had the team working for him. Williams on the other hand, with an organization equal to that at McLaren, had the best engine/car combination, and two of the top four drivers, yet they lacked the harmony to win both Championships which, on paper, they really ought to have done.

The season had been a great one for Grand Prix racing, though the gulf between the top three teams and the rest (with the later exception of Benetton) was wider than usual. Even during the McLaren monopoly of 1984, half a dozen teams looked capable of winning, at times. In 1986 former front runners Brabham and Ferrari were never serious contenders, and while Ligier did well, they did not threaten the status quo. As for the rest, they all tried hard and did their best, some making progress while

Less than a lap after Keke Rosberg had retired, a rear tyre exploded on Mansell's car along the straight, and he demonstrated a remarkable depth of skill as he brought the car to a standstill. Piquet was brought in to change his tyres, and thus left Prost in the lead. He not only won the Australian Grand Prix, but also became the first driver to retain the World Championship since the Australian Jack Brabham in 1960.

others drifted backwards, but clearly the divide between the 'haves', with Tag/Porsche, Honda, Ferrari, BMW, and Renault engines, and the 'have nots', with lesser engines, was not getting any less.

PROPOSALS

Politically, 1986 had been quite momentous as well. I have not been slow to criticize the many failings of the FIA, CSI/FISA, and M. Balestre

over the years, but following the various early season accidents, their prompt actions and initiatives were good to see. Particularly important was the realization of the need to curb both the ever increasing speeds of the Grand Prix cars, and the rapidly escalating team costs. Contrary to form, FISA threw out ideas, instead of dictats, to all concerned, and offered to discuss and consult with the teams, drivers and organizers on ways of achieving these aims. Some of the FISA proposals, such as the running of a qualifying race the day before a Grand Prix, to

250

Grand Prix Results 1986

GRAND PRIX	DRIVER	CAR	NO	1ST PRACTICE Time/Posn	2ND PRACTICE Time/Posn	3RD PRACTICE Time/Posn	FINAL GRID POSN	FINAL PLACING	RETIRED CAUSE OF	HIGHEST POSN IN RACE
BRAZILIAN Jacarepagua 23.3.86	A. Prost	McLaren-TAG MP4/2C-3	1	1min 28.74sec 4/25	1min 28.10sec 10/25		9-25		Lp 31 Engine failure	1st
	K. Rosberg	McLaren-TAG MP4/2C-2	2	1min 28.76sec 5/25	1min 27.71sec 7/25		7-25		Lp 7 Engine failure	5th
SPANISH Jerez 13.4.86	A. Prost	McLaren-TAG MP4/2C-3	1	1min 23.70sec 4/24	1min 22.89sec 4/24		4-24	3/8		2nd
	K. Rosberg	McLaren-TAG MP4/2C-2	2	1min 23.95sec 5/24	1min 23.00sec 5/24		5-24	4/8		3rd
SAN MARINO Imola 27.4.86	A. Prost	McLaren-TAG MP4/2C-3	1	1min 26.27sec 3/26	1min 26.18sec 4/25		4-26	1/6 WINNER		1st
	K. Rosberg	McLaren-TAG MP4/2C-2	2	1min 26.96sec 6/26	1min26.39sec 6/25		6-26	5/6		1st
MONACO Monte Carlo 11.5.86	A. Prost	McLaren-TAG MP4/2C-3	1	1min 26.06sec 4/26	1min 22.63sec 1/26		Pole	1/12 WINNER		FL 1st
	K. Rosberg	McLaren-TAG MP4/2C-2	2	1min 25.66sec 2/26	1min 24.70sec 9/26		9-20	2/12		2nd
BELGIAN Spa-Fran-corchamps 25.5.86	A. Prost	McLaren-TAG MP4/2C-3	1	1min 55.04sec 3/25	1min 54.50sec 2/25		3-25	6/13		FL 6th
	K. Rosberg	McLaren-TAG MP4/2C-2	2	1min 56.35sec 7/25	1min 55.66sec 8/25		8-25		Lp 7 Engine failure	9th
CANADIAN Montreal 15.6.86	A. Prost	McLaren-TAG MP4/2C-3	1	1min 29.54sec 6/25	1min 25.19sec 2/25		4-25	2/12		1st
	K. Rosberg	McLaren-TAG MP4/2C-2	2	1min 29.35sec 4/25	1min 25.53sec 4/25		6-25	4/12		1st
DETROIT, USA 22.6.86	A. Prost	McLaren-TAG MP4/2C-3	1	1min 43.37sec 5/26	1min 40.72sec 7/26		7-25	3/10		2nd
	K. Rosberg	McLaren-TAG MP4/2C-2	2	1min 43.73sec 7/26	1min 40.85sec 9/26		9-25		Lp 13 Broken transmission	9th
FRENCH Ricard-Castellet 6.7.86	A. Prost	McLaren-TAG MP4/2C-3	1	1min 07.27sec 5/26	1min 07.27sec 4/26		5-26	2/12		1st
	K. Rosberg	McLaren-TAG MP4/2C-2	2	1min 07.55sec 7/26	1min 08.18sec 7/26		7-26	4/12		3rd
BRITISH Brands Hatch 13.7.86	A. Prost	McLaren-TAG MP4/2C-3	1	1min 09.78sec 6/26	1min 09.33sec 6/25		6-22	3/9		3rd
	K. Rosberg	McLaren-TAG MP4/2C-2	2	1min 09.48sec 5/26	1min 08.48sec 4/25		5-22		Lp 8 Broken transmission	5th
GERMAN Hockenheim-ring 27.7.86	A. Prost	McLaren-TAG MP4/2C-3	1	1min 43.37sec 3/26	1min 42.17sec 2/26		2-26	6/12		1st
	K. Rosberg	McLaren-TAG MP4/2C-2	2	1min 42.48sec 1/26	1min 42.01sec 1/26		Pole	5/12		1st
HUNGARIAN Hungaroring 10.8.86	A. Prost	McLaren-TAG MP4/2C-4	1	1min 33.11sec 5/26	1min 29.95sec 3/26		3-26		Lp 24 Accident	3rd
	K. Rosberg	McLaren-TAG MP4/2C-2	2	1min 34.15sec 6/26	1min 30.63sec 5/26		5-26		Lp 35 Broken rear suspension	5th
AUSTRIAN Österreichring 17.8.86	A. Prost	McLaren-TAG MP4/2C-3	1	1min 24.35sec 2/26	1min 25.29sec 8/26		5-26	1/11 WINNER		1st
	K. Rosberg	McLaren-TAG MP4/2C-2	2	1min 23.96sec 1/26	1min 23.90sec 3/26		3-26	9/11	Lp 48 Electrical fault, but classified	2nd

ITALIAN Monza 7.9.86	A. Prost	McLaren-TAG 1 MP4/2C-3	1min 26.89sec 8/26	1min 24.51sec 2/27	2-27		Lp 28 Disqualified	**5th**
	K. Rosberg	McLaren-TAG 2 MP4/2C-2	1min 26.74sec 7/26	1min 25.38sec 7/27	8-27	4/11		**4th**
PORTUGUESE Estoril 21.9.86	A. Prost	McLaren-TAG 1 MP4/2C-1	1min 19.69sec 3/27	1min 17.71sec 2/27	3-27	2/14		**2nd**
	K. Rosberg	McLaren-TAG 2 MP4/2C-2	1min 20.56sec 6/27	1min 18.36sec 7/27	7-27		Lp 42 Engine failure	**5th**
MEXICAN Mexico City 12.10.86	A. Prost	McLaren-TAG 1 MP4/2C-5	1min 19.29sec 6/26	1min 18.42sec 5/26	6-26	2/13		**2nd**
	K. Rosberg	McLaren-TAG 2 MP4/2C-2		1min 19.34sec 10/26	11-26		Lp 33 Damaged susp flat rear tyre	**5th**
AUSTRALIAN Adelaide 26.10.86	A. Prost	McLaren-TAG 1 MP4/2C-5	1min 19.79sec 2/26	1min 19.65sec 4/26	4-25	1/11 WINNER		**1st**
	K. Rosberg	McLaren-TAG 2 MP4/2C-2	1min 21.30sec 5/26	1min 26.78sec 7/26	7-25		Lp 63 Thought engine had blown up	**1st**

determine grid positions – thus having two starts instead of one – were clearly hideous, and thankfully rejected. Others, such as executing a volte-face and banning turbo-engined cars from 1989, and doing away with special qualifying tyres, were both sensible and generally well received.

Indeed, the only major blemish on a difficult year was the $5,000 fine Alain Prost received for his comments about being allowed to start the Italian Grand Prix from the pit lane, only to be black-flagged and disqualified when well into the race. He had been risking his life unnecessarily, even coming back into the pits for a new nose cone, while the organizers dithered, and said as much. When told of the decision to disqualify Alain, Ron Dennis tried to get the organizers to change their minds, which held up matters still further. The organizers took half an hour to reach their decision, but Alain's criticism was justified.

Prior to the 1987 season, one proposal to curtail the speeds and costs of Grand Prix racing was abruptly taken out of FISA's hands. Pirelli withdrew, leaving Goodyear as the sole tyre suppliers. Goodyear were under the threat of a take-over, and met this by cutting back on peripheral activities. Racing tyres were regarded as being of promotional and developmental value, and not as core business. In addition, binding contracts with Lotus, Ferrari, Williams and McLaren meant that Goodyear were not prepared to service the other teams.

The options were rather stark; Grand Prix racing would consist of eight cars from the above teams, or could use F3000 cars and tyres, as happened in 1952 when Formula 2 rules predominated. There was far too much money invested in current machinery to take this road, so Goodyear's other proposal was gratefully accepted. The four teams' contracts were rescinded, and Goodyear undertook to supply all teams with ten sets of a standard tyre (suited to the circuit in question) per car entered for each race meeting, at a fixed price. Four sets of wet tyres per car, if needed, per car/race meeting would also be supplied.

It was a take-it-or-leave-it offer and, though hard on the contracted teams, was the only way out. The tyres could be divided as the teams saw fit, so car 1 could have nineteen sets and car 2 just one set, to last for the whole meeting: race, qualifying and testing. This also solved the problem of special qualifying tyres.

Other changes which were to affect the speeds of the cars concerned the retaining of the

195 litres (43 gallons) of fuel per race (to be reduced for 1988), and the reduction of the turbo boost to 4 bar. This would restrict power outputs from the BMW-quoted 1,050bhp, in race trim, to around 850bhp or thereabouts, and keep speeds down. Another change, as a prelude to the turbo ban for 1989, was the re-introduction of normally aspirated engines of 3.5 litres, as a separate category within Grand Prix racing. In that category, drivers would complete for the Jim Clark Cup, and constructors for the Colin Chapman up. Four teams, fielding five cars, were to compete in this new category, most notably Tyrrell, as Renault had pulled out of supplying engines to its customer teams.

This did not affect McLaren as such; they were too busy integrating a variety of changes into their framework. At the forefront of these was the move to new, purpose-built headquarters in Woking, incorporating the very latest in office design and workshop information technology systems. It is a highly functional building, with every need catered for under one roof, whether it be design offices, dining facilities, or a display area for cars and trophies. The general appearance and tidiness are as far removed from one's image of the racing workshop as one can imagine, and reflects the determination of McLaren International to remain at the forefront of Grand Prix racing.

Ron Dennis recruited new key personnel, marking a subtle change in policy since John Barnard's departure for Ferrari. Foremost among these new recruits was Brabham designer Gordon Murray, whose numerous cars had been mostly successful, occasionally brilliant, and always original. He became the Technical Director, but did not step straight into the shoes vacated by Barnard. Steve Nichols took over the responsibility of designing the 1987 car, assisted by Tim Wright and Neil Oatley, the ex-Williams and Haas-Lola (which had just folded) engineer. Thus the engineering design team was substantially strengthened, while a new direction was taken, by not entrusting a new car to one person, as had been the case with Barnard. In the long term, this foresight on Ron Dennis's part yielded substantial dividends in a number of engineering areas.

To the racing enthusiast, the most public of personnel changes came with the retirement of Keke Rosberg. The year 1986 had not lived up to expectations as far as his move to McLaren was concerned, and the hoped-for battle between himself and Alain had been little more than a walkover in favour of the latter. This happened mainly because the whole McLaren set-up was geared towards Alain Prost and his style of driving. Keke had not enjoyed the best of working relationships with Barnard, and his rugged, extrovert driving style was not suited to the MP4/2C, at least not until later in the season. Even so, he had been thoroughly outdriven by Prost, and as a result his respect for the Frenchman grew enormously, as indeed Prost admired the way Rosberg coped with all the problems he suffered during the year.

Keke Rosberg was replaced by Stefan Johansson, another extrovert character, who had impressed after two seasons with Ferrari. He arrived with the reputation of being a highly competitive racer, yet a bit unenthusiastic about long practice sessions, and in that way somewhat resembled his late compatriot, Ronnie Peterson. With Prost as number one, the matter of practice sessions was not likely to be too crucial for the team, since Prost undertook most of the developmental testing. Johansson had never won a Grand Prix though was clearly capable of doing so; but he was without doubt the understudy to Prost, and probably did not rank in the top five drivers at that time.

FAREWELL TO THE TAG ENGINE

For 1987 Williams still posed the greatest challenge. They retained Piquet and Mansell, although their obvious antipathy towards each other might well work against them, as it had in

1986. These two drivers – Piquet, blindingly fast, supremely talented, yet tactically astute; and Mansell, enthusiastic, possessing huge determination, and powerful to the extreme – were favoured, along with the FW11B car and the very powerful Honda engines. Even before the season began, few would have bet against this combination winning something, McLaren and Alain Prost notwithstanding.

Lotus, if anything, were expected to be an even stronger rival than in 1986. After Renault's withdrawal, Lotus, Ligier and Tyrrell had to make alternative engine arrangements, and Lotus came up trumps, attracting Honda. They were to receive engines identical to those supplied to Williams, and accepted Japanese driver Nakajima as their number two in place of the unlucky Dumfries. Senna remained, and with the 'active' suspension Lotus 99T car, though bereft of John Player sponsorship, Lotus were ready to challenge for the top honours again.

Of the other teams, perhaps Ferrari held out the most promise, with the Barnard-inspired F1/87 car; new 90 degree V6 engine; and Berger joining Alboreto behind the wheel. Plenty of potential there, but was the Ferrari team the best to put together a winning package from these elements?

Brabham had not won a race in 1986, for the first time since 1979, and with Murray's departure, looked like a spent force. They retained exclusive use of the BMW 'flat' engine, in the new BT56, while de Cesaris joined Patrese as a driver; in all, not too promising. Benetton had shone towards the end of 1986 and promised to be interesting challengers in 1987. They had lost Berger to Ferrari, but recruited Boutsen in his stead – a fair swap. They also retained Fabi. However, with BMW pulling out, Benetton needed an engine. The demise of the Haas-Lola team meant that the Ford Cosworth V6 became available, and Benetton were the benefactors. There was the little matter of its competitiveness to consider, but signs were promising. Thus, with entries from Minardi, Zakspeed, Ar-

rows, and Osella; with Tyrrell, Lola, March, and AGS in the 'second division' non-turbo category, the new season began in Brazil.

Well, not quite. FISA had performed well during 1986, almost too well, and so it proved. In December, a FISA council set the cost of the drivers' 'super licence' at 5,000 French Francs, plus, 1,000FF per Championship point scored in 1986. These are not large sums of money to top drivers but, perhaps expecting trouble, the decision was kept quiet for three months. Naturally, many drivers were upset at the way this was imposed, particularly the more successful ones, and Alain Prost outlined the drivers' point to FISA. He was concerned that the rates might be arbitrarily raised for 1988, without consultation. (FISA were not above such tricks, as we know.)

Prost's meeting with FISA resulted in a comprise being reached: drivers accepted the new charges, but the latter would not rise above inflation for the next five years. Too good to be true? Balestre, now aided by Ecclestone as the FIA's Vice-President of Promotional Affairs, did not wish to be seen losing face and announced that there had been 'no compromise', merely that the drivers had obeyed the rules . . .

Everyone except Ligier (in dispute with Alfa Romeo, their new engine suppliers) gathered in Brazil for the first race of 1987. McLaren's MP4/3 featured an all-new chassis, body, and cooling system, while the Tag/Porsche engine, front suspension, and wings were substantially modified; it was, in effect, an all-new car. There were a few problems to be sorted out before the race itself, and Prost found that the car handled badly in corners and was unable to match the Williams on the straights. A retreat to traditional settings was made, and these worked excellently; the car handled well, and was fast.

Williams served notice of their intent during qualifying. Mansell and Piquet held the front row of the grid, 2 seconds ahead of Senna, in third place. Prost was 3 seconds slower, in fifth place but, as so often happened in the past, he was fastest in the race morning warm-up, after

Stefan Johansson

There was a period in the mid-1980s when it seemed that Johansson was destined to become a consistent Grand Prix front runner, picking up the occasional victory. Today, on the eve of the 1991 season, after seventy-eight Grands Prix, he still has not won a race and, as a driver for the AGS team, is unlikely to in the near future.

Swedish-born Stefan is the marketing man's ideal Grand Prix driver. Good looking, with an extrovert personality, and a 'charging' driver to boot, Johansson has been popular with all the teams he has driven for. He was the 1980 British Formula 3 Champion, and moved up to Formula 2 for the next two seasons, with a private Toleman, and then with Gordon Coppuck's Spirit team. It was with the latter that Johansson made his Grand Prix debut in 1983, with the Honda turbo engine, though he had failed to qualify for the 1980 British Grand Prix, in a Shadow.

The next season saw Stefan without a Grand Prix drive, until he deputized for the injured Brundle at Tyrrell, and then joined Toleman near the season's end. With Senna moving to Lotus, Johansson was retained by Toleman for 1985, but the team had tyre supply problems and could not compete. Then, when Arnoux was suspended by Ferrari, Johansson fell on his feet and landed the number two seat to Alboreto. The Swede soon showed himself to be a worthy and loyal driver, actually leading the San Marino Grand Prix until he ran out of fuel, and his 'never say die' driving made him popular with both the Ferrari team and the Italian fans.

Stefan did even better the next year, enhancing his reputation as a good race driver, if not so hot at testing, but 1986 was a disappointing season for Ferrari, and Stefan took the vacant seat at McLaren. As Prost undertook the majority of testing, Johansson's mediocrity in that area did not matter too much, and he soon established himself as a sound number two, though not really able to challenge Prost. In such a role, Johansson could not be faulted, but with Senna coming on to the market, McLaren had to dispense with his services.

Thereafter, Johansson spent a year with the shambles at Ligier, followed by two seasons getting the new Onyx team from the slowest of pre-qualifiers to the occasional points-scoring finish. Neither of these teams, nor his new drive at AGS, are worthy of his talent, yet it looks as though time has passed Stefan by. He was unlucky enough to arrive at Ferrari and McLaren when both suffered hiccups in their normal performance, and even Ligier might have performed better than they did. As it is, Johansson holds the unwanted distinction, along with de Cesaris, of being the only Marlboro-McLaren drivers never to have won a Grand Prix race in their career to date. That is a harsh epitaph for such a talented, loyal and popular driver and, had he not been dealt so duff a hand, Stefan Johansson might have been remembered in more glowing terms.

---

the setting had been revised. Stefan qualified in a steady tenth position.

As starting time drew near, the sultry heat was about 110°F in the shade, and cockpit temperatures were off the thermometer scale. Racing in a 200mph car, when clothed in thick overalls and helmet can be simply horrendous. As expected, the Williams pair contested the lead with Senna during the opening laps, but Prost nursed his tyres, car, and himself, and kept the leaders in view. First Piquet went into the pits, then Mansell, and finally, on lap 13, Senna . . . and Prost was in front. He lost the lead during his tyre stop, but normal service resumed on lap 21, and he drove, virtually unchallenged, to victory. It all sounds so easy!

Stefan drove a brave, efficient race, holding second place at one time, to finish third. He was seriously dehydrated by the end – a harsh reminder that Grand Prix driving is not as easy as it sometimes seems. What of Williams? Piquet came a distant second and Mansell sixth, and lapped, after a puncture.

The San Marino Grand Prix provided Mansell with his first win of 1987, while Prost retired when an alternator belt snapped and his engine cut out. Johansson came fourth. Prost had won twenty-six Grands Prix to date, one short of Jackie Stewart's long-standing record, and the next race was at Spa, his favourite circuit. The occasion looked irresistible for Prost.

As usual, the Williams pair sat on the front row, with Senna 1 second behind Mansell, and

Prost a frustrated sixth, 2 seconds adrift. Johansson was back in tenth position, again. Spa is formed by two sections of public road, linked by an 'infield' stretch, and winds its way around the Ardennes in southern Belgium. It is perhaps the most challenging circuit in use. The Honda-engined cars were in another league from the rest, particularly on the long straightish sections, but a Grand Prix covers nearly 200 miles, so anything could happen.

Mansell roared off, chased by Senna, Piquet, and the rest. Near the end of lap 1, Boutsen and Berger tangled; while Streiff's Tyrrell got away from him, early on lap 2. The car hit the barriers; the engine and chassis separated; and teammate Palmer crested the rise at *Eau Rouge* and found his path blocked. He rammed the wreckage, and the race was sensibly stopped.

At the restart, Senna led Mansell away, and just after they entered the infield section, Mansell tried to overtake. It was a bit of a dicey move – Mansell managed to get his car in front when they touched wheels, and off they went: Senna for good, and Mansell effectively out of the running. Piquet's subsequent lead did not last long, as his engine management system failed, and with Berger's retirement and Alboreto's gears failing on lap 10, Prost took over the lead, with only Fabi to worry about.

Johansson really got to grips with things and moved into second place, removing any threat from behind, but Prost's computer had failed again, and he did not know the fuel situation. A link was set up via the on-car radio and Johansson's still functioning computer, but because of interference, Prost could not hear anything. He watched Ron Dennis and Steve Nichols each time he passed the pits. If they were standing around calmly, then all was well – as you know, McLaren are right at the cutting edge of modern technology!

But it worked, while Johansson's car ran out of fuel 200 yards short of the finish. Fortunately, he was far enough ahead to retain second place, but on-car computers and radios were not in favour with the drivers.

Two modern classics? The hideous one in the background at least gets Detroit noticed. Prost meanwhile keeps his eyes off the monstrosity and gets on with the job in hand, at the United States Grand Prix.

With this comprehensive victory, Prost equalled Jackie Stewart's record and moved into the lead of the World Championship. Johansson, with his third consecutive finish, was now second, while McLaren led the Constructors' Championship. Everything seemed rosy, but the sheer power of the Honda engines was readily apparent, and McLaren could not rely on luck in every race.

All this might have been expected to make the headlines, but it was the additional value-for-money show that attracted all the attention. Senna and Mansell had indulged in their third collision, and this time the Englishman had decided to sort things out. Believing Senna to be at fault, he went to the Lotus pit and began to

Prost's brilliant start from fourth place on the grid to take the lead of the British Grand Prix, before Copse Corner, is shown here. He is about to block off Piquet with Mansell, Senna, Fabi, Boutsen, Alboreto, and Johansson, up into eighth place, behind. Prost's lead did not last; Piquet was past by Maggots Curve, and Mansell along the Hangar Straight. Such was the power of the Williams team.

measure the size of Senna's neck with his hands, while contemplating whether he might not look prettier with a less protruding nose. The Lotus mechanics helped save Senna's more recognizable features, while the press had a field day, with criticism flying around from all angles. It might not have done the 'corporate image' of Grand Prix racing any good, but at least it showed a bit of spirit.

Thereafter, the season ran away from both Prost, and McLaren. The next eight races were all won by Honda-engined cars, with Senna, Mansell, and Piquet each winning two on the trot, and Mansell and Piquet three apiece. Prost tended to be the best of the rest, though Ferrari and Benetton were thereabouts. The Tag/Porsche engine was now no match for the Honda, although Prost comfortably led the German Grand Prix before the alternator belt snapped, robbing him of a certain victory.

Amidst all this sharing of victories, it was possible that Prost might have picked up enough points to stay in contention. Instead, with a string of five second places to go with his wins,

Piquet piled up a formidable points tally, while Prost could only manage three third places. McLaren became less harmonious to a degree, as often happens when a winning team is knocked from its perch. Mechanical troubles – some major, like engine failures, others trivial, such as battery failure – caused problems for both drivers in over half of these races.

To suggest that McLaren had ceased competing would be very wide off the mark indeed. New aerodynamics, an uprated engine specification, and even a new alternator belt were tried. Their effectiveness remained limited by the power of the Honda engine, especially as installed in the Williams chassis. Even Senna had been unable to cope with them, the 'active' suspension on the Lotus not working as well as the conventional Williams. Then, to boot, Williams introduced their 'self-levelling suspension' car, similar in concept to that used by Lotus, and it won first time out, in Italy. It was all 'go' at the front.

In the meantime, Prost, whose Championship chances had all but vanished, had still not

257

won his record-breaking twenty-eighth race, and apart from in Germany, had not looked likely to. Then came the Portuguese Grand Prix, following on from testing, during which a few of the electrical bugs were ironed out.

Prost qualified in third place on the grid, behind Berger on the pole, and Mansell; this looked promising. A second start was needed, and though Mansell led initially, Berger was soon by, and the Williams retired a little later. Prost, as usual, was using his brain more than most, and settled back to let things sort themselves out. By lap 30 he was fourth, but by the time Berger regained the lead, after his tyre stop, Prost moved into second place, 20 seconds adrift, with half the race left. He had nursed both the car and himself; fuel and tyres were good; and so he began to set about the Ferrari.

A long, determined pursuit began, and Berger responded by upping the rating. You could see that Berger was really trying, as he hopped over kerbs, slid around on tyres worked to their limit, and used the full rev range of the engine. Prost was different though. The car pursued the same smooth lines as before, there was no sliding around in corners, and it looked for all the world as if he had his grandmother on board! Yet there was no doubt that Berger was giving his all. You could see that, and you could also see, first on your stop watch, and then with your eyes, that Prost was gaining. Prost's pursuit was relentless, but it was no picnic either. His brakes were overheating, the tyres overworked, and Prost was going flat out as well, though it was not apparent to the observer.

Berger knew what he was doing, and traded lap records with Prost. Despite all his efforts, still the McLaren got closer. How could Berger shake off the red-and-white car? Berger's lead was down to 3 seconds, and with two laps to go it looked enough, but the pace was awe-inspiring; Berger dare not ease off. Then, he overdid it and spun, while Prost drove through to that record-breaking victory, while Berger recovered to finish second. Prost was desperate to win, even turning the turbo boost up, at the risk of fuel economy, and had never driven so hard in his life. It was the most appropriate way to beat the long-standing record of Grand Prix victories, and desperately unlucky on Berger – but his day was not far off.

END OF AN ERA

That was just about it for McLaren. Prost's second and Johansson's third place, well behind Mansell, in Spain, followed by Johansson's fighting third place in Japan, brought the curtain down on the Tag/Porsche era. Mansell won two of the remaining races, before his accident in Japan rendered him *hors de combat* for the season, and thus handing Piquet the World Championship. Berger, meanwhile, won the last two races for Ferrari – John Barnard's work paying dividends.

A brief, highly successful era came to an end with the chequered flag at the Australian Grand Prix. McLaren consigned the Tag/Porsche engine to history, and embarked on a new association with former rivals Honda. The Tag/Porsche engine had powered McLaren to twenty-five wins in four short years, of which Alain Prost recorded nineteen. No other team, not even Ferrari, could beat that, and only Jim Clark, between 1962–1965, could equal Prost's record.

Much of the credit for this outstanding performance was heaped on to the engine, and yet was it really the class of the field? McLaren provided the perfect car for the engine, but only two drivers actually won races with that combination. For those dragging up the age-old argument that the drivers are not important anymore, this says quite a lot. So did Mansell's display in 1985–1986 when, with identical machinery, he won eleven races to Piquet's six, and enjoyed some appalling luck on the way.

McLaren's switch to Honda was not without its misgivings, nor was it taken lightly. Ron Dennis said that at the time, 'No one could see the logic; we were winning with the Tag/

During what was a difficult season for McLaren, with their Tag/Porsche engine being outclassed by the Honda V6, Stefan Johansson battled on manfully. Here in the Spanish Grand Prix, he leads Warwick's Arrows, on his way to a satisfactory third place.

Despite not having the best machinery at hand, Prost and Johansson performed well throughout 1987. Prost was clearly the superior driver, but Johansson was not far behind, as seen here during the Spanish Grand Prix. Johansson's performances with the MP4/3 were often good, and deserved better drives than subsequent seasons have brought.

Patrese's Brabham proved difficult for Johansson to get past in the Spanish Grand Prix. As you can see, the Italian looks to have a few extra tricks up his sleeve, apart from the usual driving tactics.

Porsche engine, and enjoyed a successful relationship with them.' However, as far as McLaren were concerned, the change was a result of their management philosophy of combating complacency by continually seeking to affect improvement.

According to Ron Dennis, 'The logical progression was to stay with Porsche and for them to design and develop a normally aspirated engine. Instead, we chose to go in a different direction; obviously the right one to take but, at that time, thought to be quite radical.' Radical it might have been, but with one year of turbo-engined formula left, the Honda was the engine to beat, and Honda had their first normally aspirated engine on test, before the ink

had dried on the contract. As Prost discovered when he visited the Honda Research and Development facility in Japan, there were one thousand people working on the racing projects, so it was better to have them on your side than against you.

Why Honda chose to leave Williams though, was a different matter. Like most car manufacturers engaged in motor sport, Honda are not in the field for the hell of it; they want to promote and sell their products. As a spin-off, racing may 'improve the breed', but that is not the primary aim. Piquet was probably the best known racing driver worldwide, at that time, and was therefore highly desirable for Honda in terms of promotion. The sight of Mansell putting one over

Grand Prix Results 1987

GRAND PRIX	DRIVER	CAR	NO	1ST PRACTICE Time/Posn	2ND PRACTICE Time/Posn	3RD PRACTICE Time/Posn	FINAL GRID POSN	FINAL PLACING	RETIRED CAUSE OF	HIGHEST POSN IN RACE
BRAZILIAN Jacarepagua 12.4.87	A. Prost	McLaren-TAG MP4/3-3	1	1min 29.52sec 4/22	1min 29.18sec 5/22		5-22	1/12 WINNER		1st
	S. Johansson	McLaren-TAG MP4/3-2	2	1min 31.34sec 8/22	1min 30.48sec 10/22		10-22	3/12		2nd
SAN MARINO Imola 3.5.87	A. Prost	McLaren-TAG MP4/3-3	1	1min 29.32sec 9/27	1min 26.14sec 3/24		3-24		Lp 15 Alternator	2nd
	S. Johansson	McLaren-TAG MP4/3-2	2	1min 30.42sec 13/27	1min 28.71sec 8/24		8-24	4/13		4th
BELGIAN Spa-Fran-corchamps 17.5.87	A. Prost	McLaren-TAG MP4/3-3	1	2min 11.20sec 9/26	1min 54.19sec 6/26		6-26	1/10 WINNER		FL 1st
	S. Johansson	McLaren-TAG MP4/3-2	2	2min 12.06sec 11/26	1min 55.78sec 10/26		10-26	2/10		2nd
MONACO Monte Carlo 31.5.87	A. Prost	McLaren-TAG MP4/3-3	1	1min 25.57sec 3/25	1min 25.08sec 4/24		4-25	9/13	Lp 16 Engine failure	3rd
	S. Johansson	McLaren-TAG MP4/3-2	2	1min 27.70sec 9/25	1min 26.32sec 6/24		7-25		Lp 58 Engine failure	11th
DETROIT, USA 21.6.87	A. Prost	McLaren-TAG MP4/3-3	1	1min 46.04sec 9/25	1min 42.36sec 5/25		5-26	3/12		2nd
	S. Johansson	McLaren-TAG MP4/3-2	2	1min 46.62sec 11/25	1min 43.80sec 10/25		11-26	7/12		7th
FRENCH Ricard-Castellet 5.7.87	A. Prost	McLaren-TAG MP4/3-3	1	1min 06.88sec 2/26	1min 07.84sec 4/26		2-26	3/11		2nd
	S. Johansson	McLaren-TAG MP4/3-2	2	1min 08.58sec 9/26	1min 09.10sec 12/26		9-26	8/11	Lp 75 Electrics Not running	8th
BRITISH Silverstone 12.7.87	A. Prost	McLaren-TAG MP4/3-4	1	1min 08.58sec 4/26	1min 09.49sec 9/25		4-25		Lp 54 Electrics Clutch	1st
	S. Johansson	McLaren-TAG MP4/3-2	2	1min 10.24sec 7/26	1min 09.54sec 10/25		10-25		Lp 19 Turbo failure	6th
GERMAN Hockenheim-ring 26.7.87	A. Prost	McLaren-TAG MP4/3-4	1	1min 43.20sec 3/26			3-26	7/9	Lp 40 Engine failure	1st
	S. Johansson	McLaren-TAG MP4/3-2	2	1min 45.43sec 8/26			8-26	2/8		2nd
HUNGARIAN Hungaroring 9.8.87	A. Prost	McLaren-TAG MP4/3-4	1	1min 30.16sec 2/26	1min 30.33sec 6/26		4-26	3/13		3rd
	S. Johansson	McLaren-TAG MP4/3-2	2	1min 31.23sec 7/26	1min 31.94sec 8/26		8-26		Lp 15 transmission seized	6th
AUSTRIAN Österreichring 16.8.87	A. Prost	McLaren-TAG MP4/3-4	1	1min 26.17sec 9/26	1min 43.13sec 7/26		8-26	6/16		3rd
	S. Johansson	McLaren-TAG MP4/3-3	2	1min 29.00sec 14/26	1min 41.71sec 4/26		14-26	7/16		7th
ITALIAN Monza 6.9.87	A. Prost	McLaren-TAG MP4/3-4	1	1min 25.34sec 6/28	1min 24.95sec 5/25		5-26 11-26	15/15		5th
	S. Johansson	McLaren-TAG MP4/3-5	2	1min 27.42sec 10/28	1min 27.03sec 10/25			6/15		6th
PORTUGUESE Estoril 20.9.87	A. Prost	McLaren-TAG MP4/3-4	1	1min 18.40sec 4/26	1min 17.99sec 3/25		3-26	1/14 WINNER		1st
	S. Johansson	McLaren-TAG MP4/3-5	2	1min 20.13sec 7/26	1min 20.23sec 7/25		8-26	5/14		5th

261

SPANISH Jerez 27.9.87	A. Prost	McLaren-TAG 1 MP4/3-4	1min 24.60sec 5/28	1min 24.91sec 5/27	7-25	2/14	**2nd**
	S. Johansson	McLaren-TAG 2 MP4/3-5	1min 26.15sec 8/28	1min 26.15sec 10/27	11-25	3/14	**3rd**
MEXICO Mexico City 18.10.87	A. Prost	McLaren-TAG 1 MP4/3-4	1min 20.57sec 2/27	1min 18.74sec 5/27	5-26		Lp 1 Damaged **5th** steering
	S. Johansson	McLaren-TAG 2 MP4/3-3	1min 22.19sec 9/27	1min 22.38sec 16/27	15-26		Lp 2 Car bent **15th**
JAPANESE Suzuka 1.11.87	A. Prost	McLaren-TAG 1 MP4/3-4	1min 42.50sec 4/27	1min 40.65sec 2/26	2-26	7/14	**FL 2nd**
	S. Johansson	McLaren-TAG 2 MP4/3-5	1min 43.61sec 8/27	1min 43.37sec 9/26	9-26	3/14	**2nd**
AUSTRALIAN Adelaide 15.11.87	A. Prost	McLaren-TAG 1 MP4/3-4	1min 18.20sec 3/27	1min 17.97sec 1/27	2-26		Lp 54 Spun off **2nd**
	S. Johansson	McLaren-TAG 2 MP4/3-5	1min 19.76sec 9/27	1min 18.23sec 7/27	8-26		Lp 47 **5th** Shattered brake disc, spun

on Piquet might make for good motor racing, but Mansell was not as well known as Piquet, whereas people the world over would more readily identify with the Brazilian driver – a case of 'If Piquet wins with Honda, it must be good, I'll buy it', as opposed to 'Mansell who?'

What concerned Honda most was that Williams allowed their number two driver, Mansell, to get away with this, and in fact positively encouraged it. After all, when Reutemann started beating Jones, in 1981, the team soon put a stop to it. Furthermore, Frank Williams ran a very tight ship indeed, and after years of struggling to keep afloat, he was not about to bail out control to his engine suppliers. Frank was very much the Captain, and had every intention of keeping it that way. He was also very patriotic, and this probably had much to do with Mansell being allowed to usurp his number one.

For his part, Mansell was very loyal and gave his all, endearing himself to the team members. He felt that he had received underpowered engines in Italy and Spain. Piquet, on the other hand, was unhappy in the team and did not get on with Mansell; he was leaving when his two-year contract expired. It was the combination of commercial reasoning, and control, which drove Honda to pull out of Williams with a year of their contract still to run. But why go to McLaren? Surely Ron Dennis controlled things at least as tightly as Frank Williams, and their drivers were no better known?

Yes, Ron Dennis keeps things very tight indeed, but he is also a great one for co-operation and delegation. It was this willingness to work as partners that swayed the day, while Honda's readiness to continue developing their turbo engine for one final season, as well as to prepare their new engine for 1989 convinced Ron Dennis of the correctness of the move.

Amid all this the sacrificial lamb was Stefan Johansson, who had performed steadfastly throughout the season and had finished sixth in the Drivers' Championship – about equal to his ability in the natural order of things. He was not a serious rival to Alain Prost, and with Senna keen to leave Lotus – also with a year of his contract left to run, and seen by Honda as their new man – he was moved out to make way. This was not too difficult a choice for Ron Dennis, because here was the fast man of the future and, alongside Alain Prost, it once again gave him the strongest driving team in the business. The way was thus smoothly paved for Piquet to go to Lotus, who kept Nakajima and the Honda engines.

With hindsight all this seems straightforward, but of course wasn't so at the time, with three teams, six drivers, and two engine suppliers involved. No one knew what the future held, and though things worked out well for McLaren, a couple of interesting 'what ifs' remain. Suppose they stayed with Tag/Porsche, and they built a normally aspirated engine for 1989? What would have happened to Honda then, bearing in mind subsequent events at Lotus? Perhaps more interesting is why didn't Honda build their own Grand Prix car after the problems with Williams? Now, that really would have been worth seeing. The next chapter might have read rather differently . . .

CHAPTER 9

. . . Mighty Oaks Will Grow

REWRITING THE RECORD BOOKS

The year 1988 marks a watershed for both McLaren and Grand Prix racing. What happened is simple; McLaren International comprehensively re-wrote the Grand Prix record books. We will concentrate on the 'why' and 'how' in this chapter, but first a quick look at what did happen in that remarkable season.

There were 16 Grand Prix races in 1988, and a McLaren driver won fifteen of them. More precisely, new-boy Ayrton Senna won eight races and became the World Champion, while Alain Prost won seven. Ten races were won in 1–2 formation, and fifteen pole positions gained, thirteen of which went to Senna. Prost gained 105 points to Senna's 94, but with only the best eleven results counting towards the Championship, Senna had 90 points to Prost's 87. In the Constructors' Championship, McLaren gained 199 points to second-place Ferrari's 65 points. All these were outright Grand Prix records! In addition, a McLaren car won each of the first eleven races, second only to Ferrari's run of fourteen wins in 1952–1953, while their four consecutive 1–2 wins was equal second to Ferrari's record of 1952. Phew, it leaves you gasping for breath.

Quite appropriately, the only race a McLaren failed to win was the Italian Grand Prix, where Berger and Alboreto recorded a Ferrari 1–2, shortly after the death of the great Enzo Ferrari – a fitting send-off for the man.

Images of Mercedes Benz in 1955; Lotus in 1978; and even McLaren in 1984, running two cars at the head of the field; are put in the shade and into perspective by McLaren's 1988 performance. The results in no way flatter the complete dominance of McLaren, from practice (where they occupied both front-row grid positions on eleven occasions) to the race (where Prost and Senna were each other's main rival). Prost finished fourteen out of a possible sixteen races, winning seven and coming second on the other seven occasions, yet he did not become the World Champion! However, that fact gives a true measure of the McLaren mastery.

There is no doubt that McLaren simply hammered the opposition, but how did this come about? And to many enthusiasts' complaints that McLaren's domination of the grid was 'boring', here is Ron Dennis's reply:

'1988 was a very unusual year, one in which the majority of competitors were uncommitted to the regulations that governed that particular period. Everybody was looking to the rule changes that were coming into force for 1989, and they were not prepared to make the time investment, or money investment, in building new cars that optimized the regulations for 1988. Our view was "Let's win 1988 first, and then worry about 1989".'

This is perhaps an over-simplification of the situation, but it gives the essense of the problem.

REGULATIONS, 1988 FASHION . . .

It was to be the last season for turbocharged

engines in Grand Prix racing, and this was the root of the problem for many teams. The turbo boost pressure was to be further reduced from 4 bar, or four times the atmospheric pressure of 14lb psi, to 2.5 bar. Power was thus toned down considerably, but there was more. The minimum weight remained at 540kg (1,190lb) while the petrol capacity was reduced from 195 litres to only 150 litres (43 gallons).

Fuel economy had played an adverse role in the races of previous seasons, and the new regulations appeared draconian by comparison. On the other hand, the normally aspirated cars of 3.5 litres capacity, while expected to nearly match the power output of the emasculated turbocharged engines, were allowed an unrestricted amount of fuel, and had a minimum weight of only 500kg (1,102lb). Thus, they could be expected to put up a better show than in 1987. Indeed M. Balestre, the President of FISA, said that he expected the 3.5-litre cars to be at least as competitive as the turbo-engined cars . . .

Since this was the last season for turbo engines, teams and engine builders were reluctant to invest heavily in a project with a very restricted life. Renault had pulled out at the end of 1986, BMW had done the same after 1987, though not really having their heart in it even then. Ford abandoned their turbo engine before it was fully developed, to concentrate resources on their new 3.5-litre engine, and the Tag/Porsche engine had been similarly discarded, when McLaren astutely joined with Honda.

Put into perspective, four of the leading six turbo engines had been withdrawn from Grand Prix racing, and the Ferrari engine was definitely not for sale, while Megatron had taken over the earlier BMW engine, developed this, and supplied the Arrows team. Zakspeed continued with their four-cylinder turbo engine, and Osella struggled on with the V8 Alfa unit, neither of which had ever looked like winning a race. As far as turbo engines went, it looked, on paper at least, a two-horse race: Ferrari vs Honda with perhaps Megatron getting a look in, somewhere.

. . . AND THE COMPETITION

What of the competitor teams who, according to Ron Dennis, were 'uncommitted to the regulations'? Ferrari were definitely committed, up to a point. They had modified their turbo engine and, after victories in the last two races of 1987, expected to be competitive. However, their car, the F187/88C, as the designation suggests, was an evolution of the 1987 car; good . . . but not the best. Moreover, they had a 3.5-litre engine under development, and felt that they might use it if all was not well with their turbo. So there was an element of doubt within the team, although one could not dismiss Ferrari, they might just as easily sweep the board, even if recent experience suggested this was unlikely. So, regarding Ferrari, Ron Dennis was probably right; even McLaren's main turbo rival left the normally aspirated door ajar, just in case.

Arrows produced the A10B, but again this was not brand new, and they had never won a Grand Prix to date. In reality, the Megatron engine was not expected to compete seriously with the Honda and Ferrari power units over a full season, but Arrows did not appear to have gone into the final turbo year half-heartedly. In the final results, they possibly did better than expected. Of the other turbo teams, Zakspeed and Osella – without being rude or demeaning to such enthusiastic outfits – could not and did not expect to challenge McLaren or Ferrari, new cars or not, and so do not really enter the equation of serious opposition.

Williams were a different matter. They had run off with the Constructors' Championship the previous two seasons, yet did not use a turbocharged engine in 1988. Here was a team to rival McLaren in many areas; they had a new car, and were far from 'uncommitted' to the regulations. Of course, their problem was the loss of the Honda engine. What were they to do, with one year of the turbo formula left, and the lack of an alternative? Yes, they might possibly have used the Megatron unit, but that was

---

Gordon Murray

Throughout the 1970s and 1980s Gordon Murray portrayed his 'pop star' image to the world of Grand Prix – not entirely inappropriate as he is a great fan of Bob Dylan, and other good things from that scene. Highly individualistic in both character and work, Gordon Murray is one of the top Grand Prix car designers of his era and, like Colin Chapman, led where others followed. While at Brabham he virtually ran his own team, and it came as quite a surprise when he left for the more structured environment of McLaren, at the end of 1986, to become their Technical Director. He has since moved out of the Grand Prix arena.

Murray was born in South Africa, where he used to race cars which he prepared. He came to Britain and joined the Brabham design department in 1970, becoming Ralph Bellamy's assistant when he joined from McLaren, in 1972, and taking over from him when Bellamy left to join Lotus a year later. Murray's first Grand Prix car design was the BT42, of 1973, and thereafter he produced a whole string of individualistic, original designs which went on to win twenty-two Grands Prix, give Piquet two World Championships, yet never won the Constructors' title.

Some of these designs were truly outstanding, yet none achieved the supremacy they deserved. This was due partly to Brabham changing component suppliers who did not live up to their promise, for example Alfa Romeo engines, Pirelli tyres, and partly to the fact that from 1980 onward it was a virtual one-car team, with Piquet partnered by whoever had enough money to buy the number two seat. Murray's seven-year partnership with Piquet was prolific though, the two working together with an ease and affinity that made the job look easy, but then Piquet departed for Williams, after a disappointing 1985, and Murray also left a year later.

At McLaren, Murray initially worked alongside Neil Oatley and Steve Nichols on the design teams, but never had, nor expected, the autonomy he enjoyed at Brabham. Earlier though, Murray had taken an interest in the Midas kit-car, and this had spurred his interest in the road car direction. It was thus a short step for Gordon to take charge of McLaren's own road 'super-car', and it is with this that he is now immersed. Details of this are a bit thin at the moment, mainly because many aspects still have to be finalized, but the promised 'best' car ever built will be just that, with the genius of Gordon behind it. Since his favourite car is the Lotus Elan – the original lithe version, not the flabby, overweight, modern thing – you can bet that Gordon will come up with a similar gem, and standard-setter, that more than meets the highest expectations of today's road cars.

One cannot help feeling that Gordon Murray ought to be back designing Grand Prix cars: at the moment, it seems that only Tyrrell are producing a car different to the rest, though the 'pregnant' looking Williams FW14 may set a new trend. Perhaps though, Grand Prix racing really has advanced beyond the stage where one man can design a new car, and where a 'design team' is essential. This will be a great shame, because it limits the role of such an individual as Gordon. True, other designers have produced cars which have won more races/ championships, Patrick Head and John Barnard to name two, but it was Gordon Murray who carried the torch of the individual genius after Colin Chapman died, and his cars were always something special.

Of one thing you can be sure though, Gordon is not being put out to grass on the McLaren road car, with his Dylan tapes, motor bike and Lotus Elan for company. When this and other projects come to fruition, we will almost certainly see the genius of Gordon being brought to bear on other cars, hopefully cars that are more accessible to you and me.

---

too much of a compromise, so what was the point? Instead, they opted to use the Judd 3.5-litre V8, a modified version of Honda's not too successful Formula 3000 engine. This gave around 600bhp compared to Honda's expected 685bhp, but bearing in mind the weight advantage and unrestricted fuel, it might have been competitive. There was no doubting their commitment to the regulations though.

Of the other non-turbo teams March, with

their 881, Ligier a JS31, and AGS, all used the Judd engine, and had this been competitive then maybe one might have pulled a surprise or two. As it happened, AGS were indifferent, Ligier collapsed into a disorganized heap, while March eventually rose to become the leading non-turbo team, usurping Williams. That did not mean they were ever more than fleeting rivals to McLaren.

Tyrrell were just about the leading Cosworth

DFZ-engined team, but none of these minnows were in with a whisper, let alone a shout, and had a turbo engine been available to them, which was not the case, it would have made little difference.

That leaves Benetton, of the non-turbo teams and, like Williams, they too had little choice in what sort of engine to use. The Ford turbo engine was coming good, though not fully competitive with the Honda or Ferrari engines. It needed time to become a race winner, and that it did not have. So Ford, rather than waste money and effort on the nigh-obsolete turbo engine, concentrated on the new Cosworth-developed DFR 3.5-litre V8, and Benetton had no real option but to take this

path because, once again, a turbo engine was not available.

Two major teams remain unaccounted for. Ecclestone withdrew Brabham from Grand Prix racing, and later sold the team, so that was that. What about Lotus? As in 1987, they used Honda engines, alongside McLaren. The Honda option was there, and they grabbed the opportunity with both hands. Apart from Ferrari, which other of the aforementioned teams would not have done the same? Lotus also had a new car, the 100T, a landmark in any firm's existence, and this did not use the 'active' suspension, but returned to more conventional means. A real challenge was expected from Hethel, but it did not materialize and, as the

Alain Prost and Ayrton Senna did work together in 1988, and here they are discussing practice statistics with the Honda technicians.

season wore on, they struggled to keep in the top five teams. It was not really a question of commitment, more one of expedience.

Would McLaren's commitment to the turbo regulations have differed had Honda not left Williams, and the Tag/Porsche engine fallen further behind? I wonder.

This leads us to the drivers. Reigning World Champion, Piquet, had decided early on to leave the Williams hot-house, and took his no. 1 to Lotus. There, he was to lead Nakajima, not really a winner, but not having a forceful partner never bothered Piquet when at Brabham. Great things were expected from the Lotus/Honda/Piquet package, if not the Constructors' title, but as the season wore on and Lotus fell off the pace, Piquet's attitude seemed to deteriorate even more, and their performances became more inept by the race.

Ferrari had the talented, enthusiastic Berger to partner Alboreto, a good pairing, perhaps second only to the McLaren duo, but they needed a superior team package to wrest the initiative from the Woking men. Berger turned in the only threatening performances to Prost and Senna all season, scoring one win and claiming one pole position – not really a fair reward for his unstinting efforts throughout a difficult year.

That left Mansell, partnered by Patrese, at Williams. After a front-row position in Brazil, which raised very false hopes for the normally aspirated brigade, Mansell only secured two points-scoring finishes all season. Both of these were second places, to Senna at Silverstone and a truly gallant chase of Prost in Portugal, but the Williams gradually lost ground to other cars, and Mansell could only do so much himself.

Boutsen and Nannini at Benetton, netting eight third places between them, performed well, but neither had won a race previously, nor did they seriously challenge for the lead this time around. The Arrows men of Warwick and Cheever just might have turned in the odd winning performance, given that they too had turbo power beneath their right feet, but they ended up fighting over the scraps. In fact it was the March pair of Capelli, in particular, and Gugelmin, who were the surprise of the season, Capelli actually briefly leading Prost in Japan.

In a season which saw four new teams, six new drivers, and two new engines, with there being thirty-one entries for most races, quality was distinctly thin on the ground. No team could match the McLaren combination of car, engine teamwork and, arguably, the top two drivers. It was this all-round package that enabled McLaren to prove such a towering force.

McLaren's commitment to the final year of turbo racing began with a brand new car, the MP4/4, designed by a team headed by Steve Nichols, and including Gordon Murray. There was little left over from Barnard's MP4 series; it was totally new, designed around the Honda engine. Six chassis were built for a life of one year only; that is commitment. A new gearbox was introduced from Silverstone onwards and virtually everything, except the engine, wheels, gearbox internals, and tyres, was made at Woking. Quality control was thus assured, and the only retirement due to a mechanical failure came at Monza when Prost's engine failed; although Senna was disqualified in Brazil after changing to the spare car, as his race car jammed in first gear at the start. No other team could approach such a record of reliability. Occasionally though, the Ferrari did look the better balanced car, which leads us to the next stage.

Honda were not easing up in the least, just because their engine had only one season of racing left. The sheer scale of their racing engine operation was truly awe-inspiring, and made one wonder how anyone else could possibly compete. The latest RA168–E V6 engine produced 685bhp at 12,500rpm, and was remarkably fuel-efficient; there were not too many occasions when a McLaren was in danger of running out of petrol. There was never any doubt at any stage of the season, which was the most powerful engine, though one must remember that Lotus had an equal share of the sixty, yes sixty, engines in the float.

The partnership between Ayrton Senna and Ron Dennis has grown to equal any of the past.

However, as Lotus were to quickly find out, the Honda engine did not guarantee race wins, let alone a virtual whitewash. The key was the dedication and teamwork of the McLaren and Honda partnership. That last word really does describe the way in which the two worked, as partners, and not just as engine suppliers to a team. McLaren went to great lengths to work with Honda, taking great strides to close the cultural gap, in both the literal and business senses. The two were, and indeed still are, supportive of each other's problems, and have a total commitment to excellence. This is what both parties were looking for when initial approaches were being made, and that is what happened.

Within McLaren, delegation is one of the roads to success. No one person can oversee everything, though it is very much Ron Dennis's show. The emphasis is on teamwork and preparation, nothing is overlooked, and no avenue left unexplored. Everybody and every job has its place within the team, and is important to its performance. The workshops would make more than adequate operating theatres, and the absence of the traditional oil, grease, smell and general mess associated with a garage, perhaps best symbolizes the aim for perfection.

The idea is inculcated into each employee, whether it be floor cleaner or team manager, not only of the importance of his or her particular job but also of the need for excellence. All very laudable and easy to write about, but needing considerable determination and dedication,

269

Ayrton Senna

Anybody watching a motor race for the first time, at the 1991 United States Grand Prix in Phoenix, would probably have marvelled at the faultless drive and imperious victory achieved by Ayrton Senna. Here he was in a brand new, virtually untried car, and he simply ran away from the rest of the field without being challenged. While others fell off the circuit, fell over each other, and fell short of the necessary quality, Senna took the pole position and won at his own, often searing pace. One could easily show our first-time viewer numerous other races in which Senna has followed exactly the same script and they would almost certainly assume that here was the best racing driver of his day, and possibly ever. For sure they would be surprised if you said that he is not the best all-round driver at the moment, and that some, no, many people consider him to be one of the most dangerous drivers ever to win a Grand Prix race, and that he was lucky not to be banned from racing.

It is too easy to explain away this contradictory phenomenon as aversion for, or jealousy of, the top man. Senna's driving has always been exceptionally forceful, from his days in FF1600, through Formula 3, to Grand Prix racing. He joined Toleman for 1984 and immediately came across as a star of the future, achieving two second places, and might have, given different circumstances, won the Monaco Grand Prix. His dispute with his team, who suspended him from the Italian Grand Prix after he signed for Lotus, also signalled that he was very much his own, ambitious man.

Ayrton spent three seasons with Lotus, winning his second race for the team, and kept them at the forefront of Grand Prix – a place subsequently shown to be rather flattering. While Senna's stature as a driver grew, so too did his reputation for reckless driving. Each victory was shadowed by a major incident, often involving Mansell, and with this came growing disaffection both with many followers of Grand Prix, and those directly involved. The root of this was Senna's overtaking method, and his blocking of cars to stop them passing him. Since joining McLaren in 1988, Senna's total of victories has outstripped his incidents but, disconcertingly, these have become more frequent, resulting in love/hate feelings for Senna the driver, and the refusal, both his peers and past 'greats', to acknowledge him as a 'great'.

Senna is a practising Christian, and takes his motor racing in the same serious vein. His life is committed to both his racing and his god, but he likes nothing better than to spend the winter break back home in Brazil with his family, away from the world of motor racing. Many have been the occasions on which Senna has been accused of arrogance on the racing circuits, but away from them he is a devoted professional and a modest man. When at Woking, he only too readily chats to those who keep the premises spotlessly clean, and will make his own way to the airport rather than have a car provided for him. That McLaren and Honda personnel hold Senna in such high regard and affection is not solely due to his immense driving ability.

At the end of the day though, Ayrton the man cannot be divorced from Ayrton the driver. If he can find a way to eliminate the important errors and become a little more tactically aware without losing his brio, then, like Prost, he will take his place among the Grand Prix 'greats', no questions asked. If he retains his sheer speed as well, then Senna may yet become the greatest of them all. Time is running out though, and if Senna keeps having these incidents, whatever the cause, he might well find his Grand Prix career being, involuntarily, shortened by the new legislation aimed at improving driving standards. His future is in his own hands, but there are already several quarters from where backing will not be forthcoming.

to carry through. McLaren have been critisized for being too efficient, characterless, and so on in 1988, but it was their aim to win every race, and if that is what was needed, so be it.

It was no surprise that the one chink in the McLaren armour concerned the drivers. Having the best car, team, and engine is not the whole answer; put in two of the best drivers and you cannot go far wrong. Prost was very much a team driver, and the most accomplished in the field. Senna was less of a team man, more introspective and dedicated beyond belief; he was possibly the fastest driver in the world, though he had a few well publicized accidents, which raised the odd question. Undoubtedly, it was better to have Senna in a McLaren car, than ranged against one, and the pairing looked what it was: unbeatable.

Much attention was focused on how Prost and Senna would get on, with their different philosophies: Prost, at home in 'his' team, happy to share any technical information, twice World Champion and going for his third title; Senna, a 'new boy', having to find his feet, and desperate to win races and the Championship. At first all went well, but a decline did set in, and the previously formidable Prost/McLaren relationship began to wane, if only a little. It was a year which proved Senna to be the faster driver, though not the best, and saw Prost rattled a bit. The chemistry was not there for a harmonious season, and so it proved, as both men were each other's main rival.

As the season progressed Ayrton appeared to get the upper hand, a fact freely admitted by Prost, and a deterioration in their relationship and, in Prost's case, with the team, set in. Let us not exaggerate this; the differences were no more than between normal working partners. As for Senna stealing a march on Prost, that was not a surprise. We have already commented on their differing philosophies and attitudes to racing, and McLaren made a big effort to accommodate Senna, even to the extent of the occasional preference over Prost.

There was nothing wrong about this; Senna had to find his feet and needed to adjust to the new environment, and Prost understood this. Senna's initial advantage came from being a faster qualifier than Prost, which probably stemmed from his knowledge of the Honda engine and his astonishing ability to execute the perfect lap. He used a different cornering style to Prost, jabbing the throttle to keep the engine buzzing well into its power band. Prost, on the other hand, used a much smoother throttle application, more economical, but more suited to the Tag engine. He tried to copy Senna's technique, but was not happy doing so.

For the races, Senna made use of Prost's car settings, as he felt that Prost was better at setting up the car, and Alain was happy to assist. Senna was also much better at lapping slower cars than Prost, and this proved advantageous on several occasions. This is not to say that Prost was substandard, but Senna was ruthless in his execution of this necessary part of racing, and he took risks. He finally came unstuck in Italy, when he was caught out lapping Schlesser's Williams, for the second time, and crashed out on the penultimate lap, handing victory to Berger. Prost was much more circumspect, and it was to cost him the Championship in Japan, as dithered behind Nakajima and also de Cesaris/ Gugelmin, while Senna sliced past without being held up.

Senna handed victory to Prost at Monaco after he clipped the apex at *Portier* and hit the barriers opposite, a rare mistake. There was little to choose between the two until Prost's victory in France, when Senna got the upper hand for the next five races. It was during this period that Prost was critizised for 'whingeing', and that his faith in McLaren began to waver.

During the French Grand Prix Prost had run over a kerb, which adversely affected the handling at the British Grand Prix. In fact it was so bad, changing from oversteer to understeer in every corner, that he gave up, and the press pilloried him. In Germany Prost ran over a kerb again, avoiding a wayward Euro-Brun, and the chassis handled worse than ever. Thereafter, he

271

never found that particular car, MP4/4–4, to his liking, and told the team as much. It is significant that when Prost finally got a new car, in Portugal, he went on to win three of the last four races with it.

Amidst all this was the matter of Honda engines. Honda claimed that engines were supplied to Lotus and McLaren in no particular order, and that no differences were made between drivers. However, in Germany Prost noted that an old engine was fitted to his car for qualifying, and he was not happy with the way he could not hold Senna in Italy either. That is why he drove the engine to destruction, and the only race failure of the season. By Japan, the penultimate race, Honda's fairness was being questioned by none other than Balestre himself. Honda and Ron Dennis were indignant at the FISA President's suggestion that they were not treating the drivers to equal equipment, but there was little doubt that Senna had the better working relationship with the Honda personnel, so perhaps a little favouritism was understandable. More pertinent perhaps, is why should Balestre get involved in team affairs? Surely it is up to a team as to which, if any, driver gets preferential treatment?

By the last race of the season, with both Championships wrapped up, all was not well in the McLaren camp. The row involving Balestre included the little matter of FISA wanting to inspect the McLaren gearboxes after the Japanese Grand Prix, as Prost's had been playing up. In truth, it was the clutch that gave Prost problems, but this unwarranted intrusion by FISA fuelled the row between the parties, which widened the cracks in Prost's relationship with the team.

Ron Dennis made light of Prost's mechanical problems, some of which have been detailed, thus giving the impression, which the press had bandied about, that Senna had won the title in equal circumstances. Prost felt otherwise, and forcibly made his point to Ron Dennis, who in turn admitted that McLaren had given Senna more than his fair share of attention, for integra-

tion purposes, at Prost's expense. Prost made it clear that this would have to change before the next season, then went out and won the last race.

If this paints a picture of a downturn in the Prost/McLaren relationship, then it is not amiss. Senna deserved his title, but given equal equipment Prost could match him blow for blow. The two were never likely to enjoy a similar working relationship as, say, Prost and Niki Lauda, considering their different outlook on racing. However, we have mentioned the ruthless streak in Senna, used particularly when lapping slower drivers. There was one occasion when he turned it against his own team-mate, pulling the sort of manoeuvre no other top-class driver would ever have done.

It happened after the third start of the Portuguese Grand Prix. As the light shone green Prost got alongside Senna and, as they raced away, gently eased him over to the edge, but not off the circuit, by the first corner. Senna brusquely chopped ahead of Prost as if he were not there, to take the lead, leaving Prost to stamp on his brakes; there was nothing unfair about Prost's move. At the end of lap 1 Prost came out of the corner before the straight faster than Senna. Through the gears they went, the speed getting ever higher: 150, 160, 170, 180mph. Prost pulled to the right to get past, and as he came alongside, Senna also moved to the right, forcing Prost towards the pit wall. Team managers holding signal boards out over the pit counter were forced to pull them back, as Prost's wheels whirled past within fractions of an inch of the wall.

The two McLarens' wheels were dovetailed as they hurtled along the straight, and an awful accident looked imminent; what was Senna doing? Unable to brake or manoeuvre any further, Prost jinked his wheel to the left and back again, forcing Senna out a little. He managed to get through, into the lead, and win the race. Senna's actions were unforgivable, though he apologized later, and Prost said afterwards that, 'If he wants the Championship that much, he

Grand Prix Results 1988

GRAND PRIX	DRIVER	CAR	NO	1ST PRACTICE Time/Posn	2ND PRACTICE Time/Posn	3RD PRACTICE Time/Posn	FINAL GRID POSN	FINAL PLACING	RETIRED CAUSE OF	HIGHEST POSN IN RACE
BRAZILIAN Rio de Janeiro 3.4.88	A. Prost	McLaren-Honda MP4/4-2	11	1min 31.98sec 3/31	1min 28.78sec 3/31		3-31	1/9 WINNER		1st
	A. Senna	McLaren-Honda MP4/4-3	12	1min 30.22sec 1/31	1min 28.10sec 1/31		Pole		Lp 31 Disqualified	2nd
SAN MARINO Imola 1.5.88	A. Prost	McLaren-Honda MP4/4-4	11	1min 41.28sec 1/29	1min 27.92sec 2/30		2-26	2/19		FL 2nd
	A. Senna	McLaren-Honda MP4/4-1	12	1min 41.60sec 2/29	1min 27.15sec 1/30		Pole	1/19 WINNER		1st
MONACO Monte Carlo 15.5.88	A. Prost	McLaren-Honda MP4/4-4	11	1min 28.38sec 2/30	1min 25.43sec 2/30		2-26	1/10 WINNER		1st
	A. Senna	McLaren-Honda MP4/4-1	12	1min 26.46sec 1/30	1min 24.00sec 1/30		Pole		Lp 67 Accident	FL 1st
MEXICAN Mexico City 29.5.88	A. Prost	McLaren-Honda MP4/4-4	11	1min18.10sec 2/30	1min 18.30sec 3/30		2-26	1/16 WINNER		FL 1st
	A. Senna	McLaren-Honda MP4/4-1	12	1min 17.47sec 1/30	1min 17.67sec 1/30		Pole	2/16		2nd
CANADIAN Montreal 12.6.88	A. Prost	McLaren-Honda MP4/4-4	11	1min 22.50sec 2/31	1min 21.86sec 2/31		2-27	2/13		1st
	A. Senna	McLaren-Honda MP4/4-1	12	1min 22.39sec 1/31	1min 21.68sec 1/31		Pole	1/13 WINNER		FL 1st
DETROIT, USA 19.6.88	A. Prost	McLaren-Honda MP4/4-4	11	1min 42.02sec 2/30	1min 43.42sec 6/29		4-26	2/8		FL 2nd
	A. Senna	McLaren-Honda MP4/4-2	12	1min 40.61sec 1/30	1min 41.72sec 3/29		Pole	1/8 WINNER		1st
FRENCH Ricard-Castellet 3.7.88	A. Prost	McLaren-Honda MP4/4-4	11	1min 08.17sec 1/30	1min 07.59sec 1/29		Pole	1/15 WINNER		FL 1st
	A. Senna	McLaren-Honda MP4/4-2	12	1min 08.46sec 2/30	1min 08.07sec 2/29		2-26	2/15		1st
BRITISH Silverstone 10.7.88	A. Prost	McLaren-Honda MP4/4-4	11	1min 11.55sec 4/30	1min 10.74sec 4/30		4-27		Lp 24 Handling	11th
	A. Senna	McLaren-Honda MP4/4-5	12	1min 10.79sec 3/30	1min 10.62sec 3/30		3-27	1/19 WINNER		1st
GERMAN Hockenheim-ring 24.7.88	A. Prost	McLaren-Honda MP4/4-4	11	1min 44.84sec 2/30	1min 45.87sec 1-30		2-26	2/18		2nd
	A. Senna	McLaren-Honda MP4/4-5	12	1min 44.60sec 1/30	1min 50.55sec 9-30		Pole	1/18 WINNER		1st

HUNGARIAN Budapest 7.8.88	A. Prost	McLaren-Honda MP4/4-2	11	1min 29.59sec 1/30	1min 28.78sec 1/30	7-26	2/13		FL 2nd
	A. Senna	McLaren-Honda MP4/4-5	12	1min 30.42sec 4/30	1min 27.64sec 1/30	Pole	1/13 WINNER		1st
BELGIAN Spa-Fran-corchamps 28.8.88	A. Prost	McLaren-Honda MP4/4-2	11	1min 54.13sec 2/30		2-26	2/15		2nd
	A. Senna	McLaren-Honda MP4/4-5	12	2min 15.196sec 4/24	1min 25.97sec 1/30	Pole	1/15 WINNER		1st
ITALIAN Monza 11.9.88	A. Prost	McLaren-Honda MP4/4-1	11	1min 26.28sec 2/30	1min 26.43sec 2/30	2-27		Lp 34 Engine	2nd
	A. Senna	McLaren-Honda MP4/4-5	12	1min 26.16sec 1/30	1min 25.97sec 1/30	Pole	10/13	Lp 49 Spun off, accident	1st
PORTUGUESE Estoril 25.9.88	A. Prost	McLaren-Honda MP4/4-6	11	1min 18.38sec 2/30	1min 17.41sec 1/30	Pole	1/12 WINNER		1st
	A. Senna	McLaren-Honda MP4/4-5	12	1min 18.03sec 1/30	1min 17.87sec 2/30	2-27	6/12		1st
SPANISH Jerez 2.10.88	A. Prost	McLaren-Honda MP4/4-6	11	1min 26.74sec 4/31	1min 24.13sec 2/31	2-26	1/14 WINNER		FL 1st
	A. Senna	McLaren-Honda MP4/4-5	12	1min 24.78sec 1/31	1min 24.07sec 1/31	Pole	4/14		3rd
JAPANESE Suzuka 30.10.88	A. Prost	McLaren-Honda MP4/4-6	11	1min 26.28sec 2/30	1min 26.43sec 2/30	2-27	2/17		1st
	A. Senna	McLaren-Honda MP4/4-2	12	1min 26.16sec 1/30	1min 25.97sec 1/30	Pole	1/17 WINNER		FL 1st
AUSTRALIAN Adelaide 13.11.88	A. Prost	McLaren-Honda MP4/4-6	11	1min 18.18sec 1/31	1min 17.88sec 2/31	2-26	1/11 WINNER		FL 1st
	A. Senna	McLaren-Honda MP4/4-2	12	1min 18.33sec 2/31	1min 17.57sec 1/31	Pole	2/11		2nd

can have it . . .' Senna did, and he got it.

That sums up why and how McLaren won hands down in 1988. Due to the regulation changes, certain teams were left fighting with one hand firmly tied behind their backs, and those that might still be expected to compete, Lotus and Ferrari, were not in the same league. McLaren had a car the equal of any, that was the most reliable; the best engine, shared with Lotus; the most awesomely efficient team; and

the best pairing, and best individual drivers. McLaren might not have been the best in every area, but they were, by a long way, the most powerful all-round unit.

The next season did not offer too much hope for the other teams either, as Honda were dealing with McLaren exclusively, having dropped Lotus – or more likely, Lotus having got themselves dropped – and reports of the new V10 were far from encouraging for the rival teams.

The only McLaren weak spot looked to be the rift with Prost. If this had not healed, and if relations between the two drivers deteriorated still further; who knows?

. . . INTERNAL STRIFE – A FAMILY AT WAR

Looking back on 1989, the results were, as far as McLaren were concerned, a logical extension of the year before. On the circuit, McLaren were still the team to beat, if not quite to the same extent as in 1988, while in other respects they took one hell of a battering. In 1976 it was the McLaren vs Ferrari rivalry that spilled over from the race tracks. In 1989 the controversy was just as bizarre, but the players were Alain Prost vs Ayrton Senna, and then McLaren. Whatever perspective is used to evaluate 1989 – the resurgence of Ferrari and Williams, the quality of entries, the standard of racing and so on – there is no way of avoiding the internal wranglings at McLaren, particularly those involving the drivers. It does not make for particularly happy reading.

Remember though, 1989 saw the return of the non-turbo age, using 3.5-litre, normally aspirated engines of no more than twelve cylinders. This heralded the first new formula since 1966, when our story began, as the banning of the 3-litre engines, from 1985, was no more than retrospective legislation; the obsolete non-turbo engines were no longer competitive anyway.

Unlike 1966, there were plenty of teams; as many as thirty-nine entries were received at some races, and pre-qualifying was reintroduced. As for engines, any thoughts that the competition, in numbers, of the turbo years was gone for good was soon dispelled when plans were unveiled. Engines to five different configurations were proposed, from ten manufacturers, featuring enough technical variations to make even the most hardened motor racing hack take notice.

Ferrari, as expected, took the route of sheer power, namely twelve cylinders in V formation, with no real concessions to planning the engine silhouette for aerodynamic benefits – that was not their style. Lamborghini entered the fray with an engine of classical V12 proportions, for Lola, while Motori-Moderni with Subaru backing, were building a flat-12 engine. Two other ambitious, twelve-cylinder engines were planned but, like the flat-12, did not appear, the 'Broad Arrow' 12, with three banks of four cylinders, from Life and MGN. This unusual shape offered the theoretical advantage of maximizing power, with twelve cylinders, and giving a more compact package than the V12. We would have to wait a full year before one of these was to show itself at a Grand Prix.

Honda and Renault produced engines to a new configuration for Grand Prix, the V10. In certain respects, these were 'compromise' engines, not quite matching the theoretical power output of a twelve-cylinder, though Honda undoubtedly had the most powerful engine in 1989, while being slightly more compact, but not as aerodynamically helpful as a V8. Anyone who thought that this latter engine would be out of its depth in such a multi-cylindered sea needed to consider Cosworth's position. With the backing of Ford, Cosworth could have chosen any route they fancied, yet they opted for eight cylinder, because this was what they knew best.

For 1989 there were two engines produced by Cosworth, the 'customer' DFR, as used by AGS, Arrows, Coloni, Dallara, Ligier, Minardi, Onyx, Osella, Rial and Tyrrell; and the new EXP development used exclusively by Benetton. Neither engine could quite match the power of Ferrari, Renault, or Honda, but time was on their side. John Judd had further developed his Honda-based V8, using a shorter stroke, and though Williams deserted to Renault, Lotus were snapped up in their place. March and Euro-Brun used this engine, while Brabham made a welcome return after their sabbatical, with Teddy Mayer as their new

Managing Director. Brabham were powered by the Judd. Finally, Yamaha decided to try their hand at Grand Prix racing, with a five-valve V8 engine, supplied exclusively to Zakspeed – the Japanese really becoming involved in the top echelon of motor racing.

There were few regulation changes, other than the banning of turbo engines, the moving of the foot-pedals behind the front-wheel axle line, and there being no limit, other than practical considerations, on the amount of fuel carried. The one change that affected a number of teams was that each team had to field two cars, so AGS, Coloni, Dallara, Osella and Rial had to find the money to fund a second car, while Onyx had to start off as a two-car team.

Quite what the reasoning behind this was is unclear; it was not as though, as in 1966, grids were a bit thin. In any case, it affected the smallest teams, those who were the least competitive, had little money, and were still learning the trade. Their drivers were mostly inexperienced at this level and, in view of the problems experienced in 1988 with backmarkers indiscipline, this only unleashed yet more 'rabbits' under the feet of the front runners. Yet safety was supposed to be a prime consideration in Grand Prix!

There is little point in listing all the Grand Prix drivers who raced in 1989, as not many featured in the McLaren story, but when it came down to true opposition, there were rather more than in the previous season. Lotus remained unchanged with Piquet and Nakajima, though the former champion disappointed once again, the Lotus 101 not really being a worthy successor to some forebears. Brabham, with the BT58, and Brundle making his Grand Prix comeback, were no longer the team they once were, but with Teddy Mayer behind them, there would be no slacking. At first they made progress, but it all dried up a little towards the end. March, divorced from the factory, failed to continue their progress of 1988 and slid back among the also-rans, while Ligier never left them, Arnoux acting like a moving chicane,

without mirrors, in the races for which he qualified.

Tyrrell, with the 018 car, had Alboreto return to the fold, to partner Palmer, and after the Italian fell out with Ken Tyrrell in mid-season, he was replaced by yet another Tyrrell protégé, Jean Alesi. Still, with the Cosworth DFR engine, the good years, not the tyres, were unlikely to return in a hurry. The same could be said about Arrows, with their A11 car, still driven by Warwick and Cheever. Lola, with Lamborghini power, driven by Dalmas and Alliot, might have been expected to produce a rabbit or two out of the hat, but failed on the whole, even when Alboreto found refuge in the team, at Dalmas's expense.

A couple of 'McLaren old boys' were still around, in the lower regions. Johansson, recovering from his year of torment at Ligier, came back with the new Onyx team. Though never for one moment expected to be a serious threat to McLaren, they showed real progress. From being the two slowest cars in pre-qualifying, at the opening Brazilian Grand Prix, to Johansson coming third in Portugal, their progress was impressive. Our old friend de Cesaris found a drive with Dallara, his seventh team in nine years, but as before, his season was marked more by what he did wrong, than what went right, and his team-mate, Caffi, was clearly the better driver.

What of the real competitors to McLaren? Williams, with the FW12C, and FW13 to follow, had lost Mansell and gained Boutsen to partner Patrese. As James Hunt said, 'Two number two drivers' – a bit harsh perhaps, but not too wide off the mark, good though they were. However, Boutsen won in Canada and Australia, in both cases after Senna had retired from the lead, while Patrese picked up four second places. They were never far behind McLaren, but neither were they often alongside, the Renault engine not quite being able to match the power of the Honda.

The same could be said of Benetton, who lost Boutsen and initially recruited the young

Ayrton Senna tests the new Honda 3.5-litre V10-powered MP4/5 in Brazil, before the season.
This was the new car/engine's first outing, and with only one car available, problems were
encountered. For a start, neither Prost nor Senna were happy with the handling on high-speed
corners, and Mansell won the race.

Johnny Herbert, a risky move since he still had not recovered from a nasty accident in F3000. Nannini was promoted to lead the team, and they made progress up the field, releasing Herbert, who was far from unsuccessful and came back briefly with Tyrrell, on the way. Nannini won in Japan, but only after the McLarens had eliminated each other. Still, the Cosworth engine was even less of a match for the Honda than had been the Renault. However, Benetton were 'up there', if not quite on a par with McLaren.

That left Ferrari, with Mansell newly arrived to partner Berger, a new car, the F189, and that new V12 engine. Only the engine did not

match the Honda either, being clearly deficient at the very top end. Yet they won three races; two went to Mansell, while Berger enjoyed the most ill-luck one could imagine with mechanical reliability. Ferrari were the only team to beat McLaren fair and square all season, and could never be overlooked. The Barnard-designed car looked the equal of the McLaren, yet the two spirited drivers were let down in the engine department, of all places, and by appalling reliability.

That, of course, leaves McLaren. Naturally, to accommodate the new Honda V10 engine, there was a new car, the MP4/5, developed from its immediate predecessor. It was designed

The McLaren MP4/5 with Honda V10 power, all ready for 1989.

by a team headed by Neil Oatley – not that Steve Nichols had been demoted, but it was another move from Ron Dennis to reduce reliance on any one individual. The major change was in the aerodynamic details, featuring a neat and tidy tapered rear, now that there was no need for all the plumbing and gadgetry of the turbo engine. There was also a return to the pre-1976 look, with an air intake above the drivers' rollover hoop, designed to force the air into the engine induction system, as fitted to many, but not all, cars.

Later at the British Grand Prix came the new transverse gearbox, and Brembo brakes, instead of McLaren's own, which permitted a re-design

of the rear suspension as well. The major benefit of the new gearbox was that it brought the weight of this unit within the rear-wheel axle line, moving the centre of gravity forwards, and giving scope to improve the handling of the car. Thus McLaren kept something in reserve, and remained one jump ahead of their rivals. During the season eight chassis were raced, two of which were badly damaged, and were subsequently used for exhibition purposes.

Honda's part in the equation amounted to providing the V10, RA109E, engine. Right from the start, this was the most powerful engine, initially developing 650bhp, and Honda kept it that way. They produced five different

Senna leads Prost, both in their MP4/5 cars, during their bitter season.

versions during the year, with either a little extra power, which eventually reached 685bhp at 13,000rpm, or the power characteristics mated to a given circuit. Whenever another engine, usually from Ferrari, seemed to be gaining, out came another improvement Honda had in reserve, to put them firmly back in the top slot. It must have been a thankless task trying to keep pace with the men from Japan.

As to reliability, Senna seemed to have drawn the short straw. He retired from the lead in the USA and Canada, when the engine management system failed – in the former race, this was possibly due to some interference from the on-car radio transmitter. Senna also suffered the

only race engine failure, again when in the lead, at the Italian Grand Prix, ironically a race characterized by bitter recriminations between Prost and Honda. Hardly a failure though.

McLaren's team work either at the circuits or back in Woking was, at the risk of sounding blasé, as before. This means comprehensive and scrupulously thorough in every detail. The partnership with Honda went through a few trials and tribulations, especially during the conflict with Alain Prost but, if anything, at least as far as can be ascertained, emerged stronger than before. Honda may or may not have given Senna better engines, but their commitment to the partnership never wavered one iota, and neither did that of McLaren. Little wonder McLaren-Honda ran out comfortable, if not peerless, winners.

Out of sixteen Grand Prix races, McLaren won ten, lost three, and gave three away. Senna's car twice let him down, when well set in the lead, and Prost picked up and carried the colours to victory, while both cars were sidelined in Canada. McLaren were comprehensively beaten on three occasions, twice by Mansell in Brazil and Hungary, and once by Berger in Portugal, but they claimed second place in each race. They only managed four 1–2 wins, but considering the opposition, that was still a major achievement. It was not always the racing that gained centre stage, however.

The problem, initially, was the relationship between Prost and Senna. After their disputes towards the end of 1988, the position remained stable throughout the winter, although Prost was slightly aggrieved by test sessions where he would spend painstaking hours setting up the car, only for Senna to come along and set the fastest time; that uncanny ability to complete the optimum lap, again. They were hardly bosom buddies, but neither were they at daggers drawn.

Senna did not do his reputation any good in the Brazilian Grand Prix, after netting the pole. His start was matched by Patrese, while Berger went even better and aimed between the leading pair as they got away. Senna, never the most gentlemanly of drivers, promptly closed the gap, and Berger, determined not to be intimidated,

Motor racing's number one driver, with the no. 2 car. 1989 was not the happiest of seasons for Alain Prost, but he came out on top for the third time.

Ayrton Senna is undoubtedly a very fast driver indeed but, as this picture shows, he is not always as neat as Alain Prost and Niki Lauda. He still wins though, and here he is on his way to victory in the 1989 Monaco Grand Prix.

went the other side. Senna, seeing Berger's ploy, tried to chop across the Ferrari's bows once again, but Berger was not going to be brow-beaten into submission and kept his foot on the throttle. Patrese, exercising his right as he was leading, moved across the corner and Senna was trapped, only this time the boot was on the other foot. It did not do Berger any good because, in the inevitable collision, he spun off and out of the race, while Senna lost his nose cone and was effectively out of the running once it was all sorted out; not the ideal start for a defending Champion. Mansell went on to beat Prost fairly and squarely, and an 'open' season's racing looked a possibility.

ANTAGONISM

The trouble began at the San Marino Grand Prix, which was stopped after Berger had an awful accident, and was trapped in his blazing car for 23 seconds. Why the car should have crashed, or indeed burst into flames, is a matter not publicly resolved, but the fact that he survived, with a couple of broken bones and relatively minor burns, says much for the protection given to the modern Grand Prix driver. This happened on lap 4, and the events at the restart were to act as a tinder-box to the relationship between the McLaren drivers.

Prior to the race, Senna had suggested to

281

Prost that, after the start in Brazil, whoever held the lead at the start, and Senna was on the pole with Prost alongside, should not be passed in the opening laps. Prost agreed to this, and Senna led the first start, while Prost did not challenge. Then came the restart. This time Prost led away, with Senna behind. Bearing in mind the 'agreement', Prost drove cleanly, but without trying to defend his lead; there was no need: Senna was second. Then, on the run down to the *Tosa* corner, Senna went through on the outside. He drew away but Prost, once he had gathered up his skirts, pushed him all the way, until he spun on lap 43, whereupon he settled for second place. The fun and games began afterwards.

Reminiscent of the scene between Villeneuve and Pironi at this very circuit, seven years before, Prost was distinctly cool at the trophy presentation, and furious with Senna. Thereafter, events became a little messy. Prost accused Senna of breaking the 'agreement' and of being dishonest. At first Senna denied proposing any such agreement, but Marlboro's John Hogan had been present when it was struck, and he said as much. Senna then compounded his error by petulantly saying that it was intended for the start of the race, not for a restart, and later still that it was only for the first corner. Whatever the exact details of the 'agreement', Senna had not acted in a sporting manner, and did not emerge in a very good light. True, he had won the race, but not in a completely clean manner.

That was not the end of the matter, oh no. Ron Dennis made Senna apologize to Prost, but he did so, shall we say, without feeling, and regretted this as he felt he had done no wrong. Prost, for his part, was sick and tired of Senna and was unwilling to trust him again, which only served to fuel matters further. Then at Monaco, Ron Dennis made what was undoubtedly a silly move. He tried to inform a highly sceptical press that there was no disagreement between the McLaren drivers, and that everything was hunky-dory. This was foolish in several respects. First and foremost, whatever Ron Dennis might have wished the position to be, it was a lie. Secondly, everybody knew it was a lie. Thirdly, Prost felt very angry about this, and although up until then Senna had been the main cause of Prost's unhappiness, with perhaps a little thought or two in Honda's direction, he saw this latest injury as threatening his relationship with Ron Dennis and the team, a relationship, moreover, which he regarded as sacrosanct. Prost had made this clear in an interview with *L'Équipe*, and in so doing had broken the bond of silence with Senna and Ron Dennis over the whole incident. This act did not help matters either.

Finally – yes there is more to this event – FISA had to stick their nose in. At Imola, Prost did not attend the post-race press conference, as is required, and instead took himself and his rage off, to avoid controversy. Obviously, something was wrong, as he was not his usual chatty self on the podium. He did behave with a certain equanimity, and avoided any newsworthy or controversial remarks that would undoubtedly have come forth in such a setting as, indeed, in most sports. However, FISA fined Prost $5,000 for keeping his mouth shut!

The following Mexican Grand Prix did not help matters either, as Senna claimed his thirty-third pole position, to equal Jim Clark's record, and in doing so qualified a second faster than Prost. When Senna was able to pull away from Prost along the straight, this raised doubts in the Frenchman's mind about the equality of Honda's engines, again, despite their announcement that any difference would amount to no more than 5bhp. He was not too happy with the team either, after they fitted the wrong tyres, slowly, at his first pitstop – a genuine error – while virtually repeating this at a second visit to the pits. With Prost qualifying for the United States Grand Prix, in Phoenix, 1.4 seconds slower than Senna, he viewed this, rightly or wrongly, as more evidence that Honda were not giving him an equal engine. On the other hand, Senna retired in this race and the following Canadian

By 1989 Prost may not quite have had the sheer speed of Senna, but like Niki Lauda before him he showed that there is more than one way of winning races, and ultimately the Championship. Unlike so many drivers, he runs around the kerbs, as depicted on his way to second place in the 1989 Monaco Grand Prix.

Grand Prix, when the engine management system broke down.

Ironically it was at the French Grand Prix, where Prost claimed his second consecutive pole position, led from start to finish, and where Senna retired for the third race on the trot – getting no further than the first corner of the restarted race when his differential failed – that Prost announced that he was leaving McLaren, purely because of Senna.

At this time, several options were being bandied about for Prost: the formation of a McLaren B team; the possibility of an Indycar team for a year (after all, former McLaren driver Emerson Fittipaldi had returned to American oval racing and had just won the Indianapolis 500); or a three-year contract, with a one-year sabbatical for 1990, to return in 1991, when Senna's contract had expired. These were serious proposals, put forward by a team who had not fallen out with their star driver.

The problem was that Prost wanted to continue in Grand Prix in 1990, so, with Ron Dennis's approval, he began talking to Williams. He also, to Ron Dennis's dismay, began talking to Ferrari, perceived to be much more of a threat by Ron, and this is when things began to get a bit nasty.

The 1989 Canadian Grand Prix was not one of McLaren's best. Neither driver finished in the points, though Senna ran among the leading cars for all the race, until his engine failed three laps from the end.

Gerhard Berger was signed to replace Alain Prost by the British Grand Prix, where Senna spun out of the lead on lap 12, but not before administering another of his 'chops' to get in front of his team-mate at the start. Prost studiously built an advantage over Mansell, until a puncture forced the charging Briton to settle for second place. At the German Grand Prix Prost and Senna, after poor pitstops for both of them, staged a battle and a half, with Prost holding off Senna until two laps from the end, when Prost lost sixth gear and had to settle for a distant second place. This battle should have stolen the headlines, but it did not.

Honda's Osamu Goto went to great lengths to tell the press that Prost now understood that his smooth driving style was not suited to the Honda engine, and that, like Senna, he had to change and keep the engine revving, particularly in the corners. He then went on to state that Prost did not know how to change gear, an absurd remark about the winner of thirty-eight Grands Prix, ten of which achieved with Honda engines! Prost's growing isolation within the team was hardened when Ron Dennis later agreed with Goto's claim. Clearly Ron Dennis was not happy with the prospect of their driver possibly moving on to Ferrari.

It was at the Italian Grand Prix that the relationship between Prost and McLaren-Honda was torn asunder. First of all it was announced that Prost would be joining Ferrari for 1990, and that went down like a lead balloon in the McLaren camp. Prost was also under pressure from former Honda drivers, Rosberg and Mansell, to speak out about the perceived inequality between the engines, as they thought they had both suffered in the past. Prost's engine management system had been set up to take into account his more delicate driving style, and in Canada this system had been fitted with a 'chip' used by Senna until then, and Prost suddenly became more competitive. In Italy, Prost was being left behind once more.

During practice Senna, as determined and forceful as ever, was nearly 2 seconds faster than Prost, and about 3mph (5kph) faster along the straight. This seemed to offer evidence that Senna did have a more powerful engine, but there were other considerations to take into account. Prost accepted that Senna was a faster qualifier than himself, though 'not by 1.8 seconds', yet Honda were quite prepared to admit that the difference in power between individual engines might be as high as 5bhp, or 0.74 per cent of 680bhp. Prost might well be around 1 second slower in qualifying, so his best practice time was 0.95 per cent slower than Senna's, and if Prost's speed along the straight was around 1.5 per cent slower than Senna's, in supposedly equal cars, then these figures are not that far adrift. I am not suggesting that a power advantage translates exactly into a time/speed superiority, but remember that Senna was usually the faster qualifier.

Honda then got involved in the war of words, by producing evidence from their telemetry databanks of on-car engine recordings, that showed that Senna was using more revs at given points in corners, which translate into a higher speed on the straights. This did not end the matters, as expected, as it was then suggested that Honda could use their telemetry systems to alter the power of the engines during a race. Honda denied that they could do this and, naturally and sensibly, said that they never would, on grounds of safety.

Just imagine, you are cornering right at the very limit, being hard pressed by a rival, when a technician suddenly decides, in mid-corner, that you could use an extra 10bhp. What would you think as the extra power pushes you over the limit, and you spin off towards the barriers? It was becoming something of a silly joke. In any case, boosted engine or not, it did not do Senna any good as his engine blew up when in the lead, with eight laps left, and Prost was the beneficiary, winning again.

It was not all over yet, because in a moment of emotion Prost dropped his trophy to the gathering of Ferrari fans below the podium. This was most unlike him – his mother looks after these prized possessions – and Ron Dennis did not approve either. He brusquely placed the Constructors' trophy at Alain's feet and left, the two having harsh words later. This act and Prost's criticism of his chassis set-up further isolated him in the team, since the latter fuss hit at his mechanics, as Prost always works at setting up his own car!

Prost was now considered a bit of 'traitor' by certain parties in McLaren, and Senna called for him to be sacked. Prost was also being criticized for his complaining, but he said, 'If I am a whinger, so be it. That is better than being taken for an idiot.' He felt that neither McLaren nor Honda were being fair, yet in Portugal a statement was released, signed by Alain Prost, Ron Dennis and Honda's Public Relations Manager, saying that the three parties would be doing their best for each other for the rest of the season, and effectively denied any engine 'favouritism'. Prost still complained about both parties, in private.

For his part, Senna had remained aloof from all this squabbling. One can view this two ways:

either that he aimed to win the World Championship and was not interested in all the innuendo and politics, or that he was more than happy to get the best engines and treatment, and kept 'mum' about it. Whatever the reason, his silence was welcome in the then current climate.

Prost's differences with Senna had been overshadowed by those with both McLaren and Honda, but they had not disappeared. Prost considered Senna to be dishonourable, and a lack of trust had undermined his position with the team, particularly after Ron Dennis's statement at Monaco, and his backing of Honda in Germany. Prost now felt that McLaren and Honda were being dishonest about engine equality, saying one thing in public, and doing the opposite in private. In Portugal, it was Senna's driving that caused a new upset, with more evidence of partiality within the team. Rightly or wrongly, there appeared to be no perceived back-handedness within McLaren before the arrival of either Senna or Honda.

TRICKS OF THE TRADE

Over the years, Senna had been involved in an inordinate number of incidents, for a driver of his ability. Prost put this down to Senna being too arrogant to give way, too forceful, and to his belief in God that made him think he was immortal. Not an objective analysis perhaps, but it did contain a grain of truth. Senna was not wholly at fault in all these mix-ups, perhaps not in the majority, but many were connected to the way he overtakes. While passing back markers, Senna could be ruthless beyond belief, but this was often understandable and usually paid dividends. He was not the most gentlemanly of drivers while tussling with direct rivals, and much of this emanated from the 'Senna chop', where he 'shut the door' on pursuing drivers, irrespective of their position on the track, leaving them to find their own way around the corner. Sometimes it worked, like in Portugal

against Prost in 1988, and sometimes it did not, as in Brazil with Berger in 1989. There was to be a repeat performance in Portugal, but with a slightly different script.

The Ferraris were the top dogs in that race and Berger was leading, while Senna was second, with Mansell closing fast. Unfortunately, Mansell had overshot his pit and, instead of driving round again, he reversed the few feet into place, an act punished by disqualification, which he ought to have known. Meanwhile, on lap 46 Mansell was in Senna's slipstream along the start/finish straight, under his wing, and going into the low sun, at 180mph (290kph) plus, when the black flag, bearing the number 27 was waved, meaning that car no. 27 (Mansell) had to go into the pits, as the official wanted to speak to him.

The next time round Mansell showed no sign of entering the pits, indeed there he was again, tucked beneath Senna's rear wing, at 190mph (305kph). Perhaps next time? No; the McLaren appeared again with the red Ferrari even closer in tow and alarm bells rang in the McLaren pit. Had Senna not seen the black flag, as he was racing Mansell? No doubt about it. More to the point, had anyone informed Senna that Mansell ought not to have been on the circuit? Over the radio, Ron Dennis told Senna to ignore Mansell, as the two cars passed the pits. Senna asked for the message to be repeated, as they hurtled towards the first corner, but before Ron Dennis had a chance, Mansell pulled to the right of Senna under braking. They were alongside when Senna produced his 'chop' again, and turned straight into Mansell, the two skating off the road into the sand, and out. Guess who was to benefit from this? Yes; Prost, who came through serenely into second place.

Two main arguments followed: one over who caused the accident, and the other about the fact that Mansell was still racing. The most unfortunate aspect of the silly war of words which followed this incident, was the rather aggressive, not to say stupid, reaction from McLaren. One could not help thinking that this would not have happened a couple of years before.

Mansell was fined $50,000, and banned from the following Spanish Grand Prix, and he got very annoyed and indignant over this, even threatening retirement. There is no doubt though, that Ferrari were responsible for allowing Mansell to continue, either knowingly or not. Initial McLaren reaction centred on the lack of response from the Ferrari management, while Mansell claimed that neither did he see the flag, nor was he made aware of it by radio. Prost, without giving anything away, confirmed that driving along the straight into the low sun made it difficult to see signs from the pits, and he was not under Senna's wing.

The real mess erupted before the Spanish Grand Prix, when Ron Dennis admitted that he had made a major error by not informing Senna of Mansell's predicament. He then challenged Mansell by saying, 'I don't buy the horse★★★★ that he didn't see the flag. He knew.' Not too eloquent, but the meaning was crystal clear. He was later to regret these comments. Surely though, if Mansell had seen the flag, so too should Senna, and allowed Mansell to pass. Senna joined in the fun by suggesting that Mansell's overtaking move had been 'suicidal'. That was the kettle calling the pot black! Senna had tried his 'chop' once too often and, like Berger, Mansell was not going to be intimidated.

Furthermore, a few weeks later Senna was to perpetrate an even more outrageous overtaking manoeuvre, that failed in similarly dramatic circumstances. Back in Spain, following an incident in practice, Senna passed eight black flags held aloft by marshalls, while on a flying lap, and did not slow down until he had finished, at the red flag. He was fined $20,000, and Ron Dennis's muted remarks were to the effect that he deserved it. Mansell certainly had something to ponder.

Senna won commandingly in Spain, but then came the Japanese Grand Prix. The 'wash' from the events at Honda's home race was to last for a considerable time and was particularly muddy.

The event got off on a controversial footing, as many teams were upset that McLaren had undertaken three days' testing at the circuit prior to the race, thus breaching an agreement undertaken by all teams. McLaren answered this by saying that the agreement did not cover their Japanese testing team, quite rightly, but then rather pettily added that it had rained during the tests, so they had not been of much use.

Before the race, Prost informed Senna (whether by note or messenger is unclear!) that he would not back off into corners, so there would be no Imola-like misunderstanding. Senna needed to win the last two races to retain the Championship, while Prost only need beat Senna once. As Senna sat on the pole, 1.7 seconds ahead of Prost, this might have looked a bit academic, but Prost was determined to win in style, took the lead, and drew away from Ayrton. Towards the end of the race Senna, driving raggedly – which suggested a touch of desperation – caught up with Prost, but there was no way past. Prost had the situation under control, while Senna probed his defences to no effect.

Time was running out; Prost was unlikely to make a mistake, and the chicane looked to be the only place to offer Senna any hope. On lap 47, with seven to go, Senna took a run up the inside where Prost had left room, for a late turn in, and got his front wheels into the gap under braking. It all looked too close for comfort. On this most important occasion, Prost was not going to be intimidated by this, and he executed a perfect 'Senna chop' on the executioner.

The two Marlboro-suicide-McLarens came to rest part on the circuit, part up the escape road. Prost was up and away, walking back to the pits, while Senna gestured the marshalls to disentangle the cars, and this necessitated Senna being briefly pushed backwards, before being push-started. Senna continued through the escape road, thereby missing the chicane, went into the pits to have a new nose cone fitted, resumed the race, and stole the lead off Nannini to take the chequered flag. He was disqualified shortly afterwards, and then the fun began.

Despite Prost having secured the World Championship, McLaren appealed against Senna's disqualification, thereby putting Prost's third title in doubt. They stated that it was their aim to win every race, and Senna had indeed won on the road. As can be imagined, Prost was somewhat less than thrilled with this. Senna had transgressed three rules: being pushed backwards on to the circuit, being given a push-start and missing the chicane. It was on the last two points that Senna was disqualified, and on which McLaren appealed.

Before looking at the startling events which followed the appeal, the Australian Grand Prix settled the Drivers' Championship when, in appalling conditions, Prost refused to take the restart, thereby ending his McLaren career, while Senna took the lead off Nannini on lap 5. By lap 14 he was out; he had run into the back of Brundle, not having seen the car amidst all the spray and water. Prost's decision not to race was justified, and Senna was not at fault over this accident, though he might have approached the wall of spray with a little more circumspection. Prost was thus confirmed the World Champion, while McLaren were long since Constructors' Champion, with nearly double the points of Williams, in second place. But the battle of words was already well under way.

By the time FISA, FIA, Ron Dennis, Balestre, the Japanese stewards, the press, Prost, Senna and anyone else who had any say in the matter had finished, the issue at stake – namely the disqualification of Senna in Japan – was no longer clear; neither was it of much interest, except to those directly involved, and the subsequent machinations had dragged Grand Prix racing through the very depths of self-deceit. The main players were either on the attack or defensive, baring all to the press or refusing to meet them, and twisting and turning, like Houdini, trying to seek an advantage. In any other sport under this spotlight, the governing bodies would have joined team and players in the dock for bringing the game into total and utter disrepute; but this is Grand Prix racing, where nothing is quite so simple.

Ron Dennis and Ayrton Senna, accompanied by lawyers, arrived at the FIA Court of Appeal in Paris, before the Australian Grand Prix, to argue Senna's case against his disqualification in Japan. They were rather stunned at the report FISA presented to the court, which raised five other allegations against Senna, to argue that he was a dangerous driver. These went back only as far as the Italian Grand Prix of 1988, and I am sure Mansell would have added a few more had he been given the chance. Furthermore, FISA

Grand Prix Results 1989

GRAND PRIX	DRIVER	CAR	NO	1ST PRACTICE Time/Posn	2ND PRACTICE Time/Posn	3RD PRACTICE Time/Posn	FINAL GRID POSN	FINAL PLACING	RETIRED CAUSE OF	HIGHEST POSN IN RACE
BRAZILIAN Rio de Janeiro 26.3.89	A. Senna	Honda-V10 MP4/5-2	1	1min 26.21sec 2/30	1min 25.30sec 1/30		Pole	11/14		11th
	A. Prost	Honda-V10 MP4/5-3	2	1min 27.10sec 3/30	1min 26.62sec 4/30		5-26	2/14		1st
SAN MARINO Imola 23.4.89	A. Senna	Honda-V10 MP4/5-1	1	1min 42.94sec 2/30	1min 26.01sec 1/30		Pole	1/19 WINNER		1st
	A. Prost	Honda-V10 MP4/5-3	2	1min 44.56sec 3/30	1min 26.23sec 2/30		2-26	2/19		FL 2nd
MONACO Monte Carlo 7.5.89	A. Senna	Honda-V10 MP4/5-1	1	1min 24.13sec 1/28	1min 22.31sec 1/29		Pole	1/15 WINNER		1st
	A. Prost	Honda-V10 MP4/5-3	2	1min 24.67sec 2/28	1min 23.47sec 2/29		2-26	2/15		FL 2nd

MEXICAN Mexico City 28.5.89	A. Senna	Honda-V10 MP4/5-1	1	1min 19.11sec 1/29	1min 17.88sec 1/29	Pole	1/15 WINNER	**1st**
	A. Prost	Honda-V10 MP4/5-3	2	1min 20.40sec 2/29	1min 18.72sec 2/29	2-26	5/15	**2nd**
USA Phoenix Arizona 4.6.89	A. Senna	Honda-V10 MP4/5-4	1	1min 30.11sec 1/30	1min 30.71sec 1/30	Pole	Lp 44 Engine	**FL 1st**
	A. Prost	Honda-V10 MP4/5-3	2	1min 31.62sec 2/30	1min 31.52sec 2/30	2-26	1/6 WINNER	**1st**
CANADIAN Montreal 18.6.89	A. Senna	Honda-V10 MP4/5-4	1	1min 21.05sec 2/29	1min 21.27sec 1/29	2-26	7/8	**1st**
	A. Prost	Honda-V10 MP4/5-3	2	1min 20.97sec 2/30	1min 22.27sec 2/29	Pole	Lp 2 Suspension	**1st**
FRENCH Ricard- Castellet 9.7.89	A. Senna	Honda-V10 MP4/5-4	1	1min 07.92sec 1/30	1min 07.23sec 2/30	2-26	Lp 1 Transmission	**1st**
	A. Prost	Honda-V10 MP4/5-5	2	1min 08.29sec 2/30	1min 07.20sec 1/30	Pole	1/13 WINNER	**1st**
BRITISH Silverstone 14.7.89	A. Senna	Honda-V10 MP4/5-6	1	1min 09.12sec 1/30	1min 09.10sec 1/30	Pole	Lp 11 Spun off, Gearbox	
	A. Prost	Honda-V10 MP4/5-5	2	1min 10.16sec 4/30	1min 09.27sec 2/30	2-26	1/12 WINNER	**1st**
GERMAN Hockenheim- ring 30.7.89	A. Senna	Honda-V10 MP4/5-3	1	1min 42.30sec 1/30	1min 42.79sec 1/30	Pole	1/11 WINNER	**FL 1st**
	A. Prost	Honda-V10 MP4/5-5	2	1min 43.31sec 2/30	1min 43.30sec 2/30	2-26	2/11	**1st**
HUNGARIAN Hungaroring 13.8.89	A. Senna	Honda-V10 MP4/5-3	1	1min 21.58sec 6/29	1min 20.24sec 1/30	2-26	2/13	**1st**
	A. Prost	Honda-V10 MP4/5-5	2	1min 21.08sec 3/29	1min 22.27sec 13/30	4-26	4/13	**3rd**
BELGIAN Spa-Fran- corchamps 27.8.89	A. Senna	Honda-V10 MP4/5-7	1	2min 11.17sec 2/30	1min 50.87sec 1/30	Pole	1/16 WINNER	**1st**
	A. Prost	Honda-V10 MP4/5-5	2	2min 12.72sec 5/30	1min 51.46sec 2/30	2-26	2/16	**FL 2nd**
ITALIAN Monza 10.9.89	A. Senna	Honda-V10 MP4/5-7	1	1min 25.02sec 3/30	1min 23.72sec 1/30	Pole	Lp 45 Engine	**1st**
	A. Prost	Honda-V10 MP4/5-5	2	1min 25.87sec 4/30	1min 25.51sec 4/30	4-26	1/10 WINNER	**FL 1st**
PORTUGUESE Estoril 24.9.89	A. Senna	Honda-V10 MP4/5-7	1	1min 15.50sec 1/29	1min 15.47sec 1/30	Pole 4-26	Lp 49 Accident	**1st**
	A. Prost	Honda-V10 MP4/5-5	2	1min 17.33sec 3/29	1min 16.20sec 4/30		2/14	**2nd**
SPANISH Jerez 1.10.89	A. Senna	Honda-V10 MP4/5-7	1	1min 21.86sec 1/27	1mion 20.29sec 1/27	Pole	1/10 WINNER	**FL 1st**
	A. Prost	Honda-V10 MP4/5-5	2	1min 23/11sec 4/27	1min 21.37sec 3/27	3-26	3/10	**3rd**
JAPANESE Suzuka 22.10.89	A. Senna	Honda-V10 MP4/5-7	1	1min 39.49sec 1/30	1min 38.04sec 1/30	Pole	Disaqualified	**1st**
	A. Prost	Honda-V10 MP4/5-8	2	1min 40.88sec 3/30	1min 39.77sec 2/30	2-26	Lp 46 Accident	**FL 1st**
AUSTRALIAN Adelaide 5.11.89	A. Senna	Honda-V10 MP4/5-7	1	1min 39.49sec 1/30	1min 38.04sec 1/30	Pole	Lp 14 Accident	**1st**
	A. Prost	Honda-V10 MP4/5-8	2	1min 40.88sec 3/30	1min 39.77sec 2/30	2-26	Driver withdrew	

289

blamed Senna alone for the Japanese incident and, in addition to breaching Regulation 56 by missing out the chicane as he restarted the race, cited eight further allegations of rule breaking. The FIA had allowed this bringing of fresh charges in court before; remember the banning of Tyrrell in 1984? It is this kind of maverick behaviour which gives the governing body such a lowly reputation.

The FISA lawyers must have combed through the rule book to seek out any possible rule that might just have been transgressed as Senna desperately, if a little naively, tried to race on. They ranged from the serious, for example causing the elimination of Alain Prost by carrying out a dangerous manoeuvre, to the laughable, including the fact that Senna had partially left the track in order to attempt the dangerous overtaking of Prost. Finally, the FISA report called for a heavy fine and a suspended withdrawal of Senna's licence for a year. And McLaren thought they were going along to appeal against a simple race disqualification!

McLaren based their appeal on the fact that Senna was being moved from a dangerous place on the circuit, right in the middle of the first corner of the chicane, when push-started. They also maintained that, as Senna faced immediate disqualification if he reversed to take the chicane, he had no option but to use the escape road, though not deriving any benefit by so doing. These were points worth arguing, although the impression was given that it was pure luck that Senna's engine fired up when pushed, while everyone could see that he got the marshalls to purposely push-start him. One just had to admire his never-say-die spirit, while noting that McLaren were not being completely honest. Still, when faced with such a kangaroo court, what does one expect?

Not much, if one goes by Ron Dennis's subsequent actions. Dennis threatened to pursue the matter in the civil courts unless the appeal was upheld, and he was right. The FIA court denied the appeal a few days later, fined Senna $100,000, and imposed a six-month suspended

ban. Which brings us back to Senna's driving. He was undoubtedly the fastest driver in 1989, and might well have been the best all-round driver as well, given that Prost performed with an understandable lack of enthusiasm on occasions, although Mansell positively shone in his development. Yet the evidence of all those incidents cannot be waved away. Right from his Formula 3 battles with Brundle, through his early Grand Prix days, he had been involved in skirmishes with other cars. Many of these, especially the more recent incidents, were a result of his slingshot entry into corners, late and wide, which, if you happened to be on the inside, translated into the 'Senna chop'.

As Prost has said, 'Ayrton is a fantastic driver, yet he will not accept that he has been overtaken, or that he cannot overtake another car . . . because he believes in God he thinks he cannot be killed or injured . . .' Prost had been saying these things for a long time and, given that Senna is too good to be guilty of silly mistakes, such as not using his mirrors, there may be, whatever Senna might say, more than just a grain of truth in this.

There was little joy for McLaren in winning the Constructors' title again, or for Prost in winning the Drivers' Championship, save that he stopped Senna from so doing. Prost claims that 'This has been my least satisfying season in Grand Prix', though one wonders, as he looks back, if he will not regard 1989 as a major achievement, considering all the political and emotional hurdles (some of which were self-inflicted) that he overcame. As for Senna, there was to be no respite for him. While the arguments continued to rage, he was deciding whether or not to retire. All this fuss just makes one wish that all the main protagonists would get into a boxing ring and settle their differences with honour, rather than drag Grand Prix racing through the mire.

Motor racing's latest 'winter of discontent' was not solely limited to Grand Prix, and featured the FISA President, Jean-Marie Balestre. It was debatable as to which of the two battles did the most harm to motor sport: Balestre vs the Auto Club de L'Ouest, over the Le Mans 24-hours, or Balestre vs Senna. Whatever his behind-the-scenes tactics, Senna had behaved with public dignity, concerning events at McLaren. Prost, perhaps justifiably, had 'gone public' on an increasing number of occasions, regarding what he considered to be unfair treatment or dishonourable behaviour, and had been labelled a 'whinger'.

Balestre had no such compunction, and when Senna finally made his feelings known, regarding the fine and suspended ban, Balestre went on the rampage. He demanded a written apology from Senna, or a Grand Prix super-licence would not be issued for 1990! The President ought to have examined his own behaviour over the years, before seeking to effect retribution for relatively minor utterances. One wondered whether McLaren or Senna might not initiate a court action against FISA, citing the limitation of freedom of speech. Still, one cannot lay the whole blame on Balestre. What of those mealy-mouthed delegates at the FIA General Assembly who gave their unanimous support to his handling of the Ayrton Senna and Le Mans cases, and the FISA Plenary which gave him a 90 per cent majority? These 'grey men' deserve to be similarly pilloried.

MORE CHAMPIONSHIPS, MORE CONTROVERSY

The controversy raised by Senna was not the only personnel problem facing McLaren before the 1990 season. Having signed Gerhard Berger, from Ferrari, to replace Alain Prost, a dispute now arose with the Italian team as to whether Prost should be allowed to drive the red cars while still contracted to McLaren. This bore the mark of 'tit for tat', and was further complicated when Steve Nichols joined Ferrari. Nichols had been asking to be appointed as Chief Designer for quite a while, and said that he would leave if not. Eventually an offer came,

with a reputed tenfold increase on his McLaren wage, that he could not resist. Ron Dennis was less than happy with this latest defection, and said as much. This kept the Grand Prix pot simmering away nicely, and added to McLaren's growing list of controversies.

None of this seemed to affect either the way the McLaren personnel work, or their effectiveness. As in previous seasons, and unlike several teams, a new car, the MP4/5B, was ready for the first race of 1990. As the designation suggests, the car was not totally brand new, but was developed from the 1989 car and, of course, used the Honda V10 engine, designated the RA100E. The package may have looked the same but each part of the car, from the aerodynamic shape to the mechanical components, was analysed to effect an improvement, or to ensure that it was still able to work as before, bearing in mind other changes.

As for the engine, six versions were introduced in the space of two years, and by the end of 1990 it was producing 690bhp and could use up to 13,800rpm. This was ahead of all rivals. The latter read: Ferrari V12 685bhp, Renault V10 660bhp, Ford-Cosworth HB V8 650bhp, Lamborghini V12 640bhp, Judd EV V8 640bhp, Ford-Cosworth DFR V8 620bhp, Judd CV V8 610bhp, and Subaru flat-12 600bhp. An 'inverted broad arrow' twelve-cylinder engine finally made its bow with the Life team, but was relatively hopeless and did not qualify for a race. Honda's continuous development also cut the weight of the engine by about 4.5lb (2kg), reduced internal friction, modified the valves (changed from butterfly to slide-operated throttles) and also changed to unleaded fuel. There were numerous minor improvements, all of which added to an increase in power, better fuel economy and improved throttle response − which, ironically, would have suited Alain Prost. The overall car engine package was thus going to be as formidable as ever.

McLaren's innate professionalism ensured that the work on the cars was unrivalled, but

Gerhard Berger

Over the years Grand Prix racing, as with most sports, has seen many drivers who have never achieved the results their talent, or effort, deserved. Gerhard Berger falls into the category of those who have won a few races, but really ought to have won more. In 1990, after winning five Grand Prix in four years, Berger – one of the acknowledged top-four drivers – joined McLaren, the best Grand Prix team, and yet failed to win a race all season. This in itself was one of the most surprising statistics of that year.

All Berger's rivals know that he always gives 100 per cent, and that he is very fast indeed. Like Mansell, he may be amiable off the track, but once on it drives like a tiger. Alongside Senna, Berger appeared to be overawed, but he led the Brazilian at times and out-qualified him on a number of occasions. There was also the problem of reliability. If a McLaren were to break down, it seemed to be Berger who drew the shortest straw, as before at Ferrari.

However, his biggest problem at McLaren was that he did not fit the car. In the first few races of the season, some of which he led, Berger was really cramped. This improved as the season progressed, but his height was a perennial problem for the team. Even in the first races of 1991 Berger was not happy with the fit of his car, a problem suffered by other large drivers, such as Mansell. This hampers Berger's ability to give his all, especially if, even subconsciously, he has to think where the pedals are, or worse, is suffering from cramp, as has been the case. One wonders why after such a length of time, McLaren are still building cars that hamper the performance of a driver. Since other drivers are also suffering, there is a case for FISA to become involved.

Berger came to Grand Prix after racing in saloon cars, FF2000, and Formula 3. He made his debut at his home Austrian Grand Prix in 1984, in an ATS, thanks to his BMW connections. Thereafter, his rise was rapid, reflecting his speed and ability. He went to Arrows in 1985, after recovering from a broken neck, and then landed a Benetton drive the following year. There, he rose from being a promising driver, to a consistent front runner, giving the team its first ever victory, in Mexico.

Ferrari soon spotted his talent, and off he went to Maranello for three years, just as John Barnard joined. The year 1987 saw him claim two more victories, while he was the only effective opposition to Senna/Prost the next season. In that year, Berger knocked Alboreto off the number one spot, and out of the Ferrari team.

Mansell replaced Alboreto, but it was another difficult season, with Berger's car letting him down time and again, and he did not secure a single points finish until the Italian Grand Prix, the twelfth round in the Championship!

At the San Marino Grand Prix, Berger survived a terrible accident (the cause of which has never been made public) when he was trapped in his burning car for nearly half a minute. It is a tribute to the efficiency of the Italian marshalls, the safety features of the modern Grand Prix car and the flame resistance of his overalls, that Berger only missed one further race.

However, Mansell's never-say-die efforts made him a great favourite at Maranello, and when Prost was recruited it was Berger whom he replaced to, hopefully, move on to better things at McLaren.

Despite what the press have said, McLaren are far from disappointed with Gerhard Berger, a fact attributable both to his considerable efforts, and not in the least to the points he gained, which helped them win the Constructors' Championship. While Berger cannot match the sheer speed of Senna (and who, at present, can?), he could, and should, be winning races. However, one fears that until he feels perfectly at ease in his car, McLaren will not see him at his best. That Berger continues to do so well, despite his size problem, says more for his determination and ability than an occasional victory.

there was speculation on the driving front. Even when Prost was less than fully committed to the team, or motivated, he was a formidable driver, and now he had gone. In his stead arrived Gerhard Berger, a hard-charging and fast driver from Ferrari, but who had endured a poor season of reliability in 1989, and had been over-shadowed by the arrival of Mansell at Maranello. Berger, one of the top four drivers, was a good 'team man', and could be expected to work better with Senna than had Prost. It was not exactly a fair swap, and with Prost, highly motivated, and perhaps harbouring a sense of revenge, ranged against them with

Mansell alongside him, Ferrari posed a real threat.

That all depended on Ferrari, now with Fiat wielding a bit more authority. The 1980s had not been their decade; they had not produced a champion driver since 1979, though having won the Constructors' Championship twice. They were seldom completely off the pace and had potential aplenty, if only that could be utilized. The last man to comprehensively turn Ferrari around had been Niki Lauda, and if there was one contemporary driver who could pick Ferrari up by the bootstraps and lick them into shape, it was Prost. And that is exactly what he set about doing.

Before long, Mansell began to find his nose being pushed out as Prost worked with Nichols at honing the Barnard-designed car (with its seven-speed, electro-magnetically operated gearbox and new version of the V12 engine) into a race-winning combination. It did not look too reliable at first, but finally gave McLaren the closest run for their money in years.

Williams looked to be strong and settled for 1990, retaining Patrick Boutsen and Riccardo Patrese, while the FW13 car made its debut towards the end of 1989 and was already a winner. Renault had been continuously revising their engine, and the overall package, including team preparation, looked highly promising, though the drivers would not be expected to match the McLaren or Ferrari line-ups. The Leyton House position was similar – retaining Capelli and Gugelmin to drive a new CG90 – but the Judd engine was down on power. Their drivers never gave up though, and if a McLaren retired, either of these might well be there to take over.

Benetton were perhaps the 'joker' in the 1990 pack. Having exclusive use of the Ford-Cosworth EXP engine just about put them on a par with Williams, and while they were to start the season with the old car, a new one, the B190, was due at Imola. Furthermore, they had made two important additions to the team dur-

ing the winter. John Barnard, the original McLaren International designer, moved from Ferrari, and though his success there had been limited, his record with McLaren showed the potential for the future.

The second recruit was regarded in a less optimistic fashion by the press. Three times World Champion Nelson Piquet, after two markedly uncompetitive years at Lotus, came to partner Nannini. When at Lotus, Piquet made no bones about not being interested in pulling out all the stops to get from twentieth position to fifteenth place, but when the car was, occasionally, running well he still showed that he had lost none of his competitiveness, and little of his speed. If he was to be a success, it was up to Benetton to give him the right car.

Of the other teams, none of which were expected to offer a serious challenge, Lotus were optimistic. It was all change at Hethel, with a new management, a new car, the 102, powered by the Lamborghini V12 engine, and new drivers in Derek Warwick and highly promising Ulsterman Martin Donnelly. Perhaps, just perhaps, they might produce something of their old form and turn a few heads. Brabham, whose ownership was a source of much speculation, were hardly expected to spring too many surprises, but their old adversaries, Tyrrell, were not knocked out, even after all these years on the ropes.

'Uncle' Ken Tyrrell had thrust his hand into his hat and produced not one, but three rabbits. He was still saddled with the Cosworth DFR 'customer' engine but, with an eye to the future, had signed Nakajima, and the Honda V10 engine was to follow in 1991. His other 'rabbits' were for more immediate use, and he retained his talented find of 1989, Jean Alesi, perhaps the best young driver in the field, providing him with the 019, a car whose only defect compared to the MP4/5B was in the engine compartment, and which, in Alesi's hands, really sang.

293

SURPRISES

The rest of the field was made up much as before, except that Zakspeed had closed their doors while the Life team, with their unique engine, entered the fray, of sorts. Thus the scene was set for the opening round of 1990, the United States Grand Prix, on the streets of Phoenix, and there were a few shocks. For a start, Berger began his Mclaren career in the best possible way by claiming the pole position, while Martini in a Minardi, de Cesaris in a Dallara, and Alesi, were ahead of Senna. The Ferrari challenge did not amount to much either, as Prost was seventh and Mansell a distant nineteenth on the grid.

The surprises did not end there either. Before the race, Berger said that if pressed by Senna he would let him through, but it was Alesi who got the jump on him at the start, while Senna settled into third position. Nine laps later Senna pressured Berger into a spin, by which time young Alesi had a nice breathing space, while Berger lost a couple of laps (being moved by marshalls) and two more in the pits, effecting repairs.

Out at the front, Alesi was having a jolly old time, lapping slower cars as though he was an old hand at such things. Senna was closing though, but anyone who thought that Alesi was going to keel over and die just because he had the menacing-looking McLaren in his mirrors

Gerhard Berger practises in his MP4/5B at Phoenix, prior to setting the pole time on his McLaren debut.

needed to think again. Senna, as is his wont, tried a few jabs down either side, which were neatly parried. Then on lap 34, at the first corner, Senna came down the inside, and got his nose in front on the exit. 'Well, that's this race over', it was thought, but Alesi stood his ground and took the inside line at the next corner to regain the lead. He was the first man to 'out-Senna' Ayrton for a long time, and it worked.

There was no way Senna was going to give up, especially when going so well, and he executed the same manoeuvre on lap 35, and got completely in front of the Tyrrell. Senna thus held the inside line for the second corner, but Alesi was not finished yet. On the run down to the next corner, Alesi was wheel to wheel with Senna, who just managed to hang on to his lead. Thereafter, Senna drove a mature race to win unopposed, despite clutch problems near the end – the same as which sidelined Berger. Young Alesi stole the headlines with his excellent second place and his hard-fought, but very fair, battle with Senna.

After the surprises of Phoenix, Senna took his customary pole position in Brazil, with Berger alongside and the two Williams and two Ferraris, back on the pace again, behind. Senna took an immediate lead, followed by Berger. The latter, however, felt uncomfortable: it was a tight squeeze to fit the tall Austrian in his car, and he was later passed by Boutsen, and then Prost. Senna briefly lost his lead to Prost after a tyre stop, on lap 34, but regained this with a series of rapid laps, which left him 12 seconds ahead by lap 40.

Senna came up to lap Nakajima, followed him through three corners, and thinking he had left a gap for him, dived to the inside. As he did so, Nakajima cut across and ran over Senna's nose cone with his rear wheel. Just as Senna had his home race in his pocket, so he was heading for the pits. A new front was quickly fitted and Senna set off, but he could do no better than third place, while Prost recorded his fortieth Grand Prix win, and first for Ferrari, who were well and truly back. Berger struggled on

gamely, plagued by understeer, a dodgy clutch, and the effects of being cramped up for so long, to finish an admirable second. For any other team, these would have been two good results, but not for McLaren!

This raised questions about Senna's driving once again. Though Nakajima admitted responsibility for the incident, one wonders why Senna, sitting on a good lead, did not wait until the next straight, when he could have used the power of his engine to the full. True, it may not be his style to sit and wait for an opening, but one could not have imagined Prost, Lauda, Stewart, or Clark coming to grief in such a manner. If Senna wishes to be considered a 'great' then these are the standards which he has to meet.

That Senna did not win in San Marino was not his fault as, after forging into an early lead, a rear wheel broke up on lap 4, and he ran off the road into a sand trap, and out. Boutsen inherited the lead, but he retired, and Berger took over. It was during his battle for the lead with Mansell, that the question of driving standards arose once again. Mansell caught Berger and began to look for a way past when, leaving the Tamburello corner at around 180mph (290kph), he aimed at the outside for the following straight. Berger, not expecting Mansell to have made a move at that point, kept to the racing line, which forced Mansell on to the grass, and he pirouetted wildly before regaining the circuit, not in a happy frame of mind. Three laps later he was out, but Berger was again struggling, and ten laps from the end Patrese took over the lead, to record his first win in seven years, leaving Berger with another second place.

Thus far McLaren were not having things all their own way, though Senna, when running, was still the man to beat. He proved this again in Monaco, with an unchallenged flag-to-flag win, the hallmark of a true master. The race needed two starts to get under way, and Berger and Prost had to race in their spare cars, after a three-way incident with Alesi. As the McLaren

HONDA RA 168E Power characteristics

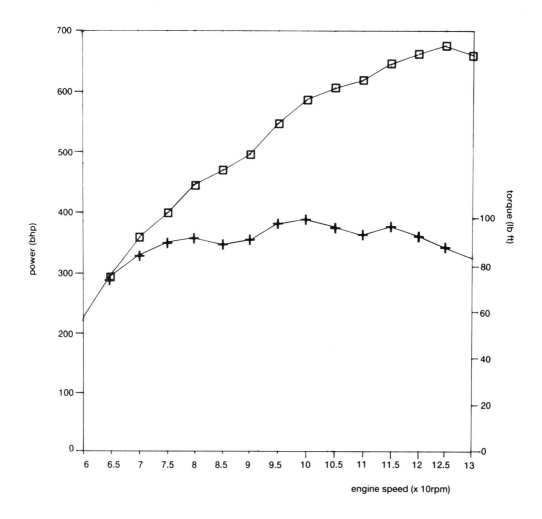

spare was set up for Senna, Berger was condemned to another uncomfortable race. When Prost retired near half-distance, Berger ran third behind the fast-learning Alesi. However, Berger was unable to mount a challenge, as he lost first gear – normally not too important, except at Monaco. Third place, just behind Alesi, was scant reward for his efforts, but added to McLaren's points tally.

With Berger leading Senna home by 45 seconds in Canada, McLaren seemed to have resumed normal service at last, except that Berger had jumped the start, and had been penalized one minute. As a result, he finished fourth, while Senna won from Piquet with another cultured drive, in both the wet, and latterly dry conditions. Unless you worked for McLaren it did not look good.

The Mexican Grand Prix was Senna's one hundredth, but he did not celebrate with a pole position, both Berger and Patrese qualifying ahead of him. By way of a contrast, Prost qualified thirteenth, his lowest place in ten years, but it was the ex-McLaren driver who came up trumps at the finish.

Prior to the race Ron Dennis decided to inflate Senna's tyres a little less than Berger's, and as Berger came into the pits on lap 13, this seemed to be vindicated. Senna led with impunity and one could not see him losing, but by two-thirds' distance Mansell and Prost were gaining; Senna had a slow puncture. Ron Dennis decided that it was better for Senna to soldier on, rather than risk sacrificing everything with a pitstop, and initially all looked well, as Mansell was held up by a backmarker. Then, on lap 55, with Mansell about to lap another slower car, Prost squeezed by to relieve him of second place. He was not going to hang around; Senna was in trouble and he was going to make the most of the opportunity. Five laps later, Prost took the lead under braking for the first corner, and a lap later Mansell did likewise. Shortly afterwards, Mansell got himself into a bit of a pickle, and Senna re-took second place. A minute later, he was out; the right rear tyre fell apart five laps from the end.

So far, so good, but the race then took on an entirely different perspective. As Mansell recovered from his spin, Berger came barging past, the two banging wheels like fairground dodgem cars. This was the signal for Mansell to launch a furious assault on Berger. Mansell was dodging this way and that, trying to get past Berger, who held firm. With a lap to go, I was reminded of the 1979 French Grand Prix. Mansell kept over to the left out of the esses, and at the following corner ran round the outside of Berger, in one unforgetable manoeuvre of immense bravery and daring, to pinch second place out of his pocket.

In its own way, the French Grand Prix was also an interesting affair, with Mansell on the pole, ahead of Berger and Ayrton. By lap 2 Berger was leading, with Senna second, while a string of cars followed in line astern, with Prost ominously making his way up into third place. Around one-quarter distance, the tyre stops were under way and both McLarens were

somewhat less than perfect; Senna resumed fifth, with Berger sixth. Capelli and Gugelmin, in the Leyton House cars, led from Prost, not having stopped to change their tyres. Eventually Prost passed Gugelmin, who later retired, and pursued Capelli relentlessly, if not quite so vigorously as Mansell had Berger – then again, one would not expect that from Prost. Rather than the thrilling, no-holds-barred slugging match in Mexico for second place, Prost exercised his tactical expertise and, like a Grand Master in chess, slipped by to win, without any drama. It might not be as exciting to watch, but as Prost has shown, and Lauda before him, the carefully planned, 'thinking' technique certainly pays dividends. Senna recovered to finish just 3 seconds behind Capelli, with Berger a distant fifth.

The British Grand Prix saw Mansell to the fore again, taking the pole ahead of Senna, and then hounding him mercilessly until he took the lead on lap 12. Two laps later, Senna spun and rejoined fifth. Before long, Mansell was leading Prost, from Berger, who was not happy with his car's handling, and was further demoted before retiring with throttle control failure, just before the finish. The Ferrari's were in another league, but Mansell had gearbox problems. Prost took over the lead and won, while Mansell retired, having lost all drive to the wheels. Mansell later announced his retirement from Grand Prix racing. Senna was grateful to accept third place, though relinquishing the Championship lead to Prost, and harboured dark thoughts about the handling of the MP4/5B cars.

This was, for McLaren, a crucial stage of the season, and it was decided to alter the car. Though the MP4/5B was a more efficient car than its predecessor, it was more temperamental, in certain conditions the downforce was inadequate, and it gave the drivers a nervous ride, making it difficult to totally commit themselves to each corner. This was most obvious at Silverstone, so McLaren took the sensitivity out of the car, making it less efficient but more predictable, and suddenly the results fell into place.

In Germany Senna and Berger lined up on the front row, 1½ seconds ahead of Prost. Honda produced more powerful, higher revving engines, and as they led away in team formation, they looked invincible. After the tyre stops Senna resumed second, to Nannini who was running non-stop, and finally got past a few laps from the finish, to win and resume his lead of the Drivers' Championship. Berger could not pass Nannini, stating that his engine 'was not of the best'. It was good enough to deprive Prost of third place though, and thus assist his team leader.

All was not well in Hungary, as Boutsen claimed the pole, with Berger and Senna on the second row of the grid. Boutsen led from the start, and Berger soon took second place off Patrese. On lap 22 Senna went into the pits for a new set of tyres because, like in San Marino, a stone had worn away part of a wheel, and he resumed tenth. Boutsen was shadowed by Berger, Patrese and Mansell, but on lap 48 Berger stopped to change tyres, and was soon passed by Senna, who was now well into his stride. Senna soon caught the leading group of Boutsen, Nannini and Mansell, and on lap 64 it all suddenly happened.

Senna ran inside Nannini at the chicane, with two wheels over the kerb on to the grass, and the resulting impact flicked the Benetton out of the way and into retirement, nearly overturning the car. Senna was able to continue unabated, and challenged Boutsen for the lead. Nannini was not very happy with the manoeuvre, having taken the only line thorugh the chicane, while Senna barged him out of the way, only half on the circuit. He commented that, 'If Senna can do such a move, so can everyone else' which rather echoed Prost's earlier remarks about Senna's driving. Considering Senna's avowed aim to win the Championship, to say nothing of his suspended ban, it was not a very intelligent move, as it could easily have resulted in his elimination and the loss of a safe 4 points, while Prost was out of it; but Senna wanted to win.

Meanwhile, Mansell and Berger resumed where they left off in Mexico, and went at it hammer and tongs. After Berger nearly succeeded in passing Mansell, their combined momentum brought them up to the leaders, and the four-way battle looked anything but settled. It did not last long. On lap 72 Berger repeated Senna's manoeuvre, on Mansell, only both cars were eliminated. The Hungaroring is not a good circuit for overtaking, but this was taking things a bit too far. Berger, who took the inside line at the chicane said, 'Mansell just moved over on me', but Mansell, as forthright as ever in these situations, said, 'There is only one line at the corner, and I had it!' Hmm . . .

That left Senna, on new tyres, free to concentrate on Boutsen, on worn tyres. Senna pressed relentlessly all the way, but Boutsen displayed admirable calm and tactics by blocking each move. On the penultimate lap they came up to lap Tarquini for the third time, and he blocked them all the way round. For once it was Senna who came off second best in this situation, and Boutsen survived the last lap to secure a well fought victory, fully appreciated by Senna.

TOP DOG

One of the most contentious arguments among racing enthusiasts these days is that concerning who is the best driver. Without meaning any disrespect to all others involved in Grand Prix racing, this really boils down to two: Ayrton Senna, and Alain Prost. It is probably true to say that Senna is the faster, while Prost is the better all-rounder, but the performance that Senna put together to win the Belgian Grand Prix is no longer in the repertoire of Prost.

On the most rewarding of current Grand Prix circuits, at Spa, Senna took the pole and then led from flag to flag, after the race needed three attempts at starting. He even retained his lead while in the pits for tyres, despite Nannini passing by on the circuit! Such was Senna's mastery that he beat Prost by 3½ seconds, after the Ferrari pitstop took 4 seconds longer than Senna's, yet the reigning World Champion never really had a serious look in. The two brilliant drivers consistently lapped at speeds the others could not even match for one lap. It is no shame on Berger to record that he came third, and was really top of a lower division, not in the same class as those two at all.

Unlike in 1989, Senna's off-track reputation had improved markedly. He had praised Alesi, in both Phoenix and Monaco; failed to criticize Nakajima in Brazil despite his disappointment; accepted responsibility for not going into the pits in Mexico to change the tyre; not whined about the lack of stability of the chassis; and was not drawn into a row with Nannini, in Hungary. After defeating Prost in Italy – the two once again being in a league of their own, with Berger only just over a second adrift at the finish – the estranged former McLaren team-mates publicly 'made up', on the winners' podium. It was all quite a contrast to the events of the year before.

Portugal saw Mansell back on the pole, but Prost, Senna, and Berger got past at the start. Gradually he worked his way up the ladder, and by lap 49 was pushing Senna for the lead. Starting lap 50, Mansell cut inside at the first corner, the one at which they had collided the year before, but there was no undue drama this time, and Mansell went through to take the lead, and win by 2 seconds. Prost was only a further 2 seconds adrift, while Berger was just 1 second behind him. Grand Prix looked to have become a four-horse, two-team race.

Senna claimed his fiftieth pole position in Spain, and then led for the first twenty-six laps, before going into the pits for new tyres. However, Prost, as tactically alert as ever, had changed his tyres a few laps earlier and was already closing on Senna. Piquet briefly inherited the lead, and as Senna was leaving the pits, he arrived with Mansell and Prost on his tail; the four leading cars in a bunch. Mansell let Prost through, while Piquet got carried away by all

the fuss and missed a gear. Before he had recovered, Prost and Senna were through, but Prost began to pull away, so Senna settled for second place. But it was not to be. Senna had felt his car begin to slide around and, thinking the rear tyres were going off, he shot into the pits for a new set. Unbeknown to him and, surprisingly, to the Honda engineers with their telemetry engine diagnosis system, he had run over an AGS undertray support rod which had pierced a water radiator. The water leaked on to the circuit just in front of his rear tyre, hence the sliding; and a lap later, he was out.

To complete a miserable race for McLaren, Berger, challenging Boutsen for fourth place, decided to make his move at the hairpin and got it all wrong. The two cars touched wheels, and Berger vaulted over Boutsen to land in the sand, ending his race. Prost and Mansell completed a Ferrari 1–2, and in so doing Prost closed the gap to 9 points behind Ayrton, with two races left.

The Japanese Grand Prix is, of course, Honda's home race, and naturally McLaren wanted to put on a good show. Apart from which, if Senna beat Prost he would become the Champion. He certainly went the right way about it, claiming the pole ahead of Prost, but therein lay a problem. The pole position was on the right of the circuit, not ideal for the run into the first, right-hand corner. McLaren had made representations to the organizers to change this, the day before the race, but to no avail, and this was to have serious consequences.

The big title decider lasted just 9 seconds before, as in 1989, the two contenders crashed. As McLaren feared, Prost, on the racing line, soon overcame Ayrton's 7 metre advantage and pulled ahead. Moreover, he was ideally placed with the best line for the cricual first corner. Prost was clearly ahead and turned into the corner, but Senna kept coming down the inside, and hit the Ferrari's rear wing, causing it to break off. The two cars slithered across the track, on to the gravel, and out. It was not all over yet, though. Berger had assumed the lead, and as he began lap 2, he went into the first corner too fast and went off on the dust from the first incident. What a day for McLaren!

Now it was Mansell's turn to lead, and perhaps salvage something for Ferrari. He came into the pits on lap 27 for new tyres, still in the lead, got over-excited about restarting, and broke a driveshaft as he set off down the pit lane. That left Piquet in the lead, and he was sensible enough not to look a gift horse in the mouth. Steadily, yet displaying all his skill, he brought the Benetton home to record his first win in three long years. Not only that, he guided his new team-mate Roberto Moreno, who replaced Nannini, injured in a helicopter crash, to second place. Piquet might have been lucky to inherit the lead, but he had to be ahead of the rest, and he did not do anything silly once there. It was a thoroughly well deserved win, but was completely overshadowed by the latest rift between Senna and Prost.

IN THE LIMELIGHT

The outfall from this put Grand Prix racing well and truly in the news. The incident will be examined later, but the two weeks before the Australian Grand Prix saw the episode highlighted, rather than fading away. Of course, the crash settled the question of the Drivers' Championship, in favour of Senna, and also, as neither Ferrari or McLaren finished, the Constructors' Championship, which McLaren won for the third consecutive year. McLaren had thus set another new Grand Prix record, as the first team to win the Constructors' Championship, and simultaneously provided the Champion Driver, for three consecutive seasons. This settlement of the two titles upset quite a number of people, as the Australian Grand Prix was to be the 500th race for the Drivers' Championship. There was never any doubt that it could stand on its own feet, without the artificial props of championships and anniversaries to support it.

Senna celebrated his title in the usual manner, by claiming pole position and, with Berger

alongside and both Ferrari's on the second row, with Alesi up there as well, as he had been all season, there was little chance of a dull race. Senna led away, as expected, and Berger slotted in behind. A lap later Mansell passed Berger, but could not catch Senna and later spun, retaining second place. He had to change his tyres, however, resuming fifth. Piquet and Prost later passed Berger, but Senna strode on until, on lap 62, when approaching a slow left-hand corner, he failed to select second gear and ran gently into the barriers; his race, and season, run.

Piquet now enjoyed the luxury of a fairly comfortable lead, and did not intend throwing it away. Behind him Prost appeared less than interested in making a serious challenge, but there was another red car going round like a bat out of hell. It was Mansell, in his last drive for Ferrari; and eleven laps after Senna retired, he was past Prost and after Piquet. His motivation, after he announced his premature retirement at Silverstone, had been questioned, but here he was fully wound up, and charging. With each succeeding lap he came closer to Piquet, but the end of the race was near, and before long they were on the last lap. Mansell was still not near enough to challenge the Benetton, but he made one daring, devil-may-car attempt by coming up the inside of Piquet, at a right-hand corner. Piquet refused to be budged, held his place, and Mansell slithered across the track, his gallant attempt just failing. He finished just 3 seconds behind Piquet, but what would the outcry have been had Mansell collected Piquet, and eliminated them both?

That brought the 1990 racing season to a close, and completed McLaren's twenty-fifth year in Grand Prix racing, and McLaren International's tenth. They had risen from the back of the field to sit proudly at the top, with every intention of remaining there. I wonder if, in twenty-odd years' time, AGS, Coloni, Dallara, etc. will have done likewise, or will they like Zakspeed or Techno disappear, having hardly created a ripple?

In a season remarkably free of controversy,

once under way, the Senna/Prost incident stood out like a beacon during a night of the new moon. It was unfortunate that this should have settled both World Championships, yet there was almost an inevitability about the whole occurrence. That Prost got away in front of Senna was of no surprise to the McLaren camp, and remember, Prost had to win, so there was no chance of him giving way once ahead. Similarly, Senna does not give up the lead so easily and, as they rushed down to that all-important first corner, some form of cut-and-thrust seemed likely.

Prost was clearly ahead, and he turned into the corner earlier than normal in order, quite legitimately, to block Senna's route down the inside. This move was far less aggressive than many of Senna's in the past, and indeed of most racing drivers at all levels. However, Senna did not back off; instead, he kept coming at Prost, hitting him hard enough to remove the Ferrari's rear wing, as Prost's route into the corner cut across that chosen by Senna. From that moment on the two drivers were once again at loggerheads.

Most independent observers at the time, and there were millions watching on television, placed the blame on Senna, a fact difficult to deny. If a World Championship is won over a season and not just a few races, so a Grand Prix is not won on the first corner. Senna is the most aggressive driver in Grand Prix racing when overtaking, but Prost, when he has the mind to, is no push-over either. However, after repeated viewings of this particular incident, and knowing how important the race was for Prost, I think Senna was a bit too optimistic to keep on going at him at that precise moment. It seems as though Senna made both a physical and tactical error of judgement, and would have been better off waiting for a more opportune moment. But that is not normally Senna's way; he likes to make things happen, and so often does it pay dividends that the odd error must be expected.

The fall-out from this incident was another matter though, and one out of which the press saw fit to make a meal or two. The Ferrari management were remarkably restrained, considering both their past record over such incidents, and the fact that they were the main losers. Prost, on the other hand, was outspokenly vociferous in his condemnation of Senna, feeling that here was yet another example of his dangerous driving, a result of his perceived indestructability. Furthermore, Prost more than hinted that if FISA did not take action to curb such driving, then he might not continue racing. More sensationally, Prost was convinced that Senna had quite deliberately and cold-bloodedly punted him off so as to ensure that he would become the World Champion. It was this which the press particularly enjoyed, and which ultimately robbed Prost of much sympathy.

Ayrton Senna was quite dismissive of the whole incident. It has to be said that had it taken place between the last two cars on the grid, it would hardly have been noticed. On the other hand he refused to accept any responsibility, possibly mindful of his suspended driving ban, a factor which alienated him to a degree. Ron Dennis tried to cool things down and keep them in perspective by claiming that it was just one of those things that happen in motor racing when two top drivers are really charging hard, which it was, but he never sounded too convincing.

Senna deservedly won his Championship, over the course of the whole season, as did McLaren theirs, but a touch of humility would not have gone amiss. Everyone makes mistakes, and Senna was no different than the rest of us in his reluctance to admit them, but professional pride can be taken too far. The incident was unique in at least one respect though. M. Balestre for once got things right when he said, 'It is a scandal that a World Championship should be decided on such a collision . . . I am sure all motor racing fans throughout the world will feel as frustrated as I do after such an appalling end to the World Championship' – which just goes to show that old dogs can be taught new tricks.

Grand Prix Results 1990

GRAND PRIX	DRIVER	CAR	NO	1ST PRACTICE Time/Posn	2ND PRACTICE Time/Posn	3RD PRACTICE Time/Posn	FINAL GRID POSN	FINAL PLACING	RETIRED CAUSE OF	HIGHEST POSN IN RACE
USA Phoenix Arizona 11.3.90	A. Senna	Honda-V10 MP4/5B-4	27	1min 29.43sec 5/29	1min 52.02sec 2/14		5-26	1/14 WINNER		1st
	G. Berger	Honda-V10 MP4/5B-2	28	1min 28.66sec 1/29	1min 53.49sec 6/14		Pole		Lp 45 Clutch	FL 2nd
BRAZILIAN Rio de Janeiro 25.3.90	A. Senna	Honda-V10 MP4/5B-4	27	1min 17.77sec 1/30	1min 17.28sec 1/28		Pole	3/25		1st
	G. Berger	Honda-V10 MP4/5B-2	28	1min 17.89sec 2/30	1min 18.50sec 3/28		2-26	2/25		FL 1st
SAN MARINO Imola 13.5.90	A. Senna	Honda-V10 MP4/5B-4	27	1min 24.08sec 2/30	1min 23.22sec 1/29		Pole		Lp 3 Wheel damaged by stone, Spun off	1st
			28				2-26	2/13		
	G. Berger	Honda-V10 MP4/5B-3		1min 24.03sec 1/30	1min 23.78sec 2/29					1st
MONACO Monte Carlo 27.5.90	A. Senna	Honda-V10 MP4/5B-4	27	1min 21.8sec 2/29	1min 21.31sec 1/29		Pole	1/6 WINNER 3/6		FL 1st
	G. Berger	Honda-V10 MP4/5B-3	28	1min 23.00sec 2/29	1min 22.68sec 5/29		5-26			3rd
CANADIAN Montreal 10.6.90	A. Senna	Honda-V10 MP4/5B-6	27	1min 20.40sec 1/30	1min 30.51sec 3/27		Pole	1/13 WINNER		1st
	G. Berger	Honda-V10 MP4/5B-5	28	1min 20.47sec 2/30	1min 33.24sec 13/27		2-26	4/13		FL 1st
MEXICAN Mexico City 24.6.90	A. Senna	Honda-V10 MP4/5B-6	27	1min 18.24sec 4/30	1min 17.67sec 2/29		3-26		Lp 63 Puncture	1st
	G. Berger	Honda-V10 MP4/5B-5	28	1min 17.23sec 1/30	1min 17.85sec 3/29		Pole	3/19		1st
FRENCH Ricard Castellet 8.7.90	A. Senna	Honda-V10 MP4/5B-6	27	1min 04.55sec 2/30	1min 08.87sec 30/30		3-26	3/17		1st
	G. Berger	Honda-V10 MP4/5B-5	28	1min 05.35sec 5/30	1min 04.51sec 1/30		2-26	5/17		1st
BRITISH Silverstone 15.7.90	A. Senna	Honda-V10 MP4/5B-6	27	1min 08.07sec 1/30	1min 09.06sec 8/30		2-26	3/26		1st
	G. Berger	Honda-V10 MP4/5B-5	28	1min 08.25sec 2/30	1min 08.67sec 5/30		3-26		Lp 6 Throttle mechanism	1st
GERMAN Hockenheim-ring 29.7.90	A. Senna	Honda-V10 MP4/5B-6	27	1min 40.20sec 1/29	1min 46.84sec 22/30		Pole	1/10 WINNER		1st
	G. Berger	Honda-V10 MP4/5B-5	28	1min 40.43sec 2/29	1min 46.63sec 21/30		2-26	3/10		2nd
HUNGARIAN Budapest 12.8.90	A. Senna	Honda-V10 MP4/5B-6	27	1min 20.39sec 8/29	1min 18.16sec 1/30		4-26	2/15		2nd
	G. Berger	Honda-V10 MP4/5B-5	28	1min 18.13sec 1/19	1min 18.70sec 2/30		3-26		Lp 72 Accident	2nd
BELGIAN Spa-Fran-corchamps 26.8.90	A. Senna	Honda-V10 MP4/5B-6	27	1min 52.28sec 2/28	1min 50.37sec 1/29		Pole	1/16 WINNER		1st
	G. Berger	Honda-V10 MP4/5B-5	28	1min 51.21sec 1/28	1min 50.95sec 2/29		2-26	3/16		2nd
ITALIAN Monza 9.9.90	A. Senna	Honda-V10 MP4/5B-6	27	1min 22.97sec 1/30	1min 22.53sec 1/30		Pole	1/14 WINNER		FL 1st
	G. Berger	Honda-V10 MP4/5B-5	28	1min 23.24sec 3/30	1min 22.94sec 3/30		3-26	3/14		2nd

PORTUGUESE Estoril 23.9.90	A. Senna	Honda-V10 MP4/5B-6	27	1min 14.25sec 1/30	1min 13.60sec 3/29	3-25	2/15		**1st**
	G. Berger	Honda-V10 MP4/5B-5	28	1min 14.55sec 3/30	1min 14.29sec 4/29	5-25	4/15		**2nd**
SPANISH Jerez 30.9.90	A. Senna	Honda-V10 MP4/5B-6	27	1min 18.90sec 1/30	1min 18.39sec 1/29	Pole		Lp 53 Puncture	**1st**
	G. Berger	Honda-V10 MP4/5B-5	28	1min 19.64sec 2/30	1min 19.62sec 5/29	5-26		Lp 56 Accident	**4th**
JAPANESE Suzuka 21.10.90	A. Senna	Honda-V10 MP4/5B-7	27	1min 38.83sec 3/28	1min 36.99sec 1/27	Pole		Lp 1 Accident	
	G. Berger	Honda-V10 MP4/5B-5	28	1min 38.37sec 1/28	1min 38.12sec 4/27	4-25		Lp 2 Spun off	**1st**
AUSTRALIAN Adelaide 4.11.90	A. Senna	Honda-V10 MP4/5B-6	27	1min 15.67sec 1/30	1min 15.69sec 1/30	Pole			**1st**
	G. Berger	Honda-V10 MP4/5B-5	28	1min 17.43sec 2/30	1min 16.24sec 2/30	2-24	4/13		**2nd**

THE WORLD'S BEST?

This brings us to consider Senna as a Grand Prix driver. First of all, I must state that I am no more qualified than the next man to assess the needs and merits of the Grand Prix driver. Having raced at the lower end of the single-seater scale only serves to remind me on what a different plane Grand Prix drivers are compared to ordinary mortals. Braking distances and turning in points for corners are done so much later than in, say, a Formula Ford, and cornering speeds are off the dial. The difference is as great as that between international football and a kick around in the park.

So, is Ayrton Senna the best racing driver around today? Ron Dennis certainly thinks so, and also that Senna is possibly the most complete driver of all time. On the other hand, Ron Dennis also states that if Niki Lauda were in Grand Prix racing now, at his best, he too would soon work out just what was needed to succeed, and then master it. Dennis's opinion cannot be taken too lightly either, as he has had the privilege of working closely with Senna, Prost and Lauda; three of the all-time greats. Senna is almost certainly the fastest driver of his age, a fact which is enough to convince his many admirers of his greatness, but there is more to being a top-rate Grand Prix driver than just racing speed.

Today, more than ever before, test driving abilities are vital to the success of the Grand Prix driver. Once again, Ron Dennis believes Ayrton Senna to be the best there has been; his professionalism and commitment to getting the very best out of the car apparent at all times. On the other hand, Senna was unable to transform Lotus in the way that Lauda transformed Ferrari, as did Prost, young though he was. There is no doubt that Senna has an empathy with the McLaren-Honda engineers the equal of any driver/team relationship of the past, and that this is a major factor in their mutual success.

One other important aspect of Grand Prix racing in which Senna excels is that of qualifying. A glance in the Appendices will show that there have been many outstanding qualifiers: Piquet, Hunt, Prost, Mansell, and even Lauda, but none have managed to maintain their period of supremacy over such a long period as has Senna. His ability to put together the almost perfect lap is unmatched, and his uncanny sense of timing when it comes to performing this out on the circuit, leads observers to suggest he is lucky in this respect. The fastest qualifier and driver, the most committed of test drivers, Senna appears to have it all; yet doubts remain.

As regards race tactics, two drivers stand out above all during the last two decades: Niki Lauda and Alain Prost. The manner and regularity in which both of these had the knack of coming from behind to win, prompted racing enthusiasts to say, 'Boring', just as some echo the same feelings about Senna's ability to win from the front. However, both Prost and Lauda did regularly dominate races and win from the front, especially in their younger years. Senna, on the other hand, does not appear to be their equal when coming from behind. The Brazilian's main tactic is his sheer speed, but motor racing is almost unique in the way a competitor relies on his equipment. Many are the fast drivers who have not succeeded – de Cesaris and Warwick to name but two. Senna is certainly no fool in this respect, yet he does not seem to have the broad tactical armoury of Lauda and Prost, which means having something for almost every occasion. Knowing when to give up, is not, I am sure, even a part of Senna's make-up.

There is one further aspect of driving which has raised the most questions about Senna's ability. Jackie Stewart has stated that Senna has suffered too many accidents and incidents to be considered a 'great'. Certainly, alongside all those drivers who have won more than one in ten Grand Prix in their career, Senna's record is very poor. The statistics are there to prove it: 1986=2, 1987=1, 1988=2, 1989=5, and 1990=3 accidents in these years. Prost, by way of comparison, has had three in the same period, two of these involving Senna, in both of which Senna received the lion's share of the blame. Not all of these were Senna's fault, but others, such as when he nearly pushed Prost into the pit wall in Portugal in 1988, which did not result in an accident, have been ommitted.

Another undoubted 'great' driver, Stirling Moss, commented that he had been racing for four years before he spun a car, because he was afraid that the car would turn over and crush him. Bearing in mind Prost's oft-quoted remarks that Senna believes in his own indestruct-

ability (rooted in his belief in God) and the massive improvement in the safety features of Grand Prix cars over the last twenty years, it could be that Senna takes too many risks. With the onset of mandatory built-in safety features of Grand Prix cars since the 1970s, there was an undoubted increase in unruly driving, with cars touching, and drivers making more breathtaking passing manoeuvres than ever before. Senna is certainly not the only forceful and aggressive driver, but if the risk factor were not so historically low, perhaps he would be less inclined to get entangled in potentially dangerous situations.

One would never accuse the likes of Fangio, Moss, Clark, Hunt and Peterson of not being forceful, and they did not have a Grand Prix/accident ratio anything like Senna's. Perhaps only Villeneuve could approach Senna's poor record, but he was on a different plane altogether.

Then again, there are accusations that Senna is intimidating, perhaps even dishonest, unsporting, and worst of all that he will deliberately force an opponent out of the way if he is held up. While Mclaren might scoff at the latter suggestion, there is a point to be made. Of the thirteen incidents in which Senna has been involved in the last five years, he has been at least the equal guilty party in nine of them, and is not wholly blameless in the others. When one considers his immense talent and judgement, that is an awful lot of errors to make.

One could argue that Senna has been the fastest driver during this period, but Prost has been at least his equal, while others such as Mansell, Piquet and Berger have all had periods of being faster, without the incidents. Other drivers were involved in eleven of those incidents, all of which could have been avoided if Senna had displayed a little circumspection. Were any of these deliberate?

Quite a number of contemporary drivers are not exactly keen on Senna's perceived intimidating driving style, especially when they are in his way. Senna does occasionally seem to be in too much of a hurry for his own good, although there have been countless occasions when this press-on overtaking style has outfoxed his rivals. There is genuine concern among some rivals, and past drivers, about Senna not allowing anyone to prevent him overtaking them, or indeed letting anyone pass him. To succeed in any sport, whether it be rowing, squash, hockey or whatever, a certain amount of aggression is needed, but it can be overdone. It does seem that every time a driver stands up to Senna, an accident of some sort happens. Perhaps more ought to resist him, and then he will have to become more selective in his tactics.

As for being honest and sporting, this is very much a double-edged sword. It is a fact of life that one cannot be completely honest, certainly not in Grand Prix racing, or else all your secrets will be given away. Senna is as honest as the next man, perhaps more so, and is not one to cheat, which in itself is very difficult in Grand Prix racing. Senna does not always display one's ideals of being 'sporting', but what is sporting to one, can be foolish to another. In any case, Grand Prix racing is more than just a sport. When certain journalists don their haloes, and proclaim Ayrton to be 'unsporting', one is always tempted to try to imagine them coaxing their lazy bodies into some form of sporting activity, and wonder if they would 'walk' when the umpire gives them 'out'; I might be unimaginative, but some how I just cannot.

I have not tried to answer any points regarding Senna's stature as a driver; it is not within my capabilities to do so. Certainly I cannot think of another driver who, almost from the very moment he sat behind the wheel of a Grand Prix car, could raise people's passions so. There are thousands who adore him as the fastest driver of all time, and therefore excuse his many errors and occasional lack of sportsmanship. Against, there are the many who think Senna reckless, downright dangerous, and a cheat, including one or two contemporary drivers, and would like to see him either banned or brought down to earth a little. As ever, the issues are far more complex than portrayed in the press, and we are not best placed to judge either. As Senna matures as a complete driver – and he still has time on his side – then there is nothing to stop him becoming the best ever, which Ron Dennis, with his unique insight into three top class drivers, is convinced he will become. One thing is certain though; and that is that McLaren are the top team of the 1980s and 1990s and will take some catching.

CHAPTER 10

'The Professionals'

By the time you actually get to read this, the 1991 season will be over and done with. One thing is for sure, the second twenty-five-year span in McLaren's Grand Prix history will have got off to a better start than did their first. As I write this, they already have two wins under their belt, one emphatic, the other rather lucky, with Mansell giving Senna something to think about.

In the meantime, the rules have changed, and at the centre of this was none other than . . . guess who? At the Italian Grand Prix, M. Balestre announced that from the San Marino Grand Prix, in 1991, all cars would be required to have a flat bottom, from the leading edge of the front wheel to the back of the bodywork. Furthermore, the minimum weight was raised from 500 to 540kg (1,102 to 1,190lb). However, a two-year breathing space for the implementation of rule changes exists to enable teams to plan ahead, and not be subjected to whims of the governing body. You would not, by now, expect such a minor technicality to stop Balestre, and he insisted that the new rules would go ahead under the aegis of safety, which allows for a by-pass to the two-year gestation period. Warwick's accident at Monza cocked a snook at the President's idea, as it immediately showed how safe modern Grand Prix cars are . . .

One dithering, though very welcome, change for 1991 was that all sixteen races would count towards a driver's points total, and not just the best eleven. To ensure that a 'winner' received the due rewards for such a feat, he would now gain ten, instead of nine, points. To round off with a good display of crisis manage-ment, the pole position at the Suzuka circuit in Japan was moved from the right to the left of the track, just as McLaren had requested. Now, I wonder what prompted this action?

Then, just when everything seemed settled, some of the car construction changes, thought to be mandatory, were postponed. The she-naningans performed by Balestre and FISA over the winter were the latest example of their in-ability and unsuitability to govern an interna-tional sport. There is little doubt that a group, such as FOCA could perform a better, more consistent job without the 'power-play' politics. In this book I have only cited certain instances of FISA/CSI/Balestre bunglings, or mis-management, but there is more than enough material for an enterprising script writer to pre-pare an ongoing comedy series.

As far as the teams go, 1991 promises to be the most competitive season for many years. Three of the established top drivers are nearing the twilight of their careers, but all are likely winners, while there are many up and coming drivers, in good cars, to really shake the apple cart. The most likely challenge to both Senna's and McLaren's Championships should come from Ferrari. Their engine can virtually match the Honda, while their car is as good and reli-able as any. In Prost, they have the most com-plete driver around, while Alesi is the most promising. It is a mouth-watering combination; the young pretender under the wing of the 'master'; old Enzo would have been mightily pleased. As ever though, it is a case of can the team hold together, and not fall apart if they are not winning, because you can be sure that the pressure from McLaren will be relentless; there

306

Gerhard Berger appears happy enough for his chances for 1991. Mind you, he has not squeezed into his car yet!

season. His efforts might even dampen the Ferrari threat, by beating them regularly.

The other favourite team to challenge McLaren is Benetton, with the rejuvinated Piquet, backed by Moreno, at last getting the chance he deserves. This combination is not unlike that at Ferrari, and with the best chassis John Barnard can produce and powerful Ford-Cosworth engines, the team will be striving to be the top dog. However, they have switched to Pirelli tyres, a move which might give them an advantage over the Goodyear teams, but they might also find themselves off the pace at times. This looks to be an interesting gamble, but history has shown, with Brabham using Alfa engines from 1976, or using Pirelli tyres in 1985, that to depart from the norm does entail risks that can ruin the whole season, for few gains.

Well, of course, you know what happened, so you can soon put me right. None of the above are surprise choices to do well, but what about some outsiders? For a start, both Honda and Ferrari are running B teams; Tyrrell using the Honda RA101E 690bhp, version six, V10 engine, in their new 020 car; while Ferrari are providing their 685bhp, 1990 V12 engine to Minardi. Tyrrell have developed their 1990 car further, and with Honda power have moved into the first division. It will not be long before Williams and Benetton are finding Uncle Ken's cars uncomfortably close, and even nipping past. Unfortunately, Tyrrell have lost Alesi, but Modena is another talented driver, and he might well break his duck and claim a victory – a sensation Tyrrell have almost forgotten. Minardi's track record is less impressive, though they have run well on occasions. Martini, in particular, should spring a few surprises, though I think that engine sharing will only serve to prove that more than a good engine is needed to win in Grand Prix racing.

Brabham are having an interesting comeback, being one of the three Japanese-owned teams. They will use the new Yamaha V12 engine, and though their V8 engine was a disaster in the

will be no let up whatsoever. If Prost is beaten early on by Senna, then he too might become disillusioned, and Ferrari will be looking to him for inspiration, not the other way round.

Williams, with Mansell and Patrese, make an interesting comparison to McLaren. In terms of sheer speed, Mansell is the one driver who can still match Senna, while Patrese is a very steady number two, quite capable of winning if Mansell falls by the wayside, rather in the mould of Gerhard Berger. The Williams team are also the closest to McLaren in terms of performing at their optimum level, at every race, and the Renault engine is hot on the heels of the Honda. They will certainly be more potent than before, but while I think Mansell will win a few races, he is unlikely to mount a serious threat over the

Zakspeed, much more is expected from the new partnership. Brundle, a top sports car driver, will lead them, and he certainly has the talent to win a race or two, while his partner will be the highly promising Blundell. If everything comes together as expected then the 'big boys' had better watch out. Leyton House, formerly the March Grand Prix team, have retained the well matched Capelli and Gugelmin for their fourth season, and have been unlucky not to have scored a victory. 1991 will see them exclusively using the new Ilmor V10 engine, and if this proves to be as effective as the Ilmor USAC engine, other teams had better watch out.

That concludes the list of likely winners, though you can bet anything that the other teams and drivers will be giving their all, which is why Grand Prix racing never stands still. It is a sobering thought that, of the thirty-four drivers entered for the races, only eight have won a race, all of whom are aged over thirty, and four have each won five races or less. That said, watch out for potential victories from Alesi, Moreno, Modena, Brundle, Capelli and Martini.

IN THEIR OWN WORDS . . .

For all the above, McLaren is the team to beat if victory is to be contemplated. The depth of McLaren's combined talent, and their ability to re-assess a situation and make the correct change in direction was ably demonstrated after the 1990 British Grand Prix. Prost had won three consecutive races, and McLaren looked to be rocking, yet they took the brave decision to make the car less efficient, but more predictable. This enabled the drivers to commit themselves to each and every corner of a given circuit, though the car might not be quite so fast, and the results started to come, which ultimately gave the team both Championships. Ron Dennis commented, 'I do not think our competitors caught us up so much as we got it wrong. 1990

was a difficult year, one in which we learnt many lessons, and we have no intention whatsoever of repeating any of our mistakes. We have thus changed our direction and strategy, for 1991.'

The MP4/6 car is a completely new design, developed by a team headed by Chief Designer Neil Oatley, though built to the traditional McLaren format of a carbon fibre composite chassis, with separate body. It has two major differences from the MP4/5B: the first being forced by rule changes necessitating reduced, and slightly repositioned, front and rear aerofoils; the second replacing the Honda RA100E, V10 engine by the RA121E, V12. This latter resulted in a slight lengthening of the car, and required an increased fuel capacity, while the extra exhaust pipes, and length, of the V12 made the aerodynamic packaging that little bit tighter. McLaren's six-speed, transverse gearbox has been retained, and though the suspension systems look identical to those of before, these have been altered to improve the cornering stability.

Aerodynamic changes, especially with the sidepods, including new radiator ducting, have seen the most radical departure from the MP4/5B. McLaren engineers were all too aware that the Ferrari seemed the better car in high-speed corners, and the winter research programmes set out to rectify this deficiency. The MP4/6 has thus improved grip, through increased downforce, and handles consistently throughout both high and low speed corners. Ron Dennis adds:

'Of course it's not a very comfortable prediction to make, but I would assume that the latter part of 1991 is going to be more successful than the former. We've got a new learning curve to go up; we have to understand the car; there are some pretty significant changes to the aerodynamic package, and, as usual, we will assemble the car very late. In view of these factors, we'll perhaps not be as competitive as we need to be for the first races, but we'll see.'

The new MP4/6.

After seeing the first two races of 1991, if Dennis's predictions are accurate, heaven help the other teams as the season progresses.

Honda's contribution is their new V12 engine, which has been developed over two years. The V10 engine was quite an act to follow, having won 50 per cent of Grand Prix races over its two-year lifespan, yet by the end of the 1990 season the V12 was producing, at around 690bhp, as much power as the definitive version of the V10, with substantial development potential. All did not appear to be quite so hunky-dory on the eve of the season, as Ayrton Senna, emerging from his winter rest for pre-season testing in Portugal, felt that the engine ought to have more power than it did. This caused some bewilderment in the press, though McLaren were quite happy, but the engine in question had its power characteristics tailored to the tighter Phoenix circuit, and not Estoril.

Ron Dennis commented, 'We at McLaren are happy with the Honda V12, though Ayrton expected a little more power. It is Honda who are not where they want to be, not necessarily where we want them to be. Wait until the racing starts.' He was right. At Phoenix, Senna proved the ability of the new car and engine, by thoroughly trouncing the opposition, despite very little testing. The only cloud on the

309

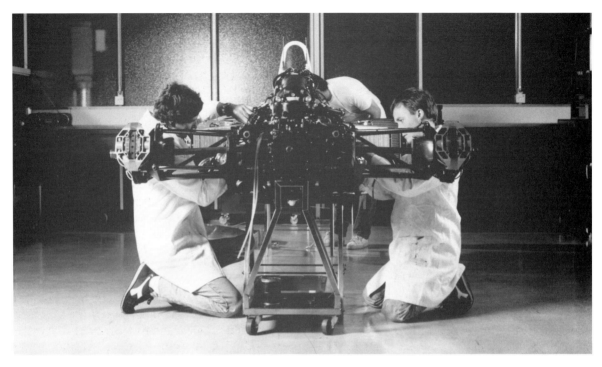

The 'patient' undergoes surgical treatment, in an 'operating theatre' at McLaren's Woking headquarters.

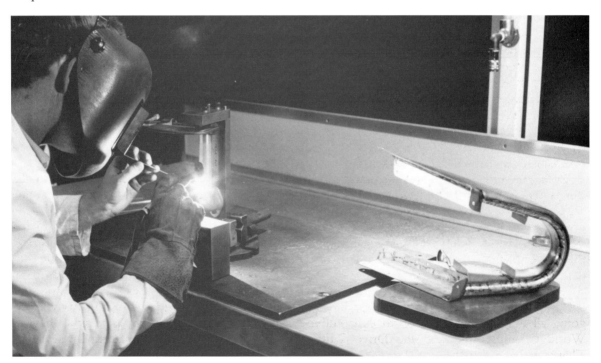

Although McLaren do not as yet have their own foundry, nearly all the parts for the cars are manufactured in-house.

horizon concerned Gerhard Berger, who could only run in sixth position; the car still not comfortably accommodating his tall frame.

PROJECTIONS

If Ferrari had the most promising driver of the future in Alesi, and best all-rounder in Prost, McLaren held the best driver line-up, both Senna and Berger being proven 'winners' in their own right. On his early 1991 form, Senna seems even more formidable than ever before; his ability to annihilate the opposition from the front remaining undiminished. However, it is his ability to overcome strong challenges that have led him into trouble, and it is only when seriously pressed that we will see if Senna can acquire the universal accolade, 'great', from both his peers and past drivers, that his dedication and talent deserve. Berger has the additional motivating factor of putting himself back into the front rank of drivers. To some people, he fell from grace a little in 1990, despite the problems he had fitting into the car. The re-emergence of Piquet as a force, plus Alesi and others, has put Berger's top four position under threat, and he will be doubly keen to prove the doubters wrong.

On the other hand, it seems incredible and, if accurate, unforgivable, that the MP4/6 cockpit is too small for Berger. Early reports suggest he is not happy with his working surroundings. If this is the case, and only time will tell, then McLaren engineers have perpetuated a major error, the very thing one would not expect from them. This will not enable the team to get the best from Berger, and will condemn him to the role of an also-ran compared to Senna.

Considering how often Ron Dennis states that it is his aim to win every race, McLaren are going all out to win their fourth consecutive World Championship and the Drivers' title. That is easier said than done, but actions speak louder than words, and the joint actions of McLaren-Honda could not be easier to read.

Tag-McLaren is a group of four, soon to be five companies, geared to keeping McLaren International, the racing team, at the head of the field. Remember 1975 when March could field a two-car team for an entire Grand Prix season, win a race, and run strongly in others, all on a budget of £50,000? Taking inflation into account, that is around £350,000 at today's prices. In the early days of McLaren International, when John Watson was a driver, there were sixty employees working for the company, but both these figures have grown somewhat. There are now 220 people working to keep McLaren at the top, and this figure, if anything, is likely to grow.

The cost? Well, March's 'inflation boosted' 1975 budget would not even pay 5 per cent of Senna's basic wage, while McLaren's costs are around £60 million! On top of this is the Honda contribution, with research centres in both Japan and England and their vast army of engineers and technicians. All this is fairly staggering, but this is what is needed in 1991, to win, and all credit to Ron Dennis who ensures that McLaren-Honda do not go without.

McLaren's commitment to 'win in style' comes above everything, but there is certainly no philosophy of 'win at all costs'. In terms of safety McLaren, as always, have set standards above the minimum laid down. Neil Oatley comments, 'We are always looking at new fibres and materials, for the composite components, to improve the crash resistance, so that our cars are as reliable and safe as we could possibly make them.' As far as Grand Prix racing can be 'environmentally friendly', McLaren have led the way here, having used unleaded fuel for several seasons, although other actions, for example the disposal of their good quality red trainers after every race, makes one wish they would throw any size 6 shoes my way!

This gives some insight as to why they are not the most colourful team around; one cannot be playing practical jokes all the time and expect to win, even in amateur sport. As for not being at the beck and call of the press all the time, for

311

Oh for the days of the design scribbled on the back of a cigarette packet. This is the name of the game in Grand Prix car design these days.

Ron Dennis this is simple. 'The press have an extremely inflated view of their importance. Their writing, nor the time I am requested to give for interviews, does not influence whether we win or not, one iota. It is my job to try and ensure that we win each race, and therefore I prioritize my time accordingly.' He might have added that if other teams took a similar approach then they might be a little more sucessful.

It is quite probable that Grand Prix racing, minus the antics of its governing body, has be-

come the most professional of all sports, and certainly the most business orientated. Undoubtedly McLaren are the most professional of all Grands Prix teams, and for this they draw an inordinate amount of hostile comments from the press, not that this worries them. Many are the articles which dismiss McLaren personnel as businessmen, devoid of enthusiasm for motor sport. Personally, I adhere to the 'amateur' ethic of competing being the motivating factor, rather than the 'professional' ethic of winning. Imagine though, if Grand Prix racing were an

This is the real 'hothouse' of Mclaren, the oven in which the carbon fibre composite car is baked.

amateur sport; most drivers would be using glorified Formula Fords, except for a few wealthy and possibly undeserving drivers who could finance their own team. An amateur team could not compete in Grand Prix racing today, and McLaren are the most realistic team, in that they do what is necessary to win in the world as it exists. They might take a very business-like approach to their work, but those working in the racing team are enthusiasts, no different to you or me.

Ron Dennis, who draws much criticism for his approach to Grand Prix racing, readily admits to being very much an enthusiast, and after ten years of attending each Grand Prix '. . . cannot envisage missing one in the next ten years. I still get a buzz out of being involved, and that is what I shall be doing for a good few years to come.' I am sure that this is true of most people involved in professional sport, but to meet the demands put on them by the press, supporters, governing bodies, owners, and to perform at the required level, requires an application, and dedication, rather different to the traditional approach. This goes for any sport, but is magnified with Grand Prix racing

313

Ron Dennis

If one had to chose a single word to describe Ron Dennis, it would have to be 'ambitious', although that would inevitably hide more than it reveals. After just ten years in charge of McLaren International, and only eight with overall responsibility, Ron Dennis has transformed an ailing top team into a force unrivalled in Grand Prix history. In so doing, he has become the third most successful team owner, after Enzo Ferrari and Colin Chapman, and comfortably managed to out-thwart the former during that time. Make no mistake, the success of McLaren International is due to Ron. He might have had the best drivers, cars, engines, team, and sponsors, all of which have contributed to the McLaren success equation, but it was Ron who brought them together and made the formula work. If the Christian god is supposed to have created man in his own image, so has Ron formed McLaren. It is *his* team, and that is the main reason it succeeds.

That said, Dennis is a much misunderstood man, one seldom flattered by the press; indeed he is often short-changed. Much of this is to do with his attitude towards motor racing; his totally dedicated, professional approach, and his oft-professed aim to win every race. However, Dennis would draw praise from Karl Marx with his dialectical materialist philosophy towards motor racing. He works out what is needed to succeed, and then gets on with it.

We might still hanker after the days when Grand Prix racing was still jolly good fun, and one could stay up partying until the small hours, put on a bow tie, go out win the race, and celebrate with a bun fight in the local hotel. That approach would not win a FF1600 race today, let alone a Grand Prix, and Dennis is as much the right team boss for his time as were Chapman for Lotus in the 1960 and 1970s, Neubauer for Mercedes in the 1930s and 1950s, and Ferrari throughout his life.

Ron Dennis joined the legendary Thomson and Taylor's and, thanks to takeovers, soon found himself at Cooper's, one of the top Grand Prix teams. He wanted to be in motor sport, and the only way he could realistically find a gap in the door was as a mechanic, not a driver, and so that is what he became. The determination to get where he wants has been in evidence ever since: through his move to Brabham in 1967, to forming Rondel Racing with Neil Trundle (the Brabham Indycar Chief Mechanic) in 1971, to running the Ecuador-Marlboro Formula 2 team in 1974, his Project Three F2 team of 1975, and his Project Four team, which eventually merged with Team McLaren to form McLaren International. That fourteen-year phase saw Ron rise from a mechanic, to become the owner of one of the top Formula 2 teams, one with Grand Prix ambitions.

Dennis needed to go into Grand Prix racing, and it was with this in mind that he recruited John Barnard to build Project Four a suitable car. He showed faith in Barnard's revolutionary idea for a carbon fibre car, though as things turned out the merger with Mclaren went ahead before the car was ready, and it became the legendary MP4. It has been in the last decade that Ron has come right to the fore with numerous successes, including: getting Tag to support and Porsche to build the turbo engine, persuading Lauda to return to racing, building the team around Prost, persuading Honda to join as partners, recruiting Senna, and recruiting Gordon Murray.

Yet still the ambitions grow, as the size of the team has done, with new premises and further plans for McLaren's own test track and, of course, the road car. He has made errors along the way, especially those resulting in the loss of key personnel, but the risks he has taken, and which have paid off, would make even the most stout-hearted go weak at the knees. Yet Ron receives little credit for his achievements.

Another criticism levelled against Dennis is that he is more a marketing man and less a racing enthusiast. This is patently untrue; he not only takes charge of the Mclaren pit at Grand prix and test sessions, but has not missed a race while in charge of McLaren, and has no intention of doing so. Let us face facts: if he were not an enthusiast, life would be much easier conducting business back at home, instead of being dragged all over the world during the racing season. He might be attuned to the needs of sponsors; the need for professionalism, commercialism, and television, but he wants to win in the Grand Prix arena, and if he perceives that the route to that goal demands Mclaren to work in a certain way, so be it. Better to be a dull winner than a happy-go-lucky loser.

It would seem that the press really have gone too far when Ron Dennis and McLaren have to actually say that yes, Ron does have a sense of humour and can enjoy himself like the next person, at the right time. Were the press as punctilious as Dennis, then images they portray would not be so inaccurate. Ron is as much a human being as anyone, with all that entails, but be sure of one thing, he knows everything that goes on at McLaren, keeps his finger firmly on the pulse, plans the way, or paths, forward and is, far more than Ayrton Senna, the man firmly in the driving seat, and steering the course ahead. Oh, and he is loving every minute of it.

because of the high cost of equipment, and putting on the events themselves. If McLaren personnel are enthusiastically watching their rivals perform, then they are not going to be winning, and that is the name of the game these days.

As time passes, so ambitions become modified, or even change altogether as goals are achieved. For a number of years now, McLaren have been seeking to set up their own test track facility and to relocate, somewhere in south-east England. There are, and have been, major problems with this, both on environmental grounds and cost. To have one's own test circuit, away from the public eye yet close to one's base, is the ideal for all Grand Prix teams, yet only Ferrari have this. It is far more difficult to set up such a facility these days, yet McLaren intend to have their own in the near future. With their road 'supercar' also due to be in production, on a very limited scale, by the mid-1990s, this will see McLaren enter a new era and will further strengthen the base from which they work. All that will remain then is for them to build their own engines, though this is not on the agenda, as yet. The partnership with Honda has a good few years to run, but if Honda do decide to either depart Grand Prix racing, or to build their own car, this could be the path McLaren will take, rather than accept second best from elsewhere.

A new testing facility, factory base, and production car, with other projects to follow, will take McLaren a further step towards self-sufficiency, and ahead of rivals. Already over the last few seasons, we have seen that only Ferrari, and fleetingly Williams and Benetton, have been able to seriously challenge McLaren, and if the gap widens still further, who knows just how difficult it will become to compete against them. There is also the likelihood that McLaren will branch out into other formulae, and this might be a reason for the recent signing of American driver Michael Andretti, the son of 1978 World Champion Mario Andretti, as a test driver.

Of one thing you can be sure, none of these possible developments will be allowed to restrict the performance of the Grand Prix team. That is sacrosanct, and McLaren's *raison d'être* is to win at the highest level of motor sport. Hence the reasoning behind Ron Dennis's thought of taking a season's sabbatical:

'Grand Prix racing is a roundabout, the speed of which one has no control over, and therefore needs total commitment at all times. Breathing spaces are too short to allow management to recover, therefore as we are poised to relocate, and at the same time re-form the company, I can't see any problem in stopping racing for a year. Ninety per cent of our costs are incurred in competing, and so the cost of standing still is minimal. We would return even more formidable than before, so why not?'

Despite the obvious risks involved, this would be a daunting prospect for their rivals.

This kind of thought and consideration for his employees leads one to think of Ron Dennis as, unwittingly, following in the footsteps of the 'benevolent capitalists' of last century. An excellent canteen, a good working environment, and relaxation facilities are provided, in the knowledge that happy, satisfied, staff will perform to a higher level and enjoy their work more, with consequent benefits to the team – their team. I wonder how history will finally portray Ron Dennis; merely paraphrase the inaccuracies written so often today, or try and look a little deeper?

Another major step forward for McLaren, apart from their moving to new premises, is the road 'supercar' project. Details are few and far between at the moment, not in the least because McLaren are not prepared to indulge in idle speculation. They will inform the world of relevant details as, and when, they have been established, but of one thing you can be sure, in the words of Gordon Murray, it will be priced '. . . higher than anything around today'. On the other hand, the car will have Grand Prix standard suspension; steering and brakes will be

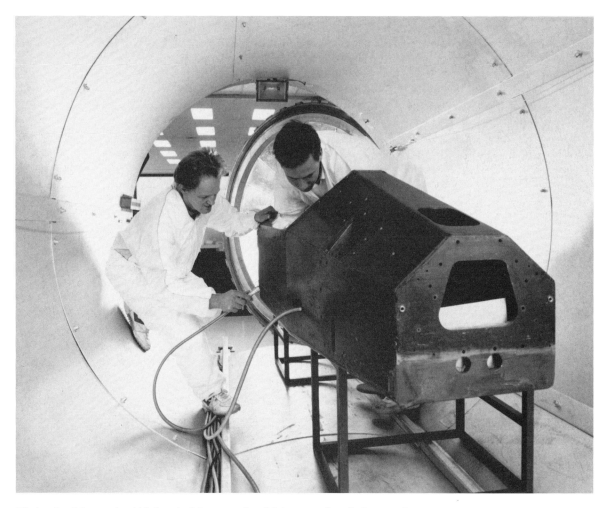

The interior of the oven in which the tub of the current Grand Prix cars are formed. Compare this to some of the earlier garage scenes; this will give a true picture of the advance in car building technology over the years. No place for tin snips and rivets nowadays.

relatively light; and it will be hand-built in the same way as a Grand Prix car is. Neil Oatley has said that, 'A lot of the technology, particularly in the use of composite materials, will come from the Grand Prix cars, transferred by the design staff.'

Obviously, the production run will be restricted, the price will see to that, but there are other projects in the pipeline which will see McLaren emerge as a true, if small-scale, manufacturer. The aim is to produce the best sports

car possible, and set new standards for road cars along the way, while McLaren's reputation in Grand Prix will ensure that nothing less than this is achieved.

An interesting project, which will come as something of a surprise to those who view McLaren as nothing more than a highly successful, if dour, Grand Prix team, is that of a museum. As you will be aware, McLaren have an ongoing display of their cars at their headquarters, along with a good selection of the

The machine tools possessed by McLaren would outstrip the budgets of most Grand Prix teams, about fifteen years ago. These pictures of the inside of McLaren's headquarters show that the team's obsession with their brand of 'professionalism' is not just empty rhetoric.

many trophies they have won over the years. In addition to this, Peter Stayner says that, 'We are gradually gathering together items of interest from the earliest days of McLaren, trophies and suchlike, with a view to creating a museum'. Since Team McLaren used to sell off any cars, or other things, that were no longer of use, this is likely to remain a long-term project, and one that will not be comprehensive.

McLaren International themselves are not known for keeping extensive archives of their activities; they are too busy going racing in the present to dwell on past successes. However, they realize the historical significance of what they have achieved, and a museum will be one way to display their achievements, while leaving the team free to carry on the winning. No firm details of the format the project will take have been established yet, but it promises to be a mouth-watering display of great historical value.

What of the future for Grand Prix racing

though? It has survived the recent recession easily enough, but is there the possibility that it will become something of an anachronism? The cost of competing has spiralled in the last two decades, yet the sport/entertainment/business, call it what you will, is perhaps less of a spectacle than it once was. Drivers are usually highly paid, yet face less risk than a good mountaineer, or rock climber. Speeds continue to rise, despite changes in engine formula and aerodynamic tinkering, necessitating major circuit alterations, which push the paying customer further back. It is also surprising how many people I have met, while writing this book, who have not heard of McLaren, despite the claims of large television audiences.

This scenario might not be the case all over the world, and undoubtedly interest has grown in Britain since I first went to a motor race, but when the advertising industry is reduced to promoting the value of advertising, you can bet the limits are being reached. This type of doom and gloom has been forecast many times before, and still Grand Prix racing continues to grow in superficial, if not genuinely enthusiastic, popularity. Times are changing and gradually, as people realize the wholesale environmental threat posed by the car, and become aware of the slaughter on the roads of the world, so the car might be used less. Other sports, particularly those easier to participate in, are either making a comeback or coming to the fore, and with the possibility of the car being used less, it is likely that motor racing in general, and Grand Prix, with its ever inflating costs in particular, will feel the pinch.

Of course, there is so much money invested in Grand Prix racing, and so many able people around, that Grand Prix teams would soon adjust to any new environment. Of one thing you can be sure, whoever writes a book after fifty years of McLaren in Grand Prix racing will review an awful lot of changes, and very likely a sport either in decline, or firmly rooted on a maximized plateau, the only way to go being down. We shall see.

The future for motor racing depends on the actions of the FIA, and in particular for Grand Prix racing, FISA and Balestre, for as long as he remains President. Clearly, if the governing bodies continue to act in the manner they have for the last two decades, then the future looks very bleak indeed. The political and personal ambitions of M. Balestre have brought motor sport into disrepute on so many occasions, that it is as though he is a Fifth Columnist, planted on motor racing by some outraged 'anti', to wreak havoc with the sport. McLaren have had rather more than their fair share of quarrels with FISA and, like so many others, have usually been less than happy with the outcome. Ron Dennis says that:

'These have been periods in McLaren's history that are best forgotten. We, at McLaren, feel strongly that there were inconsistencies of interpretation placed on some of the incidents surrounding the Suzuka affair, in 1989, and likewise, the outcome of *all* the controversies have been less than satisfactory. The one thing that has been consistent throughout is that we acted correctly, honestly, and in a manner that is completely consistent with the rules, regulations, and statutes laid down by the governing body. I don't think that all the other parties involved could claim the same thing.'

In this book I have highlighted several of these controversies, quite a number of which have not directly involved McLaren. It is for you, the reader, to make up your own mind on this matter, both concerning the sport as a whole, and McLaren in particular, and though I have my own opinions on the matter, those incidents that I have covered are by no means exhaustive.

Perhaps the greatest claim for motor racing, over nearly a century, has been that 'racing improves the breed'. This has certainly been true, though as with most things, it goes in cycles. Grand Prix cars have not looked much like our road cars with a few odd exceptions, since before the last World War, but that does not mean they are of no use to the car industry. Within the period covered by this book, we have seen four-wheel drive tried and discarded, a revolution in tyres, the introduction of turbocharged engines, the use of high octane, low lead fuels, a major rise in engine efficiency (why else are Honda, Renault, Ford, Ferrari, Lamborghini, Yamaha, etc. heavily engaged in the sport?), the importance of aerodynamics and, just in case you were thinking this usefulness had been exhausted, survival cell technology, and the use of new materials.

Ron Dennis confirms this, and adds:

'The materials technology that we are currently using, composite structures, plastics, etc., are pioneering in their application, and will undoubtedly flow through to the automobile industry as the cost of these materials drop. As production techniques improve, there are many other areas on Grand Prix cars that have still to contribute to the ever increasing safety-conscious automobile manufacturers. The sophistication in our braking and suspension systems, the ability for structures to absorb energy, all of these things will ultimately flow through to the car that is driven by the general public.'

He might well have added 'starting with our own road car'! With all this to come, and no doubt more in the long term, Grand Prix racing's future seems assured, although I still think that the rate of growth of the last two decades will not be matched.

Which leaves us to consider the future of McLaren. Five years from now, even if Grand Prix racing remains unchanged, will see McLaren in a rather different shape than it is at present. With a move to new premises, the acquisition of their own test track, a road car, and a museum all in the offing, some at least will have borne fruit. Based on past experience, it is unlikely that either Senna or Berger will still be driving for the team, while even Honda might have departed, although a McLaren car not

Inside Story

McLaren are based in one half of a large, smoke-glazed building occupying 60,000 square feet (5,570 square metres), at the Woking Business Park. Viewed from any angle – except when the big transporter lorries are in evidence – it does not fit one's impression of a Grand Prix team's premises, more that of a medium-sized company, or an insurance company, and the former is what Tag/McLaren is. There is no evidence of the sights, sounds and smells of the traditional garage: mechanics coated in oil, dirty tools lying around the floor, bits and pieces everywhere. The areas where the cars are built up have been described as 'operating theatres', such is their cleanliness, while the rest of the building could quite easily, to my mind, be the NASA headquarters.

Inside, grey wood wall panels abound, providing a uniform, functional environment in which to work. By the entrance lobby stand seven complete Grand Prix cars, the most successful chassis from the last seven seasons, all wound up and ready to race. Yet, not only is there not a drop of oil or grease anywhere, but you would be hard-pushed to find a speck of dust. A good selection of the many trophies and awards won over the years, both enhances the display and completes the message being put over: 'We go motor racing to win, and to win in style. We are proud of what we have achieved, and this is attributable to our dedication to getting every possible aspect of our performance, just right.' This was conveyed by the surroundings, but it is a sentiment echoed by each employee, from the bottom to the top. 'Team spirit', and 'success breeds success', are two phrases regularly used to explain a run of success, but there is more to the equation in reality. There is more to winning than 'team spirit'; McLaren's key to success is good management, and motivation.

Ron Dennis's personal management philosophy begins with a commitment to everything, and every detail. He expects professional behaviour from all team members, though this leads to derisory comments in the press. Everybody has their own idea of what is meant by 'professionalism', so let us hear what, exactly, Ron Dennis's definition is. It is, 'The obligation to call on, at every opportunity, the expertise, experience, and mental abilities that are available to you, with total commitment, and in a manner that is quantifiable to oneself as being reflected in continuous effort.' Peter Stayner, the head of McLaren's marketing services, adds, '. . . and to be seen to be doing the job in the correct, best way'.

One can now begin to appreciate why McLaren have their own way of doing things.

wearing the familiar Marlboro red and white colours would be a sure sign of changes being rung. There is thus plenty of room for things to happen.

Perhaps the question most regularly asked about Mclaren is, how much do they depend on Honda? Or, 'It's the Honda engines that win them all the races, isn't it? Look what happened to Williams'. Ron Dennis regards the relationship with Honda as a genuine partnership, and like all partnerships, if one half leaves, then performance suffers. Remember, in two seasons with Honda turbo engines, and Ayrton Senna and Nelson Piquet as two of their four drivers, Lotus only won two races; an engine is not everything. There is absolutely no reason whatsoever to suggest that the McLaren-Honda partnership will not go on for many years to come, and Ron Dennis adds, 'If the partnership ends, it will be for reasons outside each other's control. I'll tell you what though, it will go on for a good while yet.'

So, there is no reason to suggest any change there but, for yet another 'what if?', supposing Honda pull out of Grand Prix or decide to build their own car, and Senna either retires or moves to another team, would McLaren 'do a Lotus', and go from the front of the grid to near the back in the twinkling of an eye? It is of course impossible to say, being as it is an entirely hypothetical question, but as Ron Dennis says, 'It is my job to ensure that there is no decline in the standards set by the team'. Ron Dennis's record, especially with the Tag/Porsche engine, suggests that the loss of the Honda engine would only cause a temporary blip in the success stakes, and that a more than suitable alternative would be found, one way or another.

Ron Dennis rates the loss of a driver as much less of a serious problem, though he considers that Ayrton Senna to be one of, if not the, greatest driver ever – a claim based on, 'The amount of commitment he brings to fulfil his objective.' Look at some of the drivers who have left McLaren in the last ten years: John Watson, Niki Lauda, Keke Rosberg and Alain Prost. All of these at their best, if they could be transported in time, would be winners today, and yet Mclaren continued to win after they had gone. There is no reason to suggest that if, and when, Senna and Berger leave, McLaren will not have found suitable replacements. After all, which driver does not want to drive for the top team in Grand Prix racing?

However, if Ron Dennis left, quite apart from the immense psychological blow that it would have on the team, things would not look so rosy. They might be the largest, most talented team in Grand Prix, but without the inspiring leadership of the man who created this successful outfit, the picture could change dramatically. Can you imagine Lotus being in their recent predicaments if Colin Chapman were still with us?

As it is, with McLaren building the best car on the grid, Honda providing the most powerful engines, Senna showing himself to be currently not only the fastest but the best driver, all backed by Marlboro, in particular, and others, McLaren, again, are the team to beat in 1991. The only cloud appears to be regarding Berger, who is still having problems fitting into his car, a most puzzling oversight from a team which oozes professionalism, as defined by Ron Dennis, from the top to the bottom. Ron Dennis acknowledges that it was this poor fitting of the car, in 1990, that contributed to Berger's results not reaching expectations, and it is to be hoped that the Austrian will not be similarly handicapped throughout 1991.

Time will give answers to all the questions raised, and as this manuscript goes through the production process, so many of these answers will be forming. Of course, you, the reader, might well have come to your own conclusions about issues raised in this book, and these may be the opposite to my own ideas, but this is the beauty of history, it is always open to new facts and interpretations. While this book had many aims, not all of which have been met, cost considerations imposing a considerable limit on the length of the script, but it is to be hoped that you have enjoyed recalling twenty-five years of Grand Prix history. More importantly perhaps, the book has attempted to offer a balance to the traditional 'build them up, and then knock them down' attitude, given to so many of our sporting heroes. McLaren are not, have never been and, despite the best efforts of Ron Dennis, never will be perfect.

This book represents my own interpretation of the team, and its changes, over the seasons, and probably does not conform to their own vision of themselves. This does not mean that it is right or wrong; as with most things in life, Grand Prix racing is not that simple. One thing does stand out in racing though, and that is being the 'winner', which is the intention of McLaren for 1991, and each succeeding season to come. It may be a little tedious watching the red and white cars take the chequered flag time and again, but it is mightily impressive.

Appendix 1

Specifications of McLaren Cars					
CAR/YEAR	**McLAREN-FORD M2 1966**	**McLAREN-BRM M5A 1967**	**McLAREN-FORD M7A 1968**	**McLAREN-FORD M7A/ M7C 1969**	**McLAREN-FORD M14A 1970**
ENGINE	Ford (USA) V8 95.3 × 52.4mm	BRM V12 84.5 × 64.8mm	Ford-Cosworth DFV V8 85.6 × 64.8mm	Ford-Cosworth DFV V8 85.6 × 64.8mm	Ford-Cosworth DFV V8 85.6 × 64.8mm
BORE/STROKE CAPACITY	2,999cc	2,999cc	2,993cc	2,993cc	2,993cc
COMPRESSION RATIOS	10:1	12:1	11:1	11.1	11.1
BHP at RPM	321bhp @ 9,000rpm	356bhp @ 9,750rpm	410bhp @ 9,000rpm	410bhp @ 9,000rpm	430bhp @ 10,000rpm
FUEL	BP	Shell	Shell	Shell	Gulf
GEARBOX	ZF	Hewland DG 5-speed	Hewland DG300 5-speed	Hewland DG300 5-speed	Hewland DC300 5-speed
BRAKES	Lockheed	Lockheed	Lockheed	Lockheed	Lockheed
FRONT SUSPENSION	Rocker arm and radius arm. Top Transverse link and radius arm	Transverse link and radius arm. Outboard springs	Double wishbones. Outboard springs	Double wishbones. Outboard springs	Double wishbones. Outboard springs
REAR SUSPENSION	Top link and radius arm. Transverse link and radius arm	Upper transverse link and radius arm. Lower reverse wishbone, radius arm. Outboard springs	Double wishbones. Outboard springs	Double wishbones. Outboard springs	Double wishbones. Outboard springs
WHEEL DIAMETER	13in	13inF 15inR	15inF/R	15inF/R	13in or 15inF 15inR
WHEEL WIDTH Front/Rear	8.5inF 12inR	8.5inF 12inR	9.25inF 13.5inR	9.25inF 13.5inR	11inF 16inR
TYRES	Firestone	Goodyear	Goodyear	Goodyear	Goodyear
WHEELBASE	96in (2,438mm)	96in (2,438mm)	94in (3,387mm)	94in (2,387mm)	95in (2,413mm)
TRACK Front/Rear	50in (1,270mm)	58in (1,473mm)	58inF 57inR (1,473mmF 1,447R)	58inF 57inR (1,473mmF 1,447mmR)	62.4inF 60.5inR (1,585mmF 1,537mmR)
WEIGHT	1,180lb (535kg)	1,180lb (535kg)	1,190lb (540kg)	1,190lb (540kg)	1,180lb (535kg)

Specifications of McLaren Cars

CAR/YEAR	McLAREN-FORD M19A 1971	McLAREN-FORD M17C 1972	McLAREN-FORD M23 1973	McLAREN-FORD M23 1974	McLAREN-FORD M23 1975
ENGINE	Ford-Cosworth DFV V8 85.6 × 64.8mm	Ford-Cosworth DFV V8 85.6 × 64.8mm	Ford-Cosworth DFV V8 85.6 × 64.8mm	Ford-Cosworth DFV V8 85.6 × 64.8mm	Ford-Cosworth DFV V8 85.6 × 64.8mm
BORE/STROKE CAPACITY	2,993cc	2,993cc	2,993cc	2,993cc	2,993cc
COMPRESSION RATIOS	11:1	11:1	11:1	11:1	11:1
BHP at RPM	440 @ 10,000rpm	450bhp @ 10,000rpm	460bhp @ 10,000rpm	460bhp @ 10,250rpm	465bhp @ 10,500rpm
FUEL	Gulf	Gulf	Texaco	Texaco	Texaco
GEARBOX	Hewland DG300 5-speed and DG400 5-speed	Hewland DG400 5-speed	Hewland DG400 5-speed	Hewland DG400 5-speed	Hewland DG400 5-speed
BRAKES	Lockheed	Lockheed	Lockheed	Lockheed	Lockheed
FRONT SUSPENSION	Double wishbones, Inboard springs	Double wishbones, Inboard springs	Double wishbones, Inboard springs	Double wishbones, Inboard springs	Double wishbones, Inboard springs
REAR SUSPENSION	Lower wishbones, top links radius rods. Inboard springs	Lower wishbones, single top links, twin radius rods. Outboard springs	Lower wishbones, or parallel lower links, Single top links, twin radius rods. Outboard springs	Lower wishbones, or parallel lower links. Single top links, twin radius rods. Outboard springs	Parallel lower links, single radius rods, twin radius rods. Outboard springs
WHEEL DIAMETER	13inF 13in or 15inR	13inF/R	13inF/R	13inF/R	13inF/R
WHEEL WIDTH Front/Rear	11inF 16inR	11inF 16in or 17inR	11inF 18inR	11inF 16in or 18inR	10inF 18in R
TYRES	Goodyear	Goodyear	Goodyear	Goodyear	Goodyear
WHEELBASE	100in (2,540mm)	100in (2,540mm)	101in (2,565mm)	104.2in (2,467mm)	107in or 105.75in (2,718mm or 2,686mm)
TRACK Front/Rear	63inF 62inR (1,600mmF 1,575mmR)	63inF/R (1,600mF/R)	65.5inF 62.5inR (1,664mmF 1,587mmR)	64.2inF 66inR (1,631mmF 1,676R)	64.2inF 65inR (1,631mmF 1,651mmR)
WEIGHT	1,230lb (588kg)	1,257lb (570kg)	1,270lb (576kg)	1,270lb (576kg)	1,325lb (601kg)

Specifications of McLaren Cars

CAR/YEAR	McLAREN-FORD M23 1976	McLAREN-FORD M26 1976	McLAREN-FORD M23 1977	McLAREN-FORD M26 1977	McLAREN-FORD M26 1978
ENGINE	Ford-Cosworth DFV V8 85.6 × 64.8mm	Ford-Cosworth DFV V8 85.6 × 64.8mm	Ford-Cosworth DFV V8 85.6 × 64.8mm	Ford-Cosworth DFV V8 85.6 × 64.8mm	Ford-Cosworth DFV V8 85.6 × 64.8mm
BORE/STROKE CAPACITY	2,993cc	2,993cc	2,993cc	2,993cc	2,993cc
COMPRESSION RATIOS	11:1	11:1	12:1	11:1	12:1
BHP at RPM	465bhp @ 10,500rpm	465bhp @ 10,500rpm	475bhp @10,800rpm	465bhp @ 10,500rpm	485bhp @ 10,800rpm
FUEL	Texaco	Texaco	Texaco	Texaco	Texaco
GEARBOX	Hewland FG400 6-speed	Hewland FG400 6-speed	Hewland/McLaren 6-speed	Hewland/McLaren 6-speed	Hewland/McLaren 6-speed
BRAKES	Lockheed	Lockheed	Lockheed	Lockheed	Lockheed
FRONT SUSPENSION	Double wishbones, Inboard springs	Double wishbones, Inboard springs	Double wishbones, Inboard springs	Double wishbones, Inboard springs	Top rocker arms, bottom wishbones. Inboard springs
REAR SUSPENSION	Parallel lower links, single top links, twin radius rods. Outboard springs	Lower wishbones, single top links, twin radius rods. Outboard springs	Lower wishbones, single top links, twin radius rods. Outboard springs	Lower wishbones, single top links, twin radius rods. Outboard springs	Lower wishbones, single top links single radius rods. Outboard springs
WHEEL DIAMETER	13inF/R	13inF/R	13inF/R	13inF/R	13inF/R
WHEEL WIDTH Front/Rear	10inF 18inR	10inF 18inR	10in or 11inF 18inR	10in or 11inF 18inR	10in or 11inF 18inR
TYRES	Goodyear	Goodyear	Goodyear	Goodyear	Goodyear
WHEELBASE	107in (2,718mm)	108in (2,743mm)	107in (2,718mm)	108in (2,743mm)	107.75in (2,737mm)
TRACK Front/Rear	64.2inF 65inR (1,631mmF 1,651mmR)	63inF 64inR (1,600mmF 1,626mmR)	64.2inF 65inR (1,631mmF 1,651mmR)	65inF 66inR (1,651mmF 1,675mmR)	67inF 66inR (1,702mmF 1,676mmR)
WEIGHT	1,325lb (601kg)	1,300lb (589kg)	1,325 (601kg)	1,300lb (589kg)	1,340lb (608kg)

Specifications of McLaren Cars

CAR/YEAR	McLAREN-FORD M28 1979	McLAREN-FORD M29 1979	McLAREN-FORD M29B/C 1980	McLAREN-FORD M30 1980	McLAREN-FORD M29F 1981
ENGINE	Ford-Cosworth DFV V8 85.6 × 64.8mm	Ford-Cosworth DFV V8 85.6 × 64.8mm	Ford-Cosworth DFV V8 85.6 × 64.8mm	Ford-Cosworth DFV V8 85.6 × 64.8mm	Ford-Cosworth DFV V8 85.6 × 64.8mm
BORE/STROKE CAPACITY	2,993cc	2,993cc	2,993cc	2,993cc	2,993cc
COMPRESSION RATIOS	12:1	12:1	12:1	12:1	12:1
BHP at RPM	470bhp @ 10,800rpm	470bhp @ 10,800rpm	470bhp @10,800rpm	470bhp @ 10,800rpm	470bhp @ 11,000rpm
FUEL	Texaco	Texaco	Texaco	Texaco	Valvoline
GEARBOX	Hewland/McLaren 6-speed	Hewland/McLaren 6-speed	Hewland/FGB 5-speed	Hewland FGB 5-speed	Hewland/McLaren 5-speed
BRAKES	Lockheed	Lockheed	Lockheed	Lockheed	Lockheed
FRONT SUSPENSION	Top rocker arms, lower wishbones. Inboard springs	Top rocker arms, lower wishbones. Inboard springs	Top rocker arms, lower wishbones. Inboard springs	Top rocker arms, lower wishbones. Inboard springs	Top rocker arms, lower wishbones. Inboard springs
REAR SUSPENSION	Lower and upper wishbones, lower rocker arms. Inboard springs	Lower and upper wishbones, lower rocker arms. Inboard springs	Lower and upper wishbones, lower rocker arms. Inboard springs	Lower and upper wishbones, lower rocker arms. Inboard springs	Lower and upper wishbones, lower rocker arms. Inboard springs
WHEEL DIAMETER	13inF/R	13inF/R	13in or 15inF 13inR	13in or 15inF 13inR	13inF/R
WHEEL WIDTH Front/Rear	11inF 18inR	11inF 18inR	11inF 16in or 18inR	11inF 16in or 18inR	11inF 16inR
TYRES	Goodyear	Goodyear	Goodyear	Goodyear	Michelin
WHEELBASE	113in (2,870mm)	106in (2,692mm)	108in (2,743mm)	106in (2,692mm)	108in (2,743mm)
TRACK Front/Rear	70inF 64inR (1,778mmF 1,626mmR)	68inF 62inR (1,727mmF 1,575mmR)	68inF 62inR (1,727mmF 1,575mmR)	69inF 63inR (1,7523mmF 1,600mmR)	68inF 62inR (1,727mmF 1,575mmR)
WEIGHT	1,378lb (625kg)	1,300lb (589kg)	1,320lb (599kg)	1,320lb (599kg)	1,320lb (599kg)

Specifications of McLaren Cars

CAR/YEAR	McLAREN-FORD MP4 1981	McLAREN-FORD MP4-1B 1982	McLAREN-FORD MP4-1C 1983	McLAREN-TAG MP4-1E 1983	McLAREN-TAG M4/2 1984
ENGINE	Ford-Cosworth DFV V8 85.6 × 64.8mm	Ford-Cosworth DFV V8 85.6 × 64.8mm	Ford-Cosworth DFY V8 90 × 58.8mm	Porsche-Tag V6 82 × 47mm	Porsche-Tag V6 82 × 47mm
BORE/STROKE CAPACITY	2,993cc	2,993cc	2,994cc	1,499cc	1,499cc
COMPRESSION RATIOS	12:1	12:1	12.2:1	7:1	7.5:1
BHP at RPM	470bhp @ 11,000rpm	480bhp @ 11,100rpm	510bhp @ 11,000rpm	700bhp @ 11,500rpm	650bhp @ 11,500rpm
FUEL	Valvoline	Unipart	Unipart	Elf/Unipart	Shell
GEARBOX	Hewland/McLaren 5-speed	Hewland/McLaren 5-speed	Hewland/McLaren 5-speed	Hewland/McLaren 5-speed	Hewland/McLaren 5-speed
BRAKES	Lockheed	Lockheed	Automotive Products	Automotive Products	McLaren carbon fibre
FRONT SUSPENSION	Top rocker arms, lower wishbones. Inboard springs	Top rocker arms, lower wishbones. Inboard springs	Push rods operating auxiliary rockers, lower wishbones. Inboard springs	Push rods operating auxiliary rockers, lower wishbones. Inboard springs	Push rods operating auxiliary rockers, lower wishbones. Inboard springs
REAR SUSPENSION	Top rocker arms, lower wishbones. Inboard springs	Top rocker arms, lower wishbones. Inboard springs	Top rocker arms, lower wishbones. Inboard springs	Top rocker arms, lower wishbones. Inboard springs	Top rocker arms, lower wishbones. Inboard springs
WHEEL DIAMETER	13inF/R	13inF/R	13inF/R	13inF/R	13inF/R
WHEEL WIDTH Front/Rear	11inF 16inR	11inF 16inR	11inF 16inR	11inF 16inR	11.75inF 16.25inR
TYRES	Michelin	Michelin	Michelin	Michelin	Michelin
WHEELBASE	105.1in (2,669mm)	105.6in (2,682mm)	105.8in (2,687mm)	105.8in (2,687mm)	110in (2,794mm)
TRACK Front/Rear	71inF 66inR (1,803mmF 1,676mmR)	71.5inF/R (1,816mm F/R)	71.5inF 66inR (1,816mmF 1,676mmR)	71.5inF 66inR (1,816mmF 1,676mmR)	71.5inF 66inR (1,816mmF 1,676mmR)
WEIGHT	1,300lb (589kg)	1,279lb (580kg)	1,191lb (540.2kg)	1,191lb (540.2kg)	1,191lb (540.2kg)

Specifications of McLaren Cars

McLAREN-TAG MP4/2B 1985	McLAREN-TAG MP4/2C 1986	McLAREN-TAG MP4/3 1987	McLAREN-HONDA MP4/4 1988	McLAREN-HONDA M4/5 1989	McLAREN-HONDA M4/5B 1990	McLAREN-HONDA M4/6 1991
Porsche-Tag V6 82 × 47mm	Porsche-Tag V6 82 × 47mm	Porsche-Tag V6 82 × 47mm	Honda RA 168E Turbo 77 × 50.8mm	Honda RA 109 V10 92 × 52.5mm	Honda RA 100E V10 –	Honda RA 121E V12
1,499cc	1,496cc	1,496cc	1,494cc	3,490cc	3,498cc	
7.5:1	7.5:1		9.6:1			
750bhp @ 11,500 rpm	750bhp @ 11,500rpm	750bhp @11,500rpm	688 @ 12,500rpm	685 @ 13,000rpm	690bhp @ 13,000rpm	700+ @ 14,000rpm
Shell	Shell	Shell	Shell	Shell	Shell	Shell
McLaren 5-speed	McLaren 5-speed	McLaren 6-speed	McLaren 6-speed	McLaren 6-speed	McLaren 6-speed	McLaren 6-speed
McLaren carbon fibre	SEP	McLaren carbon fibre	McLaren/SEP	Brembo/SEP	Brembo/SEP	Brembo
Push rods operating inboard auxiliary rockers, lower wishbones. Inboard springs	Double wishbones and pushrods	Double wishbones and pushrods	Unequal length wishbones, pushrod/rollertrack system	Double wishbones and pullrods	Double wishbones and pullrods	Inboard coil spring/dampers activated by push rod
Push rods operating inboard auxiliary rockers. Inboard springs, top and lower wishbones, rear lower toe link	Double wishbones and pushrods	Double wishbones and pushrods	Unequal length wishbones, pushrod rocker system	Double wishbones and pullrods	Double wishbones and pullrods	Inboard coil spring/dampers activated by push rod
13inF/R	13inF/R	13inF/R	13inF/R	13inF/R	13inF/R	13inF/R
11.25inF 16.25inR	11.75inF 16.25inR	11.75inF 16.25inR	11.75inF 16.3inR	12inF 16.3inR	12inF 16.3inR	12inF 16.3inR
Goodyear	Goodyear	Goodyear	Goodyear	Goodyear	Goodyear	Goodyear
110in (2,794mm)	110in (2,794mm)	111in (2,819mm)	113.2in (2,875mm)	114in (2,895mm)	115.7in (2,939mm)	115.7in (2,832mm)
71.5inF 66inR (1,816mm F 1,676mmR)	71.5inF 66inR (1,816mm F 1,676mmR)	72.5inF 66inR (1,841mmF 1,676mmR)	71.8inF 65.76inR (1,824mmF 1,670mmR)	71.6inF 65.75inNR (1,819mmF 1,670mmRO)	71.8inF 65.75inR (1,824mmF 1,670mmR)	71.8inF 65.75inR (1,824mmF 1,670mmR)
1,191lb (540.2kg)	1,191lb (540.2kg)	1,190.5lb (540kg)	1,190.5lb (540kg)	1,102.3lb (500kg)	1,102.3lb (500kg)	

Appendix 2

CAR	RACES	DNQ	POLE POSITION	FINAL POSITIONS						OTHER	RETIRED	FASTEST LAP
				1st	2nd	3rd	4th	5th	6th			
M2B	5							1	1		3	
M4B	2						1				1	
M5A	11							2		4	5	
M7A	45			4	3	1	4	4	3	8	18	
M7C	16				1	2	2	2		3	7	
M7D ALFA	5	4								1		
M14A	28				2	3	3	1	1	6	12	
M14D ALFA	5	3								1	1	
M19A	29			1	1	3	2	4	1	8	9	1
M19C	19				3	6	1	2		4	3	1
M23	176	11	15	16	11	13	12	10	11	46	45	9
M26	69	4	2	3		3	4		5	20	30	1
M28	14	1				1	1		1	5	5	
M29	47	2					3	3	5	11	21	
M30	3								1	1	1	
MP4	51			5	3	4	3	1	4	10	21	3
MP4/1C	24	2		1	1	3		1	3	4	9	1
MP4/1E	7									1	6	
MP4/2	32		3	12	5	1	1		1	2	10	7
MP4/2B	31		2	6	2	4	2	1		1	15	
MP4/2C	32		2	4	5	3	4	2	2	1	11	2
MP4/3	32			3	3	6	1	1	2	7	9	2
MP4/4	32		15	15	10		1		1		5	10
MP4/5	32		16	10	7	1	1	1		2	10	8
MP45B	32		13	6	4	8	3	1			10	5

McLaren Car Performances

Appendix 3

McLaren Grand Prix Champion Constructors

1974,   1984,   1985,   1988,   1989,   1990

McLaren Grand Prix Champion Driver

1974 (Fittipaldi),   1976 (Hunt),   1984 (Lauda),
1985 (Prost),   1986 (Prost),   1988 (Senna),
.1989 (Prost),   1990 (Senna)

McLaren Can-Am Champion Constructors

1967,   1968,   1969,   1970,   1971
Record 43 race wins

McLaren Can-Am Champion Drivers

1967 (McLaren: 1st – Hulme: 2nd)   1968 (Hulme:1st – McLaren: 2nd)
1969 (McLaren: 1st – Hulme: 2nd)   1970 (Hulme)   1971 (Revson)
Hulme: Record 22 race wins

Leading Constructors Grand Prix Records

	RACES	STARTS	WINS	POLE POSITIONS	FASTEST LAPS	POINTS	CONSTRUCTORS CHAMPION
FERRARI	473	1136	103	110	118	1675	8
MCLAREN	346	748	87*	67	62	1546.5	6
LOTUS	428	1124	79	107	70	1337	7

*Includes 1976 British Grand Prix

McLaren Indianapolis 500 Record

1971 Revson: 2nd   1972 Donohue (Penske): Winner
1973 McClusky: 3rd   1974 Rutherford: Winner
1975 Rutherford: 2nd   1976 Rutherford: Winner
1977 Sneva (Penske): 2nd   1980 Sheva (O'Connell): 2nd

Appendix 4

McLaren Constructors and Drivers Records									
MCLAREN CONSTRUCTORS				**DRIVERS**					
YEAR	POSITION	POINTS	CHAMPION OR RUNNER-UP	DRIVER	POSITION	POINTS	DRIVER	POSITION	POINTS
1966	7th	3	Brabham	McLaren	14th	3			
1967	8th	3	Brabham	McLaren	14th	3			
1968	2nd	49	Lotus (62 pts)	Hulme	3rd	33	McLaren	5th	22
1969	4th	38	Matro-Ford (66 pts)	Hulme	6th	20	McLaren	3rd	26
1970	5th	35	Lotus (59 pts)	Hulme	4th	27	McLaren	4th	6
				Gethin		1			
1971	6th	10	Tyrrell (73 pts)	Hulme	13th	9	Gethin		0
1972	3rd	47	Lotus (61 pts)	Hulme	3rd	39	Revson	5th	23
1973	3rd	58	Lotus (92 pts)	Hulme	6th	26	Revson	5th	38
1974	1st	73	[Ferrari (65 pts)]	Hulme	7th	20	Hailwood	11th	12
				Fittipaldi	1st	55			
1975	3rd	53	Ferrari (72½ pts)	Fittipaldi	2nd	65	Mass	8th	20
1976	2nd	74	Ferrari (83 pts)	Hunt	1st	69	Mass	9th	12
1977	3rd	60	Ferrari (95 pts)	Hunt	5th	40	Mass	6th	25
1978	8th	15	Lotus (86 pts)	Hunt	13th	8	Tambay	13th	8
1979	7th	15	Ferrari (113 pts)	Watson	9th	15	Tambay		0
1980	9th	11	Williams (120 pts)	Watson	10th	6	Prost	15th	5
1981	6th	28	Williams (95 pts)	Watson	6th	27	de Cesaris	18th	1
1982	2nd	68	Ferrari (74 pts)	Watson	2nd	39	Lauda	5th	30
1983	5th	34	Ferrari (89 pts)	Watson	6th	22	Lauda	10th	12
1984	1st	143½	[Ferrari (57 pts)]	Prost	2nd	71½	Lauda	1st	72
1985	1st	90	[Ferrari (82 pts)]	Prost	1st	73	Lauda	10th	14
1986	2nd	96	Williams (114 pts)	Prost	1st	72	Rosberg	6th	22
1987	2nd	76	Williams (137 pts)	Prost	4th	46	Johansson	6th	30
1988	1st	199	[Ferrari (65 pts)]	Prost	2nd	87	Senna	1st	90
1989	1st	136	[Williams (74 pts)]	Prost	1st	76	Senna	2nd	60
1990	1st	121	[Ferrari (110 pts)]	Senna	1st	78	Berger	3rd	43

Appendix 5

McLaren Grand Prix Drivers Records															
DRIVER	RACES	DNQ	DNS	POLE POSITION	FRONT ROW	1ST	2ND	3RD	4TH	5TH	6TH	OTHER PLACINGS	RETIRED	DSQ	FASTEST LAP
A. Prost 1980, 1984–1989	110		2	10	33	30	21	12	2	3	6	7	25	2	23
A. Senna 1988–1990	48			36	6	20	6	3	1		1	3	12	2	8
J. Hunt 1976–1978	49			13	9	10*	2	3	3	1	1	8	20	1	6
N. Lauda 1982–1985	61	1	2		1	8	5	2	4	3	2	3	29	2	8
D. Hulme 1968–1974	86		1		14	6	5	10	9	7	10	15	24		4
E. Fittipaldi 1974–1975	29		1	2	2	5	6	2	3	1		6	5		1
J. Watson 1979–1983, 1985	76	2			1	4	3	6	5	4	8	17	26	1	2
P. Revson 1972–1973	23			4	2	2	4	3	3			4	5		
B. McLaren 1966–1970	40		3	2	1	4	2	3	4	2		4	17		
J. Mass 1974–1977	49					1	1	6	5	4	5	9	18		1
G. Berger 1990	16			2	7	2	5	3	1				5		3
S. Johansson 1987	16					2	3	1	1	1		3	5		
K. Rosberg 1986	16			1		1		4	2			1	8		
M. Hailwood 1974	11							1	2	1		3	4		
M. Donohue 1971	1							1							
J. Ickx 1973	1							1							
P. Tambay 1978–1979	29	2							1	1	3	11	11		
D. Gurney 1968, 1970	6								1	1			4		
B. Redman 1972	3									2		1			
P. Gethin 1970–1971	14										1	6	7		
A. de Cesaris 1981	16		1								1	4	10		
A. de Adamich 1970	10	5	1									3	1		
D. Hobbs 1971, 1974	3											3			

J. Scheckter 1972–1973	6					1							2	4		
B. Giacomelli 1977–1978	5												2	3		
J. Oliver 1971	3												2	1		
G. Villeneuve 1977	1												1			
D. Bell 1969	1													1		
B. van Rooyen 1969	1													1		
G. Galli 1970	1	1														
S. South 1980	1	1														
McLAREN TOTAL	732	12	10	65	80	87*	60	61	50	39	41	118	246	8	56

* Denotes inclusion of 1976 British Grand Prix as a McLaren win.

Appendix 6

Comparison of Selected Grand Prix Drivers' Records 1966–1990						
DRIVER	**RACES**	**WINS**	**POLES**	**FASTEST LAP**	**WORLD CHAMPIONSHIPS**	**POINTS**
Fangio	51	24	28	23	5	277.14
Moss	66	16	19	20		186.64
Brabham	126	14	13	16	3	261
Hill	176	14	13	10	2	289
McLaren	102	4		3		196.5
Clark	72	25	33	28	2	274
Stewart	99	27	17	15	3	360
Hulme	112	8	1	9	1	248
Fittipaldi	144	14	6	6	2	261
Lauda	171	25	24	25	3	420.5
Hunt	92	11*	14	9	1	188
Watson	152	5	2	5		169
Piquet	188	22**	24	23	3	459
Prost	169	44	20	34	3	669.5
Mansell	149	16	15	16		289
de Cesaris	150		1	1		38
Senna	110	26	52	15	2	395

★ Includes 1976 British Grand Prix.
★★ Excludes 1982 Brazilian Grand Prix.

Index